TRADITIONAL ABORIGINAL SOCIETY
Second Edition

TRADITIONAL ABORIGINAL SOCIETY

Second Edition

Edited by

W.H. Edwards
Faculty of Aboriginal and Islander Studies
University of South Australia

First published 1987 (reprinted 5 times)
Second edition published 1998 by
MACMILLAN PUBLISHERS AUSTRALIA PTY LTD
627 Chapel Street, South Yarra 3141
Reprinted 2003

Associated companies and representatives
throughout the world

National Library of Australia
cataloguing in publication data

Traditional Aboriginal society.

　　2nd ed.
　　Bibliography.
　　Includes index.
　　ISBN 0 7329 4094 X (hbk).
　　ISBN 0 7329 4082 6 (pbk).

　　1. Aborigines, Australian – Social life and customs. I.
　　Edwards, W. H. (William Howell).

306.0899915

Typeset in 10 pt Times by
Typeset Gallery, Malaysia

Printed in China

Cover design by Cath Lindsey/Design Rescue
Cover image: Clifford Possum Tjaptaltjarri 'Corkwood Dreaming', Hank Eves Gallery of
Dreaming

Contents

Introduction

The first edition of this volume, published in 1987, developed out of my experience as a lecturer in Aboriginal Studies at what was then the South Australian College of Advanced Education, now the University of South Australia. Aboriginal Studies was first taught in a tertiary education institution in Australia in 1968 at Western Teachers' College in Adelaide, one of the colleges in the line of amalgamations that led to the establishment of the university in 1991. The first subject in Aboriginal Studies was taught to meet the needs of teachers in Aboriginal schools, who expressed a desire to learn about the culture and history of their students. This developed into majors in teaching awards and eventually to diploma, degree and postgraduate courses in Aboriginal Studies and the establishment of a Faculty of Aboriginal and Islander Studies in the university in 1992.

The Faculty has brought together people trained in a variety of disciplines, including anthropology, psychology, history, religion, education, sociology, management and archaeology. The approach to the study of Aboriginal Studies is thus multidisciplinary. Aboriginal members of staff and Aboriginal and Islander students have contributed to the value of the studies as they have reflected on their own experiences. Throughout the history of these studies, many of the students have been enrolled as external or distance education students. As many of them live in areas with limited access to adequate library services, considerable attention has been given to the preparation of readers, prepared under copyright regulations, and made available through the Distance Education Centre (now the Flexible Learning Centre). Experience in preparing such readers has contributed to the idea of publishing this volume. The response to, and use of, the first edition has encouraged Macmillan to publish this second edition. This form of publication makes the materials available to a wider readership.

When I began working with Aboriginal people in 1958, there were few books available to assist people to gain an understanding of Aboriginal cultures. There were no Aboriginal Studies courses and the teaching of anthropology was very limited. In 1966 Ian Hogbin and Les Hiatt edited a volume, *Readings in Australian and Pacific Anthropology*, which contained four chapters on Australian Aborigines. In their introduction they commented on the lack of materials available to meet the needs of an expanding student population. Since then, the Australian Institute of Aboriginal and Torres Strait Islander Studies and new university departments of anthropology have been established. Extensive fieldwork was sponsored by the institute and the departments, and in response to the needs of Aboriginal communities in establishing their claims to land in relation to land rights legislation. Many books and articles have now been published on Aboriginal culture and history. Staff and students face the problem of selecting from the large amount of materials now available. Many of the articles are published in journals which are not readily available. A few volumes have been published to provide selections of articles around themes such as mythology (Hiatt 1975) and religion (Charlesworth, Morphy, Bell & Maddock 1984). The present volume is designed to cover the main themes related to the study of traditional Aboriginal societies.

In selecting articles I have had two main aims: first, I have sought a cross-section of articles to cover the main themes related to the study of human societies. I have included two or three articles on some themes, but the exigencies of space have limited the selection on some themes to one article. Second, with the needs of first-year tertiary students in mind, I have given preference to articles which contain a good proportion of descriptive material on the societies as well as raising analytical issues. In addition to these aims I have sought to include articles which cover a variety of regions in Australia.

Some reviewers of the first edition noted the lack of contributions by Aboriginal writers. In preparing that volume I had aimed to include such writings but at that time found it difficult to find appropriate material. Two chapters in this volume are by Aboriginal people. I had hoped for more, but those who could contribute in this way are occupied at present with political and other activities associated with land title and reconciliation issues. However, it is fitting that the opening chapter is by a prominent Pitjantjatjara woman who lived her early years in a largely traditional setting. Her story of enculturation and learning in this setting was recorded in her own language and translated. An earlier publication of this story has been used widely in Aboriginal education courses, and its inclusion in this volume will make it more accessible. The values and structures expressed in the story are relevant to other chapters in the volume. In the chapter on art, Howard Morphy illustrates the social and religious contexts of Aboriginal art by reference to the bark paintings of the Yolngu people of north-east Arnhem Land. He emphasizes the religious nature of this art and its function in connecting people to the powers of the ancestral past.

A major section of this volume is given to chapters on the economic life of Aboriginal societies. The writers take up issues raised in the volume *Man the Hunter* (Lee & De Vore 1968). Since its publication, studies have been concerned with such issues as the respective roles of males and females in economic activities, the applicability of the term 'affluent' to Aboriginal societies and the ways in which groups and individuals lay claim to the rights to utilize the resources of specific areas of land. Fred Myers opens this section with his study of the Pintupi use of resources in a desert region and their concept of land ownership. The scarcity of resources in the region necessitated frequent movement and accordingly they recognized both local rights and the need to share with neighbouring groups. Myers questions the adequacy of earlier models to account for the complexities of Pintupi organization and emphasizes that indigenous ideology, as well as the need to adapt to ecological conditions, regulated relations within the society.

Jon Altman has examined the affluence hypothesis in the light of fieldwork in north-central Arnhem Land and questions the adequacy of some of the studies on which this hypothesis was based. He argues also that the male and female contributions to diet were more balanced than previously acknowledged. Chase and Sutton describe hunting and gathering activities in another tropical region. Their research among three groups in Cape York, North Queensland, reveals significant differences in the economic and social life in this region as people adapted to different ecological conditions. They question the applicability of the term nomads for these people who utilized an abundance of resources within a limited region.

Annette Hamilton reflects on her fieldwork with the Janggundjara in the north-west of South Australia to examine the debates on Aboriginal relationships to land and land ownership. Her chapter provides an outline of contributions to this debate. She argues that earlier models of patrilineal descent overlooked the complexity and multiplicity of ties to land which are held by both males and females, and that attempts to distinguish between economic and religious groupings and their ties to land, tend to minimize the extent to which the economic operates within the religious system. She suggests that for the Janggundjara, the concept of patrilineal descent relates more to the ancestral totemic species than to the biological father.

As an Aboriginal woman who has listened to evidence given by women in land claims in the Northern Territory, Queensland and New South Wales, Marcia Langton also demonstrates that the models enshrined in the *Aboriginal Land Rights (NT) Act 1976* were inadequate. She writes in this recently published paper of the gendering of landscape and social organization, of the range of women's rituals and the significance of their knowledge. Women are active participants in negotiations and in the passing on of rights and knowledge. Thus she concludes that matrifiliation and matrilateral recruitment principles are integral rather than peripheral in determining rights.

Two chapters on kinship have been included. Lee Sackett, in the light of his fieldwork at Wiluna in the central desert area of Western Australia, questions the use of earlier models which sought to explain marriage alliances. To survive in a region in which there were periods of severe hardship, Aborigines needed a wider network of exchange than allowed for in the earlier models. He suggests that alliance should be seen as part of a wider system of belief. In the other chapter on kinship, Robert Tonkinson outlines the structures of social organization in another Western Desert group, the Mardujarra. While illustrating the complexity of social organization in Aboriginal societies, he identifies clearly the basic principles of the kinship system, the role of kinship in patterning behaviour and the relationship between these structures and the wider religious values of Mardujarra society. This chapter is included because it provides an excellent introduction to the study of Australian Aboriginal kinship.

Discussion of traditional Aboriginal politics in recent decades has centred on whether Aboriginal societies can be described as egalitarian. My own chapter is a review of the earlier contributions to this debate. It introduces students to a range of literature on this topic and I am including it in this edition on the basis of the response from students. Les Hiatt has made a long-standing contribution by seeking to clarify issues relating to land tenure, kinship and politics. In his chapter, originally the 1984 Wentworth Lecture for the Australian Institute of Aboriginal Studies, he reviews the more recent contributions of Myers, Bern and Chase and demonstrates that our understanding of Aboriginal political life has been advanced by these studies. Christopher Anderson reviews references in the literature to Aboriginal people who appear to have achieved status as *bosses* despite the prevailing emphasis on egalitarianism. He draws on his fieldwork in Cape York to demonstrate that some individuals were able to achieve status, beyond that gained through their religious knowledge and ritual status, by their personal attributes.

One of the tasks given to the Australian Law Reform Commission was to report on the extent to which Aboriginal law should be recognized within the Australian legal system. A preliminary report, issued as a discussion paper, contained a chapter on traditional Aboriginal society. I have included this chapter because it provides a good summary of the findings of Elkin, the Berndts, Maddock and Meggitt.

W. E. H. Stanner was one of the most insightful and influential researchers and writers on Aboriginal religion. His chapter, 'The Dreaming', has been a foundational contribution to the study of Aboriginal religion. Although it has been published in other volumes I include it here as an essential reading for first-year students. Stanner interprets Aboriginal myths and rituals as expressions of a deep philosophy of life. Some of the language in the chapter, reflecting the usage of the time when it was written, may offend some contemporary readers. In an editor's note I encourage readers to persevere beyond this to gain the insights revealed in the chapter.

The chapter by Deborah Rose on religion first appeared in a missiological journal, *Nelen Yubu*, and its inclusion in the first edition of this Reader made it available to a larger readership. She draws on her research among the Ngaringman and Ngaliwurru people of the western border region of the Northern Territory to expand on the approaches of Stanner and Eliade in emphasizing the cosmic dimension of Aboriginal religion. She notes the problems associated with attempting to convey Aboriginal religious concepts in Western language categories, and contends that in Aboriginal thought there is a sense in which all life is sacred.

Diane Bell, in her chapter on Aboriginal women's religion, argues that a feminist ethnography leads to a more dynamic reading of Aboriginal religion. Earlier androcentric studies had undervalued the role and participation of women and perceived males as the power brokers and females as pawns. She draws on her fieldwork in central and northern Australia, which included participation in women's rituals, observing women's role in initiation ceremonies and land claims research to conclude that women engage as players in negotiating power, status, authority and distribution of resources in the religious domain.

Another chapter by Deborah Rose has been included in this edition because of the increasing interest in Aboriginal ideas about the environment. She contrasts Western and Aboriginal views, noting that areas which white Australians refer to as wilderness are viewed as tame and settled by Aborigines, while areas white Australians refer to as settled are viewed as wild and wilderness by Aborigines. She has developed this position further in her book *Nourishing Terrains: Australian Aboriginal Views of Landscape and Wilderness* (1996).

The final chapter, by Gaynor Macdonald, has been written for this volume, following discussions I have had with the writer about the use of the term 'traditional' in the title of the book. By using this term I am indicating that the emphasis is on the organization, structures and values of Aboriginal societies as they were before European contact. Most of the chapters are based on studies undertaken in regions in which many of these structures and values have been able to survive during the periods of research. The author of this chapter reminds us that this emphasis has the dangers of ignoring the dynamic aspects of tradition and of excluding Aboriginal societies, which have suffered greater interference and the greater loss of traditional knowledge and customs, from recognition and rights. From her research and involvement with the Wiradjuri people of central New South Wales, she argues that Wiradjuri traditions, especially relating to kinship and association with country, have been both continued and transformed, and reveal continuities in the deep structure despite surface changes.

In concluding this summary of the contents I am conscious that there are many other articles which could have been included to enhance the quality of the volume. The problem for an editor is not so much that of selecting what to include, but in deciding what to exclude. For example, I had hoped to include a chapter on tradition and native title. However, people I have approached to suggest they write such a chapter are busy with their participation in the negotiations. Also, it is intended that the contents of this volume will remain useful as a text for a decade, and anything written on native title now may soon be out of date in the light of negotiations and legislation. Several articles and books are available on the present situation relating to native title. I am grateful to Nicolas Peterson, Bob Tonkinson, David Trigger, Annette Hamilton, Gaynor Macdonald, Jim Birckhead and others who gave generously of their time in offering suggestions. I accept the responsibility for the final selection. My thanks also to the authors of chapters and publishers of the original articles for their permissions and support. The original sources are acknowledged at the beginning of the chapters. Colleagues in the Faculty of Aboriginal and Islander Studies of the University of South Australia and my family have offered support and encouragement in the project.

My thanks also to Brian McCurdy, who supported the original proposal and, as Publishing Director, guided me through the preparation of the first edition. In the same role, Peter Debus has been patient and helpful as I have prepared this edition. My thanks to him and other staff of Macmillan who have assisted in this production. I trust that this edition will continue to be helpful to staff and students, and that perhaps in a small way, as readers become more aware of the structures and values of Aboriginal societies, it may contribute to the process of reconciliation in Australian society.

Bill Edwards

References

CHARLESWORTH, MAX, MORPHY, HOWARD, BELL, DIANE & MADDOCK, KENNETH (eds) (1984), *Religion in Aboriginal Australia: An Anthology*, St Lucia: University of Queensland Press.

HIATT, LES (ed.) (1975), *Australian Aboriginal Mythology*, Canberra: Australian Institute of Aboriginal Studies.

HOGBIN, IAN & HIATT, L.R. (eds) (1966), *Readings in Australian and Pacific Anthropology*, Melbourne: Melbourne University Press.

LEE, R.B. & DE VORE, IRVIN (eds) (1968), *Man the Hunter*, Chicago: Aldine.

ROSE, DEBORAH BIRD (1996), *Nourishing Terrains: Australian Aboriginal Views of Landscape and Wilderness*, Australian Heritage Commission.

Contributors

Jon Altman, a graduate of the University of Auckland, obtained his doctorate in anthropology at the Australian National University, where he is now Professor and Director of the Centre for Aboriginal Economic Policy Research. He has researched and written extensively on Aboriginal economic development, the impact of mining and land rights.

Christopher Anderson gained his doctorate in anthropology at the University of Queensland. He is Director of the South Australian Museum in Adelaide, where he was previously Head of the Department of Anthropology. He has undertaken fieldwork in North Queensland and central Australia.

Diane Bell is the Henry R. Luce Professor of Religion, Economic Development and Social Justice at the Holy Cross College, Massachusetts. She was previously Professor of Australian Studies at Deakin University. Following extensive fieldwork with indigenous peoples over the past two decades, she has published widely in journals on art, anthropology, history, law and women's studies.

Athol Chase is Associate Professor and Head of the School of Australian Environmental Studies at Griffith University. Since the early 1970s he has been engaged in social anthropological research among Aboriginal people in Cape York Peninsula and has carried out similar work in the Daly River and Hermannsburg areas of the Northern Territory.

Bill Edwards, a graduate of the University of Melbourne, is an Adjunct Lecturer in the Faculty of Aboriginal and Islander Studies at the University of South Australia where he lectured in Aboriginal culture and Pitjantjatjara Language, 1981–96. He was superintendent of Ernabella Mission, SA, during 1958–72 and Minister of the Pitjantjatjara Parish of the Uniting Church in Australia from 1976 to 1980. He interpreted during Pitjantjatjara and Maralinga land rights negotiations in the late 1970s and early 1980s and for the Royal Commission into British Nuclear Testing in Australia. He is now researching Aboriginal mission history and Pitjantjatjara oral history.

Annette Hamilton is Professor of Anthropology at Macquarie University. She carried out field research at Manangrida, NT, during 1967–69, and at Mimili (Everard Park station, SA) in 1970–71. During the 1980s she acted as Anthropological Advisor to the Royal Commission into British Nuclear Testing in Australia, and worked on several land claims in central Australia. More recently she has been working in Southeast Asia, and maintains an active interest in relations between indigenous/tribal peoples and the state on a comparative basis.

Les Hiatt is a Visiting Fellow at the Australian National University and the Australian Institute of Aboriginal and Torres Strait Islander Studies. He was Reader in the Department of Anthropology, University of Sydney. He undertook fieldwork in Arnhem Land over many years and has written extensively on Aboriginal kinship, religion and land. His latest book is *Arguments About Aborigines: Australia and the Evolution of Social Anthropology* (1996). He was President of the Australian Institute for Aboriginal Studies from 1974 to 1982 and co-editor of *Oceania*.

Nganyintja Ilyatjari is a leading Pitjantjatjara woman who spent her early years in her father's country at Angatja in the Mann Ranges, north-west South Australia, before her family moved to Ernabella Mission where she was one of the first school children and later a school assistant. She later moved with her husband and children to Amata, nearer to her homeland, and in recent years has established a centre at Angatja where she educates tourists and younger Pitjantjatjara people in traditional ways.

Marcia Langton is a professor and occupies the Ranger Chair in Aboriginal Studies, Northern Territory University. She is Chair of the Australian Institute for Aboriginal and Torres Strait Islander Studies and a member of the Council for Aboriginal Reconciliation. She was formerly employed as an anthropologist by the Central and Northern Land Councils and was part of the Aboriginal negotiating team for the *Native Title Act 1993*.

Gaynor Macdonald is a graduate of the University of Sydney and has worked for many years with Wiradjuri people in central New South Wales, conducting a long-term study of the impact of the *Aboriginal Land Rights (NSW) Act 1983*, through the work of the Wiradjuri Regional Aboriginal Land Council. She has taught anthropology at the University of Western Sydney and at Charles Sturt University, Albury. She is now a consultant involved in native title research.

Howard Morphy is Professor of Social Anthropology at University College, London, having previously lectured in Anthropology at the Australian National University. He has undertaken field research in north-eastern Arnhem Land and written on Aboriginal art, religion and social organization. From September 1997 he will be an ARC Senior Fellow at the Australian National University researching Narritjin Maymuru's biography.

Fred Myers is Professor and Chair of the Department of Anthropology at New York University. He has done extensive fieldwork with the Pintupi people of central Australia and worked on a land claim. He is the author of *Pintupi People: Sentiment, Place, and Politics among Western Desert Australian Aborigines.*

Deborah Bird Rose is a Senior Fellow of the North Australia Research Unit, Institute of Advanced Studies of the Australian National University. Following extensive fieldwork in the Victoria River region of the Northern Territory she has worked with Aboriginal claimants on land claims and with the Aboriginal Land Commissioner as consulting anthropologist. She has written widely in the fields of land rights, religion, and indigenous and colonizing cultures of land management.

Lee Sackett received his doctorate from the University of Oregon (USA) following anthropological fieldwork in the Wiluna area of Western Australia. Formerly a Senior Lecturer in Anthropology at the University of Adelaide he is now employed by the Central Land Council in Alice Springs on land rights research.

The late *W. E. H. Stanner* (1905–82) was Professor of Anthropology and Sociology, Institute of Advanced Studies, Australian National University, until 1970. He engaged in fieldwork among the Mirambata people of the Northern Territory in the 1930s and wrote extensively on their religious life. His publications include *On Aboriginal Religion* (1964) and *White Man Got No Dreaming* (1979).

Peter Sutton is a freelance anthropological consultant working on native title research and a limited term lecturer in the Department of Anthropology, University of Adelaide. Former Head of the Division of Anthropology at the South Australian Museum, he has worked extensively since 1969 with Aboriginal people in Queensland, the Northern Territory, South Australia, New South Wales and Tasmania.

Bob Tonkinson is Professor of Anthropology at the University of Western Australia where he has taught since 1984. He received his doctorate from the University of British Columbia and has taught at the University of Oregon. He has extensive research experience among Aboriginal people in the Western Desert of Western Australia and among Melanesians in Vanuatu.

1
Traditional Aboriginal Learning: How I Learned as a Pitjantjatjara Child

NGANYINTJA ILYATJARI

As a child I lived at a place called Angatja. My father, mother, grandmother, older brothers, aunts and uncles taught me there and I learned from them. My mother taught me about her bush foods. She collected the plant foods and prepared them and I learned by watching her. I learned also from my father. He taught about meat foods, cooking the meat, making spears, joining parts of the spears tightly with sinew and going out hunting for meat. My mother would take me out with her. We two went out together to collect small animals and plant foods, hitting sand goannas, and sometimes collecting bush honey. I watched her and gathered some foods and when we all came together in camp we ate the meat and plant foods. My mother gathered various plant foods, native millet seeds, pigweed, roots which grew in the rocks and other seeds. These foods were available in autumn. Other foods were found on trees in spring. These fruits included mistletoe berries, mulga apples, native plums and quandongs. Also the native fig trees grew on small rocky hills.

They taught me many things and at night the men told stories. One man would tell one and when he finished another would relate one. They talked and we all just listened. We all listened together and nodded our agreement and learned, the children and women together. They talked in turn and when they finished we slept.

They taught me many things such as how to carry firewood on my head. My mother carried firewood on her head and I learned how to carry it and throw it down in the camp. Mother would give me a digging stick to dig, a small one, and I learned how to dig. I would dig a hole as mother dug for rabbits. As a child I learned by digging small holes. Mother would pull big witchetty grubs (from tree roots) and I learned to look for the right trees and dig for them.

We would tell stories and then my father and mother would send us off. They gave us meat, damper and water to take to our older brothers. We took them to our brothers and having given them the food and water we sat with them for a while and watched them as they played. Those boys played with spears and we watched them. Our older brothers camped

Tape transcribed and translated by Bill Edwards.[1] Published in *The Aboriginal Child at School: A National Journal for Teachers of Aborigines*, **19**(1), 1991.

apart and the older ones taught the younger ones, and we girls would go over and watch and learn with them. They played with spears as if spearing kangaroos and learned. Having learned they went off the next day and their father gave them spears and they went out together to look for meat and learned to spear. All this work was truly good.

Again at night the men taught the children to dance the ceremonies, teaching night after night to sing and dance. Another evening they would imitate kangaroos and practise spearing. They practised with spears, missing the targets. Just as in the Army they learned to shoot with rifles, in the same way they learned to spear, to be fighting men. They learned to dodge the spear and to watch the prey carefully.

The women taught how to winnow the seeds, separating the seeds from the grass, and we learned by watching. We asked: 'How do you winnow? Teach us.' They taught us in this way: 'Take the wooden dish.' We took a dish and put seeds into it and shaking and shaking it we learned. We learned how to grind the seeds on grindstones and having ground them we ate. And we spun hairbelts. The women spun hair into belts and we learned all this.

The children played games. When we had done all the work and learned how to work, the children came together and we girls imitated the women. We made windbreaks and collected firewood as we had learned. We sat in the shelters and made fires and played at being women looking after babies. Having watched all this work we sat apart and made out we were women, making shelters, lighting fires and telling stories. We children did this together having listened to all these things.

We learned all of our ways correctly at Angatja, about the different plant foods, the various meat foods, the water holes and the camps. Father and Mother taught us the names of all the places as the whole family together looked after them, brothers, aunts and sisters. We who were related to those places lived there together, grandfather, grandmother, my uncle, my aunt, my father and another of my fathers, and my elder sister. We travelled around close to our camps and as we moved around together we learned. As they taught and taught us we learned about all of the places and their stories. All the waterholes have names and as we moved around we camped at the named waterholes. We travelled around these places, going around from Piltati to Umpukula and from Umpukula to Angatja, and we would visit some of the smaller places. What were the names of some of them? Nyikina, Kurkaratjara, Araltji and Malukulu were some of these small camps. We would camp at them for a short while and they taught us their names and then took us to the large places and taught us. They would tell us: 'These are small places that do not have water.' They taught us about the camps, the creeks and the hills and we learned everything.

And we learned the stories of the country. They kept telling them again, again and again. Father told me many stories and I learned. He would say to me: 'You are hearing stories all the time. You keep asking for another one.' I would say: 'You know all the stories.' My elder brothers also told stories and as they told story after story I listened and listened and learned. I think about these old times and I wish we could live like these old times again. We should always live as we did in those old times when all our work was beautiful and straight.

Yes, we listened then to the story from the land, from the places to which we are related, from our very own camps. The knowledgeable men danced invisibly. We heard about these knowledgeable men of the spirit, from the ancient spirits. The spirits lived in their own places where it is said they performed the beautiful ceremonies. And a man would say, 'I have received this beautiful ceremony', and they would perform the ceremony of that place. For example, there is the story of a bird related to the camp named Miniri. Only the boys danced then, not the girls. The boys only danced, not us. It is only now that women dance for money but in the past the girls did not dance. They did not dance the Seven Sisters ceremony then, only now. They started to do it, not when we were at Ernabella, but at Amata. Some of the women received ceremonies from the North. But only the men danced then.

Sometimes during the day or in the evening, as we sat in the bush shelters our older sisters told us stories,[2] placing leaves on the ground to represent men, women, children and the youths who camped apart from the others. They placed leaves representing old men and old women and told the stories, relating the women's stories. They would tell a story about an old woman and her husband who was blind. The woman called out: 'Bring some firewood. It's freezing.' And a daughter got up and brought some firewood. She lit a fire, got some wood and threw it down. And a son put wood there and they made a windbreak and left them.

Someone else would tell a story about a man who wanted a young woman. They told these kind of stories, about a man, or a good child, or a bad child who was hit. A child who was bad was punished. Another story was about a man who wanted two wives. His first wife hit him and abused him. These are the things they taught us using the leaves: living good lives, about a man getting plenty of meat and about sharing everything. They placed leaves also to represent our relationships and moieties. 'These are people of our moiety, and those are from the other moiety. This is a daughter and this is an uncle.' Mother would teach us and we watched.

They taught us to avoid snakes and to be afraid of them and about ants that bite and to fear them and watch out for them. 'This one bites. It is bad. Keep away from them.' They pointed out the green ants and the meat ants that bite. 'Watch out for these, watch carefully in case they bite you. Be careful, watch out and hit them. Beware of poisonous snakes.'

They told us: 'Don't talk about some things or you will be hit immediately. Avoid all those things. Don't go near the mens' places. Don't look at them. Turn around and go straight in the other direction, or you will be killed. Don't go back. Go straight ahead and don't be disobedient.'

And they taught us about the plants and to choose the edible ones only, the desert raisins, bush tomatoes, native gooseberries and mistletoe berries. These ones we learned to eat, but not some others such as the emu bush and poisonous vines and herbs. These are bad. They taught us how to make shelters with spinifex grass, branches and posts and how to light fires. The men showed how to light fire by rubbing sticks together. They taught us to go carefully across the land, to look for good campsites and to look for the direction of the wind when making a camp. 'If the wind is blowing this way, build the windbreak that way, and if it changes to another direction watch and if it is blowing that way build it this way, to the east.' And when lighting fires we saw which way the wind was blowing and made the windbreaks accordingly. They taught us these things.

They taught us to read the tracks on the ground. Mother, grandmother, older sister, aunts, uncles and grandfather drew prints in the ground and taught us to read the prints of men, women, children, dogs, monsters and evil spirits. At night we children were afraid to go far away in case the wind took us away. We were safe in the camp. 'All the children stay with your mothers, fathers, older brothers and other relatives all the time. Don't go out on your own. Don't stay on your own but together with father, mother, brothers and other relatives.' Everyone looked after a child. As we grew older we looked after the younger ones. Everyone looked after the youths and the boys. All were happy and the whole family looked after everyone and cared for them, sisters, uncles, aunts, all together.

They were always teaching us about the plant foods, the honey foods, the edible scale on the gum leaves, the stories, the meat foods, making string from sinews, threshing spinifex grass to make gum and all these kinds of work, men's work and women's work. We learned the women's work and watched the men's work, such as making spears.

Our mothers gave generously to the children and taught them to share quickly. And if a child kept something selfishly or stole, thinking: 'This is mine,' the mother would hit and say, 'No! Give it! It's hers. You give it to her.' And we gave it immediately. If a child went too close to a woman and her baby the mother rebuked her: 'No! Go this way.' Mothers taught us to go straight. 'Don't play around close to the men but go off a little way,' they would say. 'Go around, not straight through here, not this way, but around the old men, the men, the young men and the old women.' Everything was good and we learned not to go around without thinking. If we did that we were hit. They would say, 'No! Go this way.' If the children played near the camp, our mothers sent us off and we would go immediately. One would get up and wave a stick and send us off: 'Run off, all of you!' And we would listen obediently and go. The children did not play near the camp. They were sent off to play at a distance. The old men and old women lay sleeping in camp and we played away from them and when we had played we would come back. The older brothers and sisters looked after the little children.

The women and older girls would go out together in case there was a man around. If one went alone a man might spear her so they went with friends for fear of men and they would come back together with lots of meat. We were learning and we were happy, eating plenty of meat and playing as children, making out we were women and learning to do the work of our mothers and fathers, cooking meat, grinding seeds, winnowing seeds, gathering foods, telling and listening to stories. We were learning about the stories, the plant foods, the meat foods, the land, and choosing good sites for camps near firewood and shelter. We learned to build camps according to the wind. We learned to observe the wind and then build shelters and windbreaks and light fires. We learned to eat the honey foods and the plant foods from the trees and we learned about the waters and the hills. We sheltered inside caves when it rained and we had no shelters. We learned to eat bush onions and to swim in the waterholes. Our mothers, fathers and older brothers taught us how to swim in the waterholes, and we learned how to dig for water and to place some spinifex grass on the water to stop it splashing. We learned everything from our fathers, just like school. We became very knowledgeable and we did our own work well.

Notes

1. The above recollections of childhood learning were related by Mrs Nganyintja Ilyatjari and recorded by Bill Edwards on 27 September 1982 at Angatja. The tape has been transcribed and translated by Bill Edwards. An earlier draft of the translation made in 1986 was published in *Learning and Other Things: Sources for a Social History of Education in South Australia*, edited by Bernard Hyams, Lynne Trethewey, Brian Condon, Malcolm Vick and Denis Grundy, South Australian Government Printer, 1988. This revised translation was completed in August 1990. Nganyintja was born in the late 1920s in her father's country near the eastern end of the Mann Ranges in the Far North-West of South Australia. After the establishment of Ernabella Mission in the Musgrave Ranges in 1937 her family moved there and she was one of the first children to attend the Ernabella School when it opened in 1940. She later became an assistant teacher at the school. She married Charlie Ilyatjara in 1950 and they had seven children. When Amata government station was established in 1961 near the western end of the Musgrave Ranges they moved there to be nearer her country. Since the late 1970s they have spent much of their time establishing a small homeland community at Angatja, in the area where she lived as a small child. There she seeks to teach young people some of the skills and stories she learned as a child and welcomes small groups of tourists who are invited to share in this learning experience.

2. Nganyintja is referring here to the story-telling method used by Pitjantjatjara women and girls and called by them *milpatjunanyi*. A woman or older girl cleared an area of sand or soil in front of her and as she told a story to younger women or girls sitting around her she held a stick in one hand and beat the ground with a rhythmical action while drawing symbols in the sand with the other hand to represent the people and places of the story. Sometimes leaves were placed on the ground to represent the characters of the story. Through these stories children learned about relationships and behaviours.

2
The Art of Northern Australia

HOWARD MORPHY

The artistic traditions of northern Australia are rich and varied and the region is characterized by an enormous range of styles and media. At Laura in north Queensland, on the rock walls of the Arnhem Land Escarpment and in the Wandjina Galleries of northwestern Australia, are rock paintings whose visual splendour rivals those anywhere in the world. The woodcarving traditions of Melville and Bathurst islands, Arnhem Land and Cape York, ranging from the abstract sculptural forms of the Tiwi grave posts to the detailed figurative carvings of northeast Arnhem Land and Aurukun, display a combination of sculpted and painted form. In Arnhem Land, too, we find what is perhaps the finest expression of contemporary Aboriginal art in the bark paintings of the region, where technical excellence combines with considerable stylistic variation as one moves from west to east. Each of these artistic systems merits in its own right a detailed examination of its stylistic expression and cultural significance. Here, we can do no more than provide a brief background to the art, a glance at its richness, a suggestion as to its significance and a hint at its meaning, in the hope that we will open an avenue towards an understanding of its complexity.

European colonization has had a major impact on Aborigines in northern Australia and in some areas that impact has been catastrophic. In the early days, entire populations were wiped out in clashes with the colonists or through the diseases that they brought with them. In some places, where Aborigines survived the initial period of contact, their populations have declined over the years through infertility and as a result of smallpox and measles. The Kakadu people of the Oenpelli area, whose forebears painted the magnificent x-ray art galleries of the Alligator Rivers region, have been reduced from a thriving population of several hundred at the turn of the century to a mere handful of survivors today through the invasion of the land by gold miners and cattlemen. Thus, living artistic traditions have been converted into sadly beautiful monuments to a near prehistoric past in a matter of decades. Elsewhere, circumstances have been more favourable and European contact has had little effect on the intensity of religious and ceremonial life. If anything, it has resulted in an efflorescence of the artistic systems analogous to that

First published in *Aboriginal Australia*, Sydney: Australian Gallery Directors Council, 1981.

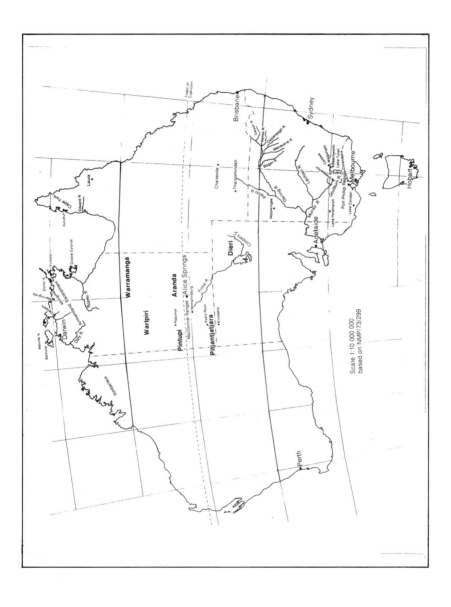

which occurred on the northwest coast of America during the eighteenth and early nineteenth centuries. In eastern and central Arnhem Land, Groote Eylandt and in parts of north Queensland and Western Australia, European contact was restricted until recently to the establishment of missionaries encouraged the Aborigines to continue to practise their had an impact on the local populations, they did not pose an immediate threat to the Aborigines' ownership and control of their land, nor did they result in a decimation of the population. In many cases, the missionaries encouraged the Aborigines to continue to practise their 'traditional' culture while at the same time acting as agents of change. Even where the missions attempted to repress traditional practices and to

Djuwany Post at Gurawuy, Trial Bay. A memorial post outside a house at Trial Bay. The post is erected with others during a Djuwany Ceremony. Ceremonial dillybags are hung from the posts and feather string suspended between them represents an ancestral track. The post commemorates a deceased clan member as well as representing one of the ancestral beings.
Photo: H. Morphy

destroy indigenous institutions, as was the case for many years on Melville and Bathurst Islands, the Aboriginal people on the whole successfully maintained their cultural identity and continuity with the past.

In recent years, in those areas covered by effective land rights legislation, Aborigines have begun to take advantage of their more favourable political situation by reasserting their control over their land, leaving the European-created settlements and dispersing to live in smaller communities. In these small outstations the manufacture and sale of art to white Australians has become a major component of the economy, which in many areas is still based on hunting and gathering. The sale of art works has had no negative effect on the value of art in indigenous contexts, where it has remained integral to ceremonial life. While the return to their land should in no sense be seen as a cultural revival, since the cultures have no need to be revived — though they continue to develop — it is a sign that Aborigines are increasingly gaining the confidence to assert their cultural values over those of white Australians.

A race's cultural survival is inextricably bound to the people's control over land and the degree of political autonomy they possess over local affairs. Aboriginal art has perhaps always been concerned with the ownership as well as the origins of the land, and in recent years Aborigines have used their art as a means of asserting to white Australians their ownership of certain areas. The continuing relevance of their art in the contemporary political context has been a factor in maintaining its vitality, though it must be added that this is underpinned by its role in traditional cultural contexts — in initiation, fertility and life cycle ceremonies. The prime motivation of Aboriginal political action has been the determination to retain cultural autonomy and has involved an assertion of cultural values. Aborigines have often seen this process as being educational, demonstrating to white Australians the rightfulness of their position, in the hope that, through understanding, justice will be obtained. While they have met with some success in the Northern Territory, in north Queensland and Western Australia their control of their land is still being threatened and their cultural and artistic systems in their present form could be in danger of extinction.

Technique and media

Aboriginal artists employ an enormous variety of media and techniques, from rock paintings to sand sculptures, from body paintings to coffin lids, and from designs woven in feather string into the framework of baskets to designs incised in ironwood clapping sticks or the stems of pipes. In some areas, such as central Arnhem Land, all of these media are employed today by members of a single linguistic group, while in other areas only some of them are used. A single ceremony in north-east Arnhem Land may involve the creation of many works of art in different media: a sculpture may be built by scraping up low ridges of sand or earth; initiates' bodies may be painted with detailed designs; painted wooden posts may be erected within the sand sculpture, with metres of feather string draped across the posts; feather string dillybags may be suspended from the lowest branches of trees or hung from the roofs of huts; surrounding tree trunks may be daubed with red paint, and carved and painted spears may be shaken by the dancers. The whole frequently represents an extravagant image of light and colour, the individual works being integrated within an overall performance by the movement of the dancers and the succession of ceremonial events that connect the objects in different ways. Not much of this artistic activity produces durable works; sometimes its expression is immanent in the action — in fleetingly experienced images of waving spears and light filtered through dust, as dancers' feet kick up the sculptured sand, destroying its form. Body paintings may last a few days, dully flaking, never as bright as when they were first put on the initiate's chest as he patiently lay still for hours in the shade of a tree. Some works such as sand sculpture are destroyed without trace at the ceremony's end. Others, such as the painted bark baskets of the Tiwi people of Melville Island, are deliberately broken up and left lying on the ceremonial ground or, as is the case with the elaborately painted Yolngu coffin lids, buried with the deceased beneath the ground soon after their completion.

However, not all works of art have so short a life. The memorial posts of northeast Arnhem Land, the hollow log coffins of the centre and west, the Pukamani posts of the Tiwi, are all intended to last well beyond the ceremony as a reminder of the deceased person they honour. Such sculptures remain for years, until eventually the rain and white ants and the forest fires reduce them to flaking stumps, soon to disappear. Painted bark huts, too, survive until the bark disintegrates. More durable still are the rock paintings and engravings, where they occur. Some of the engravings and some of the earliest paintings may outlast

Wet season bark hut at Manggalod on the Mann River in Central Arnhem Land shows one of the main secular contexts of the art-paintings on the bark walls of a young men's house. *Photo: H. Morphy*

Boys being dressed with feather decorations during a public phase of a circumcision ceremony at the Yirrkala. *Photo: H. Morphy*

not only the generations that produced them but also the cultures. The earliest works from the Laura region are probably some tens of thousands of years old, though others were produced well after European contact. In parts of western and central Arnhem Land and in the western Kimberleys, rock painting traditions carry on into the present day, though the sequence of past cultures whose works are also represented on the rock walls has yet to be determined. In the Wandjina Galleries of the Kimberleys the paintings have been maintained, though with some changes in the form, through being repainted every so often by Aborigines ceremonially renewing them, multiple layers of pigment attesting to the many generations over which this has continued.

Because of the variety of media employed in producing works of art, a detailed discussion of artists' techniques would involve an exploration of a wide area of Aboriginal technology, the technology of weaving and string making, of spear manufacture and carving. Some works of art, for example sand sculptures, require relatively little technology (though a great deal of technique); others such as the feathered string dillybags of north-east Arnhem Land are the product of complex technological subsystems involving techniques of weaving, dyeing, feather string making and so on. Here I will restrict myself to looking at the techniques of painting, though even here I will have to make generalizations that do not account for the complexities of regional variation.

On the whole, Aboriginal artists employ a palette of four colours — red, white, yellow and black. Natural pigments are used, red and yellow ochres, manganese, charcoal, pipeclay and limestone. The pigments may be picked up from the ground, obtained directly or through trade, from quarries. Sometimes the traded pigment is prepared by being ground down and made into bricks set in stringy bark moulds. The source of ochre may be important in ceremonial paintings, different ochres having different religious connotations reflected in subtle aspects of their colour. The preferred red ochre used by one of the moieties throughout northeast Arnhem Land is a heavy plum coloured haematite which has a naturally burnished effect when painted on the skin. The main source of this pigment is Elcho Island, from where it is traded to the surrounding region.

The pigments are prepared for use by grinding them and adding water and some kind of fixative before applying them to a surface. In northeast Arnhem Land red and yellow ochre and manganese are rubbed onto a stone palette that has first been dampened slightly with water. As soon as sufficient pigment has been rubbed off, a fixative is added — in the past the juices from the stem of a tree orchid or a seagull's egg, today a soluble wood glue — and combined with the powder.

The most specialized items of the painter's equipment are the brushes he employs. The main outline of a design and colour washes over large areas of a painting or as a background cover are sometimes applied with frayed pieces of stringy bark or the chewed end of a stick, though today commercial brushes are often used. The pigment may even be rubbed onto the surface using the hand, defining the outline of a figure with a finger. Detailed work, in particular the infilling of a design, may be done with a brush specially designed for the task. Such brushes vary regionally according to painting style and the technique employed. One of the most widespread brushes used is one that consists of a long strand of human hair bound to a thin stick. Such brushes are used to produce the thin lined, cross hatched infill characteristic of Arnhem Land painting. The brush is dipped into the pigment, then the hair laid on the painting before being drawn across the surface. In some areas, a feather or a thin palm leaf rib is used instead of human hair. Another specialized brush is restricted to Melville and Bathurst Islands, where it is used for producing dotted infill. This brush, consisting of a small comb cut from wood, is used to make multiple dots, thus speeding up the painting process.

In order to exemplify the painting process, I will briefly go through the main stages in the production of a bark painting by the Yolngu people of northeast Arnhem Land. The same procedure is followed for all

Sand sculpture belonging to the Yarrwidi Gumatj clan representing a sacred site at Caledon Bay. The sculpture made at Yirrkala represents a Macassan house on stilts. The sculpture is used as part of a mortuary ceremony to guide the deceased spirit back to his clan lands. *Photo: H. Morphy*

paintings on flat surfaces, be they body paintings, paintings on memorial posts or bark or coffin lid paintings. A seasoned and fire-flattened sheet of bark is prepared for painting by roughly sanding over the inner surface. The surface of the bark is then painted all over in a single colour, usually red but occasionally yellow or black. This provides the ground colour for the design. The figures and main design elements are next marked out in either black or yellow. This is done rapidly and, according to the Yolngu, 'roughly', as the outlines will not show on the surface of the finished painting. The final stage consists of infilling the design with cross hatching. To start with, the ground between the figures, and sometimes the interior of the figures themselves, is covered with white parallel lines. After a section has been covered with one set of lines, a second set is painted across it, this time in white, red, black or yellow, frequently in alternating colour sequences. Occasionally, areas are covered with dotted infill and sometimes with a combination of cross hatching with dots. Once the infill has been completed, the outlines of the figures and geometric patterns are redefined with fine lines painted with a hair brush. The whole process is one of adding colour and definition, the painting being transformed from a dull and flat surface to one that shimmers with the brilliance of the cross hatching — a brilliance that the Yolngu expect from their paintings.

A basically similar technique to the one outlined above is followed throughout Arnhem Land and on Melville and Bathurst Islands and Groote Eylandt, though very different effects are achieved according to the way in which technique is combined with shape to produce form. Thus, in western Arnhem Land the background to the figures tends to remain free of infilling, while the figurative representations are infilled; the reverse is practised in northeast Arnhem Land. Elsewhere in northern Australia very different techniques of painting are employed and to different effect. The Wandjina paintings of the Kimberleys and the more abstract painted shields of the Queensland rain forest, for example, are not covered with infilling, the surface consisting of areas of boldly and thickly applied pigments.

Art and social context

Aboriginal art is owned. Although there is some decorative art, simple geometric designs that can be applied by anyone to the mundane objects of everyday life, on the whole designs can be painted and art objects manufactured only by those who have the inherited right to produce them. The system of ownership or distribution of rights in paintings varies widely throughout the continent. Throughout much of northern Australia, rights are vested in patrilineal clans or sections of those clans. This applies in particular in the case of northeast and central Arnhem Land, the western Kimberleys and southwest Cape York. In western and southern Arnhem Land, other principles operate as well, ownership being linked to membership of a particular subsection and possibly to certain linguistic groups.

In northeast Arnhem Land, paintings, songs, dances and secret names are owned by patrilineal clans of around fifty members. A person also has certain rights in the paintings of his mother's clan and mother's mother's clan. People have differential access to the clan's paintings according to their age and sex. Greatest authority is vested in the hands of senior members of the clan. It is they who decide when to teach younger members of the clan how to do the particular paintings and it is they who decide when to explain to them the significance of the designs. Young clan members can produce paintings only with the consent of senior clan members and do not have the authority to pass on information about their meaning to outsiders.

Women, although they have rights similar to a man's in a clan's paintings, are not expected to exercise them in the same way. Women are excluded from many of the contexts in which paintings are produced, from the men's ceremonial ground and from the hut in which a coffin lid is being painted or a sacred object being made. Women are not taught the meaning of paintings in the formal way in which it is explained to male initiates and, indeed, according to public ideology, women are not supposed to know the 'inside' or restricted meanings of even their own clan's paintings. Although today women of some clans occasionally participate in painting initiates for a circumcision ceremony, and assist with the painting of coffin lids, this is very much the exception. On the whole, control over paintings and of the distribution of knowledge about the paintings is exercised by the senior male members of the clans. Certainly women do get to see the paintings and almost certainly are taught and learn as much about them as their brothers. Certainly senior women are consulted about the use of the clan's paintings in ceremonies and do play a decision-making role with regard to them. However, women's knowledge about paintings and the decision-making role they play is not part of the public structure of relations within society, belonging rather to a more informal system. Publicly, women assert that men have a superordinate role and greater access to knowledge about paintings than women. Indeed, increasing access to knowledge of paintings relative to women and uninitiated men is acknowledged to be a major feature of male initiation, one that enables men to exercise a dominant role in ceremonial life and is a reflection of their powerful position in society.

The pattern of relations between men and women and its expression in the control of the artistic system is not the same throughout northern Australia. In central and western Arnhem Land, control over art by the men is emphasized more than in the east. More stress is placed on denying women knowledge of the art, and on the whole women do not produce paintings, not even assisting their husbands or brothers with the infill on bark paintings made for sale. In some areas of western Arnhem Land women have their own ceremonies from which men are excluded. However, there are no societies in the north, as there are in central Australia, in which women own a large body of designs which are kept secret from the men. Secrecy is perhaps least emphasized on Melville and Bathurst Islands. Among the Tiwi the major ceremonies that are performed today are public mortuary rituals in which all aspects of the performance are witnessed by men and women alike, and people are not denied access to knowledge on the basis of their sex. Men, however, are still the major producers of the art, of the Pukamani poles and baskets made for the deceased.

Although secrecy is an important component of Aboriginal artistic systems, it would be wrong to think that most art objects are displayed

Crocodile Dance at Aurukun. The saltwater crocodile man took all women for his wives and would let no other man have any, so the freshwater crocodile man speared him in a combat. *Photo: Australian Institute of Aboriginal Studies (E. L. Cranstone).*

Catching the bonefish at night by men in a canoe. The dance is performed around the rack of fish. *Photo: Australian Institute of Aboriginal Studies (E. L. Cranstone).*

only in restricted contexts. Some objects are seen only by initiated men, being manufactured and revealed in restricted contexts. However, they may be shown informally to senior female clan members. Some paintings are publicly seen only in a modified form, the body paintings of initiates being masked by smearing them before the young men return to the public arena. Still more objects are manufactured in secrecy but displayed openly, such as the memorial posts and hollow log coffins of the Yolngu. In the majority of cases a great deal of artistic activity takes place in open contexts, or else the works themselves can be seen by all members of the society. The carved figures of Aurukun, the grave posts of Arnhem Land and of the Tiwi, many of the rock paintings of the Alligator River region, feather string dillybags, sand sculptures and bark paintings are all of open access. Frequently it is not a particular design that is restricted, but the place in which it is displayed or the occurrence of the design on a particular object. The design on the body of an initiate may be restricted, but the same design as a bark painting may be public. Rock paintings at one site may be public, whereas rock paintings of another site which overlap in content may be prohibited to people without permission or authority to go there. And it must be emphasized that the right and authority to produce paintings and objects are closely guarded even if access to the objects is not restricted.

Art, ceremony and value

Aboriginal art is religious art. Although we have stressed in the previous section that rights in paintings are particularly important, that they are owned by social groups, and that access to them depends on a person's status and group affiliation, they should not be thought of simply as a commodity. Paintings and other works of art are manifestations of the Ancestral Past, of the Dreamtime, when the world creative powers transformed the earth through their actions, determining the form of the landscape as it is today. Not only did they create the rivers, lakes and streams, the shape of the hills and valleys, the stars in the sky and the forests on earth; they also gave order to the world by naming the flora and fauna and the places that they journeyed to, and by establishing the form of social life, clans and moieties, marriage rules and the structure of ceremonies. They passed on to the human groups who succeeded them on the land a system of existence that was complete in all respects and which human beings simply had to fit into by following the rules that had been established.

In each place, the Ancestral Beings entrusted areas of land to particular groups: in northeast Arnhem Land and many other places to clans, and elsewhere to totemic cult groups or linguistic groups, to hold in perpetuity. Ownership of the land was, however, conditional on the human groups following the law that had been established by the Ancestors and in particular on them performing the ceremonies that re-enacted the creative events of the Ancestral Past. The Ancestral Beings indeed did not cease to exist with the creation of human beings; rather, they moved aside, often merging into the landforms that they created, removing their physical presence to beneath the surface of the earth. They did, however, retain the power to intervene in the life of man and, indeed, remain a vital force in ensuring the continuity of human existence and in maintaining the fertility of the land. The Ancestral Beings are the source of conception spirits necessary to initiate each pregnancy; they provide a source of power to ensure growth and human wellbeing, and they ensure a plentiful supply of food.

The paintings and sacred objects produced in ceremonies are not simply representations of Ancestral Beings, nor are the ceremonies themselves simply re-enactments of Ancestral Events. They are, in a sense, manifestations of the Ancestral Beings and recreations of the events that they took part in. The paintings that are produced are in many cases the paintings that Ancestral Beings had painted on their chests, or designs that have become associated with the Ancestral Being in some other way: the mark made by the tide washing over his body, or the pattern burnt into his skin as a bushfire rushed past him. The designs are Ancestral designs and are thought to contain aspects of the power of the Ancestral Beings themselves. Painting a design on a person enables him or her to be placed in direct contact with the Ancestral Past — the paintings themselves, as controllable manifestations of the Ancestors, providing people with the means of tapping the sources of Ancestral power.

We can thus see why it is so important for people to guard closely their rights in paintings, for groups to ensure that other people do not steal their designs. Looking after the paintings, songs and other components of their sacred law is not only a necessary part of fulfilling their obligations to the Ancestors who have entrusted them with their land.

Young dancers painted with pipe clay at a mortuary ceremony at Yirrkala. White pigment is characteristically painted on bodies in mortuary ceremonies and is believed to protect participants against pollution. *Photo: H. Morphy*

The paintings also provide them with their own channel of communication with the Ancestral Past, a channel of communication that can be passed on to subsequent generations of the clan or cult group.

Paintings are produced in ceremonies for a number of purposes: sometimes their function is highly specific; on other occasions it is more generalized. Mortuary ceremonies provide a major context for artistic expression. In many parts of Arnhem Land the deceased's body or, more frequently today his coffin lid, is painted with designs that represent one of the Ancestral Beings of his clan or of a closely related clan. In this way, the deceased is put in contact with the spiritual world of the Ancestral Past and the powers of the Ancestral Beings are summonded to help guide his or her spirit to the clan lands whence it came, to join the reservoir of spiritual essence associated with his clan's Ancestors in their land. Later on, when the spirit is thought to have completed its journey, the bones of the deceased may be placed in a hollow log coffin, or a memorial post may be erected in his honour. In either case, designs will be painted on coffin or post which remind people of the deceased and which represent the Ancestral Beings he has rejoined. Initiates may at the same time have paintings done on their chests which connect them to the deceased, or else they may be placed in contact with the memorial posts through ritual actions, thereby transferring some of the power of the Ancestral Beings associated with the dead person on to a new generation of clan members.

In some areas the degree of elaboration of the mortuary ceremonies depends in part on the status of the deceased and of his clan. On Melville and Bathurst Islands the more important the person is the more likely he is to have a large number of Pukamani poles carved for him on his death — a factor which reflects in turn on the prestige of his family and of the groups responsible for organizing the ceremony.

Ceremonies are often concerned with the interests of members of a society as a whole, in ensuring the wellbeing and solidarity of the group. In such cases, paintings and sacred objects are often thought to function at a more general level, ensuring the fertility of women, the vitality of children and the productivity of the land. In the area of Aurukun and the Mitchell River in north Queensland, different clans are responsible for the maintenance ceremonies for different species linked totemically to their group. Members of the clan paint their bodies with representations of different ancestors and manufacture carved figures which are used in dances that re-enact events in the lives of the Ancestral Heroes. The repainting of the Wandjinas in the Kimberley rock shelters is thought, among other things, to encourage the arrival of the wet season rains and to ensure the recovery of the land after the long period of dry weather

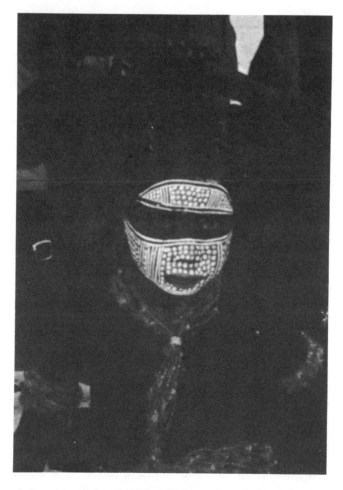

A face painting representing 'bubbling fresh water' on a boy being initiated into the first stages of the Djungguwa-malk ceremony held at Gurawuy, on Trial Bay, northeast Arnhem Land. *Photo: H. Morphy*

Flying Fox Clan Dance. Two brothers of the flying fox clan killed large numbers of their own totem animal but could not cook them. The short sticks are red flying foxes and the long ones are black flying foxes. *Photo: Australian Institute of Aboriginal Studies (E. L. Cranstone).*

that precedes it. And throughout Arnhem Land, in ceremonies such as the Kunapipi, the Djungguwan and the Yabaduruwa, paintings and sacred objects are made in ceremonies that focus on themes of growth and fecundity. Although the ceremonies operate at a societal level, symbolic actions can direct the Ancestral power created by the ceremony towards particular individuals and groups by painting designs on people of a particular age group or status, by placing them in contact with paintings on cave walls, and by rubbing sacred objects against their bodies. A painting on a person's body thus not only signifies his status and membership of a social group, but also places the person in direct contact with Ancestral Power, establishing an individual relationship between the person and the Ancestral world.

Art and meaning

Aboriginal art is about meaning. Individual paintings and carvings are products of systems of communication which create meaning by encoding relationships between things, by relating people and place to the world of the land-transforming Ancestral Beings. However, just as there are many spoken languages throughout northern Australia, so too are there many systems of visual communication, each with its own characteristics. Here we can look at only some of the general principles that underlie them, illustrating them with examples drawn mainly from eastern Arnhem Land.

Much Aboriginal art consists of Ancestral designs — designs which are themselves manifestations of the Ancestral Beings. The Ancestral Beings are complex entities which exist in many dimensions and which, during their lives on earth, underwent many transformations of form. Some took the form of rocks, trees or elements such as water and fire. They were not, however, the inanimate rocks of today; as rocks, they could walk the countryside and talk to other Ancestral Beings and perform creative acts. Sometimes, it is true, they acted in the manner of rocks, rolling down a hillside in a landfall, tearing down trees and scouring the earth, but, unlike the rocks of today, their action was guided by thought and had intended consequences in the formation of rivers and valleys and the shaping of the earth. Such Ancestral Beings transcended the boundaries between animate and inanimate forms. Others changed shape, frequently oscillating between animal and human form, sometimes combining aspects of the two simultaneously — for example, leaping great distances as a kangaroo and throwing a spear as a man. Then there are others who cannot be thought of as single objects outside their existence as Ancestral Beings. The Wild Honey Ancestor of northeast Arnhem Land consists of the whole complex of objects associated with wild honey: the hive and the bees, the tree in which the hive is found, the honey they produce and the the man looking for honey, the smoke used to stun the bees and the dillybags in which the honey is placed; all things associated with wild honey are attributes of the Wild Honey Ancestor.

Just as the Ancestral Beings themselves take many forms, so do the objects and paintings that represent them. Some paintings focus on a particular aspect of the Ancestor, representing figuratively one frozen aspect of its form. A figurative representation of a kangaroo on a western Arnhem Land rock wall may signify the site where the Ancestral Kangaroo in animal form rested in the rock shelter. Elsewhere, a painting of his dissected body may represent the place where he was caught and killed by other Ancestral Beings and cut up in readiness for cooking. A single representation seldom conveys alone the significance of the events that occurred in a particular place. In the rock shelter there may also be other manifestations of the Kangaroo: boulders that were created from his dismembered limbs, a depression in the rock where the spear that killed him fell. The concept of the Ancestral Being is the sum of all its manifestations, and the songs, dances and stories that connect them.

Some representations of Ancestral Beings are more abstract, consisting of geometric elements that signify attributes of the Ancestor and the events in which he was involved. The Wild Honey Ancestor of eastern Arnhem Land, for example, is represented by a complex diamond pattern (Figure 2.1). The diamonds themselves represent the calls of the hive; the cross hatched infill signifies different components of the hive, the grubs, the honey and the bees; the cross bar that bisects some of the diamonds represents small sticks that are found in the hive, while the dots within the circles represent the bees swarming from the entrance to the hive. At another level, elements of the design signify attributes of the fire used to smoke out the bees: the white cross hatching is the smoke, the red is the sparks and the white dots the ash. At another level still, the

entrance to hive
filled with bees

cells of hive

sticks in honeycomb

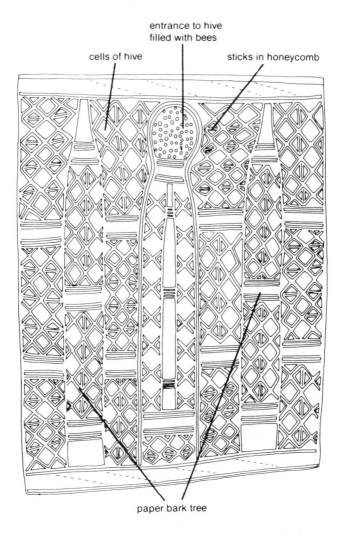

paper bark tree

Figure 2.1
A Wild Honey Ancestors design from a painting by Dula Ngurruwuthun of the
Muwyuku clan from northeastern Arnhem Land. The painting represents
aspects of the Wild Honey Ancestor in the paper bark swamps. The diamond
pattern represents the cells of the hive and fresh flowing water. According to
the infill, the diamonds represent cells filled with honey, grubs or eggs. The
elongated figures to each side represent paper bark trees and the central figure
the entrance to the hive. *Joan Goodrum.*

diamond pattern itself represents the rippling of fresh water as it flows
beside the paper bark trees in which this particular type of honey is
found. The Wild Honey Ancestor is all of those things and more.

As well as providing images of the Ancestral Beings and of the
Ancestral Past, the paintings link the Ancestors to particular places

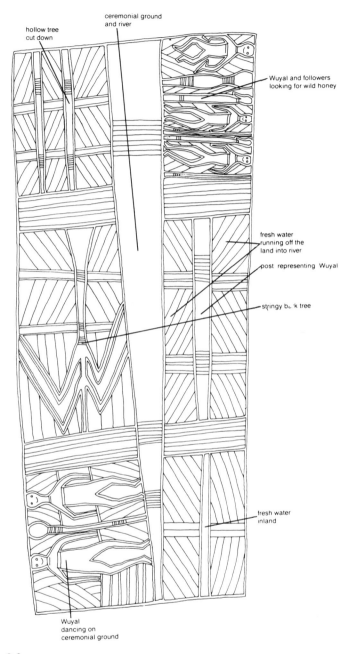

Figure 2.2
The Ancestral Being, Wuyal, creating land and ceremonies, after a painting by
Mithili Wanambi of the Marakulu clan, Yirrkala. A ceremonial ground and
river form the central part of this painting, with Wuyal depicted dancing on the
ground and then searching for wild honey with some of his followers. Other
non-figurative elements in the design represent trees and fresh water running
off the land into the river. *Joan Goodrum*.

associated with their creative acts. Sometimes this is done directly by the location of the painting: the kangaroo on the rock wall is a manifestation of that Ancestor in the place it created. In other cases, it is done by encoding in the painting meanings that refer to particular places. In northeast Arnhem Land, each painting, as well as being an image of the Ancestor and an account of events that took place on the journeys that he took across Arnhem Land, represents topographical features of the landscape in the area in which the events took place.

A painting by Mithili (Figure 2.2) demonstrates the way in which Yolngu paintings from northeast Arnhem Land encode the relationship between Ancestral Beings and the places that they created. The painting represents at one level the journey of Wuyal, a Dhuwa moiety Ancestral Being who travelled through Arnhem Land in search of honey. He travelled with his companions, who carried with them spears and spearthrowers. At various places they came upon stringy bark trees filled with wild honey, which they cut down to obtain the honey. Sometimes, when the trees fell, the impression they left in the ground became the site for a ceremony. Wuyal erected painted posts in the ground by which he would be commemorated, and his followers performed dances around the posts, thus creating the ceremonies that the Yolngu perform today. Sometimes the trees, cut down in the high country, rushed headlong down to the sea, gouging out valleys and river beds. Details of the painting can be matched with features of a particular watercourse to reveal a detailed map of the landscape, which in turn can be related to the mythological events that formed it. As people become more familiar with the landscape through journeying across it, the more complex becomes their understanding of the paintings. The paintings play a major role in mediating between experience of features of the 'real' world and the Ancestral events that led to their creation, by providing concrete objects that link the two realms.

Paintings also establish links between Ancestral Beings and specific human groups. In one sense, this is a function of the fact that paintings are owned: only people with rights in paintings can produce them. However, in parts of Arnhem Land this aspect of the system has become highly formalized, and the relationship between Ancestral Being and social group has become part of the meaning encoded in the painting. In the Yolngu area, each clan has a set of designs which are unique to it. The designs consist of repeated sequences of geometric elements which differ in some dimension or detail of combination from those of every other clan. These signify not only the clan to which the painting belongs, but also the Ancestral Being with which the clan is connected. The linked diamond design which represented the Wild Honey Ancestor is one such example. Now the Wild Honey Ancestor is not unique to one clan. Wild Honey, and the Fire Ancestral Being closely associated with it, travelled widely through northeast Arnhem Land, crossing the territories of many clans of the Yirritja moiety. Each clan associated with Wild Honey or Fire has a diamond design as a manifestation of that Ancestral complex. However, each clan's diamond design differs in some respect from that of every other clan. The first diamond design we discussed belongs to the Munyuku clan, and can be defined as consisting of large equilateral

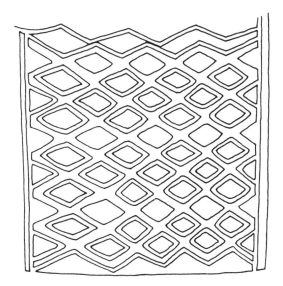

Figure 2.3
Dhalwangu clan design from a painting by Yanggarring from Yirrkala in
northeastern Arnhem Land. *Joan Goodrum.*

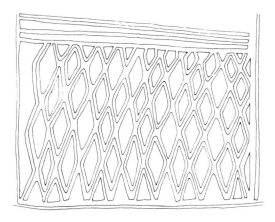

Figure 2.4
Gumatj clan design from a painting by Liawulumu of Yirrkala, northeastern
Arnhem Land. *Joan Goodrum.*

diamonds (Figure 2.1); the Dhalwangu clan has smaller equilateral
diamonds (Figure 2.3), while the Gumatj clan (Figure 2.4) has large
elongated diamonds. The set of clan designs thus expresses the
relationships between social groups, and enables each clan to establish its

own unique relationship with an Ancestral Being who may have journeyed over the territory of a large number of clans.

Each painting, and sometimes each part of a painting, has many levels or layers of meaning associated with it. As we saw in the case of the Wild Honey design, the meaning of the diamond design varies according to the interpretative perspective adopted: it signifies a particular clan, the cells of a beehive or running fresh water and, depending on the infill, the cells may be filled with honey, grubs or a small stick. Similarly, a painting may be interpreted as a map of an area of land or as a record of events that took place on the journey of the Ancestral Beings who crossed that land. These different levels of meaning are integrated with the system of initiation in such a way that some meanings will be more widely known than others. When a person is being taught about the significance of a painting, he does not learn all about the painting at once, but is given only a certain amount of information. Later on, as he grows older, he will be told further things about the painting. Not all his knowledge will be gained through formal instruction. Other knowledge will be gained through learning songs and seeing dances performed that are related to the painting, and, as we have suggested already, through visiting the places represented in the painting and learning more about their mythological significance. Overall, this means that, as a person grows older and passes through the system of initiation, he acquires a deeper knowledge of the significance of a painting. It is not that what he learns first is wrong, but that it is only part of the story. Each time he learns something new about a painting, it provides him with information that can be related to what he already knows. He may first be told that a painting represents a hunting scene in the bush. Then he may learn that the hunters are in fact Ancestral Beings and that the painting represents events in their lives. Later still, he may be shown how the painting is a map of an area of land. He will then be in a position to relate one interpretation to another, learning how mythological events led to the shaping of the landscape and why a particular rock has the shape it does.

Style, form and content

Style is the characteristic way in which form is organized to express content in a particular artistic system. It is the product of a particular way of expressing meaning. To discuss style in art without reference to meaning would be rather like describing an internal combustion engine without reference to its function — it would be missing the point.

Paintings in northeast Arnhem Land consist of a number of different components and different types of represenatation. The main components are a base colour, a border, dividing lines and figurative and geometric representations. Certainly, it would be possible to describe the art in purely formal terms as, for example, 'consisting of a number of figurative representations with the area between the figures being entirely filled with elaborately cross hatched geometric designs'. However, in order to understand the significance of the style and to discover the principles that underlie it, it must be seen as a system of meaning in the context of a particular culture.

The geometric and figurative representations encode meanings in different ways. The figurative representations are iconic: they look like the object they are intended to represent. Their meaning at one level is easy to interpret as long as one is familiar with the representational conventions employed by the Yolngu artist. Certainly, their meaning is not exhausted by the initial interpretation. If a figure represents a kangaroo, one must still ask what the significance of the kangaroo is in the context of the picture as a whole, and what it signifies to members of the culture. However, at one level and a necessary level, the representation means what the artist intended it to look like. The geometric art encodes meaning in a different way. On the whole it is not iconic. Each element can mean a variety of things in different contexts and it is impossible to interpret its meaning without being told by the artist and without being familiar with the system. The geometric art also encodes different kinds of meaning from the figurative art. In the first place, it is multivalent; each element can mean more than one thing: a diamond can signify a cell of a hive, running water and a particular clan; a circle may mean a waterhole, a campsite, a hole in the rock and so on. In the second place, the geometric art can encode certain kinds of meaning more efficiently than the figurative art. For example, as we have shown already, it can encode the relationships between social groups through similarities and differences between the patterns owned by each clan.

The fact that the geometric art must be interpreted before it can be understood makes it particularly suited to an initiation system in which certain information is restricted to people of a particular status. Until a person is instructed in the meaning of the geometric component of the art, he will not be able to understand it. Until he is initiated into its significance, he will be left only with the surface messages he received from interpreting the figurative representations. The multivalency of the geometric art also makes it an excellent means of encoding the messages which the initiate will finally learn from the art; for what is learned, as we have seen, concerns the relationships between things. In the geometric art, the relationship between ancestral action and topographical form can be encoded in a single element. To take a simple example, a circle may represent an Ancestral Being placing his digging stick in the ground and the impression it made. It may at the same time represent a waterhole that is found today in a part of the country, a waterhole that was created by his action.

The style of northeast Arnhem Land paintings is thus, in part, the product of two different systems of representation being used in combination to create meaningful forms that function in a particular sociocultural context.

Much less is known about the structure and significance of artistic systems in northern Australia, outside northeast Arnhem Land. However, if we consider as an example, the 'x-ray' art and 'Mimi figure' art of western Arnhem Land we can see it contrasts with that of north-eastern Arnhem Land in a number of respects. The art of the rock walls and bark paintings of western Arnhem Land is predominantly figurative. The wide variety of different types of figurative representations is the result of the exploitation of two complementary principles of iconic representation: elaboration and schematization or reduction of form. Animal species are most frequently represented in an elaborated manner, with great attention being paid to both internal and external features of the animal concerned. The figures include details of the external form of the animals that enable it to be readily identified, and they often include representations of the internal organs as well — in particular, the heart, lungs, liver and intestines. Human subjects, in contrast, are usually represented in a more schematic way, sometimes reduced to stick figures. In the case of the more schematic figures, the emphasis tends to be on action, the figures having a dynamic form showing the people running, throwing spears, dancing and so on. The elaborated and schematic figures do not represent, respectively, two discrete styles. Not only do figures exist that represent all states on a schematic elaborated continuum, from extremely elaborated to highly schematized; but both principles may be employed in different figures in the same painting or even on different sections of the same figure.

The x-ray and Mimi art of western Arnhem Land like the Wandjina paintings of the Kimberleys seem to be concerned with creating tangible images of events in the Ancestral Past, of the form of Ancestral Beings and of the spiritual dimension of existence. Whereas the art of northeast Arnhem Land provides a means of encoding the relationship between Ancestral Beings, groups and the land, thus enabling individuals' life experiences in the everyday world to be transformed into knowledge of the Ancestral world, the art of western Arnhem Land projects images of that alternative reality onto rock surfaces, so that the Ancestral dimension can be directly experienced. Unfortunately, until more is known about western Arnhem Land art, about the intention of the artist and the effect of the images, this remains a hypothesis and the details of the process of 'other world' creation will remain unknown.

Before concluding this section, something must be said by way of a qualification. Most Aboriginal societies produced a large variety of art objects which often appear to reflect different styles — paintings produced in one context looking very different from those produced in other contexts. In northeast Arnhem Land, there are a number of categories of art. Paintings produced in public contexts, in particular at the time of early contact with Europeans, tended to be predominantly figurative. Paintings produced in closed contexts were, like those described above, elaborately infilled paintings which included a large geometric component. In western Arnhem Land the situation was (and is) remarkably similar. Paintings produced for public contexts were largely figurative, whereas those produced in restricted contexts were predominantly geometric.

In both cases, European tastes focused on one category or 'style' of art rather than the others, so that style has been thought of as the characteristic style of the area. In western Arnhem Land, Europeans focused on the figurative x-ray and Mimi art of the rock walls and bark paintings, whereas in northeast Arnhem Land the emphasis has been placed on paintings in which clan designs fill the area between the figures. There certainly are major differences between the different categories of art in western and eastern Arnhem Land, but most Europeans are unaware that exclusively figurative paintings also exist in the east, and that entirely geometric paintings are also produced in the west.

Conclusion

In this chapter we have been able to do no more than skim the surface of the artistic systems of northern Australia. There are many Aboriginal cultures in northern Australia, each with a rich inheritance of paintings linked to the land they own. The paintings and carvings represent a way of looking at the world and of ordering life's experiences in terms of relationships between a human and an ancestral domain. The paintings can be fully understood only when related to the songs and dances and ritual events that accompany their production and revelation in ceremonial contexts; that is to say, only when they are seen integrated within the overall fabric of the cultures that produced them. The art encodes meanings which help to endow everyday events and familiar features of the landscape with cosmic significance, by referring to and conjuring up images of the ancestral past.

References
BERNDT, R.M. (ed) (1964), *Australian Aboriginal Art*, Sydney: Ure Smith.
BRANDL, E.J. (1973), *Australian Aboriginal Paintings in Western and Central Arnhem Land*, Canberra: Australian Institute of Aboriginal Studies.
CRAWFORD, I.M. (1968), *The Art of the Wandjina*, London: Oxford University Press.
EDWARDS, R. (1979), *Australian Aboriginal Art*, Canberra: Australian Institute of Aboriginal Studies.
ELKIN, E.P., BERNDT, R.M. and BERNDT, C.H. (1950), *Art in Arnhem Land*, Melbourne: Cheshire.
GROGER-WURM, H.M. (1973), *Australian Aboriginal Bark Paintings and their Mythological Interpretations*, Vol. 1, Canberra: Australian Institute of Aboriginal Studies.
KUPKA, K. (1972) *Peintres Aborigines d'Australie*, Paris: Musée de l'homme.
McCONNEL, U. (1935), 'Inspiration and Design in Aboriginal Art', in *Art in Australia*, May, 1935, 49–68.
MORPHY, H. (1977), 'Yingapungapu—Ground Sculpture as Bark Painting', in P.J. Ucko (ed) *Form in Indigenous Art*, London: A.I.A.S.
MOUNTFORD, C.P. (1956) *Art, Myth and Symbolism, Records of the American-Australian Scientific Expedition to Arnhem Land 1948*, Vol. 1, Melbourne: Melbourne University Press.
MOUNTFORD, C.P. (1958), *The Tiwi: Their Art, Myth and Ceremony*, London: Phoenix House.

3
Always Ask: Resource Use and Land Ownership among Pintupi Aborigines of the Australian Western Desert[1]

FRED R. MYERS

Introduction

> My country is the place where I can cut a spear or make a spear-thrower with-
> out asking anyone. (Western Desert Aboriginal man, quoted in Tindale
> 1974:18)

In this chapter I discuss the relationship between spatial organization and
the use and control of resources among Pintupi-speaking Aborigines of
Australia's Western Desert. The relationship of environment, technology, and social organization among hunter-gatherers has intrigued
scholars since Rousseau. Like him, many subsequent commentators have
seen in the description of food-collectors important implications for
various grand theories of 'human nature'. Such theorizing has often
seemed persuasive because of an implicit idea that foragers are *closer to
nature* than other people. Consequently, the problem of hunter-gatherer
territoriality has only infrequently been seen as involving 'thick
description' (Geertz 1973) of people's social lives and cultural constructs.
This has severely hampered effective understanding of hunter-gatherers
in a number of ways.

Like Radcliffe-Brown, most writers have recognized a spatial
component in social organization among hunter-gatherers. This is
particularly true for Australian Aborigines, among whom social
aggregates ('bands' if you will) are often identified with place names. Yet
the fact of this relationship between social group and place, perhaps
between 'band' and 'territory', has given rise to differing interpretations.
Essentially, there have been two traditions of understanding territorial
organization among hunter-gatherers.

One tradition has identified certain units of social organization, called
them 'bands', and asked how these units matched to 'land'. Radcliffe-
Brown (1930), for example, described the typical Australian society as
made up of patrilineal, patrilocal bands ('hordes'). Having discovered

First published in *Resource Managers: North American and Australian
Hunter-Gatherers*, Symposium of AAAS, held in San Francisco, 3–8 January
1980, Westview Press, Boulder, Colorado.

the existence of patrilineal descent groups with a relationship to named places, he argued that these 'local groups' owned and defended their territory, living largely within their group boundaries and thus conserving resources for their own use. This view saw the convergence between stable and enduring social groups and tracts of land as being straightforward and one-dimensional. It is now clear that confusion results from simply equating territorial organization with descent group organization and that it is wrong to assume that local groups had constant, impermeable boundaries. In other words, this approach ignores the contexts in which organization takes place and fails to relate cultural concepts to the multiple dimensions of social reality.

A second tradition, reacting to the inadequacy of the first. has argued that permanent organizational units do not exist, and has maintained that analysis of hunter-gatherer territorial organization must start with resources. This approach treats adaptation to resources as the principal structural feature of foraging societies. The culmination of this approach (Lee & De Vore 1968, 1976) emphasizes the flexibility of actual residential groups, openness of access to resources, and focuses on behavior (land and resource use) rather than the ideology so important to earlier theorists (especially seeing the contrast between residence and patrilineal ideology). While correctly pointing out that people did not live within exclusive, bounded, and defended patrilineal territories, and pointing to the importance of regional systems among foragers (Lee 1976), this model has assumed that territorial organization is to be understood only in relationship to actual on-the-ground aggregates of people. Ignoring ideology as 'epiphenomenal', this model fails to attend adequately to what a 'band' is (see Peterson 1983) or to the connected question of how regional systems operate. Using the analyst's criteria for what constitutes a 'resource', this approach distorts the nature of groups and the nature of their relationship to land, and thus does not really depict the processes through which adaptation occurs.[2]

While a focus on 'adaptation' — examining links between environment, technology, and social institutions — does point out the importance of certain material concerns in the organization of social life, analysis in this tradition tends to incorporate a 'functionalism' which does not consider the emergent internal structure of relations in particular hunter-gatherer societies. Anthropologists have been more willing, it seems, to identify the goals and values of society with 'caloric survival' when considering hunter-gatherers than for other sorts of societies. The human being as culture-user is largely ignored. With primary analytical attention given only to physical resources, beginning with human-environment interaction, no sufficient place is allowed for the specific cultural notions of resource and value. Thus, the fact that the Pintupi and most Aborigines differ from other hunter-gatherers such as the San in their conception of The Dreaming, 'totemic landscape', and male ritual hierarchy, has been reduced, at best, to similarities in maintaining access to land, and the San are now seen as the archetypal hunter-gatherers without all that 'cultural clutter'.

This too simple dichotomy between ideology and material/practical concerns tends to plague our understanding of hunter-gatherers. While some analysts have been too ready to relate indigenous concepts like the widely-used 'one country man' to our own sociocentric models of territorial organization (emphasizing local groups, 'bands', and 'hordes'), others have been too ready to dispense with the indigenous concepts altogether.

Neither of the traditions I have summarized seems adequate to account for the complex processes of territorial organization among the Pintupi. Consequently, I want to offer a third approach to the problem which maintains that what our informants say and think about their social lives may be of help in devising adequate analyses of the relationship between social organization and resources. One important tradition in anthropology sees the goal of anthropological understanding as effectively 'construing' (or translating) other people's central cultural constructs by relating them to action in their social world. We cannot really understand other societies without performing this task; even if we hope to explain a state of affairs by reference to some cross-culturally relevant 'objective structure', we must first accurately describe that state of affairs. Thus, I want to show that there are other structures involved in territorial organization than those simply of adaptation to resources and that we can get at these by attending to what our informants say. The necessity of such 'think description' is evident among Australian Aborigines for whom land as a sacred estate is a 'resource' around which organization occurs. While I cannot demonstrate it here, it is also true that as an objectified token of relationships among persons, this 'resource' is considered necessary for the reproduction of society and survival in the Aboriginal world. Attention to 'ideology' in both of these ways is essential to understanding long-term adaptation. In the rest of this paper, I focus on one of the prime constructs of the Pintupi social world, investigating the structure of territorial organization as contained in the concept of 'country' (*ngurra*) and as used by persons in the process and activities of daily life — in the process of claim, negotiation, and achievement. Finally, I show how the relationship between ownership rights and local organization remains vital to long-term adaptation. (One of the few attempts so far to do this has been Rose 1968.)

A Pintupi Life History

Pintupi Aborigines from the Western Desert traditionally occupied an arid region south of Lake Mackay with an average yearly rainfall of five to ten inches (120–240 mm), a few permanent and semi-permanent waterholes, and a terrain consisting of sandhills and plains broken up by some groupings of rocky outcrops. Water constitutes an important constraint on life in the desert. Small marsupials and lizards provided most of the protein in the Pintupi diet, the bulk of which was made up of vegetable foods and fruits seasonally available. As in the area of Gould's research (1982) just to the south, with the unpredictability of rain, local and seasonal variations in resources were common. Band sizes varied from 10 to 25 persons during most parts of the year.

My research with Pintupi people at Yayayi settlement in the Northern Territory in 1973–75 showed an individual-oriented approach to be the most useful way of conceptualizing Pintupi social life. Pintupi constantly maintain that society, as they see it, is boundary-less potentially, that individual networks and ritual links extend beyond any definable group. No one, it was pointed out, lived entirely in one place, with a single set of people, at one waterhole, as if in 'a paddock'.

I recorded several life histories of men who had lived as hunter-gatherers relatively uninfluenced by the presence of white Australians. The narratives indicate that Pintupi moved around, changed residential groups, visited, and regularly encountered new persons and places. Consideration of one of these life histories will allow us to relate statements about group life, group membership, relatedness, and living arrangements to the complex and multiple domains of social reality as experienced by Pintupi. The particular life history I am using for this summary was gathered from a 65-year-old man from the Lake Macdonald region in 1974 (see Myers 1976 for details). He had been living at Haasts Bluff and Papunya settlements since 1948, moving to Yayayi in 1973.

The physical details of Shorty Lungkata's account are clear. They indicate that persons travelled widely, not confining themselves to a 'band area' in the sense that most sociocentric pictures of band territories imply. Shorty's travels regularly took him through areas which he ascribes to several different named groups of people: Mayutjarra, Walbiri, Pitjantjatjara, the *Yumari* mob, and others. In his and others' life histories, the composition of co-resident groups (on-the-ground groups which I call 'camps') was highly variable and fluctuating. We find Shorty living sometimes with various individuals and their families, and at other times with people unrelated to the former. Shorty considered all of these people to be his 'one countrymen'.

We see the regular exploitation of certain seasonal items: *mungilpa* (a seed bearing plant that grows bountifully in claypans) near Lake Macdonald, the euros at *Turpalnga* in the hills south of the lake, and seasonal water supplies. These are constraints on the movements of individuals and groups, but it is clear that there is no band as a group of individuals travelling constantly from point A to B to C and so on. Individuals or small aggregates of families move through the landscape for purposes of their own, see evidence of other people nearby, go to visit them, travel with them for a while, and then return to their own, more typical grounds.

In the hot time, from November to February, people gathered at the large permanent waterholes to wait for rain to come and bring water to the smaller and temporarily dry waterholes. Shorty's account indicates a general pattern of spending the hot time at one of the main waters in his 'own country' as the latter is most narrowly conceived, the waterholes of *Walukirritjinya*, *Turpalnga*, and *Pirmalnga*. When the rains came, he moved out of these to travel northwards, or southwards, sometimes east with a small group, drinking at the temporary water sources and foraging for small animals, since vegetable foods were not yet ripe. The availability of these small, temporary sources of food and water allowed people to travel freely across the country, and it is during these seasons that Pintupi travelled to distant places to visit affines and other relatives. Shorty often travelled considerable distances before turning back; usually he returned to his own large waters for the summer. Later in his life, when he was married with two wives from the north, he stayed longer there; in some years he did not return to his 'own country' at all, residing instead with these northern affines as well as with his elderly and remarried mother. Thus we find him frequently around the Buck Hills (*Tjitururrnga*). That Shorty's children were all conceived in the north indicates that typically he resided there for some time.

Shorty's narratives tell of wide-ranging movement and temporary co-residence with people of various locales. There was neither expectation nor reality to the idea of people hunting and gathering within a single 'band area' with occasional visits to other bands. Shorty's commitments and obligations to a variety of individuals who were spatially separated was the pattern common to all the narratives collected. According to Shorty, after a young married couple resided with the woman's parents for a while, these people might say, 'Oh, you should go visit your parents; they must be worrying for you'. Shorty constantly reiterated that if they saw the smoke of fires in the distance, they went to visit people, since it 'was not far' and they were all 'related'. Others came to look for him, inviting him to visit their country for large gatherings when resources were available — or for companionship. Similar shifting residence patterns obtain today, and for the Pintupi even now the local group does not constitute the boundaries of society or kindred.

Life Cycle

The course of the life history shows that a processual view is necessary, not only of residential groups and their formation, but also of individuals' life cycles. I can describe this best as an expectation expressed by Pintupi. Young men said that they were 'travelling men', that they could not settle down because they were too restless. Several men told me that they were always fighting when they were young men, or that they used to do other dangerous things like stealing from whites: 'I was a young fellow then, but I'm married now.' The widest range of travel that men described occurred with regularity during their young adult years, when they were too young to marry and when they sought to make connections and acquire ritual knowledge vital for maturity and political success in the society. The approach of marriage usually brings on commitments to future affines. Young men begin to travel with their 'affines', providing them with meat and helping them in expectation of receiving a wife. After marriage, they seem to remain with their affines, or to move between their own country and that of affines.

Like their male counterparts, apparently, women at this age are not yet considered responsible. Thus, a young married woman remains with her parents, her mother does much of the cooking and looks after the children, and her kinswomen can help in the birth of children. As she grows into her responsibilities, the couple begin to make a camp more distinctly their own.

Ultimately, as a couple becomes old, the man begins to stay more consistently in his own 'country' or the country to which he has become attached. Shorty described a number of such old men and characterized them as being highly localized, residing mainly close to their more important sacred sites. Data from the other life histories support this contrast between the movement of young and old men, indicating a life-cycle pattern. Thus composition of bands reflects various developmental processes in Pintupi social life as well as the constraints of resource availablity. (Peterson 1970 and 1972 discusses processes like these.)

One Countryman

The Pintupi conceptualization of their social reality is expressed in the concepts I gloss as 'country' (*ngurra*) and 'one countryman' (*ngurra kutjungurrara*). Proper understanding of this concept brings us close to comprehending the content, quality, and processes of Pintupi social life and local groups. The problematic word is *ngurra*, and its ambiguity is a consequence of its polysemy: it can mean either 'camp' or 'country' (named place). The concept of 'one countryman' does not refer necessarily to people who occupy one bounded territory (or 'country') nor to any sociocentrically defined group. If either of these conditions were true, all members of a person's set of 'one countrymen' would have the same co-members, but in fact they do not. The concept is individual-centred: each person has his own set of 'one countrymen'. It refers to those with whom one is likely to 'camp', that is, to co-reside. Its usage, then, indicates the social reality experienced by individuals who do not always live with the same residential group or even within the same 'range' or exploitative area. One man explained that he considered various people to be his 'one countrymen' because they 'used to travel together', even though their homelands were, he acknowledged, separate.

But people are also organized around *ritual* ties to the land — to *ngurra* as named places or 'country' created by mythological ancestors in The Dreaming — that is, to what Stanner (1965) called 'estates'. The people who share ownership of a 'country' as an estate can also call each other 'one countryman'. Ownership of 'named places', as Stanner noted, consists of rights to the ritual, sacred objects, and stories associated with these Dreaming places. What is relevant here is that these 'country'-owning groups are overlapping, and individuals are able to affiliate with more than one group, each defined by ownership of a common place. Without the evidence of context and purpose, in talk about 'land' and people, the distinction between local groups and ritual groups is often blurred, although they are not co-extensive. Pintupi conceptions of local organization are two-tiered, and this complexity is contained in the polysemy of *ngurra* as 'named place' and as 'camp': the classification of people as 'from one *ngurra*' can refer either to ritual groups or to ego-centred social networks.

To understand the concept of 'one countryman' as delineating the widely extended set of persons with whom one might reside and co-operate helps us to understand the link between social relationships and space: the flexibility of territorial boundaries and fluidity of groups. While who is a 'countryman' is open to negotiation, what seems important is that people 'from one country' should help each other and that claims to be 'countrymen' open up access to resources and labour. Because people who live together co-operate in the food quest and share resources, the egocentric concept of 'one countryman' defines the set of productive relations necessary and appropriate for the conditions of Pintupi life, where one expects to live temporarily and co-operate with a variety of persons and groups. It combines access to resources and access to labour over a broad 'range'.

Resource Use and Defined Areas

Despite the individual variations in movements and rights of exploitation, there also seem to be definable resource nexuses of the sort once simplistically described as 'band territories'. The significance of these defined areas — particularly their relationship to social units — requires analysis.

No set of individuals lives entirely, for even a single year, within the boundaries of a single such area. In fact, Pintupi social groups are characterized by considerable flexibility and permeability of boundaries in regard to rights to use the resources of such 'ranges'. Exploiting camps are bilateral, composition actualized from numerous organizational categories, including kinsmen, affines, and ritual partners. Pintupi individuals have highly variable ranges, depending on their particular social relations, which are not limited to a band or its territory. Rights to land as 'range' (i.e., use rights) are multiple and easily gained, limited it seems only by initiative, and acquired through 'ownership' or social relations to 'owners'.

Such openness of access for individuals does not mean that there are not any 'objective structures' defining the limits and patterns of association. Sharp, for example, described patterns of land use similar to those of the Pintupi in another part of Australia (western Cape York Peninsula):

> People gather and hunt, ordinarily, in whatever country they will. Thus there is practically a standing permission which opens a clan's countries to all . . . (1934:23).

However, at the same place he points out that '. . . this permission may be withdrawn by the clan for those who are *persona non grata*'. Sharp maintains that 'owners' (in this case, a patrilineal clan) hold the right to exclude people but says that such a right is exercised only in exceptional cases, 'in which there is an actual or pretended drain on the resources of the land' (1934:23). At bottom, Sharp is trying to accommodate freedom of access to some mechanism for monitoring population/resource relationships.

There are defined resource-areas, sociocentric 'ranges', in Pintupi territorial organization; they are defined primarily around the permanent or semi-permanent waterholes to which people return during the dry summer. In other seasons, these people may disperse and use small waterholes to visit persons in other ranges in the way I have described above. There, rights to forage are acquired as part of residence, as a 'one countryman'. In every range, there are known resource points to which people go at times of the year when they know food is available. One example of this is the *mungilpa* seed plant in Shorty's country, a resource said to grow in great quantities in specific places after rain. Repeatedly in telling his life history Shorty described people coming in large numbers from far away to collect *mungilpa* seeds. The Buck Hills offered wild yams; and here, too, people frequently gathered. Clearly, visiting and congregating at periods and places of temporary abundance was common. As many analysts have seen, such periodically abundant resources offer no adaptive advantage for 'rationing' by one group, and Pintupi informants insisted that they would never send someone away from their country unless he or she committed some wrong. The value placed on 'compassion' (Myers 1979) as well as the opportunity to be reciprocated at some future time, inclines people to share resources. Thus, a person extends rights to use resources in his country to all his 'countrymen' with the expectation of reciprocal privilege. The case also shows the deficiency of approaches which focus on local groups as basic units and on local scarcity as compelling reciprocity. Instead we should attend to the positive qualities (which Aborigines emphasize) of *increasing societal intensity* by taking turns hosting larger groups, and allowing greater overall efficiency of resource use.

Given seasonality and local variation in resources, one could expect that the Aborigines developed a schedule of movements to take advantage of the seasonal appearance of food and water. Some consistency and recurrence in the travel histories of individuals support this assumption, although variation among persons from a single range shows that individual movements were also scheduled to take advantage of other possiblilities, such as visiting certain people and seeing particular sacred sites. This, of course, reproduced those significant, regional-systemic relations of production. It seems sensible, then, to think of hypothetical bands moving through an optimal pattern of resource scheduling, with individuals affiliating themselves to these groups as they move from place to place, travelling with them for a while, and moving on. The size of this abstract band may remain relatively constant while the actual composition may vary greatly. Nonetheless, the important requirement is that individuals must affiliate with the residential group to use the land. The results of this will become apparent.

The state of resources determines where people may be, but not necessarily where they actually are, or precisely who is there; and this is what a model of territorial organization should comprehend. It seems most reasonable, following the Pintupi concept of 'one countrymen' as people who share a 'camp', to argue that bands are largely the outcome of individual decisions, and the actual composition can be explained only through understanding the processes of individual affiliation.

We must be careful in interpreting assertions — such as the Pintupi make — that a person is from a particular country as referring to 'range'. (Shorty was from *Walukirritjinya*.) Such statements are largely predictive, reflecting the social reality that people are likely to return to their home area, especially in the summer, the period of greatest strain on localized resources and when movement is most difficult. While return to home waters has the effect of controlling the number of people at any waterhole, of controlling population in an area at a time of year when resource capacity is most diminished, how this occurs is also significant, because it does not come about through 'defence'.

Because permanent water is scarce, seasonal congregations at sites of an abundant resource are relatively large, and because there are no intermediate waters, individuals do not really have the option of moving away should conflict or dispute arise. That considerable strain occurs in large groups is well documented, and at the end of the period of their occurrence the life histories indicate an increasing desire to move away into different and smaller groups. To be among more distant 'kin' in such circumstances has the disadvantage that — while disputes are more frequent — one's support is weaker. Nonetheless, it supports this view of the processes by which adaptation occurs that every individual questioned had spent some summers away from the country with which he was most closely identified. While there is a probability that a person will be 'in his own country', it is not unusual for people to be away during the summer.

If, as these descriptions indicate, territorial organization is not simply the division of people into territorially discrete, mobile, but permanent bands, what *is* the content of 'band organization'? The content of such organization is not, apparently, a band's exclusion of others from access to resources. In this case, the importance of defined 'ranges' has too often been misconstrued. What seems vital to a foraging adaptation is sensitivity to the relationship between population and resources (Peterson 1975:59), knowledge of resources available and location of people. The processes by which this is accomplished are discussed below; understanding them, again, depends on understanding Pintupi cultural constructs.

Always Ask

Since it seems apparent that denial to access of resources is infrequent, how do the Pintupi manage the regulation of population to resources? To understand this we must learn how Pintupi think about resources, for in their view the utility of resources does not constitute a reason to maintain exclusive access to them. Access is freely granted, but people still must know how many persons are exploiting an area and where they are in order to plan strategies of exploitation.

Tindale notes what seems to be the major focus of Western Desert concepts of 'ownership' (although he does not develop it analytically) when he writes that a man told him, 'My country is the place where I do not have to ask anyone to cut wood for a spear-thrower' — the quotation with which I began the chapter (Tindale 1974:18). What is indicated here is that the content of 'ownership' is the right to be asked. What a Pitjantjatjara man once defined as 'The first law of Aboriginal morality' — 'Always ask!' (Freeman 1974: personal communication) — provides a key to much of the confusion about local organization.

Pintupi are very concerned that they be consulted over matters in which they have rights, and this is particularly true in matters concerning land. When a group of men visited an ochre mine in the Gibson Desert, for example, a few men chipped off some of the material for later use. Subsequently, at a meeting in Docker River, the primary custodian of the place (because he was conceived there) threatened to spear them and made a great show of anger. His rights had been violated because they had not asked him before digging up the ochre. This notion continues in relations with whites. Men grumbled about white people driving out to Pintupi country without asking anyone for permission to go. They never refused anyone permission as far as I was aware, but they felt that their rights were being violated if they were not asked.

The main point to be drawn from this and other examples is the nature of rights and duties in Pintupi culture, something much overlooked when we talk about 'ownership' among peoples with different sociocultural systems. For the Pintupi, to own something is to have the right to be asked about it. The norms of kinship and general reciprocity (or compassion) force one to grant the request, but one should be asked. Given the political economy of Pintupi social life, what do they seek to gain as 'value' here, and what do they lose? What they seek is prestige, the chance to be first among equals (Fried 1968), or more properly, I think, to maintain personal autonomy. All of this is satisfied when others recognize one's rights; recognition achieved, what else is to be gained by forbidding access? Consequently, it is important to understand that while use rights to land are freely granted, one must 'ask' in order to obtain them.

People acquire rights to use land by joining a residential group which is already exploiting it. As Peterson (1975) points out, the boundaries to such groups are 'defended' with rights of entry; people who want to join a group do not simply walk into its camp, no matter how close their relationship. They must announce their presence by lighting a fire at some distance from the camp, waiting there for members of that camp to come, to identify them, and, ultimately, to bring them into the camp. They must 'ask', and 'one countryman' links make it possible to do so.

This process is an etiquette of 'asking' to be admitted to the group and to rights to use the resources. The Pintupi maintained they would not send anyone away, which seems to conform to other data I have. Shorty told me of Pitjantjatjara men traversing his country in order to go west to cut special *mulyati* wood for spears; but the narrative implies that they had established this right with residents beforehand. What makes people angry is unannounced travel, going in a secretive fashion. Consequently, when moving into another's range one should ask or somehow announce one's presence as a form of deference, usually with smoke. Such behaviour, as Peterson says (1975), allows foragers to assess how many people are exploiting a territory and what strategies to employ. The content of Pintupi ownership — the right to be asked — accommodates this argument.

The Pintupi are eager for information. Knowledge of resources, of people and their whereabouts is the basis of their local organization, telling them where they can go next and allowing them to assess the relation between population and resources. Are poor returns on foraging a result of personal inefficiency, chance, or overpopulation (Peterson 1975:59)? Information allows people to decide on travels and to avoid coming upon a string of previously exploited areas; it is also important in assessing the intentions of visitors.

Even now, when people visit Yayayi from other settlements, it is clear that their behaviour is somewhat 'restrained', that they exhibit 'embarrassment' or 'deference' (*kunta*, also 'shame') at seeming to assume too much. They do not rise to give speeches at public meetings, they do not grab for themselves from local supplies in the same way that long-term residents do. If they do not explicitly ask, they are tentative in announcing intentions, assuming very little: they are always 'asking', making sure that it is all right to do as intended.

In this context I think we are better able to interpret Pintupi statements about their travels. Smokes from certain directions were known to be from 'that *Yumari* mob', or 'that *Walunguru* mob', indicating that they were someplace that a knowledgeable person could figure out, given the time of year and location of the smoke. If they were on good terms with those people and if resources allowed, they might go to visit. Shorty told me that one did not have to ask *formally* because everyone was 'family', a term he used for frequent co-residents. For these people there would be a minimum of formality in incorporation into the exploiting group.

If we take this a step further, if we follow Shorty much further from his country, we find him reporting that someone is 'guiding him' through their country. This seems a more formal sort of arrangement: someone must be able to vouch for him as he gets further from familiar places, to give information about him, to guarantee his good intentions to residents. Individuals' travels are not unrestricted in extent. At greater distances, travel is less frequent. Because people are less well known, it is more dangerous. Strangers are suspected of evil intentions, of being dangerous because one does not know how to predict their behaviour. This suspicion restricts population movement, confining people to some extent.

After travelling in the cool part of the year when movement is possible, people regularly return to their own major waters. The reason for such return seems always to be sentimental rather than what I might call jural. As they travelled further and further, Shorty used to say, 'We got homesick and turned back to our own country'. The narratives usually continue with Shorty describing his movements and then mentioning a place with emotion: 'My own country at last!'

Ownership

I have stressed, in contradiction to the patrilineal, patrilocal model, that Pintupi residential groups are to be understood through the concept of 'one countryman' as those who potentially share a camp and co-operate in the food quest. Through actualizing this potential social relation, individuals acquire rights to forage, to *use* land, in a number of ranges. Therefore, rights to use the resources of a range are relatively permeable to access by others, although there seems to be considerable variation in actual boundedness around different resources (see Dyson-Hudson & Smith 1978).[3]

A number of problems remain in understanding the relationship between regulation of resources and local organization, and these also require attention to ideology, to the concept of 'countryman' and land ownership. Here we find another puzzle in Pintupi organization: if residence is not patrilocal, neither are the land-owning groups patrilineal. Furthermore, individuals seem to belong to more than one such group. Various means exist by which individuals may make claims of identification with the 'country', and these form the cultural basis for its ownership.[4] Without providing detail here, what I want to emphasize is that there are multiple pathways by which individuals may achieve ownership rights, patrilineality being only one sort of claim, and that individuals have claims to more than one country. It is through political process that *claims* of identification are converted into rights over aspects of a country and knowledge of its esoteric qualities.

Ownership consists primarily in control over the stories, objects, and ritual associated with the mythological ancestors of The Dreaming at a particular place. Access to knowledge of these esoterica and the creative essence they contain is restricted, and one can acquire access only through instruction by those who have previously acquired it. Important ceremonies are conducted at some sacred sites, and other sites have ceremonies associated with them that men (particularly) may perform to instruct others in what happened in that important period in which all things took on their form (i.e., The Dreaming). Because knowledge is highly valued, and vital to social reproduction, men seek to gain such knowledge and to be associated with its display and transmission. It is, in fact, their responsibility to 'follow up The Dreaming' (Stanner 1956), to look after these sacred estates by ensuring that the proper rituals are conducted. Men acquire prestige when other men defer to their knowledge in the telling of a story or the performance of a ceremony. They may convert control of knowledge into authority over younger men and women.[5]

Since knowledge and control of country are already in the hands of 'owners', converting *claims* to an interest in a named place requires convincing the owners to include one in knowledge and activity. Identification with a country must be actualized and accepted by others through a process or negotiation.

With each significant place, then, a group of individuals can affiliate. The groups may differ for each place considered; the corporations forming around these sacred sites are not 'closed'. Instead, there are descending kindreds of persons who have or had *primary* claims to sites. Of all those 'identified', only a portion are said to 'hold' a country and to control its related rituals. These primary custodians are the ones who must decide whether to teach an individual about it; it is they who decide on the status of claims. Men are rather congenial to teaching 'close kin' about their country and to granting them thereby an interest in the place. For claimants who are remote genealogically, or not co-residents, there is less persuasiveness to claims. These processes make it likely that claims of a patrifilial core will be acceptable: it is men who control these rights, and because at the height of his influence a man is likely to live in his own country, it is predictable that he will pass it on to his sons. Rights are also passed on to sisters' sons, who are also frequent co-residents. If such persons or those with other sorts of claims (conception from The Dreaming, a more distant relative from it, and so forth) take up residence in an area and convince the custodians of their sincerity, my data suggest they can become important custodians too. Conversely, failure to maintain some degree of regular association with a place seems to diminish a claim. This is a process, then, by which one sort of 'one coutryman' status may be transformed into a more enduring one.

The fact that men seek to gain access to rights for many 'countries' leads to extended associations of individuals with places, surrounding a core of those with primary claims. The Pintupi data show numerous individuals with extensive estate-rights. Individuals also have very different personal constellations of such rights (see also Strehlow 1947).

Ownership and Long-Term Adaptation

How is 'ownership' and the ideology of ownership related to territorial organization and regulation of resources? To approach this, we must attend to the processes which lead to shifting and temporary distortions in the shape of defined areas. There are two dimensions of this problem.

First, in the long term, the notions of 'country' and 'country' ownership provide for extended networks of related countries and related people. Gould (1969) and others (Peterson 1969; Strehlow 1965, 1970) have discussed the importance of such links in maintaining reciprocal access to resources in different territories, providing a system of 'countryman' relationships overarching those based on simple kinship ties. Since The Dreamtime ancestors travelled widely, the activities of an ancestor or group of them may link together places on a path of hundreds of kilometres, all a part of a continuous story. The continuity of stories is used as a way of classifying named places into larger systems, and persons who own a place/part of the story have a claim to be considered for other parts. For some purpose, all those 'countries' on a Dreaming path are considered to be 'one country', and those who own different segments may be considered 'one countrymen'. Such systems of stories are in a continual process of being reworked, providing an ever-changing charter of who and what are identified as 'one country'. Again, 'countryman' relations define potential productive ties.

Second, rights to 'country' provide a basis for the localization of people in areas. As Peterson (1970) argues, and as my data corroborate, the emotional identification of persons with particular places leads older men to reside around their own primary sacred sites. This ensures that people will return to marginal areas, to exploit the entire region, and

makes for increased efficiency in a regional system, potentially supporting a larger population. The Pintupi pattern of claim and negotiation —
along with extensive identification with sacred sites — must be related to
this process. Given the harshness of conditions, population density was
low in the Gibson Desert. This means that the group of men residing
'regularly' in a range and looking after the 'country' there was small.
Given the vagaries of demography, such groups are likely to die out
(Peterson n.d.a). My own data indicate that even two generations ago
such emptying out occurred and was followed by new people moving into
the vacated area, taking over responsibility for the 'country'.

Thus, the secondary rights to 'country' as estate (see Myers 1976;
Barker 1976; Peterson, Keen & Sansom 1977) provide for what was
surely a predictable process of replacement of country-holding groups.
The present shapes of boundaries of 'country' ownership seem to
represent a stage in the process by which members of one group have
extended their claims and responsibility to nearby 'countries', essentially
combining them. The fact that they are considered to be part of 'one
country' reflects their ownership by one group. Peterson (n.d.a) suggests
that the processes of claim, extension, and movement are only a stage in
the cycle by which the resource nexus of a range will eventually re-
establish itself simply from the process of following the scheduling
pattern of resources.

Not Having to Ask: Spatial Organization and Pintupi Politics

There are, however, other processes and structures to consider in
understanding 'land ownership' in relation to territorial organization.
These can only be understood with reference to Pintupi concepts of
'ownership' and Pintupi politics. In discussing the content of ownership
rights as the 'right to be asked', I maintained that such requests are
unlikely to be refused, although I pointed out that permission might be
overtly denied, or withdrawn in some cases from *personae non gratae*.
Nonetheless, as Tindale's informant indicated, in one's own country,
one does not have to ask. In our sociocultural system, we are concerned
primarily with the outcome of such a request, since we identify the utility
of resources with what we can get for them by turning them into a
product. To extend this assumption to the Pintupi (or, I think, to many
other hunter-gatherers) is misguided. In terms of Pintupi politics and the
prime goal of personal autonomy, one places major value on not having
to ask. To live in another person's country means that one must defer to
him as the 'owner'. Visitors are freely extended rights to use resources,
but in decisions about where to go, or how to deal with disputes, they are
clearly 'second class citizens'. This is something I failed fully to understand on my first field trip, although it was apparent enough. One need
only go out to visit a man's *own* country to see the difference it makes in
his bearing, authority, and interest.

A botanist with the Commonwealth Scientific and Industrial Research Organization in Central Australia, Peter Latz, described to me his experience trying to discuss ethnobotany with a Pintupi man in the Loritja area in which the latter had been living for 30 years: he found the man rather unenthusiastic, but this changed radically when they went out to Lake Macdonald — his 'own country'. I have watched Pintupi defer quietly to the traditional owners of their current residential area, seen the limitations of their influence and the insecurity of their tenure. Finally, I have watched the transformations that take place in the demeanour of such men when we have visited their own country, where they know The Dreaming stories best, where they know who died, where what happened, and in which they need not defer to anyone. Here they have what they value: the freedom to do as they please without asking anyone. It is young men who travel most widely and extensively in other poeple's country precisely because, for them, deference to another, especially to a senior man, implies no decline in personal autonomy.

If we need further confirmation of how important this content of ownership is, let us consider what happens when there is trouble in a Pintupi community. When trouble occurs outsiders leave. My informants told me in life histories that at the first sign of danger or insecurity they went back to their 'own' country. Ember's recent paper (Ember 1978) about patrilocality and defence, while otherwise almost totally inappropriate for the facts of hunter-gatherer life, has the merit of pointing out the influence of personal and political relations for spatial organization. One of the things she fails to see, however, is that such 'danger' conditions are not constant, that boundaries (or patrilocality) may be more marked at some times than at others.

Conclusion

I hope it is now clear that to fully understand the regulation of resources among the Pintupi we have to consider the internal structure of relations within the society, a structure which does not merely reify 'ecological necessities' but which has taken on its own emergent values. What seems important about the Pintupi is not that they 'adapt' but that they create such societal intensity while managing to conform to the ecological constraints of a harsh region. Life here is not simply life in a small band; particular groups are merely temporary manifestations of society.

Understanding Pintupi spatial organization necessitates looking beyond local groups, adopting the Pintupi view of their society as a wider, totalizing, less bounded structure. Furthermore, it necessitates giving attention to the emergent structures and processes by which a regional system maintains itself. What I have tried to show is that the structure of this society as a regional system materializes only over time. Analysts have rarely considered such systems in temporal depth. Pintupi cultural concepts, however, do incorporate a time dimension and consequently orient us more adequately to the significant processes of territorial organization. Finally, this shows that we must attempt to understand something about what the participants in a system think, in part because their models may be more instructive than ours in defining the particular logic of a sociocultural system and also because indigenous ideology is part of the very material processes we hope to understand.

Notes

1. Field research with the Pintupi was supported by NSF Dissertation Improvement Grant No. GS 37122, Australian Institute of Aboriginal Studies, Living Stipend, and NIMH Fellowhsip No. 3F0IMN57275-01. This paper is based on part of my PhD dissertation written under the direction of Jane C. Goodale at Bryn Mawr College. I gratefully acknowledge the many helpful discussions I have had with Nic Peterson, Nancy Williams, and Bob Tonkinson on the subjects considered here. Much of my thinking was formulated through these discussions. I also want to thank Danny Maltz, Mario Davila, and Bette Clark whose critical comments on the early drafts of this paper are responsible for what clarity there is. The failings which remain are, of course, my responsibility.
2. Yengoyan (1976:122) has criticized some of the culturally biased assumptions in the models of ecological analysis.
3. Attention to resources and the process of band formation is instructive in connection with the meaning of territoriality, especially in indicating some variation in permeability of boundaries for different items. Shorty described large congregations, including people from far away (like Walbiri), near Lake Macdonald at seasons when *mungilpa* was available. Growing in large quantities near claypans filled with water, and abundant in August and September, this resource supported large populations often gathered for ceremony. At such times people with relatively distant ties might come to exploit the resource, conforming to Dyson-Hudson and Smith's (1978) model that unpredictable and dense resources are exploited through information sharing and a high degree of nomadism. At other times of year, however, when water is a scarce resource (as in summer) and only a few well-known permanent waters are available, the data indicate that people returning to their 'own country' are more localized in separate 'local groups' in what Dyson-Hudson and Smith describe as a 'home-range' form of resource utilization.
4. Elsewhere I have described in detail Pintupi ideas about the landscape as a culturally constituted environment and argued for the necessity of understanding the *logic* of these claims (Myers 1976).
5. For an extended analysis see Myers (1980).

References

BARKER, G. (1976), 'The ritual estate and Aboriginal polity', *Mankind* **10**:225–39.
DYSON-HUDSON, R. & E. A. SMITH (1978), 'Human territoriality', *American Anthropologist*, **80**:21–41.
EMBER, C. (1978), 'Myths about hunter-gatherers', *Ethnology*, **17**:439–48.
FRIED, M. (1968), *The Evolution of Political Society*, New York: Random House.
GEERTZ, C. (1973) 'Thick description: towards an interpretive theory of culture', in *The Interpretation of Cultures*, New York: Basic Books.
GOULD, R. A. (1969), 'Subsistence behaviour among the Western Desert Aborigines of Australia', *Oceania*, **39**:253–74.

GOULD, R. A. (1982), 'To Have and Have Not: The Ecology of Sharing among Hunter-Gatherers' in N. M. Williams and E. S. Hunn (eds), *Resource Managers: North American and Australian Hunter-Gatherers*, Colorado: Westview Press.

LEE, R. (1976) '!Kung spatial organization: an ecological and historical perspective', in R. B. Lee & I. De Vore (eds), *Kalahari Hunter-Gatherers*, Cambridge, Mass: Harvard University Press.

LEE, R. & DE VORE I. (eds) (1968), *Man the Hunter*, Chicago: Aldine Press.

—— (1976), *Kalahari Hunter-Gatherers*; *Studies of the !Kung San and their Neighbors*, Cambridge, Mass: Harvard University Press.

MYERS, F. R. (1976), *To Have and to Hold: A Study of Persistence and Change in Pintupi Social Life*, PhD thesis, Bryn Mawr College.

—— (1980), 'The cultural basis of politics in Pintupi life', *Mankind*, **12**:197–214.

—— (1979), 'Emotions and the self: a theory of personhood and political order among Pintupi Aborigines', *Ethos*, **8**:343–70.

PETERSON, N. (1969), 'Secular and ritual links: two basic and opposed principles of Australian social organization as illustrated by Walbiri ethnography', *Mankind*, **7**:27–35.

—— (1970), 'The importance of women in determining the composition of residential groups in Aboriginal Australia', in F. Gale (ed.), *Women's Role in Aboriginal Society*, Canberra: Australian Institute of Aboriginal Studies.

—— (1972), 'Totemism yesterday: sentiment and local organisation among the Australian Aborigines', *Man*, **7**:12–32.

—— (1975), 'Hunter-gatherer territoriality: the perspective from Australia', *American Anthropologist*, **77**:53–68.

—— (1983), 'Rights, residence and process in Australian territorial organization', in N. Peterson and M. Langton (eds), *Aborigines, Land and Land Rights*, Canberra: Australian Institute of Aboriginal Studies.

—— (n.d.b), 'Territorial adaptations among desert hunter-gatherers: the !Kung and Australians compared', typescript.

PETERSON, N., I. KEEN & B. SANSOM (1977), 'Succession to land: primary and secondary rights to Aboriginal estates', in *Report of the Joint Select Committee on Aboriginal Land Rights in the Northern Territory*, Canberra: Australian Government Publishing Service.

RADCLIFFE-BROWN, A. R. (1930), 'The social organisation of Australian tribes', *Oceania*, **1**:34–63.

ROSE, F. (1968), 'Australian marriage, land-owning groups, and initiations', in Lee & De Vore (1968).

SHARP, R. L. (1934), 'Ritual life and economics of the Yir-Yiront of Cape York Peninsula', *Oceania*, **5**:19–42.

STANNER, W. E. H. (1956), 'The Dreaming', in T. A. G. Hungerford (ed.), *Australian Signposts,* Melbourne: F. W. Cheshire.

—— (1965), 'Aboriginal territorial organization', *Oceania*, **36**:1–26.

STREHLOW, T. G. H. (1947), *Aranda Traditions*, Melbourne: Melbourne University Press.

—— (1965), 'Culture, social structure, and environment in Aboriginal Australia', in R. M. and C. H. Berndt (eds), *Aboriginal Man in Australia*, Sydney: Angus & Robertson.

—— (1970), 'Geography and the totemic landscape in Central Australia', in R. M. Berndt (ed.), *Australian Aboriginal Anthropology*, Nedlands: University of Western Australia Press.

TINDALE, N. B. (1974), *Aboriginal Tribes of Australia*, Berkeley: University of California Press.

YENGOYAN, A. (1976), 'Structure, event, and ecology in Aboriginal Australia: a comparative viewpoint', in N. Peterson (ed.), *Tribes and Boundaries in Australia*, Canberra: Australian Institute of Aboriginal Studies.

4

Hunter-Gatherer Subsistence Production in Arnhem Land: The Original Affluence Hypothesis Re-examined

J. C. ALTMAN

In this paper I set out to examine data collected among contemporary North-Central Arnhem Landers, which indicate that men's economic contribution today far outweighs women's.[1] This situation appears to be a consequence of access to market foodstuffs, market technology and cash from production for market exchange and welfare benefits. Initially, I document this situation with data collected over 296 days during 1979 and 1980, and then attempt to explain why the significance of the women's subsistence economy has diminished rapidly, while the men's hunting economy has remained resilient. On the basis of these data and an assumption that women's production must have met current production shortfalls under traditional conditions, I attempt to estimate men's and women's relative subsistence production in pre-contact times. My position is that in Arnhem Land men's and women's subsistence contribution must have been similar. This view, which is similar to Meehan's (1982), is counter to an orthodoxy that views women as the major producers in traditional Aboriginal society. Some wider ramifications of this finding are subsequently examined.

The Study Area and Data Base

The area where I undertook fieldwork is depicted in Figure 4.1. My research concentrated on the economy of Momega outstation that was occupied by a band of about 30 eastern Gunwinggu. In formal economic and demographic terms, Momega is little different from about 20 other outstations in the Maningrida region (Altman 1982c).

Data on the relative economic contributions of men and women were

First published in *Mankind*, **14**, 3 (April 1984), 179–90. This version is based on a paper presented at the Australian Anthropological Society Conference, Adelaide, August 1983.

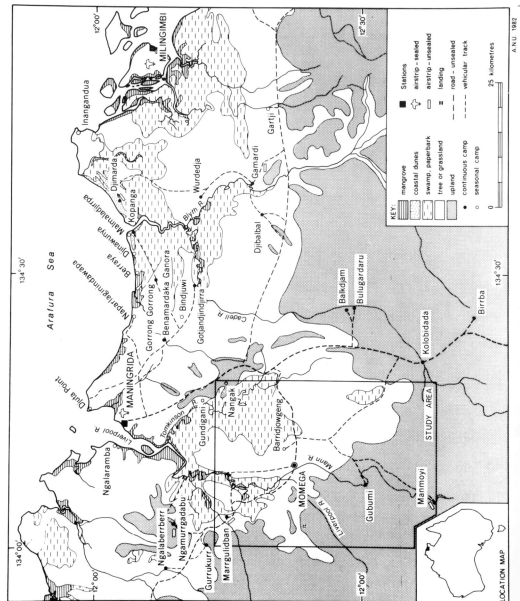

Map 1.   Outstations in the Maningrida region, North–Central Arnhem Land,   May 1979–November 1980.

Figure 4.1 Outstations in the Maningrida region, North-Central Arnhem Land, May 1979–November 1980.

collected while I was documenting the significance of the subsistence sector to the outstation. In Table 4.1, data collected over 10 months on estimated foodstuff consumption at Momega are presented. Bush foodstuffs are returns from hunting, fishing and gathering activities. Market foodstuffs are procured either at Maningrida township or from a

Table 4.1 Summary table of estimated foodstuff consumption at Momega outstation per capita per day: October 1979 to October 1980

Month	Season	Kilocalories (Nos.)					Protein (g)				
		Bush	%	Market	%	Total	Bush	%	Market	%	Total
October/November	Late dry	1696	62.9	1000	37.1	2696	112.7	87.6	16.0	12.4	128.7
November/December	Early wet	1751	54.9	1439	45.1	3190	129.8	85.6	21.8	14.4	151.6
December/January	Early wet	849	31.2	1872	68.8	2721	60.7	68.8	27.5	31.2	88.2
January/February	Mid wet	984	36.0	1749	64.0	2733	79.7	69.7	34.6	30.3	114.3
February/March	Mid wet	1051	38.4	1683	61.6	2734	85.1	71.0	34.7	29.0	119.8
March/April	Mid wet	1209	43.1	1593	56.9	2802	103.6	78.6	28.2	21.4	131.8
April/May	Late wet	1455	50.1	1453	49.9	2908	153.8	84.7	27.9	15.3	181.7
May/June	Early dry	1304	45.6	1559	54.4	2863	118.7	86.1	19.2	13.9	137.9
August/September	Mid dry	1411	47.2	1575	52.8	2986	128.2	82.3	27.6	17.7	155.8
September/October	Late dry	1493	52.6	1346	47.4	2839	98.9	82.5	21.0	17.5	119.9
Mean		1320	46.2	1527	53.8	2847	107.1	79.7	25.9	20.3	133.0
Standard deviation		299	9.5	241	9.5	152	27.4	7.3	6.3	7.3	25.8

mobile store that visits the outstation fortnightly. The aggregate data indicate that the Momega band produced 46 per cent of kilocalories and 81 per cent of protein foods that I estimated they consumed. These figures accounted for 53 per cent of a hypothetical energy requirement benchmark (set at 2,500 kilocalories per capita per day) and 164 per cent of the protein benchmark (set at 65 g per capita per day) respectively. When subsistence produce is valued at market replacement value, it constitutes 64 per cent of the outstation's social accounts. Hunting and gathering remain the dominant productive sector of the economy.

Table 4.2 *Men's and women's relative returns from subsistence production over the seasonal cycle: October 1979 to October 1980*

Month	Category	Men's production (percentage)	Women's production (percentage)
October/November	Kilocalories	95.1	4.9
	Protein	91.2	8.8
November/December	Kilocalories	95.8	4.2
	Protein	92.9	7.1
December/January	Kilocalories	94.8	5.2
	Protein	92.7	7.3
January/February	Kilocalories	96.1	3.9
	Protein	93.2	6.8
February/March	Kilocalories	94.1	5.9
	Protein	91.3	8.7
March/April	Kilocalories	86.6	13.4
	Protein	89.9	10.1
April/May	Kilocalories	74.4	25.6
	Protein	73.3	26.7
May/June	Kilocalories	73.2	26.8
	Protein	71.1	28.9
August/September	Kilocalories	90.4	9.6
	Protein	85.6	14.4
September/October	Kilocalories	98.8	1.2
	Protein	97.3	2.7
Kilocalories:	Mean (standard deviation)	89.9 (9.1)	10.1 (9.1)
Protein:	Mean (standard deviation)	87.9 (8.8)	12.1 (8.8)

The significance of the subsistence sector is hardly surprising, for these activities are very obviously the main production undertaken at outstations today. Time allocation data indicate that of total hours spent in production by adults, 72 per cent is devoted to hunting, fishing and gathering. What is interesting is that when subsistence production is divided between men's and women's contribution, men produce the majority. As data in Table 4.2 indicate, on average 90 per cent of kilocalories and 88 per cent of protein was produced by men, although there was some variation over the seasonal cycle.

This finding is reinforced by data in Table 4.3 on the relative contribution of flora and fauna to total bush food returns. During all months, fauna contributed over 90 per cent of subsistence production (in kilocalorie terms) while indigenous flora (fruit, vegetables and nuts) were relatively insignificant. In Gunwinggu society today, a strict sexual division of labour is still maintained: men are the hunters, women the gatherers, while fishing is a mixed activity, with only men involved in fish trapping. Time allocation data indicate that 81 per cent of hunting and 60 per cent of fishing was undertaken by men and 86 per cent of gathering was by women. Men are the main utilizers of fauna, while women's activities concentrate of flora exploitation.

It appears from these data that traditional utilization of flora by women — or carbohydrate production — has declined dramatically. Before examining the reasons for this transformation, it is interesting to examine whether other economic activities have emerged to supplant women's subsistence production. The most significant development has been the emergence of artefact production for market exchange. This sector accounted for 26 per cent of the collective cash earned at Momega, but only 10 per cent of total cash and imputed income. While women on average spent slightly more time on craft production than men, in dollar terms men accounted for 82 per cent of total artefact production. This distortion is due to the fact that 'the market' values men's art far higher that women's craft. Since the advent of the payment of unemployment benefits, even in the non-productive social security sector men receive 59 per cent of cash payments.

Economic Transformations

The current subsistence production system at Aboriginal outstations in Arnhem Land must be seen in its historical context. The establishment of missions and a government settlement from the 1920s to the 1950s resulted in Aboriginal population concentration at these centres. Associated with this was a gradual decline in the significance of hunting and gathering activities, predicated on a land-extensive, non-sedentary production system. By the 1960s, it was generally accepted that Aborigines would totally assimilate into the market economic system. Aborigines became increasingly dependent on market commodities, welfare handouts and employment in settlement services, physical infrastructure construction, make-work schemes and in jobs with predominantly training components (Altman & Nieuwenhuysen 1979).

In the 1970s, the decentralization movement (Coombs 1974) motivated by a dissatisfaction with life at settlements and also by the land rights issue, resulted in many traditional estates being re-occupied. As social security entitlements of Aborigines were paid in cash rather than in kind from the late 1960s, people were able to reside out bush and finance their limited market dependency. Aborigines also produced artefacts for sale to earn cash. The main goods that people required were the carbo-hydrates flour and sugar and simple market technology like shotguns and ammunition.

Access to market commodities has resulted in the supplantation of women's traditional subsistence production of bush carbohydrates, but a resilience or possible supplementation in men's production. One could argue that without these transformations Aborigines would not have returned to live at outstations. A key question that arises is why this set of transformations occurred.

Table 4.3 *Relative contribution of flora and fauna to the Eastern Gunwinggu bush foods diet: October 1979 to October 1980*

		Percentage kilocalorie contribution of					
		Flora				Fauna	Miscellaneous
Month	Season	Vegetable	Fruit	Nut	Total		(bush honey)
October/November	Late dry	0.9	0.4	0.1	1.4	98.6	0.0
November/December	Early wet	0.1	2.2	0.0	2.3	97.7	0.0
December/January	Early wet	0.9	2.3	0.0	3.2	96.2	0.6
January/February	Mid wet	0.1	0.9	0.0	1.0	98.5	0.5
February/March	Mid wet	2.0	0.7	0.0	2.7	97.1	0.2
March/April	Mid wet	7.1	0.6	0.0	7.7	91.8	0.5
April/May	Late wet	4.0	0.0	0.0	4.0	96.0	0.0
May/June	Early dry	5.4	0.0	0.0	5.4	94.6	0.0
August/September	Mid dry	3.1	0.0	0.0	3.1	95.5	1.4
September/October	Late dry	0.0	0.6	0.1	0.7	98.1	1.2

From an economic perspective, there are a number of reasons. First, access to market technology has increased the efficiency of men's production, particularly in hunting, where shotguns and rifles have been readily incorporated, but also in fishing. Women's production efficiency in gathering remained fairly stable. The traditional ironwood digging stick was replaced by a metal variety, but this did not significantly improve gathering returns. It is also important to note that introduced fauna like feral water buffalo, cattle and pig were readily hunted by men and utilized, but no introduced and exploitable floral species flourished in the region.[2]

Secondly, while gathering may have realized predictable returns, this was the least efficient sector of the traditional economy. The *maximum* returns that I observed on day-long gathering expeditions were about 600 kilocalories per woman hour. Men could produce 4–5 times this maximum rate *on average* (see Table 4.5). With market carbohydrates being readily available and storeable, the supposed regularity of women's produce vis-a-vis men's has become an insignificant consideration. I will argue below that traditionally men's subsistence production may have been more predictable than generally acknowledged in the literature.

Finally, market substitutes for bush carbohydrates are cheap, storeable and readily available, while substitutes for the flesh foods that men hunt are not only expensive but are also not readily available out bush and highly perishable. Given that the cash income levels of Gunwinggu are low by Euro-Australian standards (about $67 per capita per month in 1980) and relatively fixed, it is reasonable decision-making to concentrate expenditure on the cheaper market commodities for which local substitutes are scarce (see Altman 1982c).

Non-economic reasons also influence this transformation. Among Gunwinggu, men's status continues to be determined primarily in the male ceremonial domain. Ritual status is gained by the accumulation of esoteric knowledge. For men, success in hunting is correlated to some extent with rapid upward mobility in ritual grading. There are other ways to gain favour in ceremonies, but success as a hunter seems to be of particular importance. Secular status also accrues to men who are successful hunters.[3]

Women's status in Gunwinggu society is not as formally graded or as hierarchical as men's. Today, there is a general acceptance among women that the market has obviated the need for regular bush carbohydrate gathering. Nevertheless women continue to display traditional skills. Such displays are generally reserved for times in the seasonal cycle when exploitable bush carbohydrates are readily available. These displays could be regarded as 'symbolic' production, for to demonstrate the retention of traditional skills, as in the making of bush bread from lily seeds, is today a source of status.

Traditional Subsistence Production: a Reconstruction

The existence of a carbohydrate shortfall between current Gunwinggu subsistence production and current consumption, and the identification of this shortfall as women's domain, allows some reconstruction of relative production under traditional conditions. Such a reconstruction is based on a number of assumptions:
1. That in the past Gunwinggu enjoyed a dietary mix of protein and carbohydrate foods that approximated the current consumption mix.
2. That a kilocalorie benchmark of 2,500 kilocalories per day per capita was a preferred intake and that 2,000 kilocalories was a minimum requirement for biological viability.
3. That similar sized band groups occupied and utilized similar sized ranges in the past, and that dependency ratios were not significantly different.
4. That men and women could have only hunted and gathered for a maximum period of nine hours per day.

I also assume that men's production levels were relatively unaltered. As noted above, currently men produce about 94 grams of protein per capita per day which is about 144 per cent of a benchmark of 65 grams per day. There is no doubt that without market technology men would have had to spend more hours in the food quest (greater than the current average of 2.9 hours per day) but there is no reason to believe that current total production levels could not have been achieved.[4]

It is women's required extra work effort that I examine closely. In Table 4.4, I initially estimate the daily per capita and monthly community shortfall in carbohydrate production utilizing the benchmarks of 2,500 and 2,000 kilocalories per capita per day. Next, I estimate the women hours that would be required for this shortfall to be produced by women in the Momega band. It is important to note that here I utilize the maximum rate I observed gathered (600 kilocalories per woman hour). This is similar in magnitude to Meehan's (1982:150) estimate of 5 kilograms of vegetable food per woman day. However, both Meehan and I do not take into account the possible effect of diminishing returns over time in our estimates. Both estimates are far higher than average returns that I metered at Momega presented in Table 4.5.

Table 4.4 *Estimation of work required by women to meet carbohydrate shortfall*

Month	Daily shortfall per capita A*	B*	Monthly community shortfall A**	B**	Women hours required A***	B***	Women hours avail.****
October/November	800	300	742,400	278,400	1,237	464	no data
November/December	750	250	594,000	198,000	990	330	978
December/January	1,650	1,150	1,780,020	1,276,270	2,967	2,127	1,350
January/February	1,500	1,000	1,757,700	1,171,800	2,930	1,953	1,332
February/March	1,450	900	1,589,490	1,040,390	2,649	1,736	1,332
March/April	1,300	800	1,213,030	746,480	2,022	1,244	1,416
April/May	1,050	550	518,805	217,755	865	453	591
May/June	1,200	700	1,517,280	885,080	2,529	1,475	insuf. da
August/September	1,100	600	896,830	489,180	1,495	815	1,104
September/October	1,000	500	725,000	362,500	1,208	604	891

*   Daily shortfall A is requirement (2,500 kilocalories per capita per day) minus avera subsistence production; shortfall B is requirement (2,000 kilocalories) minus avera production.
** Monthly shortfalls A, B are daily shortfalls A, B × days metered × average populatic
*** Monthly shortfalls A, B divided by 600 kilocalories (assumed women's production rat
**** Hours available are total hours spent today in non-productive activities.

Table 4.5 *Men's and women's bush foodstuff production, work effort and efficiency (hourly return) over four months (in kilocalories)*

Month	Kilocalories produced Men	Women	Hours spent in food quest Men	Women	Hourly kilocalo returns Men	Won
November/December 1979	1,329,716	58,296	462	510	2,878	11
January/February 1980	1,120,759	45,483	822	348	1,363	13
April/May 1980	460,143	158,328	444	573	1,036	27
August/September 1980	1,038,671	110,301	795	546	1,307	20

Even assuming the above rate of return, a substantial number of women hours are required to meet even the lower benchmark requirements. Women hours available are hours spent today in non-productive (outside the home) activities up to a maximum of nine hours per day. During four months out of eight for which there were sufficient data women would have been able to produce the shortfall to a benchmark of 2,000 kilocalories, but in no month could the benchmark of 2,500 kilocalories be met.

There are a number of ramifications arising from these findings. It is quite clear that Gunwinggu who reside at outstations today consume a higher kilocalorie intake of about 2,800 per capita per day than would have been possible under traditional conditions. Furthermore, the work effort required by both men and women in subsistence production would have been far higher than the current average 2.6 hours per adult producer per day.[5]

This finding is similar to those of Meehan (1982) and Hawkes and O'Connell (1981). Meehan's work among the Anbarra is perhaps of greater comparative relevance because Kopanga (see Map) where she conducted fieldwork is only some 60 kilometres from Momega. Meehan (1982:150) notes that Anbarra women in 1972/73 would have to dig yams on 7, 14, 17 and 28 days of a four month survey period to provide the kilocalories purchased today. What Meehan does not make clear is that this work effort is additional to subsistence work effort already undertaken by Anbarra women. The most extreme example occurred in April 1973, when shellfish were collected by women on 28 out of 30 days (Meehan 1982:55). For energy requirements to be met from women's subsistence production in a hypothetical pre-contact economy, during that same month, vegetables would have *also* required gathering on 28 days (Meehan 1982:150).

Meehan (1982) and my (Altman 1982a) reconstructions of pre-contact subsistence economies in Arnhem Land call to question McCarthy and McArthur's (1960) time allocation studies conducted in 1948 at Fish Creek and Hemple Bay. It has been noted elsewhere (Jones 1980) that their study had a number of shortcomings. First, it was conducted over a short period and was therefore unrepresentative of the seasonal cycle. Secondly, the groups surveyed were not demographically normal — the group at Fish Creek consisted of adults only. Finally, over the survey period, subjects were asked not to consume market foodstuffs to which they had access. In short, the data were collected under artificial circumstances.

At Fish Creek, men spent 3 hours and 44 minutes per day in food related activities and women 3 hours and 50 minutes, while at Hemple Bay the corresponding figures were 5 hours and 9 minutes, and 5 hours and 7 minutes. It is primarily on these data (and Lee's [1968] data on the !Kung) that Sahlins (1972) built his influential 'original affluence' argument. It now appears that by accepting these data, Sahlins grossly overestimated the amount of leisure time available to Aborigines in the past and that in Arnhem Land at any rate affluence is more a modern than an original phenomenon.

These data also suggest that under traditional conditions men may have produced a greater proportion of the total diet than previously acknowledged. Prior to the 1970s, it was generally assumed that about 70 per cent of food (by weight) was gathered by women (see Lee 1968, Meehan 1974). More recent emphasis on the kilocalorie and protein contributions of men's and women's subsistence production in Arnhem Land undermines this figure. Meehan's data (1982) and mine (see also Jones 1980) suggest that in pre-contact times men and women produced about 50 per cent of subsistence produce (in kilocalorie terms) each over the seasonal cycle.

In general in hunter-gatherer studies, women are depicted as the steady producers while men provide the less certain but more prestigious large game (Lee 1980). The reason for this apparent dichotomy is that women's produce (which is gathered or collected) is immobile, while game, men's produce, is mobile. The former returns are regarded as predictable and the latter as less predictable.

I would suggest that among Gunwinggu this dichotomy is not, and was not, particularly important, and that the unpredictability of men's hunting and fishing activities may be somewhat over-emphasized. I make this assertion for two reasons. First, in Arnhem Land during certain seasons, particularly the wet seasons, there are few resources available for women to exploit. The mainstay of the subsistence economy during these seasons, when Gunwinggu occupy elevated locations, is macropods. During January-February 1980, the wettest month in the seasonal cycle, bush foods at Momega consisted almost entirely of agile wallabies. During this month men hunted 26 times and were significantly successful — one or more macropods being shot — on twenty-two days, giving a success rate of 85 per cent. Women's production during this month was at its lowest point (see Table 4.2) owing to ecological constraints. Even under modern conditions, Momega residents would have experienced an acute food shortage without this game. Secondly, I would argue that men's game is a relatively predictable resource given the production process utilized during certain seasons. Examples of such predictable subsistence production are fish trapping (with conical fish traps), fish drives (with hand held nets) and game drives, with and without fire. These production processes, combined with Gunwinggu knowledge of the terrain, animal behaviour and seasonal vulnerability, often make subsistence returns quite predictable.

Wider Considerations

The proportions of female to male subsistence contributions, by weight, varied according to Lee (1968) from 70/30 for the Dieri, Aranda and Walbiri to 50/50 for the Murngin. Meggitt (1964) suggests ratios of 70/30 to 80/20. None of these assessments was based on quantitative data. The orthodoxy in Australian anthropology has assumed that women were the major subsistence producers. This assumption has been used in diverging manners. Most anthropologists have suggested that as women were the main providers, the expropriation of their subsistence surplus (above their own needs) is further proof of their secondary status in Aboriginal society. This apparent fact has been used to provide an economic rationale for gerontocratic polygynous regimes (Hart and Pilling 1960). Other anthropologists (like Hamilton 1975 and 1981, and Bell 1983) have argued that the fact that women were the main providers gave them a degree of autonomy in the economic domain.

Recently, on the basis of quantitative reconstructions, Meehan (1982) and I have suggested that under traditional conditions the female/male subsistence contribution in kilocalories was 50/50. Furthermore, among Gunwinggu in recent times, this ratio has altered radically to 10/90. What do these data contribute to the question of production and autonomy?

An initial point that I would like to make is that in the past, analyses may have given undue emphasis to large gatherings of Aborigines at settlements, missions and pastoral stations. From my experience at Momega, it seems that when people are living off the land, they reside in extremely small groups for most of the year (85 per cent in the Momega case). At its most cohesive, the Momega band numbered a monthly average of 44 people, but during some seasons in the annual cycle, particularly the late wet and mid dry, the band splintered into smaller household cluster units. At its most cohesive, the band resided at the Momega wet season camp, divided into 9 households in three spatial household clusters. There was also a young men's camp at Momega, but each young man was affiliated to a household that was his commensal unit.

Concentrating for now on the band group, there appear to be three inter-related questions: (1) who produced what over the seasonal cycle and who was dependent on whom? (2) what was the method of distributing subsistence produce and who decided what was given to whom? and (3) what was the composition of production teams and who decided what subsistence activities should be pursued? I attempt to answer some of these questions with reference to the Momega case.

As already noted, there are times even today when the Momega band is almost entirely dependent on men's hunting returns for protein foods. Such dependence occurs during the wet seasons when women's produce is not available. Women's greatest subsistence contribution is made during the late wet and early dry today. There is no doubt that in pre-contact times, the flora utilized during these seasons would have been more thoroughly exploited. Overall, men may have been the key producers during the late dry, early wet and mid wet seasons, and women during the late wet and early dry. The mid dry may have been a time of equal production. The point is that over the seasonal cycle, with 50/50 production, interdependence appears to have been the norm.

The extent of autonomy could arguably be more closely linked to how bush foods were distributed, rather than who produced them. At Momega, I collected detailed data (see Altman 1982a:222–6) on primary sharing of subsistence produce. For both males and females, the initial obligation is to one's household, closely followed by the household cluster, and then beyond. The strictness of sharing rules varies depending on the produce and the general availability of bush foods in camp. The strictest rules apply to the division of large game, like macropods, emus, crocodiles and now feral buffalo, all hunted by men. But these rules applied not only because it was men's produce, but also because it was immediate surplus game. It was difficult to gather quantitative data on secondary and further distribution rounds, but there was no evidence that either sex had sole responsibility for such sharing.

Decisions about the composition of production teams or the subsistence activities to be undertaken may indicate autonomy. At the band level, there are four different types of production teams: individual male, male only, female only, and mixed. Furthermore, teams can be household-based, household cluster based or involve co-operation between clusters. For 60 days when the band was most cohesive, I analysed data on team composition (Altman 1982a:202–12). During this time, 127 groups left Momega in the food quest — 48 per cent were mixed teams, 43 per cent were male only and 9 per cent were female only. The most common production team was household-based (49 per cent). followed by teams that involved co-operation between clusters (35 per cent) and then cluster-based teams (16 per cent). Today, the women's only team is least common, and this may be linked to the decline in the women's gathering economy. However, I add a proviso here. When women today make their greatest subsistence contribution, the band tends to camp close to exploitable resources. In fact there is a significant correlation (see also Meehan 1982:64) between physical proximity to exploitable women's produce and its significance in the diet. In general women's only teams do not forage far from camp. This is linked to a concern (among men) for women's safety. When production teams are mixed, this is usually a result of consensus decision-making between senior men and women in the band. The unit that appears to have the greatest production autonomy however is the household, and here too decisions are generally made by consensus. Decisions about resource utilization tend to be dominated by men. This is linked to their current distorted contribution to the bush foods diet. However, ultimately it is the local environment and the seasonal cycle that dictate what resources are available. Gunwinggu have fairly fixed seasonal movements aimed at utilizing available resources at various 'resource bases' on the range. No doubt under traditional conditions when people were equally dependent on women's produce, the tradeoff between rates of subsistence return would have dictated what subsistence strategy was pursued.

Now I turn to the situation when the bands gather for regional, mortuary and exchange ceremonies. In the literature, this time is generally depicted as the period when men are preoccupied with ceremonial activities and are entirely dependent on women's produce. From my experience, ceremonies do not preclude men's hunting or fishing activities, and may in fact encourage them. Among Gunwinggu, the important times for ceremonies are the early dry and late dry seasons. During the former, eastern Gunwinggu gather on the Tomkinson flood plains. Even today, senior men engage in fish trapping and harvest massive quantities of barramundi and catfish that support large gatherings. The conical fish trap used is an item of traditional technology. During the late dry ceremonies, males often partake in large-scale fire drives that are managed by elders. Again I have witnessed massive meat surpluses at such drives, although introduced technology (guns) was utilized. In the past males may have been dependent on females for sustenance particularly as ceremonies reached their finales. Among eastern Gunwinggu, women were also responsible for the manufacture of lily pod bread that was a trade item at Mamurrang exchange ceremonies.

In general, Gunwinggu aim for balance in the diet (see Meehan 1982 and Peterson 1973), and there is little reason to believe that adherence to this aim would have abated during ceremonies. At such times, hosts may well have aimed to demonstrate to visiting groups the richness of their country and the strength of their ceremonies (emically correlated with the increase of natural species). A varied and abundant provisioning of guests would have been one way of doing this, which again points to interdependence in production.

Finally, let's examine the contemporary situation, for it seems that this too can be interpretated in various ways. There is no doubt that men today provide the majority of subsistence produce among Gunwinggu, but does this mean that they are any more or less autonomous? Conversely, has the decline in the women's economy resulted in a decline in their autonomy? It seems to me that the questions cannot be unambiguously answered. For as shown above, to bridge the 'carbohydrate gap' under traditional conditions would have required greatly increased work effort for women. Today, with access to market goods and cash income, both men and women have the freedom to choose whether to work or not. Today one can argue that it is women who expropriate men's produce, but are men necessarily exploited? If men's power in Gunwinggu society is linked to expropriating women's material surplus, one may well ask, expropriate what? And if women's autonomy which appears significant at the band level is linked to their current low production levels, one may well ask how great was it in pre-contact times?

Conclusion

In the contemporary context, there has been a marked transformation in the subsistence economy of Gunwinggu hunter-gatherers in Arnhem Land. This transformation has been in the relative subsistence contribution of men and women. There has been a rapid decline in the significance of women's production, but the men's hunting economy has remained resilient. This transformation can be explained, to a great extent, by economic factors. The ready availability of cheap market carbohydrates has resulted in the supplantation of women's produce, bush carbohydrates. Market foodstuffs are procured with cash earned by producing artefacts for market exchange and from welfare payments. Men's production has remained significant because men have incorporated simple market technology into traditional production processes, and have adapted hunting skills to exploit introduced feral game.

The resilience of the men's hunting economy must also be explained by non-economic factors. In particular, there appears to be a correlation between men's hunting prowess and men's rate of success in the ritual realm. As eastern Gunwinggu men continue to strive to accumulate ritual status as a key goal in their lives, so they continue to pursue hunting success.

Assuming that in pre-contact times Gunwinggu enjoyed a balanced diet, then the carbohydrates currently procured must have been produced by women, for carbohydrate collection is women's domain. A reconstruction of traditional subsistence production using optimal gathering rates indicates that this shortfall could only have been bridged during some months in the seasonal cycle. Coupled with the fact that men's traditional hunting technology was inferior to introduced equipment, there are two key ramifications to this finding.

First, to meet subsistence requirements under traditional conditions would have required substantial work effort from both men and women. This suggests that Sahlins' (1972) depiction of Arnhem Landers as the 'original affluent society' was erroneous — if affluence is measured in work-effort terms. Secondly, it seems that over the seasonal cycle men's and women's subsistence contribution to the diet was more equitable than previously believed.

Notes

1. The fieldwork on which this paper is based was undertaken from April 1979 to November 1980 and was funded by the Australian Institute of Aboriginal Studies while I was a research scholar in the Department of Prehistory and Anthropology, ANU. I would like to thank Dr Nicolas Peterson and Dr Simon Harrison for comments on an earlier draft of this paper and Dr Diane Bell for some comments in discussion.
2. During some months, 20 per cent of the bush foods diet consisted of feral water buffalo (see Altman 1982b).
3. See Sackett (1979) for a discussion of this point in the Central Australian context.
4. It is not clear whether introduced and indigenous grazing animals compete for resources. It seems likely that there is some competition, particularly between feral water buffalo and macropods. I assume that under traditional and modern conditions, the biomass available was similar and that the contribution of introduced game to the contemporary diet was formerly provided by greater utilization of macropods.
5. Elsewhere I have hypothesized that the increased availability of time and access to market foods has resulted in an escalation of ceremonial activity today (see Altman 1982a).

References

ALTMAN, J. C. (1982a), *Hunter-gatherers and the State: the Economic Anthropology of the Gunwinggu of North Australia*, unpublished PhD thesis, Australian National University.
—— (1982b), 'Hunting Buffalo in North-Central Arnhem Land: a Case of Rapid Adaptation Among Aborigines', *Oceania*, **52**(4): 274–285.

—— (1982c), 'Maningrida Outstation: a Preliminary Economic Overview' in E. A. Young & E. K. Fisk (eds), *Small Rural Communities. The Aboriginal Component of the Australian Economy, Volume 3*. Development Studies Centre, Canberra.

—— & NIEWENHUYSEN, J. (1979), *The Economic Status of Australian Aborigines*, Cambridge: Cambridge University Press.

BELL, D. (1983), *Daughters of the Dreaming*. Melbourne: McPhee Gribble.

COOMBS, H. C. (1974), 'Decentralization Trends Among Aboriginal Communities', *Search*, **5**:135–43.

HAMILTON, A. (1975), 'Aboriginal Women: the Means of Production', in J. Mercer (ed.), *The Other Half: Women in Australian Society*, Melbourne: Penguin.

—— (1981), 'A Complex Strategical Situation: Gender and Power in Aboriginal Australia', in N. Grieve & P. Grimshaw (eds), *Australian Women: Feminist Perspectives*, Melbourne: Oxford University Press.

HART, C. W. M. & PILLING, A. R. (1960), *The Tiwi of North Australia*, New York: Holt, Rinehart & Winston.

HAWKES, K. & O'CONNELL, J. (1981), 'Affluent Hunters? Some Comments in Light of the Alyawarra Case', *American Anthropologist*, **83**(3):622–626.

JONES, R. (1980), 'Hunters in the Australian Coastal Savanna', in D. Harris (ed.), *Human Ecology in Savanna Environments*, London: Academic Press.

LEE; R. B. (1968), 'What Hunters do for a Living', in R. B. Lee & I. Devore (eds), *Man the Hunter*, Chicago: Aldine.

—— (1980), 'Existe-t-il un Mode de Production "Forrageur"?', *Anthropologie et Sociétés*, **4**(3):59–74.

MCCARTHY, F. D. & MCARTHUR, M. (1960), 'The Food Quest and Time Factor in Aboriginal Economic Life', in C. P. Mountford (ed.), *Records of the American-Australian Scientific Expedition to Arnhem Land, Volume 2: Anthropology and Nutrition*, Melbourne: Melbourne University Press.

MEGGITT, M. J. (1964), 'Aboriginal Food-gatherers of Tropical Australia', in *Proceedings and Papers of the Ninth Technical Meeting of IUCN, Nairobi, Kenya*, International Union for the Conservation of Nature and Natural Resources, Morges, Switzerland.

MEEHAN, B. (1974), 'Woman the Gatherer', in F. Gale (ed.), *Woman's Role in Aboriginal Society*, Canberra: Australian Institute of Aboriginal Studies.

—— (1982), *Shell Bed to Shell Midden*, Canberra: Australian Institute of Aboriginal Studies.

PETERSON, N. (1973), 'Camp Site Location Among Australian Hunter-gatherers: Archaeological and Ethnographic Evidence for a Key Determinant', *Archaeology and Physical Anthropology in Oceania*, **8**:173–93.

SACKETT, L. (1979), 'The Pursuit of Prominence: Hunting in an Australian Aboriginal Community', *Anthropologica*, (n.s.). **21**:223–46.

SAHLINS, M. (1972), *Stone Age Economics*, Chicago: Aldine/Atherton.

5
Australian Aborigines in a Rich Environment

A. CHASE & P. SUTTON

1. Anthropology and Ecology

Anthropologists have for many decades borrowed from general ecological theory, and some have even adopted 'human ecology' or 'cultural ecology' as the framework for their research. While not denying the importance of economic and other modes in which people interact with their environment, most anthropologists, however, have found that a 'human ecology' framework leans too far away from the cultural side of the human condition.

On the other hand, anthropological approaches which relegate the material context of society to the status of mere background, or to the role of simply providing imagery for mentalistic culture, seem to us to go too far in the opposite direction. Such heavily synchronic approaches cannot contribute very much to the larger questions of human sociocultural history and evolution, which we regard as legitimate long-term pursuits of anthropology.

2. The Australian Context

Australian Aboriginal data have always been a critical touchstone for anthropological theories, and the ecological interest in hunter-gatherer exploitation patterns has provided new interest in Aboriginal research. Better known Australian examples of this ecological approach are to be found in Lee & De Vore (1968), Bicchieri (1972), and from a specifically archaeological perspective, in Mulvaney & Golson (1971). Gould (1973) deals with the ecological theme in an overview of Australian archaeology.

During the last seventy years or so, the predominantly *social* ethnographies of Australian Aborigines have revealed the complex systems of

First published in a slightly longer version under the title 'Hunter-gatherers in a rich environment: Aboriginal coastal exploitation in Cape York Peninsula' in A. Keast (ed.) *Ecological Biogeography of Australia*, The Hague-Boston-London: Dr W. Junk bv Publishers, 1981.

kinship and marriage, religion and totemism that form part of the ideologies under which social groups operate and considerations of the biophysical environment were at the best scant and gave no serious consideration to dynamic processes of interaction with environments.

In recent years, however, some anthropologists have called for more ecologically oriented studies of the exploiting groups (for example, see Stanner, 1965, and Peterson, 1976a:68). Only when this is done can meaningful comparisons be made of human systems: first within the Australian continent, and secondly within the wider context of hunter-gatherers and others elsewhere in the world.

3. Aborigines and Tropical Coastal Environments

As Stanner (1965) has rightly noted, there has been an over-emphasis on Central Australian arid zone Aboriginal populations in the anthropological literature and this is mainly due to their isolation from European contact and the persistence of traditionally oriented groups. There is a need for balancing this by ecological studies of coastal groups who, together with those inhabiting the permanent riverine systems of the continent, comprised the majority of pre-contact Aboriginal population. There have been few systematic investigations of those areas where marine as well as terrestrial environments were heavily exploited, and where the resource base was bountiful rather than restrictive.

The northern tropical coastline of Australia presents an area where Aboriginal hunter-gatherers operated within such habitats, and the complex patterns of plant communities, marine environments and animal life in these tropical areas provided opportunities for resource exploitation which can hardly be exceeded elsewhere on the Australian continent. Among the more interesting general ecological questions which arise from this apparent plethora of natural resources is, first, the explanation of a fairly constant hunting and gathering mode of existence throughout the continent, in both these abundant areas and the more arid inland areas, and, correlated with this, the failure of tropical agricultural systems from adjacent Papua New Guinea and the Torres Straits Islands to gain a foothold on adjacent areas of the Australian mainland.

When Aboriginal man-environment interactions are looked at within a wider perspective of neighbouring human systems, Cape York Peninsula offers itself as a research area of prime ecological importance. Its close proximity to the Torres Straits Islands and the southern coastline of New Guinea, and its apparently favourable niches for possible agricultural activities, have recently attracted research interest (Harris, 1976; Walker, 1972). Yet such apparently straightforward questions pose problems for the anthropologist. As Forde (1934) noted some time ago, human cultures cannot necessarily be seen as stages within a generalized model of economic development, but possess complete economies within themselves and these are the product not only of the availability of natural resources, but also of the cultural dimensions which result from people living in groups with established traditions.

In examining man-environment interactions *within* the Australian mainland, Cape York Peninsula presents a unique area. Due to its length and progressive narrowness, the Peninsula provides an extraordinary length of coastline in proportion to its area. In its central area north of Princess Charlotte Bay, the most remote inland location is only some 110 kilometres from either coastline, and the large western sea inlets at the mouths of such rivers as the Archer and the Wenlock reduce the distance from saltwater even further. Because of this geography, the great majority of Aboriginal populations inhabited the coastal margins and it is from these that our three examples are chosen, not merely to demonstrate the ecological processes of coastal peoples, but to show, as well, the considerable range of interactions across a variety of coastal habitats unique within Australia in their diversity and richness.

4. Cape York Peninsula and its Aboriginal Inhabitants

4.1 The natural environment

The area is impressive with its wide range of highly diverse plant communities, geological variation and marked seasonality and these combine to provide a uniquely wide range of environments for human occupation. These range from the reef and island studded eastern coastal area, with its mangrove-lined estuaries, open dunes, saltpans and beaches, dense coastal scrubs and riverine vine-forests, to the flat Carpentarian shoreline with its low dune systems, seasonally inundated grass-plains and lagoons. Intermixed with these, and comprising the central area of the Cape, are large areas of melaleuca and eucalypt dry sclerophyll forests, deciduous vine thickets, heathland, and gallery rainforests along the rivers and creeks. Coastal margins on both sides of the Peninsula exhibit the greatest variation in habitat type and complexity of distribution (see Pedley & Isbell, 1971, and Harris, 1976), and these, together with the large sinuous river systems which almost transect the Cape from the 600 metre watershed on the east coast, appear to have been focal occupation areas for pre-contact Aboriginal populations.

The strongly marked seasonal variation (see Figure 5.1) fluctuating from the heavy monsoon rains of December-April to the extreme dry of early December, brings cyclically large areas of inundation, flooded rivers and strong vegetation growth, and this progressively subsides until at the end of the year rivers and creeks are reduced to chains of shallow ponds or dry beds. At this time much of the terrain becomes parched and free-ranging beef cattle, which support nearly all of the white occupation of the Cape, undergo stress.

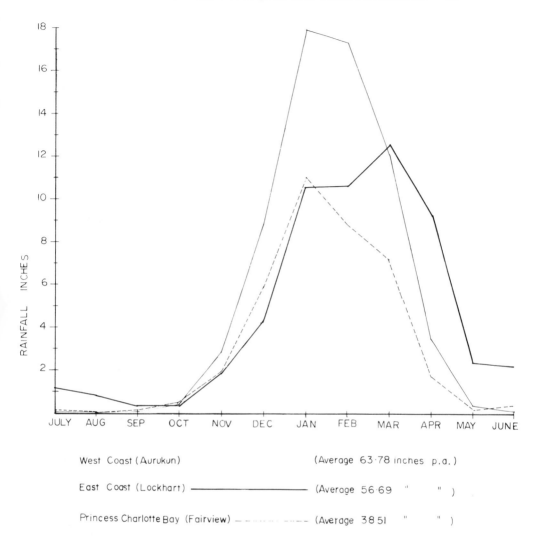

Figure 5.1. Comparative rainfall (monthly averages) for three locations closest to case study areas. Information from Bureau of Meteorology, Queensland.

4.2 The Aboriginal occupants

Cape York was occupied before white contact by members of several hundred small kin groups whose numbers appeared to vary between 10 and 50 people. Each individual recognized a homeland or 'country' which was inherited through the father's line. This intense mosaic of recognized territories was divided (in a somewhat fluctuating fashion) into larger conglomerates on the basis of such factors as common languages or dialects, shared localities, shared ceremonial interests, wider intermarriage and wider kinship ties. Such complex (and shifting) dimensions of organization, and the lack of congruence among the various boundaries make it difficult to apply the notion of 'tribe' to these populations, and the reader is referred to Peterson (1976b) for a fuller discussion of the difficulties in applying such a concept to Aboriginal Australia.

4.2.1 Languages

From the 16th parallel north, there were about 45 distinct Aboriginal languages spoken on the Peninsula a century ago before European contact, and these consist of several hundred dialects. The west coast, the far northern tip and Princess Charlotte Bay were areas of concentrated linguistic diversity. In some cases, clusters of separate languages were spoken by people whose territories were no more than twenty kilometres apart and who were multilingual. Before European intrusion, some languages appear to have had as few as 60–100 speakers, while others had, and in some cases still have, several hundred speakers. Examples of recent work on these languages may be found in Sutton (1976).

4.2.2 Technology

The common technology for these people consisted of woven bags and baskets, multiple-and single-headed spears often consisting of jointed sections and barbed with bone and stingray spines, a highly distinctive type of spearthrower decorated with baler shell plaques, elegantly sheathed firesticks, hafted stone axes, and a wide variety of shell, seed and feather ornaments.

Dependence on marine resources by coastal groups is reflected in the manufacture of large dugout canoes with single or double outriggers, and detachable head harpoons for hunting turtle and dugong. These were found along the length of the east coast and on the west coast as far south as the Archer River mouth. From the Archer south, smaller inland water craft were made from the bark of *Eucalyptus tetradonta*, and used in the shallow waters of the large estuaries and inland waterbodies. Shelters varied seasonally from simple windbreaks and platform roofs to more solid structures of bark and leaf thatched huts which were used for protection in the wet season from the rain and the clouds of mosquitos which infest much of the area.

Ceremonies (generally held towards the end of the dry season) were numerous, and rich in song, dance and accompanying mythology. Elaborate decorations and body paint designs accompanied these, and in the case of the 'hero cults' described by Thomson (1933), included the only use of a Melanesian-type drum with a skin tympanum recorded in Aboriginal Australia. The apparent technological connections to Melanesia through these drums and outrigger canoes, as well as elements of the secret ceremonies, have been commented on by Thomson (1933, 1956).

For further information on Aboriginal material culture for Cape York Peninsula, the reader is referred to Craig's area bibliography (1967).

In summary, the material technology of Cape York Aborigines provided an efficient means of coping with the problems of regular extraction of resources from the various habitats, including marine environments. The elaborate ceremonial and kinship systems, together with extremely detailed knowledge of floral and faunal components of their universe, combined with this material culture to create effective life systems which flourished until the intrusion of Europeans.

4.2.3. Contact

With early political concern for foreign invasion of Australia, the colony of Queensland pushed a telegraph line northward in the 1870s along the spine of Cape York to Thursday Island. The establishment of cattle stations along the protective flanks of this line and the discovery of gold on the Palmer River rapidly brought adventurers and settlers into the area, and by 1890 Aboriginal populations in central and southern Cape York were under severe contact pressure. With the decline of the Palmer fields, mining exploration moved northwards, and this together with the rapidly growing sandalwood, pearling and trepang industries created a pincerlike pressure on the groups occupying the eastern and northwestern areas.

By the turn of the century, many of these groups had been displaced into refuge camps around the larger settlement areas, sometimes eliminated by ruthless settlers, or recruited as labourers on the hundreds of luggers then plying the coasts. The establishment of a chain of missions and reserves early in the century along the west coast did much to prevent heavy depredations for this area, especially south of the Archer River, and today this area contains the largest populations of traditionally oriented people.

Today, the Aboriginal population is largely concentrated at the missions and government settlements along the east and west coasts, with smaller groupings around the few small towns where they depend on the cattle industry for employment.

5. The Nesbit River Region

5.1 Environments

The *Umpila* dialect area occupies about 55 kilometres of narrow coastal plain and low hills from the Massey River to as far north as Cape Sidmouth. Like the Flinders Island groups discussed later, the range of the bands occupying this area includes both terrestrial and marine environments. Beyond the beach the exploited areas took in estuaries, sandbars, fringing coral reefs, and extended several kilometres offshore to encompass a number of small islands, cays and reefs. On the mainland, their territories for the first two kilometres or so inland are composed of low parallel sandridges separated by tree-filled swales and swamps, saltpans, and occasionally wider open stretches of fresh water. Behind these complex and varied habitats, the land opens out into dry sclerophyll forests of eucalypt and melaleuca which continue the remaining five or six kilometres to the foothills of the coastal ranges, the eastern slopes of which are clad in dense monsoonal forest. All of these inland zones are dissected every 15 kilometres by a series of large creeks, rivers and braided streams which are bordered by narrow riverine rainforest. At the mouth of these waterways, the beach changes into mangrove-fringed inlets and small deltas, and in the case of the Nesbit River, a large bight bordered by dense mangrove growth and protected from the ocean by a long sandbar.

The area is difficult to traverse whether along the beach or inland in the wet season, when the swales, pans and swamps are filled to capacity, but most of this surface water has disappeared by the late dry season. The area is floristically complex with numerous clearly demarcated plant habitats, and the general area is rich in bird, mammal, reptile and fish species.

Nesbit people carefully distinguish the habitats and environments of their territories, and the following examples of progressive zones from the sea to the first line of vegetation behind the beach reveals the degree of classification which can occur over a small distance:

kuytu kulu	deep sea water
kuytu atya	seawater shallow enough to stand in
kuytu nganta	kneedeep seawater
ngaluna	seawater edge
malnkan	intertidal beach zone
tuyinu palnpana	zone where water has deposited rubbish
yi' an	raised sandy area above tidal influence where camps can be made
malata	windsheared scrubs of foredune area

Similar lists could be given for other environments and, as well, beach areas can be referred to by other terms, e.g. tide-rippled beach, wind-blown sand, dirty sand, etc. Plants and animals are also exhaustively classified.

5.2 Demography and local organization

Together with the coastal groups as far north as Shelburne Bay (*Uutaalnganu, Kuuku-Ya'u* and *Wuthathi* dialect areas) and those immediately to the south (*Kuuku-Yani* and *Umbindhamu* dialect areas), the people of the Nesbit Region formed a chain of local groups some 200 kilometres long who classified themselves environmentally as *pama malnkana* ('sandbeach people') or *pama kaawatyi* ('east-side people'). This distinction contrasts with the *pama kanityi* ('on top people') or *pama iityulityi* ('west-side people') who occupied the inland regions from the coastal ranges westward, and who spoke the closely related *Kaantju* dialect. To these inlanders, the coastal groups were *pama pakatyi* ('down below people').

The shared perception of the coastal groups as members of a broad beach-side culture reflected first, a recognition of patrimoiety division and, secondly, a common linked pattern of localized initiation ceremonies which, to one early researcher, seemed unique in Australia through their New Guinea elements (Thomson, 1933). Furthermore, *pama malnkana* see themselves sharing a common marine pattern of exploitation of dugong and turtle by use of outrigger canoe and harpoon and, as well, possessing the right powerful magical knowledge to ensure success in the capture of these animals. This combination of perceived ceremonial links, social organization and patterns of marine exploitation, together with minor dialectal variation, appeared to set a model of the widest social universe of interaction.

Other coastal peoples from further south, and more especially those of the remote inland, were considered potentially dangerous, only partly human, and eaters of human flesh. *Kaantju* speakers from the immediately adjacent inland territories were excluded from this ethnocentric viewpoint, reflecting the occasional marriage, trading relationships and sometime ceremonial participation which linked some of the neighbouring inland and coastal groups.

The Nesbit River area consists of seven patrilineal territories which divide the coastal lowlands into roughly parallel segments, each forming a strip from the ocean back to the mountains (see Figure 5.2). These vary in size from the smallest at the mouth of the Nesbit River of approximately 35 square kilometres to the largest in the Cape Sidmouth vicinity of approximately 70 square kilometres. To such landbased calculations, however, must be added the marine environments extending eastwards beyond the beachline to include reefs, bars and the small off-shore islands. All of these are seen as being equally part of 'country' along with the landmass, and contain mythological sites.

As well as this territorial division, the landscape is also segmented on the basis of the two named patrimoieties (*kaapay* and *kuyan*) which divide people, land and certain animals and plants into two realms of existence. The complete coastal strip for all *pama malnkana* thus consists of alternating moiety areas.

Male members of a patrilineal group were localized with regard to their territory, though the reader is referred to the distinction between people sharing ownership, or more correctly custodianship, and the composition of a band exploiting such a territory at any given time (see Stanner, 1965).

Reconstruction of pre-contact populations for the area is now extremely difficult, though from genealogical reconstructions it appears that local group populations may have been in the range of 15 to 30 people. Total population for the area under discussion would therefore have been somewhere in the vicinity of 150 people, with an average density of one person to 2.5 square kilometres of land area.

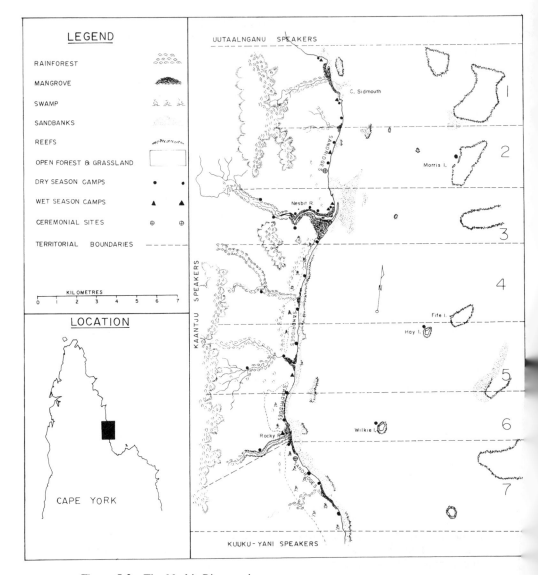

Figure 5.2   The Nesbit River region

5.3 Seasonality and mobility

Thomson (1934) reported the remarkable sedentism of the coastal groups from this area of coastal Cape York, and this is confirmed by present-day informants who spent their younger days in traditional camps. Specific camping sites for a group over an annual period had a total range of only several kilometres of beachfront and immediate hinterland. Camps were moved most often, a few hundred metres at a time, in the early dry season of June to August, when water sources along the beach were most plentiful, and an often-stated reason for the moves was the fouling and general pollution of campsites, rather than the need to find new resource bases. Campsites are always on sandy places, most commonly at named locations along the foredune area of the beach, though groups retreated some hundred metres inland to the narrow wooded sandridges when climatic conditions made beach habitation unpleasant. Named sites occur at intervals of about 300 metres along the entire habitable coastline. Six seasonal periods were recognized by *Umpila* speakers:

ngurkita (wind from northwest)	Monsoonal rain period, February to April
kuutulu (wind from southeast)	End of main rains, April to June
kaawulu (wind from southeast)	Early dry season, June to August
kayimun (hot sun)	Dry season proper, September to November
matpi pa'inyan (cloud build-up)	Impending storms, November to December
malantityi (stormtime)	Storms presaging the monsoon, December to February

Resource exploitation for this area can be viewed in two general categories: first, continuing exploitation of resources which are not particularly seasonally dependent, though access to them may be influenced by seasonality; and secondly, temporary exploitation of resources which are highly seasonal in occurrence and which are usually localized to specific habitats. (See Figure 5.3.)

5.4 Marine exploitation

The first category is dominated by the general saltwater marine environment where fishes, shellfish, crustaceans and the large green turtle and dugong can be taken opportunistically across the entire seasonal range. While seasonal variation in terms of perceived 'fatness' and other edible criteria may occur for these, and while broad climate criteria will affect availability through weather conditions, tide variation and clearness of water, they are nevertheless generally available. Beach camps throughout the year allow constant surveillance of the sea and estuaries, and permit rapid exploitation when the opportunity arises. Possession of outrigger canoes (paddled) capable of carrying three or four people considerably increased the exploitation range of these marine environments, and allowed these coastal people to extend their activities from the immediate shoreline to the more remote islands, cays, sandbars and reefs.

These marine environments also possess resources of the second category, which are prolific for short periods of the seasonal range. From the end of the wet season rains in June, vast flocks of Nutmeg

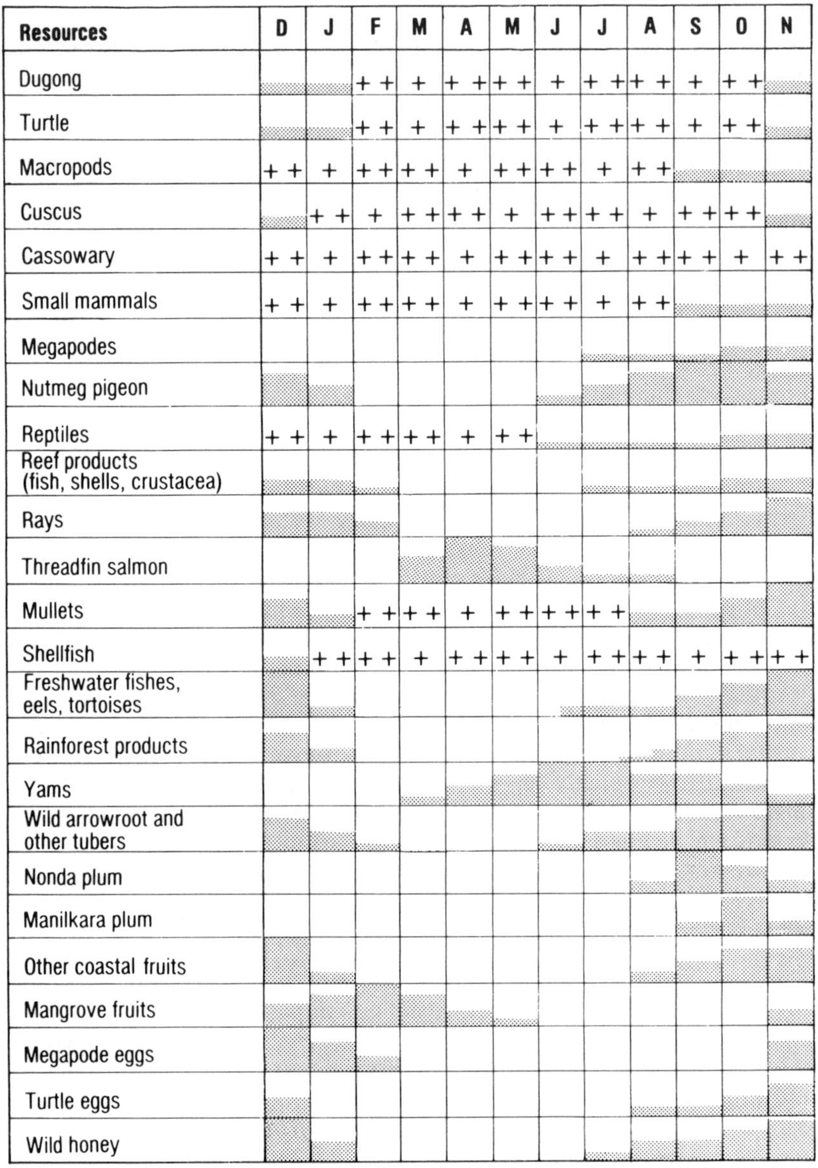

Resources	D	J	F	M	A	M	J	J	A	S	O	N
Dugong			+ +	+	+ +	+ +	+	+ +	+ +	+	+ +	
Turtle			+ +	+	+ +	+ +	+	+ +	+ +	+	+ +	
Macropods	+ +	+	+ +	+ +	+	+ +	+ +	+	+ +			
Cuscus		+ +	+	+ +	+ +	+	+ +	+ +	+	+ +	+ +	
Cassowary	+ +	+	+ +	+ +	+	+ +	+ +	+	+ +	+ +	+	+ +
Small mammals	+ +	+	+ +	+ +	+	+ +	+ +	+	+ +			
Megapodes												
Nutmeg pigeon												
Reptiles	+ +	+	+ +	+ +	+	+ +						
Reef products (fish, shells, crustacea)												
Rays												
Threadfin salmon												
Mullets			+ +	+ +	+	+ +	+ +	+ +				
Shellfish		+ +	+ +	+	+ +	+ +	+	+ +	+ +	+	+ +	+ +
Freshwater fishes, eels, tortoises												
Rainforest products												
Yams												
Wild arrowroot and other tubers												
Nonda plum												
Manilkara plum												
Other coastal fruits												
Mangrove fruits												
Megapode eggs												
Turtle eggs												
Wild honey												

The heights of the columns show the relative importance of the subsistence item in the diet. Where the whole column is shaded, this indicates a major dependence or preference, which is responsible for major allocation of activities and possible relocation of camps. + + + + + + indicates that the resource is available over long periods and is therefore less seasonal. How much is harvested then depends on secondary factors such as tides, weather conditions, and distribution within the habitats.

Figure 5.3 Resource availability and exploitation for the Nesbit region of East Cape York.

Pigeons (*Miristacivora spilorrhoa*) arrive and nest on the close off-shore islands, and the parent birds, eggs, and later, the squabs were taken in large quantities in canoe raids to the islands. In the late dry period from October to December, large shoals of mullet (e.g. *Valamugil seheli*) arrive in the estuaries and were speared from the shallow sandbars at creek and river mouths, and at the same time beaches and islands were combed for turtle eggs. With the end of the strong and constant southeast winds in November, seas become calm for periods of the day, and canoes could be used continually to search for the mating green turtles and the ever-present but elusive dugong. With the cessation of the monsoon in June, large schools of estuarine fish such as *Eleutheronema tetradactylum* (beach salmon) invade the muddy shallows along the coast feeding on the influx of shrimp.

5.5 Land exploitation

Plants and animals of the terrestrial environments (including the freshwater marine environments) are, in terms of exploitation, highly seasonal. Whilst various birds and small animals are taken throughout the annual cycle, major exploitation is concentrated upon such annual occurrences as the arrival of waterfowl who flock to the swales and lagoons from about August onwards, when the drop in waterlevel allows prolific growth of aquatic plants. At this time, progressive drying of the landscape allows burning off of the small isolated grassplains in the coastal hinterland, and these firings are carried out systematically as part of game drives for wallabies and other small animals, and to attract birds such as ibis who rapidly arrive to feed on the disturbed insects and grubs. At the end of the dry season when creeks, rivers and waterholes are at their lowest, the riverine vine forests were combed for cuscus, cassowary and echidna, and the small pools and shallow river stretches fished for eels, tortoises and freshwater fishes, often by means of plant poisons. At this time, scrub turkey and jungle fowl mounds contain incubating eggs, and these were a much sought-after delicacy.

As numerous studies have shown, vegetable foods provide the staple food supply for hunter-gatherer groups across the annual range, and this is an extremely predictable and available base for coastal Cape York people. The highly diverse and complex plant communities of this coastal strip provide a series of fruitings which, though more abundant in variety during the dry season, is nevertheless continuous and progressive throughout the year. The most important of these, in both quantity and quality are the various yam species, of which the prolific *thampu* (*Dioscorea sativa*) is the most favoured. This yam grows along the coastal dune scrubs, and is harvested at the end of the wet season in July, when the vine withers, and it remains available until the first rains of December, when new growth recommences. Yam scrubs are recognized as 'owned' by the groups within whose territory they lie, and were the subject of prohibitions, even when outside groups were invited in to share particularly bountiful crops. The care and attention given to exploitation of this resource was directed towards carefully husbanding a yam supply throughout the dry period. A continuity of supply for future seasons was assured by a specific gathering technique which left the top portion of the tuber together with the vine undisturbed on the ground ready for regrowth.

From the mid-dry onwards, a variety of trees and shrubs start producing edible fruits and these are again found most abundantly in groves along the coastal dune systems and along the riverine vine forests. Most notable among these are *Parinari nonda*, the prolific 'emu apple' of Cape York, *Syzygium suborbiculare*, or 'red lady apple', *Rhodomyrtus macrocarpa* or 'finger cherry', and a variety of succulent and sweet berries such as *Eugenia carissoides, Chrysophyllum antilogum* and *Pouteria sericea*. Most favoured of these late dry fruitings is the 'wongay plum' (*Manilkara kauki*), a tree which occurs in dense groves along the beaches and river estuaries. The prolific fruiting of this tree was the major food resource for population concentration at specific coastal ceremonial grounds for initiation ceremonies, and minor variation in fruiting time could be manipulated by harvesting the fruit in a green condition, and force-ripening by burial in the ground. A number of specific trees (e.g. *Euroschinus falcatus*) are recognized whose leaves when used as wrappings assist in this process. These times of ceremony provided the most dense population concentrations for the area.

With the arrival of the wet season in February, people grouped into larger, relatively permanent beach camps, using bark-thatched huts to protect them from the rain and the clouds of mosquitos. Flooded creeks, rivers and channels made movement difficult at this period, and the exploiting bands relied on what could be described as second-order vegetable foods: those which required preparation to remove harmful or irritating substances and to improve palatability. These foods required increased labour and effort, worthwhile only when better foods were unavailable, and when constant attention could be given to their preparation. Examples of this utilization were pods and fruits of certain mangroves (*Avicennia marina* and *Bruguiera gymnorhiza*), vines ('matchbox bean' or *Entada scandens*) and tubers of 'hairy yam' (*Dioscorea* spp.) and 'wild arrowroot' (*Tacca leontopetaloides*). This period is described as hard and difficult, a reference not only to a reliance on less preferred foods and increased labour, but as well to the psychological difficulties of being camp-bound, crowded and having to live in near-constant rain.

This brief discussion of the food resource base and seasonal mobility allows some analysis of occupation patterns. The full resource schedule of some hundreds of plants as well as animals occurs across a wide range of both terrestrial and marine habitats with the mountainous inland and the outer reef zone as its extremes. Constant camping on the immediate beachfront provides a strategic location at the centre of a complex environmental mosaic and allows rapid exploitation of general ocean and estuarine foods as opportunity arises. At the same time this location provides a central base for operating outward in either direction on land or on sea to harvest seasonally specific plants and animals.

6. Cape Keerweer Region

Donald Thomson's seminal paper on Aboriginal seasonal ecology (Thomson, 1939) was based on fieldwork partly carried out in this part of western Cape York. Sutton's recent work (1978) in the area supports Thomson's major generalizations, and in this section we deal with complementary information based on detailed fieldwork still in progress.

61. Environments

The Cape Keerweer region consists of flat, open flood-plains containing a complex system of channels. These lie between two major parallel ridge systems of sand and, in some areas, shellgrit, rising only a few metres above the surrounding country. From the months of December to April dramatic monsoonal rains flood the area, leaving only the ridges above water and sodden ground. From August to November the country rapidly dries out, leaving a few major permanent water bodies on which bird and animal life concentrate. At this time, the country becomes parched, with large areas of cracked mudflats, saltpans and grass plains, broken only by narrow corridors of woodland along the ridges. The Kirke River, which dissects the area, fans out into a huge shallow tidal lake before reaching the sea at Cape Keerweer. It is largely filled with salt or brackish water in the dry season, and fresh water in the monsoon.

This seasonally inundated complex extends several kilometres inland where it meets sharply defined dry sclerophyll woodland covering the gently rising watershed of the hinterland. This extremely clear demarcation of environmental zones is characteristic of the whole area, and the map, although slightly schematized, illustrates this fact (see Figure 5.4). One of the local languages, *Wik-Ngathan*, recognizes, among others, the following salient environmental types:

aak nhinthen ngaan	sandridge country (*aak* country, *nhinthen* ridge, *ngaan* coarse sand)
aak nhinthen theepenh	shellgrit ridge country (*theepenh* small bivalve spp.)
aak nhinthen put	sclerophyll woodland (*put* 'bloodwood')
aak thangk	grass plains
aak peth	saline mud flats
aak kunchel	dense scrub (often vine thickets containing large *Ficus* spp.)
punth	1. tidal creek, 2. intermittent channel
puthen	beach

6.2 Demography and local organization

Members of lineages whose countries are in this area largely lived and intermarried along the coastal strip. They did not interact closely with hinterlanders. Coastal territories are much smaller than inland countries, with correspondingly higher population densities (each country is

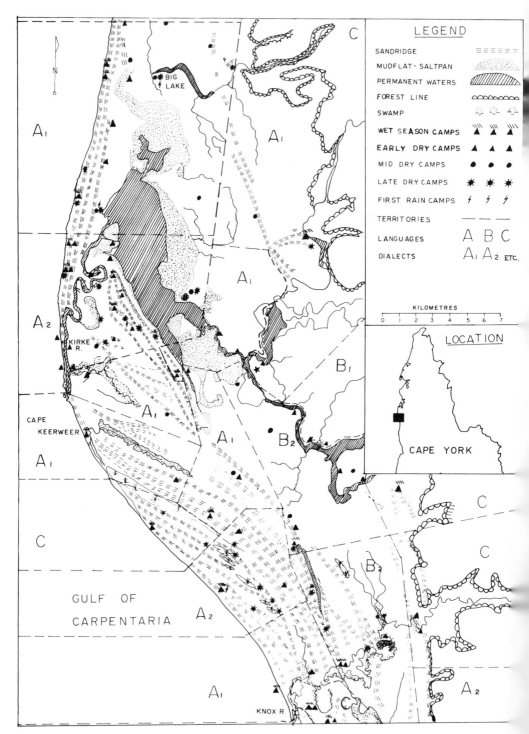

Figure 5.4   Cape Keerweer region

associated with a single lineage). A single language may be spoken by several distinct lineages, whose countries are non-contiguously scattered along the coast, separated by countries of those with other languages. All adults are polylingual.

6.3 Mobility and seasonality

In the Cape Keerweer region, exploiting groups were based on the countries of focal males. These men and their entourages spent the monsoonal period on a small number of recognized wet season camps in the males' countries. With the coming of the dry season and the reduction of surface waters, people increased their mobility and moved over nearby territories as well as those of focal males. The demarcation of territorial access was firm, and vigilantly policed, perhaps more than elsewhere in Cape York Peninsula.

Those lineages with adjacent countries in a particular environment are frequently subgrouped and named by a reference to their locality, such as *kuuchenm* 'those from the acacia (ridges)', *puthen nhikenem* 'those from the beach halfway (between two rivers)'. These environmental associations do not always correspond closely with political ties or sharing of resources, and most such subgroups have no dialectal unity.

In the *Wik-Ngathan* language the seasons are:

kaapm	rainy season (usually late December to March; literally 'northwest wind')
onchen	early dry season (usually March to May; the first part of this phase is *onchen min*, 'good *onchen*').
nhoom penthang	middle dry season (usually June to August; literally 'bushfire burning').
keyen	late dry season (usually August to the first rains).
paayem	first rains (usually about November/December; literally 'from the shoots' — i.e. plants shooting).

Those focal males with territory on the beach spent *kaapm and onchen* based on the beach ridges, where their solid shelters, filled with smoke to exclude mosquitoes, gave protection from wind and rain. In February or March, vast areas of swamp and grass-plain are visited by magpie geese which build nests and lay eggs. The first eggs are traditionally buried, since 'the geese will fail to lay more if they are consumed by people'. The onset of the exploitation of the eggs is thus delayed some time by what is clearly a cultural factor. At this time of abundant egg supply, bark canoes were made from *Eucalyptus tetradonta* so that nests located on the ubiquitous water could be robbed (a canoe of this type was made and used for this purpose in 1975, but aluminium dinghies are becoming more plentiful).

Although we have stated that many groups were resident on the beach in the monsoonal period, their *focus* was at least partly on the inland even at that time, exploiting the eggs, birds and fish of the inland waters as well as the inshore saltwater environment. This focus is reflected linguistically: unlike the Nesbit River people, who have many specific terms for species of turtle and age/sex categories of dugong, the Cape Keerweer peoples have only a single term for all sea turtles and another for all dugong. Their vocabulary is, on the other hand, rich in minor distinctions among types and maturational stages of the sharks, rays, tortoises and other species found in the lakes, lagoons, rivers and swamps which lie behind the beaches.

Those without beach country spent the wet on the other ridges of the floodplain, often effectively marooned for many weeks. They did, however, become mobile earlier, about April or May, while those on the beaches were often unable to move inland until July or August when the 'cold' winds of the plains abated. At about this time, organized grass-burning of all available plains took place, and wallaby, bandicoot, rat, goanna and other grassdwellers were 'harvested'. Groups from adjoining countries would cooperate to burn plains, and in some cases where the plain was on a territorial border the meat was taken by each group back to its own country for consumption.

In the late dry season, major mobility resulted in brief gatherings of quite large numbers of people, involving coastal groups from various parts of the long strip between the Archer and Holroyd Rivers (about 120 kilometres). These travels were to visit relatives, perform rituals of various kinds, engage in pitched battles at cremations, jointly exploit concentrated food resources, and often to escape conflict, boredom or parental domination. A distant coastal journey of up to 60 kilometres was possible, but it had to be brief and formally agreed upon, and was not a common occurrence. The outer limits of normal seasonal range were possibly about 15 kilometres inland and 35 kilometres along the coast.

But the seasonal pattern and degree of mobility of individuals and groups varied considerably, depending on the country foci of members of their kinship network and the vicissitudes of variable seasonal abundance, population strength and the changing status of conflicts. In contrast with the Nesbit River region, territories are not long narrow tracts leading inland from the beach, and territorial relationships are more complex. (See Figure 5.5.)

In the Cape Keerweer region, we may broadly distinguish between people with territorial, kinship, ritual and other associations mainly on the coast, those mainly on the sclerophyll uplands, and those midway between them who have links with both but who basically belong with the coast-dwellers. One major ecological pattern is common to them all, which distinguishes them from their east coast counterparts at Nesbit River: their food resources were mainly immobile, concentrated and seasonally specific (swamp tortoises etc. are included in the 'immobile' category). Vegetable foods and animals found on or near the large permanent fresh, brackish or salt water bodies played the dominant role. These are not general in distribution nor exploited as opportunistically as were the turtle, dugong, reef fish and shellfish of the east coast. The only Cape Keerweer people known to have exploited a wide range of shellfish,

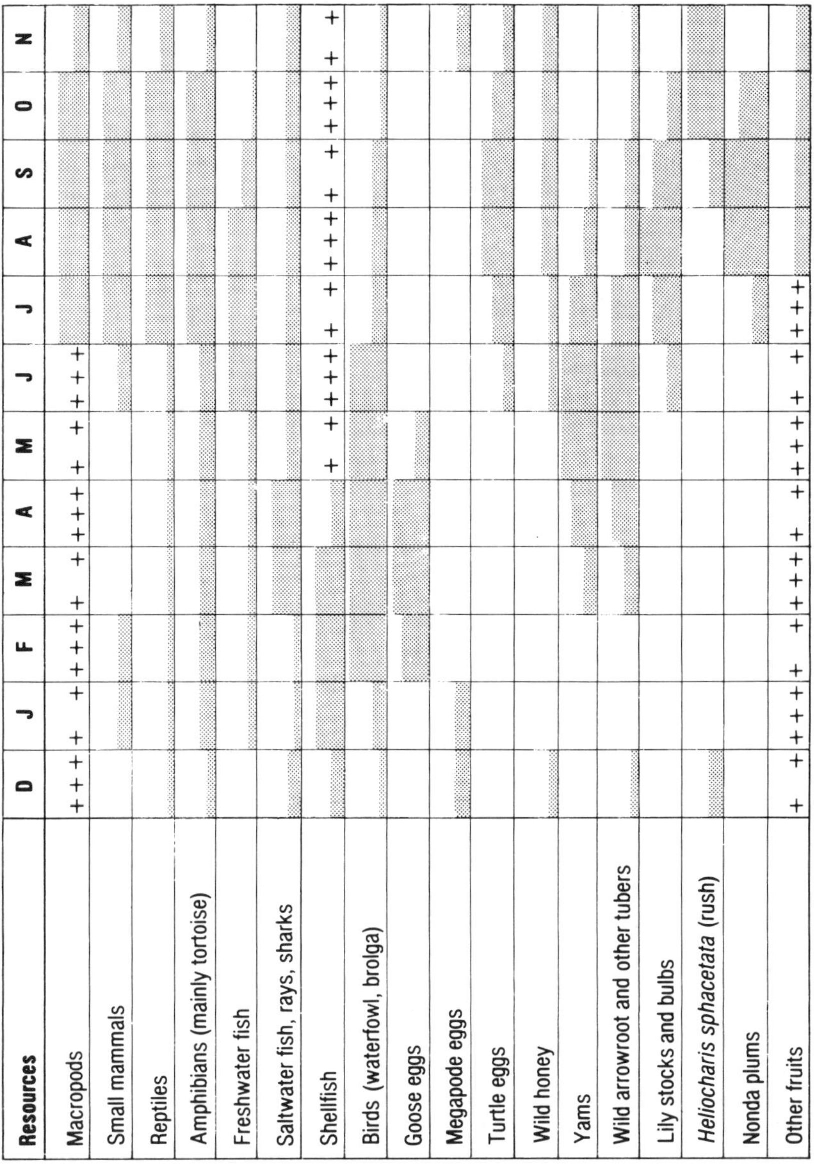

Resources	D	J	F	M	A	M	J	J	A	S	O	N
Macropods	+ +	+	+ + +	+	+ + +	+	+ +					
Small mammals												
Reptiles												
Amphibians (mainly tortoise)	+	+	+ +	+	+	+	+	+	+	+	+	+
Freshwater fish	+					+ + +	+ + + +	+	+	+	+ + +	+
Saltwater fish, rays, sharks												
Shellfish												
Birds (waterfowl, brolga)												
Goose eggs												
Megapode eggs												
Turtle eggs												
Wild honey												
Yams												
Wild arrowroot and other tubers												
Lily stocks and bulbs												
Heliocharis sphacelata (rush)												
Nonda plums												
Other fruits	+	+ + +	+ + +	+	+ +	+	+	+ +				

The heights of the columns show the relative importance of the subsistence item in the diet. Where the whole column is shaded, this indicates a major dependence or preference, which is responsible for major allocation of activities and possible relocation of camps. + + + + + + + indicates that the resource is available over long periods and is therefore less seasonal. How much is harvested then depends on secondary factors such as tides, weather conditions, and distribution within the habitats.

Figure 5.5 Resource availability and exploitation for the Cape Keerweer region of Western Cape York.

for example, are those who spent the wet on beaches just north of Knox River on the shellgrit ridges locally known as 'starvation country'. Nesbit River people usually inhabited the beach strip throughout the year. Cape Keerweer people, on the other hand, seldom stayed at a location for more than one or two of their five seasons. Cape Keerweer people are basically mainland focused, even those living immediately on the coast. The sea intrudes into their countries up tidal creeks and rivers, but the sea itself is not their major focus.

7. Flinders Islands Region

The authors were able to partially map this area in 1974 with the last traditionally-knowledgeable man from Cape Melville, Mr Johnny Flinders. Sutton (1976) has been making a salvage study of traditional culture and languages in the area since 1973. (See Hale & Tindale (1934) for some earlier ethnography.)

7.1 Environments

From the eastern edge of Princess Charlotte Bay, a dissected sandstone plateau runs southeast along the coast parallel to the Great Barrier Reef, with peaks rising to just over 600 metres. The Flinders Group of islands is a continuation of this plateau. Both islands and mainland are generally rugged, infertile and lacking concentrations of surface water. Annual rainfall is low by tropical coastal standards, particularly around Bathurst Heads and the islands. Cape Melville is dominated by massive granite outcrops, at the foot of which are some very small patches of rain forest. There are mangrove complexes on the islands but on the mainland they are confined to the western half of Bathurst Bay and the shores of Princess Charlotte Bay. The headlands and beaches have close fringing coral reefs and reefs occur extensively around the island perimeters. In the flat areas between the coastal mountains of Bathurst Bay, there are small swamps and salt pans. The Bathurst Bay coastline and two islands of the Flinders Group are notable for rock shelters, many containing prolific paintings.

The language of those Aborigines whose countries were in the Flinders Group-Bathurst Bay area emphasizes a particular dichotomy which was of great importance to them as mainland-island commuters: that of saltwater (*ugu*) versus fresh water (*aadi*). Animals are frequently described as *ugwawa* (belonging to saltwater), or *aadi marrmiwa* (belonging to fresh water). Species names are sometimes compounded with the terms *ugumilin* or *aadimilin,* respectively 'habitually associated with saltwater/fresh water'.

The other natural element with great cultural prominence in this area is wind and Cape Melville, in particular, is noted for cyclones, fierce storms and sudden squalls. The local expression for 'waves' is *waya-ulpa,* literally 'wind-heaps'. The orientation of the cardinal direction terms is based on the direction of prevailing winds:

waya iiparri	south wind, cyclone, cold land breeze
waya akathi	southeast wind (prevailing in dry season)
waya uwali	northwest wind (the monsoonal 'warm breeze')
waya ungkarri	north wind
waya ikiiniya	east wind

7.2 Demography and local organization

The pre-European demographic situation was already radically disturbed by the 1920s (Hale & Tindale 1934:79). We are now able to reconstruct the pattern, but not absolute numbers.

People belonged by patrilineal descent to land-holding units whose countries were, at least around the coast, clearly defined. They had access to countries other than their own, particularly those of their mothers. They did not live exclusively in their own countries, but lived in a definable range with home-country as base (see Figure 5.6). Each lineage was exogamous and the majority of people from the six lineages married spouses from the area between Kennedy River and Starcke River. Many different languages were spoken in the region, and most known marriages occurred between partners affiliated to different languages. Everyone was at least bilingual, normally knowing both their father's and mother's languages, as well as one or two others, but being affiliated only to that of their father. The composition of residence-groups was linguistically diverse.

Here, as in the Cape Kerweer region, there are no 'dialectal tribes' in the sense used by some Australian Aboriginal population studies (Birdsell 1968, 1976). There are cultural-geographical categories, not based on language affiliation, which form part of the reference-system of the population and play powerful roles in breeding, mobility and resource utilization. Yet, on close inspection, these categories are not shared equally across the regions. Every individual in a small-scale population has his own social network and geographical range. Every lineage has its own (sub-)dialect.

7.3 Mobility and seasonality

Movement of peoples in this area varied with the seasonal cycle. However, the area is distinctive in the wide geographic base of major camping sites which were used independently of the time of year. People from the Cape Melville-Bathurst Bay area had, besides the narrow beach line, a number of large, wooded, terrestrial islands to exploit and the overall domain of these groups could be seen as a series of discrete land areas separated by relatively short stretches of water. By careful use of prevailing winds and tides, and early morning calms, people could move freely from one to another of these land areas in their canoes. Permanent water was available at the two largest islands (Stanley and Flinders) and along the mainland beach.

In this way, a wide variety of habitats (particularly marine) was open to exploitation, and old camp sites show the importance of certain large

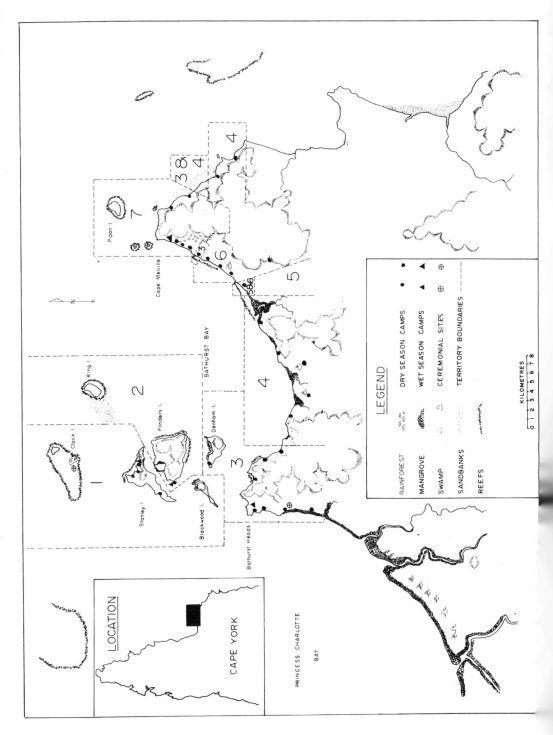

Figure 5.6   Flinders Islands group

reef shellfish in the diet. Fish, shellfish, dugong and turtle are plentiful in all the waters of the area; the latter two were traditionally hunted with harpoons.

The widest journeying, however, was in the dry season when individuals and groups from Bathurst Head to the Starcke and Kennedy Rivers visited one another. Movement was by an established and recognized system of footpaths or named 'roads', and these follow inland ridges and shortcuts behind capes and hills.

The Bathurst Bay coastline, though extremely narrow, contains a wide variety of fruit-bearing trees and shrubs. The more common are: *Manilkara kauki, Syzygium suborbiculare, Mimusops elengi, Securinega melanthesoides, Siphonodon pendulum, Carallia brachiata, Persoonia falcata, Ficus racemosa, F. obliqua* var. *obliqua*, and *Canarium australianum*. Cycad (*Cycas media* (*sensu lato*)), yams (especially *Dioscorea sativa* var. *elongata*), and mangroves (such as *Bruguiera gymnorhiza*) provided vegetable staples.

The area is notable for the large number of rock art sites, usually associated with occupational shelters on both the narrow coastal strip and the islands. Voyaging by canoe, men made the hazardous crossing to Clack Island for ceremonial practices and to decorate the sandstone walls, and drinking water had to be carried in shell containers to this barren rock outcrop.

The island and coastal bases for these peoples meant extensive exploitation of saltwater marine environments, and while, like Nesbit people, they placed importance on opportunistic hunting for dugong and turtle, the large area of sheltered waters in the lee of the islands and headlands perhaps provided a more predictable supply of these animals.

From the restricted information available on this area there appears to have been a very small number of wet season camps. The major bases for this time of the year appear to have been restricted to the western side of Flinders Island, the northeastern side of Stanley Island, and in natural rock shelters at both Bathurst Heads and Cape Melville.

At least three of the islands (Blackwood, King and Pipon) were exploited on day trips, but were never used for overnight camps. Two of these (Pipon and King Islands) had no water supplies, and Blackwood island was a major mythological site and was held to be the dead body of the 'whale' (*aarrga yithal*).

There are two social/political categories of major importance which make it clear that certain groups habitually used coasts while others habitually stayed inland: *aba thinta* (inland people) and *aba thikirr* (coastal people) (Flinders Island). Flinders Group people were friendlier with other 'saltwater' people around Princess Charlotte Bay than with their nearer neighbours from inland around Jack Lakes.

8. Discussion

This paper has presented brief reconstructions of man/environment interactions from different coastal areas of Cape York, and has attempted to demonstrate the considerable range of these interactions despite the outward similarities of coastal environments and tropical Australian hunter-gatherer systems.

In one sense, all ecological systems involving Aboriginal man were unique, representing the complex interplays between particular human groups, each with their idiosyncratic combinations of language, sociality, technology, religious outlooks and other cultural features, and the particular combinations of biophysical environments within which they operated.

Our aim has been to demonstrate the flexibility of hunting and gathering systems in exploiting the highly diverse biophysical variation that the Peninsula exhibits, and to show some of the cultural processes that are involved in this exploitation. To understand the evolution of these systems will need a commitment from archaeological research which has so far been absent. Some general conclusions are given below.

8.1 Differential resources bases

First, Cape York Aboriginal populations, which were distributed most densely along the major river systems and coastline, appear to have suffered no great hardship in the gathering of food resources. Certainly, the availability of these resources was nowhere near as critical as in other more arid zones of the Australian mainland, and this point was made earlier by Birdsell (1953) in gross terms when he related population densities, rainfall and food resources for the continent.

In Cape York, potential seasonal stress in the late dry and early wet seasons was ameliorated for the coast-dwellers by a sequence of fruitings of trees, shrubs and vines along the coastal dune thickets, sandridges, riverine vine-forests and other littoral areas. As well as these plant resources, the regular and dramatic monsoonal influence (see Figure 5.1) brought annual migrations of large temporary animal populations. The appearance of geese and other waterfowl after the wet season, and their concentration on the dwindling surface waters was of critical importance, particularly on the west coast with its extensive systems of swamps and riverine channels. The use of fire in dry season game drives was common to all areas. Similarly, the arrival of mullet shoals in the late dry, and other fish species such as threadfin, salmon and grunter in the wet season represented a similar seasonal resource in all saltwater environments. Turtle eggs were available seasonally at varying times on Cape York coasts, and the presence of reefs and islands off the east coast provided their own specific resources.

Against all of these, which form a class of resources which we have described as *highly predictable, extremely specific* (in terms of time on the annual calendar), *abundant*, and involving little hazard to obtain, there exists a second category of resources which are *less predictable, general in terms of time, less abundant* and, in important instances, diffficult to reach. Along the east coast, including both the Nesbit and Flinders areas, Aboriginal groups possessed sea-going outrigger canoes and harpoons which allowed them to take dugong and turtle, both providing copious quantities of food when captured. These animals are

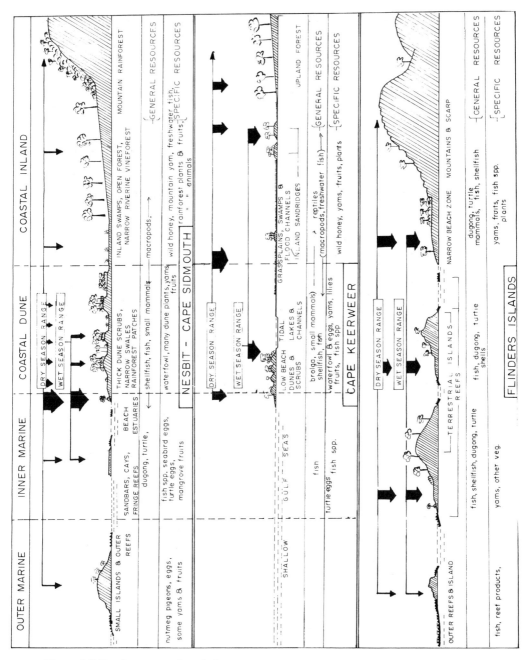

Figure 5.7 Food resources in relation to environmental zones.

present throughout the year, but move erratically along the coastlines in search of food and their capture is therefore largely opportunistic. As well, variable wind and sea conditions, together with the hazards of hunting them, make the availability of these as food resources far less predictable than the items discussed earlier. Climatic factors also operate to constrain the gathering of seasonally specific and predictable resources from the offlying reefs, islands and sandbars along the east coast.

While the west coast area discussed also possesses resources of this general category on the mainland, particularly wallaby obtainable on the large open grassplains, and, in common with all other coastal areas, various beach and estuarine fish species and shellfish, the Carpentarian marine environment lacks reefs and offshore island systems. Aboriginal groups from this area possessing neither the outlying marine environment components of the east coast, nor the seagoing canoes of the other groups, were unable to rely on resources much beyond the beachline and the estuaries.

Habitats and resources use can be summarized by suggesting a series of environmental zones:

1. The outer marine zone on the east coast contains environmental features not found on the west coast. These are most notably coral reefs and islands. While both areas have dugong and turtle populations, only east coast people with their large sea-going canoes are in position to exploit this area effectively.

2. The inner marine zone consisting of beaches, estuaries, creek mouths etc., contains similar resources such as shellfish, certain non-migratory fish species, and crustaceans, and they are exploited effectively, although land-form variation and other factors present differential abundance of these items.

3. Coastal land zones vary considerably: rainforest patches, heathland, hills and uplands, and densely forested swamp areas form a complex mosaic on the east coast. On the west coast, low flat grass plains, seasonally inundated channel systems, saltpans, and a low series of sandridges provide a more open system in which the seasonal inundation makes a dramatic impact. Both areas are rich in seasonally specific plant resources which provide a concentrated abundance. The west coast area in particular has spectacular seasonal concentrations of waterfowl, and the open terrain provides greater access to the generally available land animal populations. The large fluctuating swamp systems in that area provide prolific quantities of fishes and animals which occupy the freshwater marine areas, and which are easily trapped in the isolated and dwindling drainage channels.

4. Inland zones for both sides of the Peninsula contain narrow riverine vine forests and large areas of dry sclerophyll forests. Beyond a few from the coast, however, these areas are the habitat of other recognized Aboriginal groups, not considered 'coastal', and often speaking different dialects.

8.2 The three regions: seasonal exploitation

In the Nesbit region, the sea-oriented groups spent nearly all the year camped immediately on the beach, moving inland on rare occasions, and only for short periods, when a highly specific resource could be predictably exploited in large quantities. An example of this is the late dry season movement up the narrow river vine forests to poison freshwater pools, and to exploit specific fruitings at that time along the forest. More commonly, they placed themselves strategically on the beach where they could take advantage of all categories of resources, particularly the large marine animals. As well, they could quickly seize opportunities to make canoe forays to outlying reefs, bars and islands. At the same time, they were perfectly placed to exploit the regular seasonal appearance of plant foods, most of which occur in the dune thickets and swales immediately behind the beachline. In addition, the coastal base allowed continuous exploitation of the general resources found along the waterline, such as fishes, shellfish and crustaceans. Movement took place up and down the coastline, finely tuned to small-scale variations in these resources, and for the purposes of camping comfort. In this way, *Umpila* speaking people wére deservedly called *pama malnkana*, or 'men of the sandbeach'.

The Cape Keerweer region presents a different pattern. Much more than east coast groups, these people were geared to the specific and temporary resource base, which is a factor of the environments in this area. Coupled with this dependence upon the specific seasonal items was the high productivity of resources. The enormous quantities of food obtainable from the inland freshwater and salt-water marine areas, and the dune vegetation communities, meant that hunting and gathering activities were directed, for significant periods of the year, *away* from the immediate beach zone and inland towards the environment complex a few kilometres wide between beach and the dry sclerophyll zone. Whereas named camping sites and ceremonial performance areas are almost totally confined to the beach edge in the Nesbit area, in the Keerweer region these are found distributed densely along immediate inland areas.

The intense social divisions, and what appears to have been quite high population figures for this region, may well be linked to the resource availability. Though we avoid simple causal relationship of a deterministic nature, the resources factors of predictability, period of availability, abundance and overlap of availability allow a correlation to be made.

Information for the Flinders Island region is not available to the degree it is for the other areas. However, despite the ethnographic shortcomings, there are general discernible features which warrant its inclusion in this comparative study. In contrast to either of the other areas, the presence of a complex of large, close terrestrial islands a short distance from the mainland presents a different set of environmental components. The many middens and other such occupational remains as extensive rock art sites, show that this island complex was used for residence at most periods of the year. Density of named camping and mythological sites and, importantly, the extension of mainland territorial boundaries, reveal a viewpoint which saw the islands as a major base. This far exceeds the inclusion of islands farther north in the Nesbit region. Use of the Flinders Islands can be seen as covering longer seasonal periods and spreading across a wider resource range.

Conclusion

The one constant ecological factor, which it is hypothesized could well be true for all the northern tropical coastline, is the extreme (by inland standards) sedentism of all three of the areas examined. Indeed, so extreme does this seem, and so localized are the regular movements across the seasonal range, that even to classify these peoples as nomads might well create a false impression. Such small scale movements in small domains, where nearly all resources (both physical and social) are usually within a day's travel, give reason for re-thinking some explanations of hunter-gatherer nomadism. Those explanations based solely on critical distance from food resources and conservation of effort hardly seem adequate.

Clearly, social resource demand is a factor to be considered, along with physical resources, and the picture for these coastal areas seems rather to be one of centrally-based groups carrying out brief excursions across the full spectrum of their environments, and involved in a web of social interactions with others of their universe.

For these people, 'forayers' may be a better descriptive term than 'nomads'.

References

BERNDT, RONALD M. (1959), 'The concept of "the tribe" in the Western Desert of Australia', *Oceania*, 30(2):81–107.

BICCHIERI, M. G. (ed.) (1972), *Hunters and Gatherers Today*, New York: Holt, Rinehart & Winston.

BIRDSELL, J. B. (1953), 'Some environmental and cultural factors influencing the structuring of Australian, Aboriginal populations', *The American Naturalist*, 87:171–207

BIRDSELL, JOSEPH B. (1968), 'Some predictions for the pleistocene based on equilibrium systems among recent hunter-gatherers', in Richard B. Lee & Irven De Vore (eds), *Man the Hunter*, Chicago: Aldine.

BIRDSELL, JOSEPH B. (1976), 'Realities and transformations: the tribes of the Western Desert of Australia', in Nicolas Peterson (ed.), *Tribes and Boundaries in Australia*, Canberra: Australian Institute of Aboriginal Studies.

BUREAU OF METEOROLOGY (1971), Climatic survey, northern: region 16 — Queensland Department of Supply, Victoria.

CRAIG, BERYL F. (1967), *Cape York* (*Bibliography series no. 2*), Canberra: Australian Institute of Aboriginal Studies.

FORDE, C. DARYLL (1934), *Habitat, Economy and Society*, London: Methuen (reprinted 1971).

GOULD, RIRCHARD B. (1973), *Australian Archaeology in Ecological and Ethno-graphic Perspective* (Module 7), Andover, Massachusetts: Warner Modular Publications.

HALE, H. M. & TINDALE, N. B. (1934), *Aborigines of Princess Charlotte Bay, North Queensland,* South Australian museum records 5(1): 63–116; 5(2): 117–72.

HARDESTY, D. L. (1977), *Ecological Anthropology*, New York: John Wiley & Sons.

HARRIS, DAVID R. (1976), 'Land of plenty on Cape York Peninsula,' *The Geographical Magazine*, 48(11):657–61.

HIATT, L. R. (1965), *Kinship and Conflict*, Canberra: ANU Press.

JACK, R. L. (1922), *Northmost Australia* (2 vols), London: Simpkin.

KAPLAN, D. & MANNERS, R. A. (1972), *Culture Theory*, New Jersey: Prentrice-Hall.

KIKKAWA, JIRO (1976), *The Birds of Cape York Peninsula. The Sunbird*, 7(2):25–41, 7(4):81–106.

LEE, RICHARD B. & DE VORE, IRVEN (eds) (1968), *Man the Hunter*, Chicago: Aldine.

MULVANEY, D. J. & GOLSON, J. (eds) (1971), *Aboriginal Man and Environment in Australia*, Canberra: ANU Press.

PEDLY, L. & ISBELL, R. F. (1971), *Plant communities of Cape York Peninsula*, *Proc. Roy. Soc Qld.*, **82**:51–74.

PETERSON, NICOLAS (1976a), 'The natural and cultural areas of Aboriginal Australia', in Nicolas Peterson (ed.) (1976b).

PETERSON, NICOLAS (1976b), *Tribes and Boundaries in Australia*, Canberra: Australian Institute of Aboriginal Studies.

SCHEBECK, BERNHARD (1968), Dialect and social groupings in north-east Arnhem Land, unpublished ms.

SHARP, R. L. (1958), 'People without politics', in Verne F. Ray (ed.), *Systems of Political Control and Bureaucracy*, Seattle: University of Washington Press.

STANNER, W. E. H. (1965), 'Aboriginal territorial organisation: estate. range, domain and regime', *Oceania*, **36**:1–26.

SUTTON, PETER (ed.) (1976), *Languages of Cape York*, Canberra: Australian Institute of Aboriginal Studies.

—— (1978), 'Wik: Aboriginal society, territory and language at Cape Keerweer, Cape York Peninsula, Australia', PhD thesis, University of Queensland.

THOMSON, DONALD F. (1933), 'The hero cult, initiation and totemism on Cape York', *Journal Royal Anthrop. Inst.*, **63**:453–537.

THOMSON, DONALD F. (1934), 'The dugong hunters of Cape York', *Journal Royal Anthrop. Inst.*, **64**:237–262.

THOMSON, DONALD F. (1939), 'The seasonal factor in human culture: illustrated from the life of a contemporary nomadic group', *Prehistoric Society Proceedings*, **5**:209–21.

THOMSON, DONALD F. (1956), 'The fishermen and dugong hunters of Princess Charlotte Bay', *Walkabout*, **22**(11):33–6'.

TINDALE, N. B. (1953), 'Tribal and intertribal marriage amongst the Australian Aborigines', *Human Biology*, **25**(3):169–90.

TINDALE, NORMAN B. (1974), *Aboriginal Tribes of Australia*, Canberra: ANU Press.

WALKER, D. (ed.) (1972), *Bridge and Barrier: the Natural and Cultural History of Torres Strait*, Canberra: ANU Press.

6
Descended from Father, Belonging to Country: Rights to Land in the Australian Western Desert[1]

ANNETTE HAMILTON

In the many debates over allocation of people to land among hunters and gatherers, the Australian evidence has repeatedly been seen as problematic. Lee (1978) has already suggested the outlines of this debate, between proponents of the patrilineal territorial band and those of the flexibly organized bilateral band. He suggests that the 'patrilineal theorists ... seek to impose an Australian model of clans on the rest of the world'. The purpose of the present paper is to show that the imposition of an Australian model of clans is by no means a *fait accompli* in certain parts of Australia itself, and that the anthropologists' theorizing (fetishing?) at the ideological level mirrors the efforts of Aborigines in certain areas to construct and impose a coherent theory of patrilineal inheritance to sites and to establish patrivirilocally organized local groups, at least at their own ideological level. Why this should be so, and the problems that stand in their way, form the main focus of this discussion.

Without wishing to bore everyone with the outlines of this debate yet again, it might be worthwhile to go back to Stanner's paper, 'Aboriginal territorial organization: estate, range, domain and regime' (1965). Stanner, replying to Hiatt's criticism of Radcliffe-Brown (Hiatt 1962), claimed that what Radcliffe-Brown had presented was an 'ideal-type' model. In spite of the Weberian overtones, we might note that this view is closer to that of Lévi-Strauss, who has repeatedly stressed that the proper concerns of anthropology are with the fundamental structures beneath the superficial distortions and apparent contradictions to be found at the level of mere empirical reality, or even in the 'native model' of reality (Lévi-Strauss 1963:281; 1968:350). He considers that observable phenomena, such as real 'hordes', are at best 'a series of expressions, each partial and incomplete, of the same underlying structure, which they reproduce in several copies without ever completely exhausting its reality' (Lévi-Strauss 1963:130). Notwithstanding the possible implications of this, the Hiatt–Stanner debate

First published in E. Leacock & R. Lee (eds), *Politics and History in Band Societies*, Melbourne: Cambridge University Press, 1982. © Cambridge University Press. Reprinted with the permission of Cambridge University Press.

led to a crucial clarification — that is, the necessity to maintain a clear distinction between economic and ritual relationships to land — so that instead of a horde there is both a ritual group and an economic group. Stanner says:

> The evidence allows us to say that each territorial group was associated with both an *estate* and a *range*. The estate was the traditionally recognized locus ... of some kind of patrilineal descent group forming the core or nucleus of the territorial group ... The range was the tract or orbit over which the group, including its nucleus and adherents, ordinarily hunted and foraged to maintain life. The range normally included the estate ... Estate and range together may be said to have constituted a domain, which was an ecological life space. (Stanner 1965:2)

Here Stanner has (a) described the patrilineal descent group as a 'nucleus' with adherents — so the horde now is no longer composed exclusively of clan agnates and their wives and children — and (b) shown that this reconstructed 'horde' uses land over and above that to which its patrilineal nucleus is exclusively connected.

Stanner's distinction between estate and range is apparently a distinction between the 'religious' and the 'economic' systems. The estate is defined by virtue of 'spiritual' ties between individuals and certain places in the landscape, whereas the 'range' is defined by the hunting and foraging activities of people in the landscape. The 'clan', that is, a group of people linked by agnatic ties, is the effective 'owner' of the estate. The 'horde', however, does not own anything, but merely utilizes the products of a number of estates (as well as the territory in between estates, which may be only hazily defined as 'owned' in the religious sense, if at all). Analytically, the two domains are quite distinct. A concept analogous to 'property' may be applied to the religious sphere, but there is no equivalent concept in the 'economic' sphere. If we assume that products of the land are the basic 'means of production', we would appear to have arrived at the conclusion that Aboriginal society lacks any form of economic ownership of the means of production. This would seem to go beyond anything which Marx envisaged as 'primitive communism'.

Marx tended to view all societies which lacked heritable private property as cases of primitive communism, although he himself preferred the term 'tribal ownership' to the other usage, favoured by Engels (Marx and Engels 1973, 1:21; Engels 1973a, 2:401). He included all cases where 'a people live by hunting and fishing, by the rearing of cattle or, in the highest stages, agriculture ... The social structure is, therefore, limited to an extension of the family: patriarchal family chieftains, below them the members of the tribe, finally slaves' (Marx and Engels, ibid.). Engels included 'the German mark, the Celtic clan, and the Indian', as well as the Roman village, as communities with a 'primitive communistic order' (Engels, ibid.) While the absence of individually held private property in these instances contrasts clearly with property ownership under capitalism, from an anthropological perspective it lumps together forms of society which exhibit marked levels of internal differentiation and an extra-ordinary variety of forms of possession of property. The same tradition has been continued by Hindess and Hirst, in their recent reappraisal of pre-capitalist modes of production (Hindess and Hirst 1975). Without examining the implications of their theory here, it is necessary to note that, rather than looking at the ownership of property (or the means of production), they instead 'define primitive communism as a mode of production governed by a mode of communal appropriation of surplus labour' (Hindess and Hirst 1975:22). Wherever the appropriation of surplus labour is collective, 'there are therefore no classes, no state and no political level' (ibid.:27). All other modes of production involve non-collective appropriation of surplus labour, and a class of non-labourers. Hindess and Hirst, therefore, group together a number of 'archaic' societies, which would include both hunters and gatherers, and a number of horticulturalists. Admittedly they further subdivide primitive communism according to whether or not redistribution can be classed as 'simple or complex' (ibid.:44ff), but that also fails to distinguish along the lines which are at issue here.

The theoretical reasons for adopting these views of pre-state societies seem compelling when viewed from the contrasting perspective of modern capitalism. But to lump together all pre-state formations as cases of primitive communism is to obscure differences between them. If these differences cannot be derived from the concept 'mode of production' then we are left to conclude that they originate in the realm of the idea, and are the product of purely mental activities.

> For instance, if an epoch imagines itself to be actuated by purely 'political' or 'religious' motives, although 'religion' and 'politics' are only forms of its true motives, the historian accepts this opinion. The 'idea', the 'conception' of the people in question about their real practice, is transformed into the sole determining active force, which controls and determines their practice. (Marx and Engels 1973, 1:43)

Marx and Engels show how German ideology is replete with the illusion that 'pure spirit', 'thought', 'consciousness', is the driving force of history. 'This conception is truly religious: it postulates religious man as the primitive man, the starting point of history; and in its imagination puts the religious production of fancies in the place of the real production of the means of subsistence and of life itself' (ibid.:44).

This approach is apparent in Australian Aboriginal anthropology. Elkin, for instance, writes:

> The most important aspect of the local group, however, is spiritual in nature ... From one point of view, the members who belong to the local group by birth own their subdivision of the tribal territory. But it is truer to say that the country owns them and that they cannot remain away from it indefinitely and still live. The point is, the Aborigines hold the doctrine of the pre-existence of spirits. (Elkin 1970:79)

More recently, Maddock (1974:27) makes similar statements: 'Aborigines regard land as a religious phenomenon ... The tie between men and land is taken back to the Dreaming ... The Aboriginal theory is thus that rights to land have to do with the design of the world, not with alienable legal title ... It would be as correct to speak of the land possessing men as of men possessing land.' Maddock recognizes the difficulties of reconciling this view with an 'economic' one: 'whether this is properly to be called ownership is debatable, for if there are owners there is nothing they can alienate'.

At one level, then, it would seem that Aboriginal society had no concept of economic ownership of land, although it would seem to have had the notion of inalienable spiritual connection between persons and particular pieces of land. Therefore it should be possible to say that all Aborigines had equal access to the means of production.[2] Strehlow would seem to agree.

> Here, then, was a land where men and women in a sense lived in those ideal communities envisaged by Karl Marx . . . where there were no social classes or castes, and where men could not be tyrannized by well organized central governments . . . Since the land rights of all tribal units and, where they existed in the Aranda form, even those of the local *njinanga section* areas were believed to have been laid down for all time by the supernatural beings, no organized wars of aggression or territorial conquest were possible in Central Australia. (Strehlow 1970:130)

And yet, while the literature frequently mentions the sharing of natural resources by people in one area with people from another, there is also mention of a rigidly possessive attitude towards one's own country and the refusal to share resources with non-kin, and even instances of armed conflicts over resources. For example, Meggitt gives an account of such a conflict between the Waringari and the Walbiri:

> the Waringari had claimed the ownership of the few native wells at Tanami and the country surrounding them, but in a pitched battle for the possession of the water the Walbiri drove the Waringari from the area which they incorporated into their own territory. By desert standards, the engagement was spectacular, the dead on either side numbering a score or more. (Meggitt 1962:42)

Another example from the eastern part of the Western Desert itself concerns a massacre of the original inhabitants of Mount Chandler, over-looking Indulkana, for the rights to water in that area (Tindale 1974:10). Isobel White (personal communication) reports that the grandfathers of the oldest inhabitants of Indulkana in 1966 had told them about it, which suggests that it occurred in the 1880s.

Tindale has consistently stressed the point that areas of land were 'owned' and were inviolable except by specific permission to enter.

> Larger disputes often involved the defence of territories or their usurpation, and the taking of women. Occasional instances of all-out attack on a tribe of people and the usurpation of a tribal area by members of another tribe are matters of history. In some instances drought has been the impelling force and lack of immediate associations or contact the spur. (1974:33)

He quotes (1974:77–8) a number of early observers, in diverse regions, such as Teichelmann (1841), J. D. Lang (1861), Gray (1878), Palmer (1884), all of whom indicate that 'tribal' areas are defined and subject to laws of trespass. It is clear, however, that these instances are concerned with 'tribal' areas, rather than the smaller segments ('clan estates', 'ranges') discussed earlier. Tindale views these 'tribal' arrangements as primarily economic. Discussing the temporary lapsing of territorial exclusivity when a particularly abundant resource was available, he says:

> The occurrence of such temporary abrogations of territorial rule in tribal distributions emphasizes the point that one of the principal factors determining the existence of tribal boundaries is economic. The ability [*sic*] of the tribal group, speaking a common language ... enables it to arrange the distribution of land-use rights among its members, either as family or hordal units, so that they can ... maintain themselves for the whole cycle of the year. (1974:80)

Without considering how such land-use rights might be allocated by the tribal group, this leads us to conclude that 'the tribe' exercized economic rights over the land it occupied, while rights within it were held communally by the tribespeople and access to its products was held in common by all of its members. We have now reached a point where Marx's definitions of primitive communism would seem to apply.

Yet the fact remains that some notion of 'ownership' or exclusive possession over certain segments of tribal land by specific persons must be acknowledged, even if this cannot be considered by us to be 'economic' in character. For example, rights over sacred sites are owned by certain specified men; access to them is forbidden to all women, uninitiated men, and children, as well as to men who own other unconnected, sacred sites, except on specified occasions. These might be classed as 'religious' in character, and not 'economic', following Marx. But let us for a moment see these relationships not in Western European terms, as pertaining to two entirely separate domains, the one of which is based in reality (i.e. material) and the other in fantasy (i.e. religion), but from the perspective of the Aborigines themselves. At once the distinction is dissolved. The apparently non-economic aspect of the man–land relationship is only so to us: to the Central Desert Aborigines it is highly, almost entirely, economic; for it is by access to these pieces of land, these sacred sites, that the reproduction of species is controlled. Strehlow's account of this is excellent:

> each Aranda local group was believed to perform an indispensable economic service not only for itself but for the population around its borders as well ... the religious acts performed by the totemic clan members of all the inland tribes at their respective totemic centres were regarded as being indispensable for the continuation of all human, animal and plant life in Central Australia. (Strehlow 1970:102–3)

The literal interpretation which Aborigines put on these powers of production is apparent from one of Strehlow's informants:

> The Ilbalintja men are always taking and boasting about their bandicoot (*gura*) ceremonies. But their ceremonies are utterly useless. Euros are to be found everywhere, and it is we who created them. The bandicoots have vanished long ago. Even we old men can remember eating bandicoot meat only when we were still mere boys. Where they have gone to since, I do not know. (Strehlow 1970:103)

The powers of a specific group of men to control the reproduction of a species, through their access to a sacred site and its associated paraphernalia, does not confer any advantages to them exclusively; indeed it is conceptualized as being for the advantage of all Aborigines in the area. But not everyone can so act, for no women can ever do so, and only those men who have fully conformed to the demands of the elders can hope to join them. We have chosen to call this 'religion', and yet the truly 'economic' nature of their religious action is apparent to Aborigines: why else do they use the English term 'business' for their ceremonial activities, and why else do they consider their entire structure of 'religious' belief 'the Law'? 'At a certain, very primitive state of the development of society, the need arises ... to see to it that the individual subordinates himself to the common conditions of production and exchange. This rule, which at first is custom, soon becomes *law*' (Engels 1973a, 2:365).

So within the Aboriginal perspective 'religious' property has an aspect of 'economic' property, since reproduction of species is held to depend on human actions over certain objects, jealously guarded and kept from all but their owners, at certain places from which all but the owners are excluded. What then is the nature of these human actions? Here we encounter one of the paradoxes of Central Australian Aboriginal society, for those who perform the actions are at one and the same time the 'owners' and the 'workers';[3] they themselves must perform the necessary actions, often using their own body products (blood, semen) from which procedures they would appear to obtain no exclusive benefit, but by virtue of which the entire Aboriginal community will gain a livelihood.[4]

In many Aboriginal languages (e.g. Bidjandjara)[5] there is no indigenous term for 'work', but the English word is used to refer to two activities only, copulation and ceremonial participation. Thus, in Aboriginal thought, the powers of production and reproduction are not held to reside in the 'real' word of material reality but in the 'religious' realm (which is, to them, no opposition at all). And so it follows that whatever ideas of property, exclusivity and control over productive forces are to be found in this society, will be found in the 'religious' rather than the 'economic' sphere, or in the interaction between them. Are we then, in reaching this conclusion, ignoring Marx and Engels, who were so vehement about the necessity to search for the well-springs of an epoch in its purely material aspects? I argue that although religious manipulations are themselves mystifications — that is, that rain would fall, plants grow, and animals be born, without the intervention of humans — nonetheless it is in the religious realm that changes in technology, articulation of man–land relationships and the elaboration of systems of exchange first come into existence, and are thereafter developed. I am arguing that it is in the sphere of the 'religious' that the first hints of truly 'economic' differentiation are to be found.

If this is true, then it becomes all the more crucial to ask, how do men come to have access to the 'religious' sector of production? In particular, how do men come to have access to sacred sites and to the symbolic acts which mediate their powers? I will return now to the eastern sector of the Western Desert, and examine in detail the situation in this area.

Traditional Local Organization in the Western Desert

The area of the Everard Ranges and its immediate surroundings is in the literature described as being part of Janggundjara country. Janggundjara is closely allied to Bidjandjara and, while a detailed discussion of the

meanings and referents of these terms will occur below, it must be noted
that these are names of dialectical variants of a single language which is
spread right across the south-central portion of Australia, to the edges of
Aranda and Walbiri country in the north-east, to the Dieri in the south-
east, to the borders of the Bight in the south, and to the coastal tribes of
Western Australia in the west. This language, nameless to the Aborigines,
has been called various terms, among the best known being Kukatja and
Luritcha or Loritja, a derogatory term used by the Aranda for their
unsophisticated neighbours. Across this whole area there is a general
continuity of language and cultural forms, including religious and ceremonial
life. But there are also differences, the most striking being the absence in
the furthest eastern areas of exogamous moieties or any form of the section
system. The four-section system has been diffusing across the desert rapidly,
and in 1970–71 had reached Amata Settlement where it was being utilized
in ritual organization but seemed otherwise little understood (notably, not
understood by women). Elkin (1938:40) has given an extensive account
of kinship in South Australia, and has documented the passage of the
section system and the necessary adjustments which different groups have
made to it. It is of interest that even in 1930 local organization in this
whole region was extremely difficult to describe. Elkin, like others, put
this difficulty down to 'migration'.

> As I see it, the movement of the groups has been constantly from the (Musgrave
> and Everard and other) central ranges to the south ... Under pressure of
> droughts and at best constant desert conditions the groups pressed towards the
> south, seldom if ever to return, lengthening the mythological tracks and cutting
> themselves off from the spread of new forms of social and kinship organization
> and terminology. Thus, there was not much intermarrying, and there was relative
> isolation.

In a footnote he adds:

> This constant migration too explains the difficulty of defining tribal boundaries
> in this desert region, for life was in a state of flux. (Elkin 1940:305)

Elkin implies that at least part of the motivation for such movement
was indigenous, rather than solely the result of white contact.

Many other writers have commented on the confusing question of tribal
boundaries and dialectical units in the Western Desert. (See especially
Tindale 1972; Berndt and Berndt 1945.)

Nonetheless, all these writers imply that boundaries did indeed exist,
and could at some time in the past have been fixed, but owing to
movements of population such boundaries cannot now be established
with any certainty. The difficulties of dealing with local organization in
this area were discussed also by Yengoyan.

> The reconstruction of pre-contact local organization was the most frustrating
> phase of the overall study. Since local organization as manifest prior to
> European contact, is no longer functioning, data on this aspect were collected
> from the living memory of tribal elders. The exact composition of local groups
> could not be determined. (Yengoyan 1970:81–2)

Without wishing in any way to minimize the disruptive effects of white
contact, the fact remains that other writers have been able to give accounts

of local organization in other areas, all of which have been affected by white contact (see the discussion in Lee and DeVore 1968:147, 211). Such accounts may offer problems of interpretation, and be difficult to reconcile to one particular model, but accounts they are, in many cases detailed and exhaustive. Probably the best example is T. G. H. Strehlow's (1965) account of the 'Njinanga' section areas, but Meggitt (1962), Falkenberg (1962) and Hiatt (1965) as well as many earlier writers have, primarily from information gained from older informants and a bit of on-the-ground mapping, been able to reconstruct at least a plausible account. Yet, for the most part, writers on the Western Desert culture area have been hard put to offer any coherent ethnographic account of territorial organization at either the 'tribal' or the 'local group' level. This is to say, various writers have discussed theoretically the nature of tribal groupings, and the nature of smaller component groups, but have found it difficult to anchor these to any particular territorial space in reality, in terms which outline the area under discussion and specify which people actually have rights of what kinds over the area, or even which people actually lived there.

The sole exception to this is Tindale, who has held to a Radcliffe-Brownian model consistently. In 1972 he described and mapped the traditional and post-1915 territories of the Bidjandjara. He then said that

> the whole population of the Pitjantjara is divided into a series of smaller groups with patrilineal descent. These groups are called clans, the basis of their clan organization is a ceremonial one and is linked with a patrilineal and patrilocal inheritance of the totem of a particular locality, an inheritance shared by all men who are directly descended from a common ancestor. (Tindale 1972:223)

> The normal living unit or local group likely to be found exploiting the area around an important totemic locality is a different one than the clan and is to be known as a horde. It tends to be composed of male members of the clan minus the older girls and women who have been sent away as wives to other clans, but plus the girls and women who have been brought in as brides for local clansmen. To these persons may be added a few casual visitors and some odd persons who for one reason or another have become attached to the local group from other clans. Such persons through the passing of time may become a part of it. (Tindale 1972:224)

This neat picture, however, cannot be substantiated in reality. 'The obtaining of accurate information on the number of such hordes present among the Pitjantjara has been difficult . . .' He estimates that there were some 30 hordal groupings and the 'remants of several less successful family lines' (ibid.). 'Pitjantjara tribespeople recognize five named regional units, which are separate and tend to live in different parts of their whole territory' (228). But he adds, 'It must not be considered that these are true sub-tribal groupings. Rather, they are generalized names associated with smaller regional groups within the whole tribal area' (ibid.).

I think Tindale has experienced as much difficulty in giving a coherent account of local organization in the Western Desert as anyone. Let us turn then to Strehlow and Berndt, who have both considered this problem.

Strehlow (1965, 1970), in contrasting the apparently rigid man–land relationship among the Aranda with that found in the Western Desert, has characterized the area as one of 'loose structure'. He points out that these groups among whom he includes the Matuntara, Andekerinja, Jankuntjatjara, Pitjantjara and Pintubi originally had no subsection systems:

> they completely lacked the main structural element of the Aranda local-group organization — its *land-based* kin-group class system. According to Yengoyan the introduction into these tribes of subsection systems superficially resembling the Aranda-type class system in recent decades has not been able to do anything to rehabilitate the local groups. (Strehlow 1970:100)

One might well dispute the relevance of 'rehabilitation' in this context, but Strehlow has pointed to a fundamental feature of Western Desert organization, which has tremendous significance for the understanding of many aspects of social organization in the area.

Berndt's contribution is of a different order. He challenges the applicability of the concept of 'tribe' throughout this area, and musters much data to support an alternative explanation (Berndt 1966). Berndt gives maps referring to 'tribes' in the eastern section in 1941 and 1944, and in the western section in 1957–59, but cautions that although the material is based on 'native information' it is inexact. Among the groups concerned are the Mandjindji, Bidnanda, Andingari, Gugada, Ngalia, Mara, Mangula and Janggundjara which have been called tribes. Elkin among others has commented on the numerous tribal names for this region, referring 'either to single hordes or to a group of hordes which could hardly be regarded as a tribe in the same way as the Aranda or Yantruwantra' (quoted in Berndt 1966:37). He adds that it is difficult to fix boundaries and names. Berndt's contention is that 'these groups are not "tribes", that there are no strict boundaries, that movements were relatively frequent, and that what we are faced with is, rather, a cultural and social bloc' (1966:39). He enumerates the linguistic affiliation of people in different camps, and notes that every individual in such a camp might offer a different set of terms to describe his grouping. For instance, a person may claim to be Bidnanda–Ngalia, and another Bidjandara–Wolundara–Mandjili. All of these are differentiated dialects. On the other hand, at Wiluna Berndt found people who claimed to speak each of the following — Mandjilu, Mandjila, Mandjildjara, Mandjilijuwa — saying that each of these was different. Certainly these cannot be called 'tribes', and Berndt could not find any real territorial linkage to these terms. He concludes that such labels have nothing more than linguistic significance, and are 'ways of classifying groups of people according to dialect variations. This is done without emphasizing "anchorage" and has no territorial significance' (ibid.:41).

Indeed, mutual intelligibility of language makes the situation of the Western Desert unusual, if not unique in Aboriginal Australia. If the boundaries of the tribe 'are the boundaries of intelligibility, then the Western Desert itself is the "tribal unit" and this involves a pre-contact population of as many as 10,000 people' (Berndt 1966:32). The amount of dialectical variation from the east to the west, and the north to the south, is still within the bounds of mutual intelligibility.[6] On the one hand, then, we have Berndt's assertion that dialectical variation is a means of classifying people and has 'no territorial significance' (1966:41). On the other, we have Tindale's assertion that each dialect group is indeed a tribe and has known territorial associations. Both writers have been in the field intermittently but frequently since the thirties (Tindale) and early forties (Berndt). There is no reason to assume bad faith on either of their parts; they are both careful and meticulous scholars, they are both familiar with Western Desert languages, they are both interested in 'the truth' about Aboriginal local organization. Why then should there be this disparity?

In my own field work I fluctuated between their two views. Berndt's reconstructions made intuitive sense, in the social context of the area where I was working. Nonetheless people repeatedly referred to the Everards as 'Janggundjara' in everyday contexts, contrasting the area with Amata and Ernabella, which they said were 'Bidjandjara'. In addition they referred to people as having one or other language, and this did indeed seem to refer to an idea of 'ngura'.

Ngura ngaiyugu? Barari, welurara! Bidjiwanga tjuta!
Country mine?   Far, west!   Bidjispeakers all!

Further questioning, however, elicited the fact that although everyone there spoke Bidjandjara, some also spoke Ngadadjara and some Mandjildjara, which were like Bidjandjara but belonged further west. The answers I received made it obvious that in some way both Berndt and Tindale were right, that there was indeed an association between dialect and territory, but that it was *independent* of any individual's or group's own territorial affiliations.

In order to consider this proposition more fully it is necessary to consider the social aspects of dialects in more detail. The prefix *bidja-* comes from the word *bidjani* — to go, while *janggun-* comes from *janani* — to go, and is the Janggundjara usage. The suffix *-tjara* means 'having'. The meaning, then, is 'those people who say *bidjani* for going' and 'those people who say *janani* for going'. The initial 'j' sound is also significant. Janggundjara say *juwa* — give; Bidjandjara say *uwa*. Janggundjara say *jalindjara* for north. Bidjandjara say *alindjara*. Janggundjara-speakers maintain that their usage is more clear and precise, since it prevents elision, whereas the Bidjandjara consider it rather vulgar and unsophisticated. Although the two dialects are almost identical grammatically there are a number of nouns, the use of which is a marker of one's own linguistic affiliations, but which are merely alternative words for the same concept. The Bidjandjara say *mina* for water, the Janggundjara say *gabi*; the Bidjandjara say *buli* for rock, the Janggundjara say *jabu*. It would be misleading to treat these words as exclusive to one group or the other. In fact any speaker of either dialect knows and uses these alternative words as it suits him/her, and may know others. For instance, the Warburton people say *gumbuli* for water, while groups further west again say *juro*. The choice of one word rather than another depends not merely on what dialect the person speaks, but on the person spoken to, the place where the transaction occurs and recent social and ritual events. A concrete instance of this occurred in connection with the shortage of rain in 1971. A party of Everards men travelled to Warburton where they handed over sacred objects in exchange for the Warburton men's singing the rain songs which they had in their custody at the time. When the men returned they brought with them the word *gumbuli* for water, and this term replaced *gabi* until the rain fell a month later. The reason given for this was that since the rain songs used *gumbuli* for water the people had to follow suit if they were to be effective in their area. The dialect form used is also an indication of social relationships between the speaker and the person addressed. When visiting Ernabella on one occasion I was brought to task for failing to switch to the Bidjandjara vocabulary when talking to Ernabella people. On the other hand, if one wishes to express disappointment with members of another group, for their stinginess as hosts at a ceremony, for instance, one uses one's own dialect forms very ostentatiously in public.

The dialects of the Western Desert, then, are not separate manners of speaking handed down unconsciously from generation to generation, but are subject to conscious modification and manipulation by their speakers. A certain speech-style communicates more than just information of immediate interest — the words a speaker chooses also make statements about him/her, about the group where s/he customarily resides, and his/her situation *vis-à-vis* others. The customary rule of courtesy is that one uses the same dialect form as most others in the place where you happen to be. The 'Bidjandjara' men in the Everards used Janggundjara speech forms. In pre-contact times the customary distribution of people would have been such as to make great mixing and ambiguities, such as Berndt (1966) encountered, unusual; instead there would have been scattered camps of people usually to be found within a particular area, whose customary linguistic form would have been Janggundjara, Bidjandjara or whatever. But the boundaries of such areas are not defined physiographically — instead they exist only by virtue of the linguistic behaviour of the people usually to be found there. This is why Ernabella is now considered a 'Bidjandjara' place. An individual's identity as a speaker of one dialect rather than another depends on which dialect he grew up speaking, before initiation in the case of men, before marriage in the case of women. Because the majority of people at any one location at any one time used one dialect form rather than another, there is a *de facto* relationship between a particular territory and a particular dialect. Nonetheless it is incorrect to describe someone as a member of the Bidjandjara tribe, the territory of which is to be found between A and B.

How then are people affiliated to territory, if not by tribal membership which conveys automatic territorial rights? I referred earlier to Tindale's view on Western Desert local organization, and discussed his opinion that the land was owned by patrilineal, patrifocal groups. Berndt would appear to follow this view:

> Those persons united by common patrilineal descent, who share a given site or constellation of sites, constitute the local group; this is the land-owning group with special spiritual and ritual ties, of which the land itself represents the most obvious ... focus ... the female members of such a group move out of it at marriage but ... they do not relinquish their totemic affiliations. We may therefore speak of this local unit as a patrilineal descent group. (Berndt 1966:47)

Although Berndt describes this group as 'land-owning' he adds a puzzling footnote:

> It is territorially based; but the local group country is defined not by boundaries explicitly demarcating it from similar units, but by the actual sites connected with the ancestral being and his acts. Such territory is, ideally, unalienable but

members of other local groups are not debarred from entry or from hunting
game or collecting food within its precincts, although they may be denied
access to a sacred site where objects of ritual use are stored. (Berndt 1966: 47,
note)

We may ask, among other things, in what sense it is 'land-owning' if
others have free access to the land and there are no boundaries? How does
a person 'join' such a group? The answer would seem to be: by virtue of
patrilineal descent. On the other hand, all accounts of Western Desert
social organization maintain that a person gains his/her totemic affiliation
by being born at a particular place, near to a particular waterhole, which
will be one among a number of such sites mythically associated with a
particular ancestral being. 'Mentioning the waterhole at which he was born
a person may say "that's my *gabi*, my country"; this is his most important
tie with the land, and he is not as a rule articulate concerning any larger
territorially-based unit' (Berndt 1966:46). The only way that the two means
of territorial connection can be reconciled is if every man is born in his
own father's country, which presumably means at or near the same waterhole-
based area where his father was born. Yet what, given the exigencies of
desert living, is the likelihood of this? Such 'countries' may be only 200
square miles (320 km) in an area where the carrying capacity is only
0.007 persons to the square mile (Berndt 1966:32, note) — which gives a
total of 1.4 persons. Berndt mentions that men have a desire to return to
their own countries when a birth is imminent, but this is an ideal which
may not be fulfilled in the majority of cases. While each country usually
contains one fairly reliable supply of water, hard years would make even
this doubtful, and in any case the country between where a pregnant woman
happens to be as birth approaches and that where her husband was born
may be virtually devoid of water. We may safely assume, then, that in many
cases children are not born in their father's totemic country. We will
return to the problem of how they gain rights in their father's estate in a
moment. But first, let us ask about the mother's totemic affiliations. All
writers on this area concur that local-group exogamy is necessary. That is,
the most important thing in arranging a marriage is that the wife should
come from an area away, but not too far away, from her husband's (see
Berndt and Berndt 1945:152(56)). One might therefore assume that the
wife's totemic affiliations would be different from those of the husband,
in which case 'patrilineal descent' would be a possibility. But this is not
the case. In fact, the preferred marriage is where both husband and wife
are of the same totemic affiliations.

> By being born near his father's waterhole (and if his father has married a woman
> born in a particular country through which the ancestral being associated with
> him has passed) the child, after initiation, becomes a full member of his
> father's cult lodge. (Berndt and Berndt 1945:23(327))

> The preference in the Ooldea region and in the Spinifex country to the north
> and north-west seems to be for a man to marry a wife of the same cult totem as
> himself, but born at a *ga:bi* outside his country. (Berndt and Berndt 1945:
> 127(373))

It should be noted that this is a preference, not a prescription. Marriages
between members of different totemic associations are just as acceptable

as those between members of the same ones. However, the reason for the preference is that it is only by such a marriage, and by being born on the same track as both parents, that a son can be guaranteed a place in his father's totemic cult. Each of the three factors is taken into account in such decisions; the presence of at least one such association is an absolute necessity, two make the case stronger, but only all three can operate as an automatic guarantee. Hence we see that there are a number of factors operating to decide the affiliations of any particular individual. The 'ideal' is that a son shall be born in his father's country, near the totemic track on which both mother and father were born. But birth at any place along the track nonetheless confers rights to that totemic complex, even if it is not in the same area where the father was born. The cult totem is the focus of ritual action for all men born on its tracks.

> the Aboriginal assumption is that all those sharing a common totemic track do in effect constitute a unit ... irrespective of their particular local groups they are members of the cult ... this is not a closed unit in the sense of being restricted to a specifically defined section of the common ancestral track. It is flexible enough to include, conceptually, more distant local groups having the same totemic identification. (Berndt 1966:48)

In what sense then can we talk of 'patrilineal descent' or of 'patrilineal descent groups'? It is true that provided a child is born on the same totemic track as his father, even if in a different 'country', then he may take up rights in the totemic complex associated with his father's country. But, if he is born both away from that country and off that totemic track, he must take the cult totem of the country where he was *born*, and restrictions will be applied to his participation in his father's ritual complex (see Berndt 1966:49, note).

It is therefore incorrect to speak of 'patrilineal descent' — rights do not accrue primarily by being born to a particular father, but by being born at a particular place. Further, the time-depth created by groups who have managed to fulfil the conditions for patrilineal descent is extremely short, no more than three or four generations. The taboo on the names of deceased persons, and the desire to erase their memory as soon as possible, ensures that no precise genealogical knowledge can be maintained. This shallow time-depth is accentuated further by the custom of naming children after their grandparents' deceased siblings; the taboo name of a dead person is revived, and handed on to someone of the appropriate sex two generations below, so that the precise identities of the deceased are obliterated and the names revived in the person of young children born on the same totemic track.

Indeed everything in Western Desert culture indicates a tendency to forget the deceased, which is in marked contrast to the situation in other parts of Australia, such as northern Arnhem Land, where a great deal of creative labour is employed in memorializing the dead, together with elaborate funeral ceremonies, double disposal in some cases, grave-posts, and so on. These are also the areas where patrilineal descent is firmly articulated and socially embedded in one form or another. By comparison, Western Desert people dig shallow graves, place the corpse inside, and abandon the site until a year or two later, when they perform a brief ceremony to ensure that all spiritual traces of the dead have disappeared. No intense creative energies are devoted to the dead — concern is much more with the not-yet-living (increase rites) and with the already alive (especially initiations) (see Berndt and Johnston 1942). Peterson (1972) has noted that there are two common ways in Australia of establishing totemic affiliations — by the question 'from which water do you come?' or else 'where is your bone country?' The former implies conception or birth at a particular place, the latter means that, no matter where a person is born or conceived, the link with the father has a physical expression in the bones of the body. This indicates a comparison between place-based claims and father-based claims to sites; among the Bidjandjara a man's father can never represent his 'bone' but is always one of the 'flesh' (i.e. the named endogamous moieties, *nganandarga* (us bones) and *djanamildjan* (them flesh), mean that all members of a person's own and alternate generations are thought of as 'bones', while the father's or son's generations are the 'flesh').

In the eastern Western Desert then, a person's primary affiliation to land is not to a bounded territory, nor yet to a single specific site within a bounded area; and it is not achieved automatically by means of descent from a particular father. Instead, a person's location as a member of a cult group, as a person entitled to know, share and perform the secret rituals of that cult (if a man), and to receive certain benefits from this position, comes about as a result of being born at a particular place, near a waterhole on the track of a particular totemic ancestor. This automatically gives rights to the ceremonies connected with that ancestor, which properly speaking follow the tracks of that ancestor across the landscape, rather than being attached to specific bounded areas of land. Symbolically, this is a sort of patrilineal descent, but the 'father' is not the real father, but instead the totemic species whose essence is reincarnated in the individual born along his track. It seems as if the principle of patrifiliation to a real father is in opposition to the principle of filiation to a symbolic ancestor; in the former case it is the 'place' of the real father which counts; in the latter, the 'place' of the hypothetical ancestor, the country in which he left his marks. In this account, then, we cannot suggest that a system of matrilineal attachments precedes a patrilineal one; instead, a system of symbolic filiation to place precedes a real one to father. However, we might note that, if the allocation to totemic group and associated rites depends primarily on place of birth, then the decision of the mother as to her whereabouts is crucial for the child's future. There is the possibility that the shift to an ideology of patrifiliation is a *de facto*, although covert, method of removing any ambiguities regarding the father–son transmission of identity which might be introduced by the mother's choice of birth-site for her child.

In summary then, I am suggesting that the confusion surrounding the nature of Western Desert local organization is not simply caused by the 'degeneracy' of social institutions as a result of white contact, or by the inability to make accurate observations on the part of observers, not even by a simple confusion between the 'ideal' model and the 'real' model. In defiance of Occam's Razor, the explanation is not the simplest explanation apparent. The whole of the Western Desert cultural area was, at the time of the arrival of the Whites, in a state of transition, in which indigenous cultural institutions were undergoing transformations without having yet achieved any kind of balance. A static model of social organization could not possibly account for the structural features found under these circumstances. Where such transitions had already occurred and been stabilized, a static account appears much more successful (see the Walbiri, the Aranda). It remains a moot point whether such a stabilization would indeed have been possible, given the ecological constraints of the area. Strehlow repeatedly attributes the social organization of the Western Desert to its extreme aridity and lack of resources. This question cannot now be decided empirically, since that particular trajectory has now ended for good, to be replaced by another of equally doubtful outcome. We may, however, construct an ideal model to account for the features of the system of local organization in the Western Desert as they might once have been, and another to describe the system as it was straining to become. Both models partake of 'crystalline structures', and could never account for any real observation of any real historical situation, but are nonetheless useful to provide a basic reference point.

The Past

The Western Desert is socially defined by the tracks of ancestors. People are born on a particular track, and join the cult totem of that ancestor on initiation. Marriages are arranged between groups of people along the same track, but geographically distant from one another. Hence there is totem-group endogamy, local-group exogamy. Persons who marry thus are common children of the one ancestor, and symbolically 'brother' and 'sister' to each other. Choice of residence is not fixed, but in any lifetime many such choices along the same track will be made. A family group may live for a time with the wife's people, for a time with the husband's, for a time with other siblings. Ultimately choice of residence depends on interpersonal relations and individual preferences, not on rules. However, persons connected with one track associate with others on that same track wherever possible. 'Following the Dreaming' means literally 'following the tracks of the ancestor' in both real and symbolic terms. Religious activities are focused on the celebration of the actions of the ancestor, and on the replenishing of productivity of both man and animal species — and just as husband and wife are 'siblings', so are living people 'siblings' of the actual animal embodiments of the ancestor. Interdependence of groups is totally at the symbolic level — kangaroo people are responsible for the supply of kangaroos, emu people for emus and so on, and the well-being of the whole depends on each group carrying out its appropriate rituals. There is no sense in which 'patrilineality' is preferred to 'matrilineality' and there is no real system of human descent at all.

Differentiation between countries along the same track occurs at the level of dialect — that is, people who usually live in one particular segment of the track speak in a particular manner by which they can be differentiated from others who live in other segments. At some places tracks cross one another, and here there may be choice of totemic affiliation and some ambiguity. Initiations are all-important, but they are initiations into the world of men connected with one particular totem, and do not concern members of other cult groups.

The Future

The totemic tracks of the ancestors remain. However, the 'countries' along them are now differentiated by more than dialect, for certain groups of men now claim to 'own' these countries whereas men born elsewhere on the track do not. Marriages are still arranged with distant groups, but the specification of totemic affiliation of the wife is of no importance, for all rights in cult activity are now defined wholly and solely by patrilineal descent. Persons who marry are no longer 'brother' and 'sister' to each other. Men take their wives to live with them at marriage in their own countries. Religious activities are no longer solely concerned with the actions of a particular ancestor by people born on that track, for other ceremonies celebrating new heroes have emerged, which ignore individual totemic affiliation and group together men of different totems in celebration of the activities of these 'species-neutral' heroes. Interdependence of groups is now articulated not in symbolic terms, but in terms of real exchange — of women, of ceremonies and of paraphernalia. The possibility of 'patrilineality' has emerged and solidified, and has overcome the possibilities of non-descent, or rather, symbolic ancestor-based descent. Dialectical differentiation remains, but is now unrelated to country or track, and has lost its socially differentiating functions. Initiations are now the concern of all men, not merely of men on the initiate's track, especially since marriages are now arranged through the initiation procedures. The likelihood is that a section or subsection system will be well integrated, on a model like that of the Walbiri or the Aranda.

Contradictions

Clearly neither of these systems can exist in reality. In the case of the 'past' system the ability to remain wholly on the track of a given ancestor is limited by seasonal factors and especially by any overall change in climate. But any leaving of the track introduces the question of totemic affiliation of children born while away. Intergroup communication is at a minimum. There are no means of integration of groups wider than the totemic cult group. Choice of marriage partners in particular is limited to those people of the same cult totem in distant but not too distant places. Such a system could have been a possibility at a time when the Western Desert had a greater carrying capacity than at present, with a greater population density and less need to exploit far-flung resources in drought times. A general decline in productivity would result in greater spreading of the population, greater ambiguity about cult-group affiliation, and a greater need to alter the principles of the social formation.

In the case of the second system, environmental constraints again militate against its successful integration. Ideally, it requires that all men live on their own 'country' and that all their children are born there. Certainly under present-day desert conditions this is absolutely impossible. A wider definition of 'country', and its articulation with a subsection system, as happens among the Aranda, might provide one possible avenue of resolution. The exigencies of drought and unreliability of food supplies mean that such 'countries' would have to be at least twenty to thirty times their present size, to allow this possibility to emerge. Alternatively, connections between men could be freed of precise connections to locality, and be articulated instead in terms of a ritual system that provided access to resources not in terms of land alone but in terms of obedience to certain ritual requisites, such access to be handed on from father to son as a matter of course. There is some evidence to suggest that this is the path which the Western Desert people were taking.

Conclusion

I have attempted to show in this paper that the question of patrilineal, patrifocal band structures is far from settled in Australia, not simply because the 'economic' unit is to be differentiated from the 'religious' unit, but because Aboriginal systems, at least in some areas, were themselves in a state of change. That these changes, in the case of the Western Desert from a place-based to a father-based system of definition of rights, occur in 'religion' is apparently a confirmation that in 'archaic' societies the structures characteristic of distinct levels as found under capitalism cannot be identified in the same way. Instead we find a collapsing together of levels, in which structures usually considered appropriate to 'economic' organization are operating within the 'religious' system. Furthermore, to the extent that these alterations in ideology (e.g. the introduction of sections through the movement of rituals between men in adjacent areas) become linked into the kinship system, the distribution of women and the nature of rights held by men over women is also altered. But here we must pause, and invoke again both Lévi-Strauss and Hindess and Hirst. For, although men act in the ritual sphere using means reminiscent of action in the economic world under capitalism, and attempt to find more and more secure ways of ensuring the transmission of rights to *ritual* property from fathers to sons, the material basis on which the male religious life rests is gained through the labour of the women. This 'real' base, how-ever, does not appear anywhere at the ideological level; men continue to act as if ritual manipulations are the sole determinant of human production, and concern themselves exclusively with defining access to the rituals which constitute their 'business world', in which women feature mainly by their absence.[7]

Notes
1. The research on which this paper is based was carried out in 1970–71 at Everard Park Station (now *Mimili*) in the north-west corner of South Australia.

I am grateful to the Australian Institute of Aboriginal Studies for its financial support, and to Sally White, Dan Vachon and Nicolas Peterson for their helpful comments. The whole question of local organization in the Western Desert remains unsettled in my mind, and the results of further research by male field workers now in the area may add a great deal to our understanding of the situation.

2. I am ignoring for the moment the argument regarding appropriation of surplus labour, and exploring the simpler 'materialist' formulation here. The subject of surplus labour will be discussed elsewhere.

3. Certain Australian societies have introduced a division of labour into the religious sphere; the Dalabon for instance separate ownership and control (Maddock 1974:38), while in north-east Arnhem Land clansmen may go to their sacred sites only with the permission of their uterine relatives who are custodians, and who are the only people permitted food and water from the site (Peterson 1972:18–19). Evidence by Aborigines in recent land-claim cases has highlighted the great significance of this relationship. The theoretical implications of such a ritual division of labour require urgent exploration, since it suggests that the idea of division of labour between men is being elaborated within the ideological sphere while the economic division of labour operates primarily along sexual lines.

4. However, this 'ideologically correct' account of Aboriginal production obscures the fact that these 'owner/workers' do in reality receive disproportionate benefits as a result of their holding the key to the secrets of species reproduction. For example, over any given year they receive a great deal more hunted meat than do young men or women.

5. Or Pitjantjara, 'b' and 'd' being alternatives for 'p' and 't' in all Aboriginal languages. There is no orthographical agreement among Australian scholars at present.

6. That is to say, an adult person from any of these areas could, on moving to another such area for a short period of time, assimilate the necessary variations in dialect very rapidly. By contrast, a speaker of one of these dialects would have difficulty in learning Walbiri, or Aranda, as quickly, even though these areas abut that of the speaker.

7. The question of women's labour has been considered in Hamilton (1980). Since completing the present paper I have further considered Aboriginal land-*ownership* in the Western Desert as a relationship between men and land established through the possession of sacred objects as signifiers. This approach has been briefly outlined in my PhD thesis 'Timeless transformation' (University of Sydney, 1979).

References

BERNDT, R. M. (1966), 'The concept of the tribe in the Western Desert of Australia', in L. R. Hiatt & I. Hogbin (eds.), *Readings in Australian and Pacific Anthropology*, Melbourne: Melbourne University Press.

BERNDT, R. M. & BERNDT, C. H. (1945), *A Preliminary Report on Fieldwork at Ooldea, South Australia*, Oceania, bound reprint, Sydney.

BERNDT, R. M. & JOHNSTON, T. H. (1942), 'Death, burial and associated ritual at Ooldea, South Australia', *Oceania*, 12(3):189–208.

ELKIN, A. P. (1937), 'Beliefs and practices connected with death in north-eastern and western South Australia', *Oceania*, 7(3):257–99.

—— (1938–1940), 'Kinship in South Australia', *Oceania*, 8(4); 9(1); 10(2); 10(3).

—— (1970), *The Australian Aborigines*, rev. edn, Sydney: Angus and Robertson.

ENGELS, F. (1973a), 'On social relations in Russia', in *The Selected Works of Marx and Engels*, vol. 2, Moscow: Progress Publishers.

—— (1973b), 'Supplement on Proudhon and the housing question', in *The Selected Works of Marx and Engels*, vol. 2, Moscow: Progress Publishers.

FALKENBERG, J. (1962), *Kin and Totem*, New York: Humanities Press.

HAMILTON, A. (1979), 'Timeless transformation: women, men and history in the Australian Western Desert', Unpublished PhD thesis, University of Sydney.

—— (1980), 'Dual social systems: technology, labour and women's secret rites in the eastern Western Desert of Australia', *Oceania*, **51**:4–19.

HIATT, L. R. (1962), 'Local organisation among the Australian Aborigines', *Oceania*, **32**:267–86.

—— (1965), *Kinship and Conflict*, Sydney: Angus and Robertson.

HINDESS, B. & HIRST, P. G. (1975), *Pre-capitalist Modes of Production*, London: Routledge and Kegan Paul.

LEE, R. (1978), 'Issues in the study of hunter-gatherers: 1968–1978', paper presented at the conference on hunter-gatherers, Paris, June 1978.

LEE, R. B. & DEVORE, I. (eds) (1968), *Man the Hunter*, Chicago: Aldine.

LEVI-STRAUSS, C. (1963), *Structural Anthropology*, New York: Basic Books.

—— 1968, 'The concept of primitiveness', in R. Lee and I. De Vore (eds), *Man the Hunter*, Chicago: Aldine.

MADDOCK, K. (1974), *The Australian Aborigines: a Portrait of their Society*, Sydney: Allen Lane.

MARX, K. & ENGELS, F. (1973), 'The German ideology', in *The Selected Works of Marx and Engels*, vol. 1, Moscow: Progress Publishers.

MEGGITT, M. J. (1962), *Desert People*, Sydney: Angus and Robertson.

PETERSON, N. (1972), 'Totemism yesterday', *Man*, N.S. **7**(1).

STANNER, W. E. H. (1965), 'Aboriginal territorial organisation: estate, range, domain and regime', *Oceania*, **36**:1–26.

STREHLOW, T. G. H. (1965), 'Culture, social structure and environment in Aboriginal Central Australia', in R. M. Berndt (ed.), *Aboriginal Man in Australia*, Sydney: Angus and Robertson.

—— (1970), 'Geography and the totemic landscape in central Australia: a functional study', in R. M. Berndt (ed.), *Australian Aboriginal Anthropology*, Nedlands: University of Western Australia Press.

TINDALE, N. B. (1972), 'The Pitjandjara', in M. Bicchieri (ed.), *Hunters and Gatherers Today*, New York: Holt, Rinehart and Winston.

—— (1974), *Aboriginal Tribes of Australia*, Berkeley: University of California Press.

YENGOYAN, A. (1970), 'Demongraphic factors in Pitjandjara social organisation', in R. M. Berndt (ed.), *Australian Aboriginal Anthropology*, Nedlands: University of Western Australia Press.

7
Grandmothers' Law, Company Business and Succession in Changing Aboriginal Land Tenure Systems

MARCIA LANGTON

Introduction

This paper examines some women's affiliations to land and the relevance of the issues to the task of demonstrating an ongoing Aboriginal connection to land in native title cases. This paper rebuts the arguments concerning Aboriginal land tenure which depict these customs and traditions as the domain only of the members of patrilineages, or groups of kin who, in common, reckon their ancestry through a male line.[1]

The established anthropological orthodoxy which was constructed from the emerging ethnographic literature from last century was that Aboriginal women were excluded from any role in the important affairs of Aboriginal societies. These were the domain of a male gerontocracy, it was believed. We now understand that this was the interpretation of men (and there were only a few women in the early part of this century — including Kaberry) whose view of humanity in general was that women were inferior by virtue of a biologically determined set of conditions. Even though, in general, such propositions are no longer acceptable, the androcentric stance of Western observation of the Other still distorts, if not the scholarship, then certainly the social institutions in which claims and other aspects of the contemporary Australian recognition of Aboriginal customary land tenure are carried out.

In the Northern Territory, it was believed in the 1970s by the anthropological and legal advocates, and still today by some participants in the implementation of the *Aboriginal Land Rights (Northern Territory) Act 1976* (ALRA), that it was principally the evidence of men that established in the first place the primary criterion of traditional ownership, that is, the existence of a local descent group or groups. The orthodox view was that descent is patrilineal, or at least determined by patrifiliation.

Since the commencement of the Act, some anthropologists have shown, particularly in land-claim research, that women play an important part in

First published in Galarrwuy Yunupingu (ed.), *Our Land is Our Life: Land Rights — Past, Present and Future*, St Lucia: Queensland University Press, 1997.

contemporary Aboriginal land tenure systems. These systems are dynamic and flexible; having survived colonization and attempted genocide, they provide important opportunities in a range of social affairs for their members. Women, it is argued, maintain Aboriginal traditions relating to land ownership by their politicking in matters to do with the constitution of contemporary customary corporations and nurturing of the social relations of the land tenure system.

It is increasingly acknowledged by anthropologists that among Aboriginal groups which have endured rapid population loss as a result of frontier violence and disease, forced removals or other impacts of colonization, the senior women of the relevant land tenure corporations take on a special role in succession arrangements to land where the original land-holding corporation has not survived.

Understanding the role of Grandmothers' Law in the transformation of land-holding patterns from small 'clans' to the wider regional groupings, and, in particular, in succession processes, is particularly important both for statutory and native title claims.

It is increasingly acknowledged that the matrikin of customary land corporations are assuming caretakers roles for estates of extinct groups, and that they play a crucial role in the formation of regional groupings which have been presented as claimant groups in some claims. Anthropologists working on some native title claims will be required to pay closer attention to these transitional arrangements for successions and reconstitution of regional customary corporations in claims in 'settled' Australia. The knowledge of senior women and their custodial responsibilities for these bequeathed lands remain important matters in the documentation of claims.

Examples are provided to explicate the apparent shift from patrilineal to cognatic systems and the role of senior women in this. It can be seen that Aboriginal measures for dealing with succession in regions severely affected by colonization rely on 'classical' forms and principles.[2]

Women's Evidence and Gendered Landscapes

Some researchers and legal representatives are aware that the involvement in land-claim research and the expert evidence of a female anthropologist (or researcher from a related discipline) or female legal representative is no guarantee that the women claimants will have a fair opportunity to present their evidence, or even that evidence of the kind they would prefer to present will be presented. Nor will a female researcher or lawyer guarantee appropriate circumstances for the hearing of women's evidence, having regard to the gender-differentiated rules relating to Aboriginal ritual knowledge. Annie Keeley[3] discusses these issues and makes important recommendations.

A senior anthropologist recently suggested that having only one anthropologist to document a native title claim would be sufficient. This comment should alert us to the problem that despite all the experience of the Northern Territory, the recognition of gendered landscapes, knowledge and social organizing principles are not yet accepted in the

Australianist canon, or regarded as critical in securing the rights of all the members of a claimant group. The suggestion was stated in these terms:

> Reliance on restricted knowledge has, however, become much less important in recent claims so that it has been possible, although it is not necessarily desirable, to prepare an adequate claim with a single anthropologist doing most, if not all the work.[4]

It is not my experience that restricted knowledge has become 'much less important in recent claims'. Nor is it my understanding that the relevance of women's evidence goes only to matters of a restricted nature. I have worked in varying capacities on many claims and have led women's evidence at the proofing and hearing stages in a number of claims. In 1994, I recorded women's evidence in the Palm Valley Land Claim in central Australia and in the Lakefield National Park Land Claim in Cape York. In both cases, the women's evidence was relevant to the proof of traditional ownership and affiliation being argued.

Women witnesses have often been silenced by the conduct and organization of land claims, and thus much of the significance of 'women's business' in the general affairs of society has been missed. When women law holders have been given an appropriate forum in which to speak, they have given partial exegeses of their life-enhancing rituals and myths (often shared in a gendered fashion with the male law holders) and thereby expanded our understanding of customary land systems. The extent to which places and country are gendered has emerged incrementally over the last two decades in the land rights literature.

Mr Justice Toohey, in his report to the Minister for Aboriginal Affairs on the ALRA remarked,

> The experience of the land claims has been that in each community there have been women prepared to speak out on matters relating to land or, by performing song and dance, to demonstrate their knowledge of the land and their affinity with it. In other Aboriginal organisations women exercise forceful and effective leadership.[5]

The Range of Women's Ritual Observances

Women's ritual observances, including ceremonies, are performative devices for emphasizing important states, emotions and events, and they give expression to a wide range of life's concerns. I have summarized them by reference to their purpose, rather than style, below:

- Place-specific or regional celebrations of stories or Dreamings which may include song cycles, dance repertoires, ritual objects and body painting, for calling up ancestors and re-enacting their exploits.
- Ceremonial repertoires include those roles which they perform in public ceremonies as well as male-oriented ceremonies such as initiation and rituals for observing important species, particularly plants, and spiritually encouraging their reproduction. The story or Dreaming places associated with the creative dramas of these species/beings are celebrated in these rituals.

- Extensive knowledge concerning midwifery, birthing rituals and practices, and rituals for investing spiritual essence and power of particular births in places and trees, and for activating certain powers in newborn infants.
- Rituals concerning both the dangerous and nourishing powers of sexual attraction, courting, marriage and related emotional states, which empower women to control these states and explain their significance to younger women.
- Keeping of practical and spiritual bodies of medicinal and healing knowledge which they apply in ritual acts for the benefit of individuals, groups, sometimes for marriages, and sometimes for states of being within groups which are seen to be detrimental to the well-being of people or places invested with the spirits of ancestors. Certain sacred sites are associated with this knowledge and power.
- Specific roles in mourning and mortuary rituals, including funerary rites, coronial inquisitions to determine cause of death, and punishment rituals.
- A range of practical and spiritual practices for aggressive purposes when conflict arises, and can take vengeance on others when they feel aggrieved, through fighting or sorcery. Dispute resolution is achieved through these and specific rituals for peace-keeping.

Gendered places have been most recently discussed by Deborah Bird Rose in a report commissioned by the Australian Heritage Commission, which she titled *Nourishing Terrains*:

> Dreamings travelled; they were sometimes in human form, and sometimes in animal or other form. But whatever the form, they were almost inevitably either male or female. Dreaming men and women sometimes walked separately and thus created gendered places. There are now women's places and men's places: places which are associated with one or the other because Dreaming made it that way. There are varying degrees of exclusion: places where men can go but must be quiet, places where they can look but not stare, where they can walk but not camp, and then there are places where men cannot go at all, ever. There are places where men cannot drink the water, cannot even look at the smoke that rises from women's country. And of course the same is also true with respect to men's places, men's country.[6]

The gendering of landscape and social organization is typical of Aboriginal life. Aspects of, and places within, the landscape are gendered, as in what is meant to be conveyed by the rubric of 'men's sites' and 'women's sites'. At the same time, the social systems of Aboriginal land law are also gendered in specific ways.

Finding the Evidence for Native Title Claims: The Affiliations to Land Through Women in Post-frontier Contexts

Understanding the legacy of colonial history in transforming the gendered landscapes and social constructs of Aboriginal life has become critical in documenting native title claims where the impact of the frontier on local group composition and constitution is salient. The impacts of successive colonial assaults on the demographic constitution of local groups have had differential effects on males and females at the macro-level, and on surviving sibling sets in generations at the micro-level. The effect on the way rights in land are held and transmitted to subsequent generations is the subject of my examination of rights to land derived from female ancestors.

Anthropologists have recently debated the requirements of proving the social and historical incidents of native title, particularly a 'continuing physical connection'. This may be rather more difficult than the task of explicating Aboriginal social relationships in terms of the definitions of the ALRA. Not least of the problems is the evidentiary rules in the Federal Court.

The task of gathering evidence for native title claims will require a different approach from that for claims under the ALRA as Peter Gray points out:

> Native title does not have any of the certainties of land rights claims. It has no statutory definition. Both the ascertainment of the native title holders and the incidents of native title are dependent on Aboriginal law. Like the law of a foreign country, Aboriginal law will have to be proved as a question of fact. It is whatever the relevant Aboriginal peoples say it is, assuming that their evidence is accepted. Aboriginal evidence as to the form in which Aboriginal law has survived in a particular area will be crucial to each claim.[7]

He speculates that there will be an 'enormous spectrum' of difference, ranging from areas in northern Australia where Aboriginal law 'will have survived in less adapted form' to south-eastern Australia where 'Aboriginal law is likely to have survived in a more rudimentary form'.[8]

It is my contention that we must now look more carefully at women's rights in land. My experience in the Northern Territory, Queensland and parts of New South Wales is that women retain bodies of knowledge pertaining to the spiritual landscape. This knowledge sometimes concerns a narrower range of issues than those involved in 'women's business' in the central desert areas where there is an intense gender-differentiated ritual life, but the principal issues of concern to women are still marked off by special ritual observances.

The paradigm in which men's evidence is the cornerstone in proving the existence and rules of customary land corporations will be less efficacious in native title claims in those areas where the massacres, epidemics, forced removals and impact of alcohol abuse, imprisonment, employment in the pastoral industry and itinerant labouring have resulted in a female gerontocracy of the remnant clans and of amalgamated customary land corporations such as 'tribes' (see Rigsby 1995).

The recruitment of members to land-holding groups through grandmothers described in land claims is not, I argue, aberrant, but the outcome of strategic decisions which form part of a repertoire of strategies for sustaining land-holding group identity and continuity.

Land Claims in the Northern Territory: The Developing Understanding of the Multiplicity of Land Tenure Principles

In his comprehensive survey of Aboriginal land rights law in the Northern Territory,[9] Graeme Neate discusses changing anthropological views of traditional Aboriginal ownership. Referring to the 'variety of forms of traditional land tenure' which has been revealed by the research undertaken in the preparation of land claims, he states that, just as some anthropologists had been asserting for many years, 'no one model can adequately describe traditional land-owning and land-usage principles and practices'. He adds that some anthropologists 'continue to put forward the orthodox anthropological model as having general application'.[10]

The principal reason for the bias in the model of the patrilineage is the definition at Section 3(1) of 'traditional Aboriginal owners' in the ALRA, as a local descent group of Aboriginals who:

(a) have common spiritual affiliations to a site on the land, being affiliations that place the group under a primary spiritual responsibility for that site and for the land; . . .

The land rights literature documents the model at work in the preparation of land claims in the late 1970s to the mid-1980s: evidence of men was privileged because, in the view of some advocates, only the evidence of men went to prove primary spiritual affiliation of the group to a site or sites on the land, and common spiritual responsibility of the group.

The range of land tenure systems adduced by anthropologists and supported by Aboriginal evidence to a number of claims includes cognatically constructed groups[11] and systems with patrimoieties supported by groups with secondary affiliations to the patri-estates (those in the matrilateral ritual roles and groups referred to as *junggaiyi* and *kurtungurlu*). There have also been claims by 'language' groups (see Merlan 1996) and by 'tribes' (see Rigsby & Hafner 1994).

Sutton has discussed different levels of land-owning groups which might be recognized for the purposes of documenting native title claims. These 'different landed entities' include: 'unilineal land-holding units, local sets of totemically or ritually linked units, language groups, named sets of distinct languages, groups holding environmentally similar country' (Sutton 1995:4).

Francesca Merlan attributes the anthropological conformity to clan-level models of relationship to country to 'traditionalism', a structure with 'an undisputed pre-colonial origin'.[12] And further.

. . . it leaves the smallest margin for ambiguity in the relation between rules for the constitution of a structure (patrifiliative recruitment), the places involved (clan countries) and the set of people associated with the structures.[13]

The 'high-level socio-territorial identity "Jawoyn" ' argued by Merlan and Rumsey in the Katherine Area Land Claim is, she suggests, 'not any less "authentic", in the sense of having pre-colonial origins, than clan'.[14] This may be a more accurate representation of relationships to country by people with multiple connections to identified areas within a region through parents and grandparents:

> It may allow for the modelling of Aboriginal relationships at a broad regional level in a way that clanship by itself may not, ... the relevant notion of country at this level is much broader than it is in the case of clan country. And there is at least a degree of difference from clan identity in the potential for application of the affiliation criterion to both mother's and father's side — that is, for an individual, there is the possibility of dual affiliations with both mother's and father's identity if these are different, producing a situation in which some people may be affiliated with more than one identity of this kind — a situation unlike the normative singularity of clan identification.[15]

The rights of women as joint members of a land-holding group, along with their fathers' fathers and fathers' fathers' progeny, is readily acknowledged in the anthropological literature and land rights law literature. So too, it has been acknowledged in that literature that women are members of the laterally organized land-managing groups that are responsible in ritual and ritual-related activity for the management of the landowners' affairs, ensuring fidelity to traditions.

These relatives and their roles are called *junggaiyi* in parts of Arnhem Land and neighbouring regions, and *kurtungurlu* among the Warlpiri, in particular, and neighbouring countries where borrowing and inter-marriage with the Warlpiri have occurred for some time.

The ritual nature of the roles is emblematic of great themes in Aboriginal life: marriageability and non-marriageability; the necessity of ensuring the transmission of rights. The distribution of people and resources across territories to maximize economic opportunity, and the social reproduction of those systems, are achieved partly through the lineal and non-lineal principles of Aboriginal land law and partly by a range of political and social factors, such as authority, knowledge, personal preference, preferred residence and so on.

Grandmothers make these decisions too, with a mind to the future of their descendants. Their own structural positions, their power and authority to recruit kin to their own groups, or even to allocate kin to groups other than their own, and decisions concerning marriage arrangements, are themselves a key part of Aboriginal land law, and are part of what is meant by the Aboriginal term, 'Grandmothers' Law'.

Marriage and betrothal negotiations are thinly disguised politics of resource distribution aimed at securing the future of grandchildren and the longevity and stability of social and territorial entities.

I suggest that the non-patrifiliative aspects of the Aboriginal land tenure systems in pre-frontier times have provided strategies for distributing kin across territory in order to maximize resource use opportunities, and that in the post-frontier era these strategies have become much more critical. The decisions of senior women are crucial in marriage arrangements: their concerns include the affiliations of grandchildren and potential descendants with land estates and resources.[16]

All kinship systems, whether Aboriginal or otherwise, are based on the potentiality of patrilines and matrilines in small-scale societies to result in group constructions which share membership; the tensions between such groups which traditionally intermarry concern the rights and authority of the respective groups over descendants and the shaping of their allegiances.

When there is great demographic stress and resource scarcity, the flexibility offered by serial matrifiliation and matrilateral connections to land in Aboriginal systems provides much-needed survival strategies. Women's rights in land are a critical part of these survival strategies. A feature of post-frontier Aboriginal society has been the leadership and stability of women with the result that they have had the responsibility of developing strategies for distributing their offspring across land and resources through marriage arrangements and through influence over residential arrangements.

Grandmothers' Law: The Authority of Women

The late C. H. Berndt, in the published versions of her Honours Thesis, 'Women's Changing Ceremonies in Northern Australia' (1950), reported that a woman passed on rights in land from her father to her daughter, because of the absence of any male members of the group to whom such rights would have passed in other circumstances. She described how these rights were transmitted by the woman from that time and how the ritual knowledge for a site assumed the status of women's 'business' by virtue of the celebration of the site through women's ceremonies alone.

There is the clear implication that this transmission of knowledge through women was both customary and a response to the impact of the colonial frontier in order to maintain traditions, when the 'classical' systems collapsed under the impact of frontier conditions.

Neate summarizes the arguments concerning succession:

> Those people are members of a local descent group who have had secondary responsibility for the sites and the land but who assume primary spiritual responsibility for them on the extinction of the people who previously had the primary responsibility. The succeeding groups have rights to forage and hunt over the land being taken over ... Recognition of the succession by all interested parties is crucial.[17]

Nicolas Peterson's article, 'Rights, residence and process in Australian territorial organisation' (1983), makes the point that affiliation to country through the mother's mother can be a key factor in succession processes. This is so because a person's mother's mother and father's father, in the ideal or abstract Aboriginal model, are necessarily in the same moiety. It is often the case, too, that 'countries' are in the same moiety by virtue of their association with a particular Dreaming Track which crosses them.

> If the two bands became joined in one large band uniting the two life-spaces into one for a while, it can be expected that sooner or later the economic logic underlying the life-spaces would result in the reappearance of the two bands. In both cases in life-spaces would reinforce any potential lines of fission in the enlarged clan. These would be realised relatively quickly given the short genealogical memory *and different matrilineally traced ties to other clans among siblings of a common father*. With the fissioning, life-space and estate

would become more or less congruent. Later this congruence might be threatened by clan extinction and the assimilation of various parts of the estate to neighbouring groups continuing the interplay between demography, residence and rights. (Peterson 1983: 140–3) (Emphasis added.)

Peterson acknowledges the role of the mothers' mothers in succession in passing, but notes in reference to *kurtungurlu* or managerial roles, that,

Two non-patrilineal interests in land are mediated by kinship: one arises from being the child of a female landowner and is usually referred to as the managerial interest and the other from a regionally variable range of kinsmen but most generally the MMB [mother's mother's brother] ... In general, the managerial interest gives a nephew the right and obligation to look after the ritual property of the MB [mother's brother], the sacred places within the estate and to stage-manage the ritual performances held by that clan. *Nieces have similar rights in their mothers' ritual property where women's ritual life is well developed. It is unlikely that these interests could lead to succession to the estate of a dying clan if patrilineal moieties are present, since that would mean a change of moiety, but it is a most important and influential interest wherever it exists.*[18] (Emphasis added.)

This is not the only pattern of succession documented. Rumsey has described succession among the Ngarinyin, Wunambal and Worrorra, which operates on a principle of inheritance of rights according to *wurnan* linkages (1966:6).

These are described as 'company' relationships elsewhere, particularly in Central Australia, where it is the *Jukurrpa* or Dreaming Story which links such estates and organizes the directional flow of the so-called wife and ritual object exchange systems.

These relationships between countries of the same moiety, as noted by Peterson, are the 'company' relationships upon which Aboriginal law men and women rely for collaboration in ceremonial performances. They are relationships through Story or Dreaming Law and involve exchange of sacred objects in some regions. Between people who can call each other close 'blood' kin, there is also the possibility of close ritual and social links.

Collaboration in religion may not be possible in regions where the frontier and protection regimes have disrupted the classical organization of Aboriginal societies, and yet these company relationships are still relied on for collaboration in social affairs and resource sharing. Inter-marriage, to some extent on the classical patterns, sustains the company relationships, even though more marriages are 'wrong way' — or not conducive of building strong alliances between the countries by locating grandchildren within a regional alliance of countries.

Rumsey also notes that the moiety division, being the most inclusive of basic categories of kin, has implications for clan succession and fusion: contiguous clans of the same inter-clan relations have previously been of a different kind (e.g. gaja-gaja, 'mother's mother–daughter's son') (1996:7).

Diane Bell did not elaborate upon the underpinning relationship between the landowner as ritual celebrant and her mother's mother in her description of Yungkurru (Bell 1993:194) because of her concern with the matrilateral relationships in the *kurtungurlu* ritual role of women.[19]

In the Yutpundji-Djindiwirritj (Roper Bar) claim and the Cox River (Alawa/Ngandji) Land Claim people who are related by virtue of their descent from particular people to whom they are related as grandchild–mother's mother are explicitly named groups: *dalnyin.* Mr Justice Kearney summarized Robert Layton's submission on the relationship between groups in this way:

> The case for the claimants is that each estate is owned by a local descent group, membership of which is normally determined by applying four criteria of descent from the grandparental generation. Members usually are said to be affiliated to the group either through their father's father, father's mother, mother's father or mother's mother. The particular affiliation determines the position the individual occupies within the group and his responsibilities. Such an approach connotes that individuals may be members of four local descent groups. It is put that individuals are miniringgi in the father's father's estate, djunggaiyi in the mother's father's estate and the father's mother's estate, and *dalnyin* in the mother's mother's estate; that is to say, they occupy three distinct positions in four estates ...
>
> It is said that these three categories within each descent group have in common spiritual affiliations to sites on the estates and perform complementary functions within the group which enable the group as a whole to discharge a spiritual responsibility for the sites and the estate.[20]

The *dalnyin* were among the principal ceremonial performers in both men's ceremonies and women's ceremonies. Of the Jarata ceremony, which was controlled by and exclusive to women, the Commissioner was able to say:

> Three things did emerge. First, a linkage between the Jarata and spiritual responsibility for Alawa country seen as a whole. Second, that women have a spiritual responsibility distinct from that which they have as members of local descent groups ...[21]

The Ancestral Beings celebrated in the Jarata were said to provide 'the mythological charter for all women's ceremonial activity',[22] including women's role in men's ceremonies. This women's ceremony, it was reported, has the effect of uniting people across estates into a regional entity, emphasizing the commonality and integrity of a region and its people, overarching the clan-based identities.

This is a feature of a number of women's ritual cults, particularly those with a wide regional or continental influence, such as the other forms of the Two Women Dreaming and the Seven Sisters Dreaming. (While it is clear that there are men's regional ceremonies which also have this effect, I am emphasizing the way in which women's ceremonies have this effect for the purposes of this paper.)

Aboriginal land tenure systems in settled Australia may exhibit some of the features of their pre-frontier forms — their descent-based nature and other social organizational features of the old clans — but these are less important than forms of regional identity. In addition to tending to identify themselves as language-defined groups or 'tribes', landowners in settled Australia increasingly identify the members of their groups on a cognatic basis, enabling groups to have multiple membership by having simultaneous potential for membership reckoned from each Aboriginal grandparent.

The selection of sources of information cited above all indicate that the principles of descent from women are not aberrant features of Aboriginal land tenure systems, but rather, like patrifiliation, provide continuity through time for the identity of land-holding groups which are thereby enabled to recruit membership cognatically. Matrifocal rituals and religious concerns further bind together kin and country and provide a wider regional range of choices and opportunities than the limited 'patriclan' identity. These strategies seem to have been employed in the aftermath of the rolling frontiers in Cape York in northern Queensland.

Land Claims in Cape York: The Post-frontier Context and Land Tenure Systems

In the Lakefield National Park Land Claim in Queensland before the Aboriginal Land Tribunal, it was argued by Rigsby and Hafner that there were higher-level regional entities, 'tribes' or language groups, which formed subgroups of the larger claimant group.[23]

Bruce Rigsby, giving evidence in the Lakefield National Park Land Claim, referred to the system of reckoning used by members of the land-owning groups as 'bilateral':

> I felt it was important recognising that it's a bilateral system of kin reckoning amongst the claimants such that men and women, links through men and women, mothers and fathers are equally important in reckoning what we're calling descent here, so that men and women both should be included as apical ancestors where both are traditional owners or were traditional owners, rather than to simply specify one or the other of husband and wife as an apical ancestor and leave the other out.[24]

A young university-educated claimant, explaining his own patrilineal connection to a named 'country' on the park, and also having connections to the estates of his grandmothers, observed:

> Yeah ... it's that kind of tension between having a main say over your main country but also having a say and an interest in the whole district, you know, which other people allow you to have, because they used to allow my grandfather that, you know.[25]

Asked to identify the factors that might influence a decision to the father's side country rather than mother's side country, and what rights would be retained, he identified 'shame' at asserting oneself inappropriately for country; put another way, there is a requirement for countrymen and women to know their place in the order of social affairs according to local customs pertaining to seniority and to take responsibility to the extent considered appropriate in relation to the interests of other kin, greater or lesser than one's own.

The witness was able to name 'countries' across a wide region, because the knowledge of these levels of identity were still features of the discourse about land in Guugu Yimidhirr (the major language now spoken in the region as a result of the history of the Hope Vale mission to which so many people were removed). The 'country' which was the subject of this evidence was in the western-most region of this language group. The Guugu Yimidhirr, while suffering removals and confinement to a reserve, nevertheless sustain larger numbers than other language groups in the area, and a considerable level of knowledge of country, sites and Story is held by a large number of elders.

He went on to explain how his father's brother, entitled theoretically to claim this same country, nevertheless, because of personal historical circumstances, chose — properly according to custom — to be principally affiliated with his mother's country (or the 'country' of the younger witness's mother's father).

Having senior patrikin or matrikin who are prepared to be 'assertive' in the exercise of their authority over country, to some extent, relieves a younger person of the decision as to whether to take 'mother's side' or 'father's side' in constructing a land-based identity. But the problem is always one of tension between the groups in which the parents are members, and the matter is never an easy one, especially when the options are not straightforward.

Acknowledging that countries or estates are never entirely independent entities because of the crosscutting links of patrifiliation and matrifiliation which tie all members to mother's country and father's country, the young witness explained further that patrifiliation is not an absolute principle of seniority in all circumstances; that the choice must be made by the individual according to the circumstances:

> There are no — my view is that there's no absolutely defined principles that apply to every situation. Like, the hierarchy that I — I conceive of in relation to Bagaarrmugu is a hierarchy that gives precedence to the father's children over the mother's children because the mother's children have access to primary land elsewhere. So that's why I would insist that [named 'brother cousin'] and myself and [other 'brother cousins'] have a slightly higher say in relation to our father's country, because their father's country — and my father told me — my cousins' country is Dyugun [names key family]; Dhaarba [names key family]; Lamalama [names key family]; Dhiidhaarr [names key family], you know. That's what my father told me. But at the same time, Aunty [name (FZ)] and all those cousins also got a right up at Bagaarrmugu. They got a say up there.
> ... If I could explain — if one of my cousins' families — their land was totally irretrievable, covered by Cairns or something. Well, in that instance I think they would have as much say to their mother's country as I would, you know. It's a — each individual makes their own assessment about how assertive they should be and how — how deferring they should be, according to where their primary focus is, and as I say, our primary focus — like my — I've got interests down at Wujal Wujal, at China Camp, through my mother, and even an interest at Rossville through my mother's mothers's mother. But those are interests that I've been welcomed to assert by the group down there, but those are not interests that I would — I would seek to assert over a whole lot of other people before me ...[26]

Asked if the practical issue of the land available for claim influenced the decisions of people in choosing to matrifiliate or patrifiliate or otherwise make a choice for a grandparent's country, the witness responded:

> Yes, I think that's a — that's a big determining factor, and one which is accommodated by — by the way in which I observe the old people to operate.

If somebody's claim through their father's father is absolutely hopeless, then it's quite natural that the father's mother's or mother's mother or mother's father is a claim that they should legitimately pursue, you know. But it is a judgment for the individual ... And I would hope that what I draw from the Aboriginal tradition is this personal responsibility to understand what right you have to assert and what responsibility you have to defer to people.[27]

Groups, such as the Guugu Yimidhirr, which have a critical demographic mass and equitable land resource base to enable the reproduction of the land-holding corporations and the stability of their identities over time, retain a corpus of the 'classical' knowledge of the old clan entities.

An elder of a neighbouring subgroup within the claim, said to be related to this younger witness, made no distinction between the rights in father's father's country and mother's mother's country. The group made a claim on the basis of the language-speaking group, the so-called 'Kuku Thaypan' language, or Awu Laya people, a group that suffered severe population loss through forced removals and the brutality of the frontier. Little of their knowledge of older clan identities survives. The elder affirmed that both patrifiliation and matrifiliation were used as principles of recruitment to his group.

Questioned by counsel assisting the Land Commissioner, he made it clear that in his group claims were made through both father's side and mother's side so that 'no-one was left out'. He indicated that he and his siblings were including descendants of both his father and uncles and their sister and that the mother's side and father's side were regarded as equal:

And is that the Aboriginal way — the proper Murri way? ... Because they said they not gonna leave their sister out because that's — dad's mum and theirs, they were close, that's why they said that they'd never leave us out also, that we all were counted that — if it's from my mother's side–grandmother's side that we are part of their blood too.
Okay. Now, are you able to tell me something about the rights that people can get when they claim through either their mum's country or their dad's country? Are those rights the same? ... Yes.[28]

The women of these groups emphasize matrifiliation or forms of distributing land rights through grandmothers and the power of senior matrikin within a cognatic context. However, in some cases which I have observed, the heads of these remnant clans and land-holding corporations are women, and there are no men of their rank to recruit members on the principle of patrifiliation; that is, there are no male members who would have a stronger right to authority in the land.

These women have chosen to pass on their rights to their father's estate cognatically. This was the case when the Queensland Government transferred to Aboriginal ownership two reserves located near the township of Laura just outside the boundaries of the Lakefield National Park. Five women descendants were the senior surviving members of the land-holding groups for the area in which two reserves were subject to transfer by the Queensland Minister for Aboriginal and Islander Affairs from a trustee, at that time a public servant, to an Aboriginal trust.

The women landowners accepted the title in their own right, and on behalf of their descendants, acknowledging that they had been passing on their own rights in land cognatically. And when a dispute later developed with Aboriginal people from Hope Vale Community asserting that the anthropologist and the government had failed to recognise their rights, these senior women sent their sons to argue their interests in court.

While some male ritual life remains in this area, there are no men of these particular groups with the knowledge from which might be elicited the traditional kind of land claim evidence that has been a feature of the Northern Territory claims. It is clear that where there are younger male members of such groups, seniority is still determined by rights to hold and transmit spiritual knowledge. Men who were travelling while employed in the pastoral industry or other forms of employment did not learn their stories and songs and perhaps were not initiated.

Increasingly in post-frontier areas, matrifiliation is used as the principle of recruitment as much as patrifiliation, not only because of reduced numbers in local populations, but also because of the risk of losing more of the population as people, especially young people, move away seeking to enhance employment chances and other opportunities. A strong stake in an Aboriginal land base offered by an elder who is willing to teach knowledge of country tends to anchor people to country and secure their commitment.

The women of this region, I have found, spend much time reconstructing genealogies and relationships following the large-scale removals of people from the land and individuals from their family groups. They sustain knowledge about people, places, names, meanings, and even if few of the original names for the sites and the countries have survived, people refer to the languages that were originally spoken in the areas. They refer to the groups affiliated with the areas over which their languages were spoken as 'tribes', as Bruce Rigsby recently explained (1995). During the women's evidence in the Lakefield claim, one senior woman witness remembered:

> ... Just going round doing some mapping with — Aunty [name of knowledgeable old woman from neighbouring group], we were sort of sitting down and she was telling us that they had a lot of Women Story. Around there, women had to go hunting themselves, fishing for themselves, and not to sort of — where men's place, they not to go there. But where women's place were kept, only women were allowed to go there ... I sat down there with her, and I said to her then — after hearing what she said, I said, 'Well, it is probably all the women in all the nine different tribes must have had the same,' she said, 'Yes.' She said, 'Sometime, when we meet up altogether' — all the tribes, Thaypan would come across to Lamalama — she said, 'The ladies would get together. The ladies would have the young girls; they would talk to them; and if there was a male, the men would be talking to the male.' And then after — I said, 'What happened then after?' She said, 'Oh, the women all agreed then that maybe it was a Thaypan lady would be marrying then a Lamalama.' But they all sort of agreed because that was — would be, in culture way, the right one they would be marrying. Those old people, I asked them, 'Why did they do that?' — so they wouldn't marry someone that was close to them.[29]

Among these groups, whose numbers have been depleted severely by massacres, forced removals and epidemics, the patri-focused descent-based entities are not so privileged, and other organizing principles assume a greater importance, enabling groups to reproduce themselves through time by relying more on matrifiliation and cognatic recruitment. The principle of filiation and serial filiation through women then appears when the offspring, or surviving offspring, over two generations are women, although when male offspring are born they inherit these inchoate rights which they may activate as adults. This is the case in sections of genealogies because of the accident of all female births or only female members surviving.[30]

Male members of such groups may have been, if not deceased, then absent as a result of imprisonment or alcohol abuse. The pattern of women tending to survive men occurs in almost every generation. In these circumstances, it is sometimes the case that a group of women hold a great deal of the core knowledge pertaining to their land tenure system. At the upper generations, there is the appearance of descent through women because of the loss or absence of males from the community. Heart disease, respiratory disease and a group of factors including alcohol abuse, vehicle accidents, and deaths involving violence are the major contributors to the high rate of male mortality.

Women in these circumstances are making decisions which shape and reconstitute, not just the internal links between people, which are cast as genealogical in the land-claim discourse, but as well the customary groupings as political entities. They are keepers and transmitters of knowledge, customs and traditions which are the basis for Aboriginal land titles.

Conclusion: Looking Down the Generations and Looking Up the Generations

It is my contention that, among the range of principles and strategies which can be pursued to fuse two land-holding groups and their estates, the relationship of grandchild–mother's mother is a crucial organizing principle in succession processes and provides the basis for prescribed negotiations by one or more groups with the community of interests in the land subject to succession. It is also my contention that women negotiate actively, legitimately pursuing their interests and those of their descendants, in many succession cases.

Anthropologists have referred typically to the MMB [mother's mother's brother] in these cases ignoring the tradition of 'Grandmother's Law' as a powerful influence on all interested parties. Aboriginal people in the cases cited readily acknowledge that the approval of the mother's mother for politicking in affairs of this kind is crucial to a successful outcome.

The members of those groups who trace descent from their mothers' mothers which have had kinship and religious ties with the deceased or non-viable group may play a key part in the succession to an estate where the members of the land-owning group have no (or insufficient) members to carry on the governance of estate affairs.

Such fusing groups are sometimes contiguous, but this is not always the case. It is the actual marriages between people at the grandparental level — and thus the alliances through marriage between estates — which determine which countries and land-holding entities are related to each other.

It may not be entirely inappropriate to refer to the principles of matrifiliation and patrifiliation, when they are used simultaneously within land-holding groups by apical heads of the groups to recruit members, as bilateral principles, as Rigsby does (note that Layton used the term ambilineal[31] (1983)). However, if the view point of a range of members across generations of a group is taken, it is more appropriate to refer to the principal of recruitment as cognatic, because the affiliation may be through one or more of the four grandparents to an apical ancestor.[32]

In the Lakefield National Park Land Claim submissions, in every genealogy recorded for the claim, the grandchildren of each upper generation level group of siblings were included; this necessarily implies a cognatic system, because the younger generations looking back to the apical ancestors must have the choices offered by cognatic principles of recruitment to allow inclusivity of this extent.

It is true, however, that from the point of view of the senior members of the group who are guiding and encouraging younger generations in decisions to do with membership of land-holding groups, depending on the circumstances of the group, these senior members will be emphasizing principles of patrifiliation or matrifiliation or bilateral principles of recruitment. These differential strategies based on generation level and options available provide the dynamism in contemporary Aboriginal land tenure systems in post-frontier Australia. This dynamism is based on the tension referred to by the Bagaarrmugu witness, that between the responsibility of deferring to elders and seniors and the need to make a viable decision on land affiliation:

> It is a judgment for the individual ... And I would hope that what I draw from the Aboriginal tradition is this personal responsibility to understand what right you have to assert and what responsibility you have to defer to people.

The choices available to individuals in native title claims will not be restricted by definitions, because of the nature of native title: this title will consist of the decisions made by the members according to their law and custom. It is necessary then to recognize the full range of principles which Aboriginal people bring to bear in constructing their sociality and identities based on the issues of land affiliation. This means that matrifiliation and matrilateral recruitment principles will be integral, rather than peripheral, in the determination of membership and rights.

Notes

1. I gratefully acknowledge the discussions and assistance of Nancy Williams, Toni Baumann, John Bern, Helen Burgess, Michael Christie, Ritchie Howitt and Peter Sutton, and others, some of whom have tried, sometimes unsuccessfully, to explain to me the intricacies of anthropological theory. All errors, misunderstandings and failings are my own. I have redrafted this paper considerably from the original and changed the argument as a result of

becoming aware of some misunderstandings which I have laboured under. It is still a work in progress.

2. I became aware after presenting this paper at the conference entitled Land Rights, Past, Present and Future that Peter Sutton had written a major work examining these issues across the continent. He kindly gave me a copy of his draft, 'Families of Polity: Landed Identity and the Post Classical Aboriginal Formation', in October 1996.

3. Keeley, A., 'Women and land: the problems Aboriginal women face in providing gender restricted evidence', in *Land Rights, Past, Present and Future*, Conference Papers, Northern and Central Land Councils, 1995: 172–85.

4. Peterson, Nicolas, 'Organising the anthropological research for a native title claim', in Paul Burke (ed.), *The Skills of Native Title Practice, Proceedings of a Workshop*, Native Titles Research Unit, AIATSIS, Canberra, 1995: 10.

5. Toohey, J., *Seven Years On, Report by Mr Justice Toohey to the Minister for Aboriginal Affairs on the* Aboriginal Land Rights (Northern Territory) Act *1976 and Related Matters*, AGPS, Canberra, 1984:49.

6. Rose, Deborah Bird, *Nourishing Terrains, Australian Aboriginal Views of Landscape and Wilderness*, Australian Heritage Commission, 1996:36.

7. Gray, Peter R. A., 'Native title procedures', in J. Finlayson and Ann Jackson-Nakano (eds), *Heritage and Native Title: Anthropological and Legal Perspectives*, Native Titles Research Unit, AIATSIS, Canberra, 1996:148.

8. 'Dreamings, songs and ceremonies will have been wholly or partly lost. The significance of sites will tend to be archaeological, rather than spiritual; sites will tend to be middens, burial places, stone tool quarries, ochre mines, canoe trees and camp sites. Identification with land will tend to be on a language group basis.' Ibid., p. 148.

9. Neate, Graeme, *Aboriginal Land Rights Law in the Northern Territory*, Volume 1, Alternative Publishing Cooperative Ltd, Chippendale, NSW, 1989.

10. A leading scholar of Aboriginal land tenure systems, and its documentation and analysis, has been L.R. Hiatt. As noted by Neate, he emphasized the processual nature of people and land relationships rather than the structural and functional relationships which have been the focus of the orthodox models which privilege patrilineages and patrimoieties. Among such anthropologists who proposed that this model has general application across Aboriginal land tenure systems were the late R. M. and C. H. Berndt. The evidence by the late R. M. Berndt and W. E. H. Stanner in the Blackburn case laid the groundwork for the definition of 'traditional Aboriginal owners' in the *Aboriginal Land Rights (Northern Territory) Act 1976*.

11. Peter Sutton has suggested to me that Roger Keesing's definition of cognatic descent is useful for what I am attempting to discuss here:

> A mode of descent reckoning where all descendants of an apical ancestor/ancestress through any combination of male or female links are included (1975: 148, Kin Groups and Social Structure, New York: Holt, Rinehart and Wilson)

12. Merlan, Francesca, 'Formulations of claim and title: a comparative discussion', in J. Finlayson and Anne Jackson-Nakana (eds), *Heritage and Native Title: Anthropological and Legal Perspectives*, Native Title Research Unit, AIATSIS, Canberra, 1996:167.

13. Ibid., p. 168.

14. Ibid., p. 168.

15. Ibid., pp. 168–9.

16. This collection is not the place for a technical discussion and I trust that I have conveyed a general sense of how these principles work for the general

reader. Peter Sutton, in correspondence to me, has written: 'I would like to add that patriclan exogamy distributes women of one land-owning group across landscapes, like matrilineal totemic phratry exogamy which makes sure that land-owning group members tend to be divided among different phratries and these were also major forces in distributing people across the landscape.' This is, as the reader would understand, why I did not become an accountant.

17. Neate, pp. 83–4.
18. Peterson, Nicolas, 'Rights, residence and process in Australian territorial organisation', in Nicolas Peterson and Marcia Langton (eds), *Aborigines, Land and Land Rights*, Australian Institute of Aboriginal Studies, Canberra, 1983:137. It must be stated here in response to this analysis, even though it is many years after, that it is not the nieces alone who would assume the custodial role in succession but the daughters and granddaughters.
19. Bell, Diane, *Daughters of the Dreaming* (second edition). Allen & Unwin, 1993:195.
20. Aboriginal Land Commissioner (Mr Justice Kearney), *Cox River (Alawa/Ngandji) Land Claim, Report by the Aboriginal Land Commissioner to the Minister for Aboriginal Affairs and to the Administrator of the Northern Territory*, AGPS, Canberra, 1985:6.
21. Ibid., p. 13.
22. Ibid., p. 13.
23. Under the *Aboriginal Land Act 1991*, the case to be proved is whether there are 'particular Aboriginal persons' having 'traditional' affiliations to the land under claim. Claims may also be made on the basis of 'historical association'. This is not as restrictive a definition as that for traditional owners as the Aboriginal Land Rights Act in the Northern Territory, even if the task is no less onerous.
24. Rigsby, B., *Transcript, Lakefield National Park Land Claim*, p. 1017.
25. *Transcript, Lakefield National Park Land Claim*, disk version, p. 1681.
26. Ibid., p. 1709.
27. Ibid., p. 1712.
28. *Transcript, Lakefield National Park Land Claim*, p. 1017.
29. *Transcript, Lakefield National Park Land Claim*, disk version, 1994, p. 108.
30. Peter Sutton has clarified a number of points for me which I have not had time to correct in this work in progress: '... historically some families go through phases where there may be up to half dozen or so linkages to a particular landed group through mothers only (MMMMM etc) — but then you'll suddenly get a crop of male links in the same family'. These are cases of 'serial matrifiliation within a non-unilineal system ... the re-establishment of stable partnerships by up-coming generations after a series of very unstable ones seems to me to be a typical reason for such a switch of filiative patterns. Getting off alcohol abuse is one factor, but one among many.' 'True matrilineal systems in Australia ... ngurlu, mardu and thiyi etc, [are] concerned with non-territorial or counter-territorial imperatives of amity, peacemaking, exogamy etc.'
31. Peter Sutton has made the point (pers. comm.) that Layton's use of the term is incorrect, and I presume that this is why Rigsby has used the term 'bilateral'.
32. In the earlier draft of this paper, I had used terms such as 'kindred', 'patrimoiety' and other stalwarts of the Australianist lexicon. Various readers questioned my use of them, and I have removed much of that type of discussion because of some confusion in my own mind about their correct usage. Peter Sutton has since solved the problem to which I was referring and communicated his thoughts — with which I agree. These issues were the concern of my earlier paper, although poorly expressed:

In classical systems people identify as a source of land interests one or more grandparent kin types rather than a named ancestor so often because it is the jural role of the grandparent, ie, their kin standing to ego as a type of antecedent, that really matters. The individual personality of the ancestor is not the foundational consideration. In urban/rural systems, the powerful figure whose name is remembered for generations can be one's M, MM, FFM MMMMM, etc ... A cognatic descent group is an ancestor-focused one, not one focused on particular kin types ... You might say that a CDG is ancestor-focused, a kindred is ego-focused, and a unilineal classical land system is focused on types of filiation to kin types. (P. Sutton, pers. comm.)

References

ABORIGINAL LAND COMMISSIONER (1982), *Yutpundji-Djindiwirritj (Roper Bar) Land Claim, Report by the Aboriginal Land Commissioner to the Minister for Aboriginal Affairs and to the Administrator of the Northern Territory*, Canberra: AGPS.

—— (1985), *Cox River (Alawa/Ngandji) Land Claim, Report by the Aboriginal Land Commissioner to the Minister for Aboriginal Affairs and to the Administrator of the Northern Territory*, Canberra: AGPS.

ABORIGINAL LAND TRIBUNAL (1994), *Transcript of Proceedings, AB93-001, AB-002, in the Matter of Aboriginal Land Claims to Lakefield and Cliff Islands National Parks*, Brisbane: Auscript.

BELL, DIANE (1993), *Daughters of the Dreaming* (second edition), Allen & Unwin.

BERN, J., LARBALESTIER, J. & McLAUGHLIN, D. (1980), *Limmen Bight Land Claim*, Darwin: Northern Land Council.

BERNDT, C H. (1950), 'Women's changing ceremonies in Northern Australia', *L'Homme*, (1):1–87.

KEESING, ROGER, *Kin Groups and Social Structure*, New York: Holt, Rinehart and Wilson.

MEGGITT, MERVYN (1962), *Desert People: a Study of the Walbiri Aborigines of Central Australia*, Sydney: Angus and Robertson.

MERLAN, FRANCESCA (1996), 'Formulations of claim and title: a comparative discussion', in *Heritage and Native Title, Anthropological and Legal Perspectives, Proceedings of a workshop*, Canberra: Native Title Research Unit, AIATSIS.

PETERSON, NICOLAS (1993), 'Rights, residence and process in Australian territorial organisation', in Nicolas Peterson and Marcia Langton (eds), *Aborigines, Land and Land Rights*, Canberra: Australian Institute of Aboriginal Studies.

—— (1995), 'Organising the anthropological research for a native title claim', in Paul Burke (ed.), *The Skills of Native Title Practice, Proceedings of a Workshop*, Canberra: Native Titles Research Unit, AIATSIS.

RIGSBY, BRUCE (1995), 'Tribes, Diaspora people and the vitality of law and custom: some comments', in J. Fingleton and J. Finlayson (eds), *Anthropology in the Native Title Era, Proceedings of a Workshop*, Canberra: Native Titles Research Unit, AIATSIS.

—— & HAFNER, DIANE (1994), *Claims to Lakefield National Park and Cliff Islands, Land Claim Book,* Cairns: Cape York Land Council.

ROSE, DEBORAH BIRD (1996), *Nourishing Terrains, Australian Aboriginal Views of Landscape and Wilderness*, Australian Heritage Commission.

RUMSEY, ALAN (1981), 'Kinship and context among the Ngarinyin', *Oceania* (51): 181–92.

—— (1996), 'Aspects of native title and social identity in the Kimberleys and beyond', *Australian Aboriginal Studies*, (1): 2–10.

SUTTON, PETER (1995), 'Atomism versus collectivism: the problem of group definition in native title cases', in J. Fingleton and J. Finlayson (eds), *Anthropology in the Native Title Era, Proceedings of a Workshop*, Canberra: Native Titles Research Unit, AIATSIS.

TOOHEY, J. (1984), *Seven Years On, Report by Mr Justice Toohey to the Minister for Aboriginal Affairs on the* Aboriginal Land Rights (Northern Territory) Act 1976 and Related Matters, Canberra: AGPS.

8
Indirect Exchange in a Symmetrical System: Marriage Alliance in the Western Desert of Australia[1]

LEE SACKETT

This paper demonstrates that restricted exchange, as presented by Lévi-Strauss (1969) and others, is inadequate to account for Australian Western Desert data. The practice of combining Aboriginal ethnographic data and alliance theory is not new — the two have been intricately interwoven from the start — but the use of actual Aboriginal data to test the theory (in contrast to the general exercise of using Australian models to prove the theory's elegance) is rare. Fox (1967:329) has attempted to prod anthropologists who have done field research in Aboriginal societies to examine their data with an alliance framework in mind. To date, however, only three investigators have accepted the challenge. The conclusions of two, Hiatt (1967; 1968) and Shapiro (1969a), suggest the theory has little or no validity for Australian Aboriginal societies, while those of the third, Maddock (1969), indicate that some kind of exchange system did operate. There is some merit in both positions. Although it appears that exchange did not necessarily proceed in the manner in which Lévi-Strauss claimed, his basic alliance concept is not totally inapplicable. Links of mutual aid existed between groups which were, at least partially, created and maintained by exchanges of women. In support of this assertion I will go beyond the matter of exchanges of women to pay attention to the question of why groups found it necessary to be involved in alliance networks, for this certainly influenced the (more apparent) exchange system.[2]

Aboriginal Kinship and Marriage

The authors of the earliest works on the Aborigines were interested in marriage classes, i.e., the apparent survivals from a hypothetically prior stage of group marriage. It was Radcliffe-Brown who first tried reducing the numerous forms of Australian kinship and marriage to a series of basic types (van der Leeden 1970:78). Additionally, to some extent he

First published in *Ethnology*, **15**, 2 (April 1976), 135–49.

stressed the necessity of distinguishing between marriage, which occurs on the kinship level, and the class or section system (Radcliffe-Brown 1913; 1930–31). Since then, field workers have made additions to or modifications on Radcliffe-Brown's pioneering work, but much of the original foundation is still with us. I shall discuss one of the widely recognized Aboriginal kinship types, commonly termed the Kariera system, and show how the uses to which it has been put have influenced not just Aboriginal studies but kinship theory in general.

The name Kariera and the system itself are derived from a northern Western Australia group. According to Radcliffe-Brown (1913: 153, 155–6) these people were characterized by (1) a recognition of two lines of descent in the second ascending generation; i.e., FF and MF, (2) marriage, whenever possible, with an actual MBD, who was also an FZD, and, following from these two points, and (3) a system of direct sister exchange.[3] As originally described, the Kariera were not so much a type as they were an example of one of the many different Aboriginal kinship and marriage systems.

In 1930–31, however, the system was elevated by Radcliffe-Brown to that of a major class within Australia. Although he continued to stress the recognition of but two lines of descent and the practice of direct exchange of sisters, he modified his previous stance on precisely who ego marries. He claimed (1939:43):

> A man may only marry a woman to whom he applies the same term of relationship that he does to his own mother's brother's daughter. If it is possible for him to marry the daughter of an actual brother of his own mother he normally does so, but of course this only happens in a limited number of instances.

This is an ideal type because it is a model (see Figure 8.1) abstracted from a large amount of data and not the actual genealogy of any particular person. The type class itself is named after and stems from the group in which Radcliffe-Brown undertook his most intensive Australian field research. Had he done his field work in another area, amongst a different group of people, it is not unlikely the ideal system would have been somewhat different, for 'true' Kariera systems are admittedly rare and localized (Radcliffe-Brown 1930: 52).

It is entirely possible, and even very likely, that the recognition of only two lines of descent is more a product of the Kariera terminological system than anything else. The Kariera people had two distinct terms for males in the second ascending generation, *maeli* (FF) and *tami* (MF), and another two for females, *kabali* (FM), and *kandari* (MM) (Radcliffe-Brown 1913:152–3). Had all second ascending generation males been grouped together under one term, as is the common practice in many areas, it is uncertain what Radcliffe-Brown would have done. Furthermore, his own analysis indicates that the Kariera did recognize more than two lines of descent, if not terminologically then at least in tracing kin network relationships. If everyone married an actual bilateral cross-cousin then there would have been only two lines. But such unions occurred only in a limited number of instances, that is ego's FF and MF would not always have been actual B to, respectively, MM and FM. Once

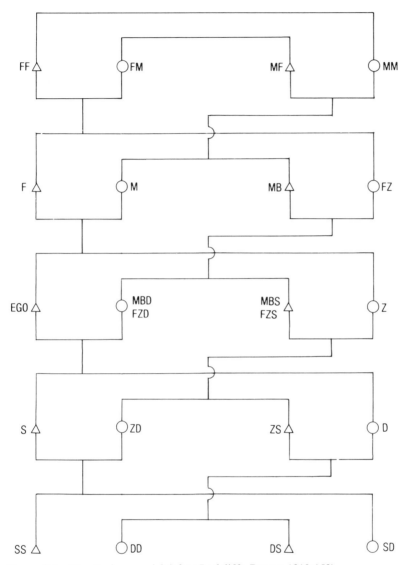

Figure 8.1 The Kariera model (after Radcliffe-Brown 1913:152)

a marriage to a more distant relative occurred and the string of direct sister exchanges was broken, other lines besides the original two were involved (at least for the offsprings of the union) and a person recognized the four lines of FF, FM, MF, and MM (see Figure 8.2).

Throughout his life Radcliffe-Brown was an advocate of a science of anthropology. To him this involved finding out all knowable things, excepting possible past occurrences, about a society and examining their relationships *vis-a-vis* one another (Radcliffe-Brown 1941:1-2, 16-17).

Consequently, and also in an attempt to emulate the hard sciences, he was a classifier (Elkin 1963:82). Such categorization, particularly with regard to Aboriginal data, is essentially subjective, however. Not only are there, for example, differences between Radcliffe-Brown's Aboriginal classification and those of other researchers, but Radcliffe-Brown himself offered different schemes at various stages of his career. Unfortunately, the delimited and described types invariably come to be regarded as archetypes with all similar forms labelled variants. This aspect is clearly evident in the Kariera case. While only a few groups conform to the ideal, many more systems approach it more closely than they do any other type. Because of their ambiguous position, however, they are seen as varieties of or deviations from the Kariera model. In most instances this variation consists of not allowing marriage to an actual MBD/FZD; i.e., the kin in this category are seen as being too close to marry, and only unions with more distant relatives are permitted (Beckett 1967:456; Tonkinson 1970: 278). Whatever the distinguishing characteristics, would it not be more appropriate, if classifications must be used, to either (1) define the type by its most numerous representatives, or (2) broaden the category to include all similarly constituted systems, thereby removing variants from the discussion?

Despite cautionary warnings, it frequently happens that ideal models, designed to represent the classes, come to be viewed as actual systems. Lévi-Strauss (1969) performed such a reification by using Radcliffe-Brown's Kariera model as the pivotal example in his theory of symmetrical alliance (Romney & Epling 1958:59). Symmetrical systems, according to most alliance theorists, consist of two groups exchanging women directly. This exchange creates or maintains an alliance between the units

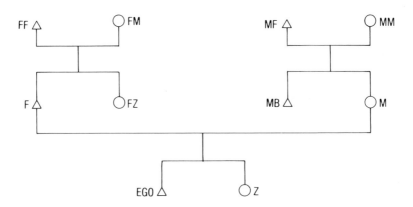

Figure 8.2   An operational Kariera model

involved. It is easy to see that such a theoretical construct is closely matched by Radcliffe-Brown's model. Indeed, Lévi-Strauss and his followers have completely accepted Radcliffe-Brown's notions of Kariera marriage, as if it was an actual MBD/FZD and involved a direct exchange of women. In fact, the only real modifications of the model, necessary to make it amenable to the theory of symmetrical alliance, is a de-emphasis of the lines of descent, and a corresponding concentration on the groups through which the lines are thought to run.

Asymmetrical alliance, on the other hand, owes far less to Aboriginal data in its original conception. This system of exchange involves a minimum of three groups, one more than is necessary for the symmetrical counterpart, and women are exchanged indirectly; i.e., a man's sister goes to one group but his wife comes from another (Lévi-Strauss 1969:233–54). Hypothetically, at least, such systems may be either matrilateral or patrilateral, whereas the symmetrical variety is always bilateral (Leach 1966:59; Korn 1973:22). Furthermore, there is the implication that asymmetrical systems are somehow more evolutionarily advanced than symmetrical ones. This is because the former are supposedly capable of indefinite expansion — by being able to integrate any number of groups above the minimal three — while the latter can grow only through fission — by splitting from the two original units into four, then to eight, and so on.

Lévi-Strauss was aware of the impracticalities inherent in borrowing material such as the Kariera model, yet he did so nonetheless (Dumont 1966:234), and in so doing he elevated the model to the level of a secondary abstraction having little or no relationship to ethnographic reality. As a consequence, the current controversies over Kariera systems and symmetrical alliance are waged in reference to systems having no actual existence. Lévi-Strauss might counter this assertion by remarking that his concern is with models in the mind and not, like the structural-functionalists, with systems as they operate (Lévi-Strauss 1960:52; Leach 1970:104–5; Barnes 1971:105).[4] But Firth (1966:2) and Hiatt (1968:174) declare that it is imperative the theories we construct relate to empirical data if these are to be anything more than intellectual exercises, and I agree.

This is not to say that alliance theory must be ruled out. On the contrary, the notion of inter-group alliance is extremely valuable, but alliance theory, especially as it has been applied to Aboriginal material, has been little more than a conception of linkages between diagrammed groups. While symmetrical alliance theory might admit that marriage may not always occur between actual cross-cousins, but prescribe union to a distant 'MBD/FZD' (viewing the positions as representing a category rather than actual individuals), no thought has been devoted to the consequences of such an admission. It is my contention that symmetrical alliance, as it now stands, is valid only for the 'suspiciously perfect' Kariera (White 1963:95) and their close neighbours, where actual MBD/FZD marriage is encouraged. For the much more numerous and widespread variant forms, where marriage takes place between distant bilateral cross-cousins and unions with actual MBD/FZD are disallowed, symmetrical alliance theory does not fit the data.[5]

Marriage in the Australian Western Desert

Aborigines throughout the Western Desert state the prescribed rule of marriage is to a cross-cousin 'a little bit far away' (Berndt & Berndt 1942:151; 1964:70–4; Fry 1950:290; Yengoyan 1970a:85), making a system which has been termed a variant of the Kariera practice.[6] As Radcliffe-Brown (1931:439) and Piddington (1970:342) note, the distance implicit in this rule is conceptualized by the people in genealogical as well as spatial terms. In other words, ego must not marry a relative from his own local group or an actual cross-cousin from another country. In all likelihood, a spatially close cross-cousin would also be an actual MBD/FZD, though the converse need not be true.

According to the Aborigines now living near Wiluna, Western Australia, there were traditionally two methods whereby a male could be promised a distant female cross-cousin as a marriage partner. Some men, it is true, were given older women as spouses, or were successful in arranging elopements, but as the proper and accepted first union of a man and a young woman necessitated wife-promising it was imperative that all men follow one or both of the practices. One form, I observed, involved the bestowal of an 'MBD/FZD' on a man by his 'FZ'. The young man who was to be promised a wife was placed a short distance from the group of kin gathered to witness and participate in the 'give away'. Next, the man's 'FZ' (*umaṟi*), who was to pledge her 'D', was separated from the main group and placed on its opposite side. The ceremonial presentation was fulfilled when a *djamu* (second ascending generation male) of the man led him to the *umaṟi* and instructed him to grasp the woman about the middle. This act obliged her to ensure the man received a spouse (ideally an issue from her womb), at some future date. The man, in return, was henceforth required to provide the woman with sufficient meat with which to properly nourish her 'D'.[7] At the time of this particular ceremony the *umaṟi* may or may not have already given birth to a daughter. It was not important that she herself gave birth to the 'D' which would eventually go to the man. Rather it was the fact that a specific woman had promised to make certain a man obtained a spouse which was most relevant.

The bestowal practice operated to institute a special relationship between the two principal actors. The *umaṟi* or taboo (Berndt & Berndt 1964:82) relationship between a man and his 'WM' was one of rigid avoidance. Indeed, the term itself was one of reference and never one of address, for one cannot call an individual by a kinship term and at the same time also avoid the person. While the 'give away' in no way altered this pattern, it did lead to the man's referring to the 'FZ' as *junggudjara* (actual or give away mother-in-law). Thus, he continued to term many females *umaṟi*, and maintain the proper avoidance (for all such women were potential 'WM'), but only one person was *junggudjara*.

Curiously, the bestowal practice was not followed by all males, for decisions as to whether or not the ceremony would be held for a man were dependent upon the desires of himself, his kinsmen, and the bestowing kin. Choice was not apparent in the second form of wife promising, *via* the male initiation rituals. These rites of passage were mandatory for all males. But, whereas in the bestowal practice it was a woman who did the promising, during an initiation it was other men who became wife pledgers.

Before a male was considered a man, and marriageable, he had to be both circumcised and subincised. As is well documented (Meggitt 1962:313), the Aborigines of the Western Desert believe the former operation to be the most important and dangerous of the two, as it involved the ritual, though symbolic, death and rebirth of the initiate. The circumcised youth was, however, only half a man (*bugudidjara*), and still ineligible to fully participate in men's activities or take a spouse.[8] Both rituals were secret, sacred, and restricted to men, although women did participate in certain of the activities. It was the men who decided such matters as who was to be initiated, when the ritual was to take place, and who the body operators were to be. In all cases, these latter persons ideally had to be distant 'MB' and 'MBS', who were not themselves actual father and son.

The 'MB' and 'MBS' who initiated ego, and held his life in their hands, automatically promised to provide him with a wife. This woman was a 'D' of the 'MB' and a 'Z' of the 'MBS', but, in the 'give away' ceremony, she need not have been the actual daughter or sister of any of the initiators. Furthermore, the body operations constituted the beginning of a new set of relationships between initiate and 'doctors'. The operators were henceforth *manggalji* to the young man and his close kinsmen, which meant they were to be avoided as much as possible in daily activity. This new behavioural pattern was reflected in the kin terminological system, for whereas ego formerly had addressed the operating 'MB' as *gaga* or *gamuru* and 'MBS' as *jungguri,* 'doctors' were now referred to as *djarbuḍa* or *wabudju* and *burga* respectively.

As can be seen, both the practice of spouse-bestowal and wife-promising operated to greatly extend one's options. It was not just one person pledging to provide ego with his or her real or classificatory daughter or sister, rather many people committed themselves to ensuring a man would receive a wife. The *junggudjara, djarbuḍa,* and *burga*, in effect, undertook to supply ego with a spouse. This situation existed because, in part, they were in most instances chosen by others. The decision that a woman would become *junggudjara* to a man was reached by her kinsmen and herself. Likewise, the men who became *djarbuḍa* and *burga* to an initiate were selected and approved by all the men present for the ritual.

Ideally, the bestower and promisers provided actual kin as the spouse, but it was more important that the future spouse of the young man came from the territory of one of the indebted. That is, while the girl may not have been the actual daughter of a *djarbuḍa,* she should have come from his country.

From the above description it becomes apparent that in the Australian Western Desert (1) marriage to an actual MBD/FZD was forbidden, and (2) direct sister exchange, as modelled by Radcliffe-Brown and completely accepted by Lévi-Strauss, was ruled out. Even if actual sisters were promised and presented to ego by his *burga* — rarely the case —

ego's sister(s) would not have gone to his own operators. These men received their wives from elsewhere, through their own initiators. Ego's sisters would have been given to the youth he helped operate on.

As the direct exchange of sisters did not and could not occur in the system, there were always more than two groups involved in the alliance network. Owing to the incest taboo, ego could not marry an actual MBD or FZD. Therefore he could not take a wife from or marry into the same group his father had married into as this unit contained his actual MBD. Nor would he have been able to marry a female from the group FZ married into. Contrary to Radcliffe-Brown's model, this means there was always a recognition of at least four lines of descent — FF, FM, MF, and MM — for the direct kin in the second ascending generation were unrelated by actual connections. Ego's father could not marry his own MBD/FZD, because ego's mother came to his father from a distantly related group. FF and FM were not actual brother and sister to MM and MF. It follows from this that the system as found in the Western Desert was quite capable of indefinite expansion, contrary to Lévi-Strauss's conclusions. The units would be incapable of such expansion only if Radcliffe-Brown's ideal model had been rigidly adhered to. If one side of the two part whole were to split into two similarly constituted units the other side would have to divide also giving rise to the two, four, eight, etc., progression. But groups did not behave in this neat manner. Indeed, in the desert system a basic two group operation was not feasible. Ego could not marry females so closely related. Women circulated indirectly — not directly — from initiator to initiate, making the system asymmetrical in its operation.

Kinship in the Australian Western Desert

Western Desert kinship formed a closed system, with ego related to all other persons in his social universe by actual or classificatory linkages (Romney & Epling 1958:68). Corresponding with the terminological system (see Table 8.1) was a system of behaviour; e.g., *umari* ('FZ') was avoided, *mama* ('F') was respected. Although there was no distinction between the terms applied to actual and classificatory relatives, it was quite possible to differentiate own (*jungara*) from more distant kin. But in most situations this was completely unnecessary as everyone knew who everyone else's kin were, and it was more important that two men behaved towards one another as brothers than the incidental fact that they were or were not consanguineally related.

In addition to forming a closed system of relationships and behaviour, kinship determined marriage. It should be recalled that among the Kariera a man married a woman whom he called by the term applied to an actual MBD (Radcliffe-Brown 1930:8). In the Western Desert this rule was not applicable, for actual cross-cousins were kept terminologically distinct from more distant 'MBD/FZD' (*njuba*) and called *djudu/ malanj* or *jingani* (Tonkinson 1966: 111–12). Likewise, male cross-cousins — the brothers of *jingani* — were termed differently from their

Table 8.1   *Western Desert kinship terminology*

djamu	FF, FFB, MF, MFB, SS, DS
gami	FM, FMZ, MM, MMZ, SD, DD
mama	F, FB
jibi	M, MZ
gaga or *gamuṛu*	MB
guṇḍili	close FZ
umaṛi	distant FZ
guḍa/maḷanj	elder/younger B, FBS, MZS, close FZS, MBS
djuḍu/maḷanj	elder/younger Z, FBD, MZD, close FZD, MBD
wadjira or *djamiḍi*	close FZS, MBS
jingaṇi	close FZD, MBD
jungguṛi, maridji, or *maguṇḍa*	distant FZS, MBS; potential or actual WB
njuba or *guri*	distant FZD, MBD; potential or actual W
gadja	S, BS, ZS
juṇḍalba	D, BD, ZD

more distant counterparts. Occasionally they were addressed as *guḍa/ maḷanj*, the same as siblings and parallel-cousins, but most usually as *wadjira* or *djamidi*, meaning close cross-cousin of the same sex. The brothers of *njuba* — distant 'MBD/FZD' — were called *jungguṛi, maridji,* or *maguṇḍa* (see Table 8.2).

The distinction between close and distant cross-cousins had a counterpart in the first ascending generation wherein father's actual sister was distinguished from his classificatory sisters. As noted, all 'FZ' or 'WM', i.e. the mothers of *njuba*, were referred to as *umaṛi*, and, because they were potential mothers-in-law, were consistently avoided. But what of the mothers of those actual (too close to marry) FZD? Had they to be avoided also? No. As they could not properly become WM, there was no necessity of avoidance, and, instead of *umaṛi*, they were called *guṇḍili* (close, patrilineally related female of the first ascending generation). There was no corresponding close/distant terminological distinction for MB and 'MB'. All such men were called *gaga*, unless chosen as ego's (or ego's brother's) initiators, in which case they became *djarbuḍa* (*manggalji*). The actual father of a man's wife could be either a *gaga* or *djarbuḍa,* depending upon whether or not his body operating 'MB' provided his own or one of his 'B' daughters as ego's spouse. (In the same way ego's wife's brother could be either a *jungguṛi* or *burga.*)

Until now the categories close and distant have been used rather loosely, because such terms are relative and definable only by reference to specific systems. That is, it is problematical whether a particular so- ciety choose to place the near/distant boundary at siblings, first cousins,

Table 8.2 *Sibling and cousin terminology*

	B	Z	FBS/MZS	FBD/MZD	FZS/MBS	FZD/MBD	'FZS/MBS'	'FZD/MBD'
Laverton (Elkin 1940)	kurda/malan	kanguna, narumba, or tudana/ malan (ya)	same as B	same as Z	same as B or toni wadjara	same as Z or toni wadjara	marit(j)i	kuri or madongu
Ooldea (Berndt and Berndt 1942)	'guda/ 'malang	'kang 'garu or 'tu 'du/ 'malang	same as B	same as Z	'malang or 'guda	'narumba	'maradu or 'maritji	'guri or 'ma 'dong
Jigalong (Tonkinson 1966)	babadu or guda/ malangu	djudu/ malangu	same as B	same as Z or njarumba	same as B or djamidi, wadjira	same as Z or jingani	jungguri or magunda	madungu
Wiluna	babadu or guda/ malanj	djudu/ malanj	same as B	same as Z or njarumba	same as B or djamidi, wadjira	same as Z or jingani	jungguri, maridji, or magunda	njuba, madungu, or guri

Note that in each case 'FZS/MBS' and 'FZD/MBD' are distinguished terminologically from other relatives.

second cousins, or further. David H. Turner (personal communication) suggests that in Aboriginal society the line was drawn on the basis of descent from the second ascending generation. That is, persons sharing a common second ascending generation ancestor (*djamu* or *gami* in the Western Desert) would have been considered close, while people not so connected were distant kin.

Although this hypothesis is supported in part by Western Desert data, the problem is perhaps more complex than Turner's explanation allows. This is suggested by the kin term *djamiḍi,* denoting close cross-cousin of the same sex. Aborigines note a connection between this term and the word *djamu* (second ascending generation male). Naturally, persons having the same *djamu* would either be siblings, actual parallel cousins, or actual cross-cousins. However, this apparently neat picture was complicated somewhat by additional factors. First, there was friendship. If, for example, two old classificatory 'B' were extremely close to one another, then it is likely that their descendants would regard each other as genealogically too close to permit marriage between the SS of one and the DD of the other, particularly if the elders were still alive.

Secondly, the *ngamuringu* practice (*ngamu* close, *ri* became) complicated matters by 'making close' certain potential spouses (*njuba*) because it was felt that a man should not have too many 'wives'. Decisions as to exactly which males and females were to be *ngamuringu* rested almost entirely with the older men. There appears to be no particular pattern in the selections, and the new relationship brought into effect by the practice was in no way extended to other kin. The change was from one of distance (*njuba*) to one of closeness (*jingaṇi* or *djuḍu/maḷanj*) in terminology, and was reflected behaviourally. The minimal restraint (relaxed) relationship existing between potential spouses became a restricted, opposite sex sibling one. The fact that a particular female was *ngamuringu* did not stop ego from being able to marry her sister, as long as the latter was not also made close, nor did it influence the avoidance relationship between himself and the woman's mother.[9]

Thirdly, there was the very real, but frequently unreported, phenomenon of the proliferation of close kin owing to polygynous and serial unions. While this aspect is only indirectly related to Turner's idea regarding closeness and distance, it becomes a problem in the determination of actual kinsmen. Meggitt (1965:146) has observed that Aborigines, because of the taboo on mentioning the names of dead persons, make poor subjects for genealogical collection, and Yengoyan (1970b:425-6) has made the dubious suggestion that they forget about the previous existence of deceased individuals and display a lack of concern regarding birth order. Rose (1965:2) alone has suggested plural and serial unions as being additional areas of perplexity. Traditionally there was no restriction placed on the number of wives a man might have at any given time, although practical concerns of acquiring, maintaining, and keeping spouses were such as to ensure that the number remained small. In addition, a man could have a number of spouses during his lifetime, some of whom died and others who left him or were given away. Women also had different spouses at various stages in their lives. As a result, any *djamu* could be traced through a large number of connecting links. He had children by his wives and his wives may have had offspring by other men. All these children would be considered close or actual siblings. They, in turn, had children of their own, giving rise to even more close relatives. By the second descending generation the near links were numerous, and made the determination of close and distant kinsmen quite complicated.

All one may safely state is that near kin were such because they shared a common ancestor in the second ascending generation. Not all remaining female cross-cousins were marriageable, however, for some were close because of associations formed in ascending generations, others had been made close by the *ngamuringu* practice, and still more, owing to the proliferation of kin *via* polygyny and serial unions, were problematical even for the Aborigines. Whether a man would have been allowed to marry the DD of a woman who was for a short time married to his own FF, but had no children by him, was one to be weighed in association with affections and the opinions of others. If the link was tenuous and best forgotten the union was allowed to take place.

Alliance in the Australian Western Desert

The prevalent model of symmetrical exchange systems is naively conceived, the notion of two groups blithely swapping women just does not hold. The prescribed form of marriage to a distant cross-cousin made confined exchange impossible. Several or even many groups were involved in the total system because an alliance established between two groups by marriage could not be renewed or re-established for at least three generations.[10] It was only when the alliance was on the verge of being forgotten, or had been, that it was reconstituted.

Alliance is too often discussed in terms of marriage and the exchange of women, but this is only the manner in which such links come into being and are maintained. But what did all this mean for the Aborigines themselves? Alliance in the Western Desert was a part of the wider, overarching belief system that helped ensure survival. The adaptive advantages of the system under desert conditions lay in the flexibility provided for spatial mobility when the availability of resources are unpredictable. If a territorial group was allied to only one other unit, then drought or lack of food resources in the group's country would not necessarily have been alleviated by a move to the area of the other. The allied area might also have been experiencing hard times or pressures owing to the influx of a new population.

In the Western Desert, the wide-spread alliance network overcame these difficulties. While each group occupied and exploited its own territory, it was linked and in contact with many other similarly structured units. The shared belief system required periodic gatherings which were facilitated by group ties of kinship and marriage. These ties were established, renewed, or validated during the ritual assemblies.

Within this system, brothers did not marry women from the same area and co-wives in polygynous unions were from different countries, being sisters in the classificatory sense only. Furthermore, ego could not marry into the groups from which his father took women. This would not only have been considered incestuous, it was unnecessary as a man had access to the country of his mother, just as he had rights within his own (his father's) territory. While mother's and wife's groups were the primary alliance units, ego also had access to additional areas through the primary links of his close kin. This meant that if a group was experiencing hard times not all its members had to go into a single other region, as would be the case with restricted exchange and symmetrical alliance. There was a degree of choice involved in the determination as to which areas persons would go to. Because of his vast network, ego had alliances with numerous groups.

Conclusion

The group to which symmetrical alliance owes so much, the Kariera, is superficially like Western Desert groups in both kinship and marriage. The main area of divergence is that in the former marriage to an actual MBD/FZD was prescribed, while in the latter it was proscribed. Since the taboo on actual MBD/FZD unions is almost universal in Australia, the Kariera were either unique in their marriage practices or more flexible in actual operation than the idealized structure would imply. Indications are that both points are true. As Radcliffe-Brown admitted, only a limited number of unions conform to the ideal. This, in itself, would not disturb the symmetrical alliance idea. Among the Kariera, however, when marriage was not to an actual cross-cousin it was to a classificatory one.

In the Western Desert, as well as other areas where variant forms of the Kariera type are found, the situation is different. Close cross-cousin marriage was prohibited. Marriage was with a distant kinsman, 'MBD/FZD', the two categories being distinguished terminologically. Furthermore, although the kinship system appears to be bilateral and capable of accommodating the direct exchange of women between an 'MBS' and 'FZS', women circulated indirectly. Men received promises of wives from 'FZ', 'MB', and 'MBS/FZS'. This served to extend options and move women unidirectionally. For example, an 'MBS' body operator would give ego a country 'Z' as a wife, but ego did not reciprocate. His Z went to the people he initiated, while his own initiator (WB) would receive women from his operators. In this way each group was allied with several others, thus enhancing the chances of survival in difficult periods. Indirect exchange was the rule. Direct reciprocity, and therefore symmetrical alliance, was impossible.

Notes
  1. The field work on which this paper is based was carried out at Wiluna, Western Australia, and financed by a Fulbright-Hays Fellowship (Australian-

American Educational Foundation Grant) and the Australian Institute of Aboriginal Studies. I wish to thank Professor Ronald M. Berndt, Dr Francis J. Murray, and Dr Robert Tonkinson for their comments on an earlier manuscript.

2. The rationale behind inter-group alliance has often been vague, or else avoided, in discussions of systems articulation.

3. Classificatory relationships will be distinguished from actual consanguineal and affinal ones through the use of inverted commas , so that, for example, F denotes ego's father and 'F' indicates ego's classificatory fathers.

4. Aptly Korn (1973:143) has asked, 'why does he [Lévi-Strauss] need to refer at all to the Kariera, the Aranda, the Dieri, the Mara, and the rest, if he is not concerned with their actual systems as forms of collective ideation and social life?'

5. This would include systems like Radcliffe-Brown's (1969:500) Kumbaingeri; and Elkin's (1964:72-75) Nyul-Nyul.

6. There is no Western Desert word equivalent to the English 'marriage'. *Guridjara* 'spouse' (*guri*) 'having' (*djara*), although close to 'marriage' includes much more, for it also pertains to persons promised to each other but not yet living together.

7. Although this ceremonial presentation is in some respects similar to the mother-in-law bestowal practice described by Shapiro (1969b; 1970), it is definitely not the 'WM' but the issue of her womb which is conceived of as being bestowed.

8. The *bugudidjara* stage means having or possessing (*djara*) the chignon or hair bun worn by initiates (*bugudi*).

9. Tonkinson (1966:121-2; 1974:51) reports a similar practice, termed *ngaranmaridi,* for the peoples now residing at Jigalong, Western Australia.

10. Dumont (1953:38) says, 'theoretically, to maintain the relation, one marriage in each generation is enough, but the more marriages of that type occur, the firmer the alliance relationship will be'. Does he mean by this that a marriage must occur between the units in every generation to keep the alliance going? Data from the Western Desert contradict this conclusion, as inter-group alliances remained intact despite the fact that marriages could not take place every generation.

References

BARNES, J. A. (1971), *Three Styles in the Study of Kinship*, London.
BECKETT, J. (1967), Marriage, Circumcision and Avoidance Among the Maljangaba of North-west New South Wales, *Mankind*, **6**: 457–64.
BERNDT, R. M. (ed.) (1970), *Australian Aboriginal Anthropology*, Nedlands: U of WA Press.
BERNDT, R. M. & C. H. Berndt (1942), 'A Preliminary Report of Field Work in the Ooldea Region, Western South Australia', *Oceania*, **13**:143–69.
—— (1964), *The World of the First Australians*, Sydney.
DUMONT, L. (1953), 'The Dravidian Kinship Terminology as an Expression of Marriage', *Man*, **53**:34–39·
—— (1966), 'Descent or Intermarriage: A Relational View of Australian Section Systems', *Southwestern Journal of Anthropology*, **22**:231–50.
ELKIN, A. P. (1963), 'Rethinking Anthropology: A Review, *Oceania*, **34**:81–107.
—— (1964), *The Australian Aborigines*, Garden City.
FIRTH, R. (1966), 'Twins, Birds and Vegetables: Problems of Identification in Primitive Religious Thought', *Man*, **1**:1–17.
FOX, R. (1967), Review of M. J. Meggitt, *Desert People*, *Man*, **2**:329–30.
FRY, H. K. (1950), 'Aboriginal Social Systems', *Transactions of the Royal Society of South Australia*, **73**:282–94.

—— (1968), 'Gidjingali Marriage Arrangements', in R. B. Lee & I. De Vore (eds), *Man the Hunter*, Chicago.

KORN, F. (1973), *Elementary Structures Reconsidered: Lévi-Strauss on Kinship*, London.

LEACH, E. R. (1966), *Rethinking Anthropology*, New York.

—— (1970), *Claude Lévi-Strauss*, New York.

LÉVI-STRAUSS, C. (1960), 'On Manipulated Sociological Models', *Bijdragen tot de Taal-, Land- en Volkenkunde,* 116:45–54.

—— (1969), *The Elementary Structures of Kinship*, London.

MADDOCK, K. (1969), 'Alliance and Entailment in Australian Marriage', *Mankind*, 7:19–26.

MEGGITT, M. J. (1962), *Desert People*, Sydney.

—— (1965) 'Marriage Among the Walbiri of Central Australia: A Statistical Examination', in R. M. & C. H. Berndt (eds), *Aboriginal Man in Australia*, Sydney.

PIDDINGTON, R. (1970), 'Irregular Marriages in Australia', *Oceania*, 40:329–42.

RADCLIFFE-BROWN, A. R. (1913), 'Three Tribes of Western Australia', *Journal of the Royal Anthropological Institute*, 43:143–95.

—— (1930–31), 'The Social Organization of Australian Tribes', *Oceania*, 1:34–63, 426–56.

—— (1941), 'The Study of Kinship Systems', *Journal of the Royal Anthropological Institute*, 71:1–18

—— (1969), Appendix, Lévi-Strauss (1969:499–500)

ROMNEY, A. K., & P. J. EPLING (1958), 'A Simplified Model of Kariera Kinship,' *American Anthropologist*, 60:59–74.

ROSE, F. G. G. (1965), *The Wind of Change in Central Australia: The Aborigines of Angus Downs*, Berlin.

SHAPIRO, W. (1969a), 'Asymmetric Marriage in Australia and Southeast Asia', *Bijdragen tot de Taal-, Land- en Volkenkunde*, 125:71–9.

—— (1969b), 'Semi-Moiety Organization and Mother-in-Law Bestowal in North-east Arnhem Land', *Man*, 4:624–40.

—— (1970), 'Local Exogamy and the Wife's Mother in Aboriginal Australia', in Berndt (1970:51–69).

TONKINSON, R. (1966), Social Structure and Acculturation of Aborigines in the Western Desert, unpublished MA dissertation, University of Western Australia.

—— (1970), 'Aboriginal Dream-Spirit Beliefs in a Contact Situation: Jigalong, Western Australia,' in Berndt (1970:277–91).

—— (1974), *The Jigalong Mob: Aboriginal Victors of the Desert Crusade*, Menlo Park.

VAN DER LEEDAN, A. C. (1970), *Australia and Melanesia: Propositions Regarding Comparative Research. Anniversary Contributions to Anthropology, Twelve Essays*, Leiden.

WHITE, H. C. (1963), *An Anatomy of Kinship: Mathematical Models for Structures of Cumulated Roles*, Englewood Cliffs.

YENGOYAN, A. A. (1970a), 'Demographic Factors in Pitjandjara Social Organization', in Berndt (1970:70–91).

—— (1970b), 'Open Networks and Native Formalism: The Mandaya and Pitjandjara Cases', in M. Freilich (ed.), *Marginal Natives: Anthropologist at Work*, New York.

9
Mardujarra Kinship

R. TONKINSON

The Aborigines whose homelands lie on the western side of the vast Gibson Desert in Western Australia have as their central reference point a giant salt lake, known to them as Gumbubindil and to Europeans as Lake Disappointment. This striking landform covers about 2000 square kilometres and straddles the Tropic of Capricorn some 600 kilometres south-east of the Indian Ocean. The people whose territories surround the lake and extend eastwards are members of several distinct dialect groups: the Gardujarra, Budijarra, Giyajarra, Gurajarra and, the largest and most easterly, the Manjilyjarra. Collectively, these groups can be called the Mardujarra, a name coined by adding to the word *mardu*, 'Aboriginal person', the suffix *-jarra*, 'having', as the desert people themselves would do. They all speak closely related dialects of the same basic Western Desert language and culturally all are very similar.

Today the groups making up the Mardujarra number about eight hundred people and live in settlements, having long since migrated from their desert homelands. It is impossible to offer an accurate estimate of their population before European intrusion, but it was probably fewer than one thousand. The desert homelands of the Mardujarra are now empty, so the use here of the present tense pretends that the situation described is one in which no Europeans have yet arrived. It is a time when the horizons around Gumbubindil are always smudged with smoke and small bands of Mardujarra hunters and gatherers are on the move.

This is an account of how the Mardujarra organize and conduct their social relationship. Much of it applies to other parts of Aboriginal Australia. The system of relatedness known as kinship plays a vital role in the social life of all Aborigines; it is important to understand why this should be so. The nature of the landscape and the amount of available food resources are important, because to some extent they limit the range of choices human beings have in deciding how to organize their society. In the Gibson Desert, one of the world's harshest environments, fresh water and food are almost always in short supply. The Aborigines are forced to spend most of their time in small groups spaced far apart and to move

First published in D. J. Mulvaney & J. Peter White (eds), *Australians to 1788*, Sydney: Fairfax, Syme & Weldon Associates, 1987. Reproduced with the permission of the author and the copyright owners.

over long distances in their search for food and water. Prolonged droughts at times force some groups to migrate temporarily into the territories of their neighbours until an adequate rainfall replenishes the resources of their homelands.

Under these circumstances, the survival of the Mardujarra depends on their ability to gain access to the land and resources of others. This depends in turn on their maintaining arrangements that guarantee a cohesive society, the members of which can agree about the very fundamentals of existence. Relatively few people are scattered over a large area, yet they need to have a sense of community based on shared values, behaviour and rules for living. Their bonds of unity must be strong enough to overcome local differences and minor conflicts in the interests of the survival of the society at large. How are these requirements satisfied in the Gibson Desert? And what binds together these small and scattered bands into a coherent society? The bonds of shared kinship are central, as are friendships and alliances founded on marriage, religion and common notions about what is fundamentally important in life. Aborigines view the world in deeply spiritual terms, and believe that every major facet of life and culture has a religious basis.

The Desert Landscape

Although marked on maps as a lake, Lake Disappointment is often dry. It fills only when there is sufficient runoff from rainfall in the catchment area. Wet or dry, the salty lake surface never attracts Aborigines, who carefully avoid even its margins. This largest single landform on the western side of the Gibson Desert remains undisturbed by humans because beneath its surface, say the Aborigines, lies another world with its own sun and heavenly bodies. The inhabitants are the Ngayunangalgu, fierce cannibal beings who will kill and devour any Aborigine who strays too close. The lake, Gumbubindil, has an important place in the myths and rituals of neighbouring Aborigines, but it is not an economic resource.

Vivid red sandhills are the most common landform in the Gibson Desert. Lightly covered with shrubs, grasses and a few trees, these long, parallel ridges stand 15 to 20 metres high and a few hundred metres apart. Between them are flat sand plains, grassed with spinifex and supporting scattered trees of several different species. The red of the sandhills is intensified in stony outcrops and ridges as well as rugged, stepped 'breakaway' formations that stand out above the dunes. In some areas, these uplands are surrounded by mulga thickets or flat gibber plains. The dry watercourses radiating out from higher areas are marked by large river gums, acacia shrubs and grasses. Shallow claypans are widespread and valuable because after rain they fill, attracting both wildlife and hunters. Rugged, narrow gorges can be found in most hilly areas and some are important to Aborigines because they have sheltered, long-lasting pools. Most also mark the site of some mythological event that occurred in the Dreaming. Some of the deeper gorges have distinctive vegetation and wildlife and their environs are favoured as summer camping spots when the searing heat dries up other surface waters and forces groups of people to retreat to their most reliable waterholes.

The Gibson Desert is a world of extremes, ranging from midsummer days when shade temperatures soar into the high forties to freezing winter dawns that turn drinking water in wooden containers to ice. Rainfall is uncommon and erratic, so it is essential that everyone knows well the location of established water sources such as rockholes, creek bed soaks, wells and the occasional spring. These are generally better protected than surface waters from an extreme rate of evaporation during the summer months. Water is indeed the most critical resource, so the desert people plan their movements according to its availability. They frequently follow well-defined waterhole routes, which are often said to mark the paths of ancestral beings who created the water sources in the course of their Dreaming adventures. Only after widespread, soaking rains can people move out to the margins of their territories and exploit the replenished food and water resources. As the surface catchments dry up, the Aborigines retreat towards longer-lasting waterholes.

Despite its difficulties for human life, the Gibson Desert is home to a variety of plants and animals that are exploited for food. Lizards, small marsupials, grass seeds, bush tomatoes (*Solanum* sp.), berries, fruits such as the quandong and wild fig, and yams (*Dioscorea* sp.) are among the most important food sources. The Mardujarra know exactly when and where foods are available. The likely location of abundant supplies of a staple food influences their itineraries. The desert environment keeps the density of population and the size of groups much lower than in more fertile parts of the continent. But cultural factors are also important in determining the size and composition of the travelling groups and influencing decisions about when and where to go next.

To the outsider, the desert seems overpowering in its immensity. Seemingly stretching forever, it dwarfs humanity. Yet the Mardujarra who call it home can read in its landforms the mythological origins of their society as well as the sources of their own being, and are thus strongly attached, spiritually and emotionally, to the land. Because their under-standing of their country is at the same time both practical and spiritual, they grow up with a strong sense of familiarity and security. They have an acute awareness not only of what can be seen but of what can be sensed; somewhere out there are other groups of kin and friends whose hunting or campfire smokes are welcome signs that all the desert's vastness is not empty.

Distant smoke means more than the mere presence of others. It promises singing and perhaps dancing; certainly talking, with animated discussion of the big meeting somewhere soon that will bring together perhaps two hundred people in many bands for a brief period of intense social activity that will be the high point of the Mardujarra year.

Local Organisation

In the Gibson Desert, as elsewhere in Aboriginal Australia, the basic social unit is the family. Many Mardujarra families are polygynous; that is, their male head has more than one wife at a time. This man is usually middle-aged or older. Few men have more than three wives at any given time and most younger husbands have only one. Women, however, commonly expect a succession of husbands; they are married for the first time in early adolescence, often as second or third wives of quite old men. Widowhood is rarely permanent and women expect to remarry within a few years of their husbands' deaths. As they get older they have more say in the choice of their next husband.

Infant betrothal is common and most marriages are arranged by senior members of the two families or groups of kin involved. The man who is chosen to perform the rite of circumcision on a youth must promise him a wife who is one of the man's daughters. After the youth has completed a long period of initiation into the secret religious life of his group, he will be permitted to claim the girl as his wife. She will normally be a distant relative, coming from a territory quite some distance away from that of her husband. People related as in-laws are expected to enter into a long-term relationship, involving the exchange of visits and gifts. For this reason, marriage is an important basis for the formation of strong alliances between groups living in different parts of the desert. In times of severe drought and food shortages in their territory, people can always go and visit their in-laws and be sure of a good reception as well as access to food supplies.

The Aboriginal group most easily discerned by an outside observer is the band, because it is the unit that travels and lives together. Among the Mardujarra the band consists most often of two to four families and seldom numbers more than about thirty people. Like other Aborigines, the Mardujarra prefer to travel in bands because this grouping, larger than the family, offers greater potential for sharing and sociability. Even so, each family generally camps a little apart from the others and has its own cooking and sleeping fires. This allows for a measure of privacy at night, especially since older boys tend to camp together away from their parents. All camps are within shouting distance, however, and many are the nights when the campsite is alive with the sounds of shouted conversations, debates or arguments before people fall asleep between the small sleeping fires behind their windbreaks.

The male adults of the band sometimes co-operate in hunting large game such as kangaroos or emus. If they are lucky in the hunt, they cook the animal near where they killed it, then butcher it and carry large chunks back to camp, where it will be distributed to all members of the band according to customary rules. If there is only one lucky hunter, he will deny himself a choice part of the animal, in keeping with Mardujarra society's strong emphasis on unselfishness in all things, especially food. To be labelled greedy is extremely shameful. In their food-gathering activities, women do not need to co-operate or to divide up the day's yield, since luck plays little or no part in their productive endeavours. They prefer to go out in groups so that they can chat while working and their younger children can play together. While boys and small girls do not have to contribute to the quest for food, they often amuse themselves by hunting small game and gathering fruit or berries to nibble as snacks; in fact, people of all ages often snack during the day. By late afternoon —

much earlier in midsummer — the family groups have reassembled in the camp. They eat their main meal of the day in the early evening.

A band varies in size and membership from time to time as social and environmental circumstances change. It achieves a measure of stability despite these fluctuations because its male heads are often related in the male line (for example, an older man, two of his married sons and a brother's son and family). At any given time, however, some in-laws or others not related in the male line may also be travelling in the band. Stability is also afforded by the fact that every band under normal circumstances spends a great deal of time in its home territory or estate. The Mardujarra like to have their children born and raised in their father's home estate area and prefer that women eventually join the bands of their husbands after marrying. Since all fully initiated men share important responsibilities as guardians of sacred sites and associated ceremonial objects in their home estates, they endeavour to spend as much time as possible in or near these areas. From time to time they must organize and perform important rituals at specific sites in their homelands, so they try to remain within reasonable distance of them for most of their lives.

Bands may occasionally split into single-family units in very good or extremely bad times. Yet favourable and unfavourable environmental conditions can also encourage larger groupings, involving members of several neighbouring bands. This may be caused either by an abundance of food in a given area or by severe shortages of water that force two or more bands to retreat to a single reliable water source, usually during the late summer.

Individual bands also lose their identity once or twice a year when big meetings are held. The site and approximate time are known in advance; in fact, if there are boys to be initiated, they and older guardians are sent out to contact as many bands as possible and to summon them to the meeting. Such large gatherings may be held at any time of the year, as long as the chosen venue offers a good source of water and enough food to supply up to one hundred people for a couple of weeks. Most venues are at or near sites of religious significance, and one motive for the meetings is to conduct ritual activities. After an initial tense period in which all outstanding disputes must be brought to settlement, ritual activities begin amid great excitement. People take the opportunity to exchange gifts with their kin, to socialize and to catch up with news and gossip, as well as to plan their future movements and discuss arrangements for the next big meeting. In the desert, such meetings are the only occasions when the society at large is visible and its vital concerns are dramatized and thus reinforced in the eyes of its members.

Estate groups play an important role in Aboriginal culture but, unlike the band, the estate group cannot easily be discerned. Its members never assemble as a group and to the exclusion of members of other estate groups, nor is its membership rigidly defined. Most men maintain strong allegiance to just one estate group but have interests in others. Women, on the other hand, often live far from their home estates after marriage and become more involved in the estates of their husbands. Every linguistic unit, such as the Giyajarra or Budijarra, is made up of a number of estate groups, the members of which are normally scattered in bands throughout or even beyond their home territories. The core of the estate group is men, women and children who are related through the male line. They share strongly felt bonds to a number of sites and tracts of country that together make up the home estate. Its boundaries may be vague, because no two people share an identical constellation of places which in sum comprises their *manda*, or country. However, many people will name the same major site as their *yinda*, 'main place' within the home estate.

People can claim affiliation with an estate group through several avenues. One is descent from the father. They may also claim membership in their mother's estate, although among the Mardujarra this link is considered secondary. Totemic links are also important. Every person is thought to have lived before as a kind of spirit essence left behind by a particular creative being or group of beings during their travels in the Dreaming. Both the place where they were left behind and the identify of the creative beings involved are always known and are important components in individual identity. Estate membership may also be claimed by those who have grown up in and around the estate.

A further avenue of estate affiliation is active involvement in rituals performed periodically by estate members. Middle-aged and older men, especially, affirm membership by demonstrating responsibility towards the care and guardianship of sites and objects that form the secret and sacred core of the estate. Indeed, religious ties to the estate are more important than ties of shared descent; strong religious bonds may be forged with men who are not close relatives in the male line. The Mardujarra show no interest in tracing their ancestry back through many generations. It matters more to know how and where each person came to be left behind in the Dreaming, a time well beyond all generational counting and yet one to which every person feels strongly connected by spiritual descent.

The initiated men who are the estate's guardians not only look after the caches of sacred objects hidden at every 'main place' throughout the Gibson Desert, but also organize the performance of rituals that belong to the estate and derive from the activities of the Dreaming beings who first created the territory. One important ritual, the *mirdayidi*, is held at every estate to induct young initiates, brought together from neighbouring estates, into the secrets of the collection of secret objects. These symbolize the unity of humans with land, spiritual powers and the Dreaming. By partaking in the ceremonial feast that is central to the proceedings, the initiates have the estate opened up to them. Having consumed the spirit of the land, they gain future access to the estate and its resources. Once they have hunted meat to pay for the honour of witnessing the sacred core of the estate and learning its powerful secrets, they also have the right to take part in ritual activities there.

The collective identity implied by the name 'Mardujarra' is not shared by individual Aborigines, who identify themselves as members of a particular linguistic unit, such as Gardujarra or some smaller grouping. They often use dialect group labels when talking of their neighbours in adjoining territories and beyond. Yet, when asked to identify themselves, people most often use the name of their 'main place'. This is generally the major site within their home estate which will be known far and wide because of its religious significance. Each dialect group is associated with a stretch of territory. Commonly agreed boundary zones separate the various dialect units, but these are not always precisely defined.

Members of each unit recognize a common identity because of their shared dialect and neighbouring territories. They claim a measure of distinctiveness because of their particular dialect and some minor elements of belief or behaviour not shared with their neighbours. But there is plenty of overlap, both physically, where hunting–gathering ranges extend into the countries of their neighbours who speak different dialects, and socially. The links of kinship, marriage, religion, economics and shared values embrace all the dialect units and extend beyond the Gibson Desert to cover the entire Western Desert area, which occupies about one-sixth of the continent. Thus the Mardujarra constitute only one small part of a huge cultural system, and in some respects are indivisible from the rest because boundaries (even dialectal ones) do little to impede the free flow of people, objects and ideas across the sparsely occupied desert.

Members of a single dialect unit never congregate as a wholly exclusive group. Even the periodic big meetings attract members of several adjoining dialect units and vary in size and composition from one meeting to the next. However, members of the same dialect unit inevitably see more of one another and are more closely related than they are to members of other dialect units because of the territorial anchorage of each unit. But given the nature of marriage arrangements, kin networks, ritual responsibilities and the many other cultural elements that favour wider unities, it would be difficult for any one group to remain separated in such a way that dialect and social boundaries coincided. Indeed, it would be suicidal for any group to attempt to close its boundaries and resources to non-members, given the vagaries of rainfall. A certain degree of exclusiveness is essential for human social groups to maintain their sense of distinctiveness, but in areas as harsh as the Western Desert the need to assert a particular identity has to be balanced against the need to remain on good terms with neighbours.

The Western Desert is the largest culture area in the continent over which there is a free flow of news, ideas, objects and rituals. Although the settlements of Jigalong and Ooldea are about 1500 kilometres apart on opposite sides of the desert, songs recently recorded in Jigalong are almost identical in words and tune to those recorded by R. M. and C. H. Berndt 22 years earlier at Ooldea. The continued vitality of desert culture depends on these open lines of communication.

The Role of Kinship

It has been said that the Australian Aborigines, perhaps more than any other people, live in a universe of kin. Social relationships in which people refer to each other using terms of biological relatedness such as 'mother', 'son', 'cousin' are called kinship systems. In Aboriginal society everybody with whom a person comes into contact is called by a kinship term, and social interaction is guided by patterns of behaviour considered appropriate to particular kin relationships. Although a person's sex and age are important in determining social status, the system of kin relatedness largely dictates the way people behave towards one another, prescribing dominance, deference, obligation or equality as the basis of the relationship.

Aborigines employ what is known as a 'classificatory' kinship system; that is, the terms used among blood relatives are also used to classify or group more distantly related and unrelated people. Classificatory systems are based on two principles. First, siblings of the same sex (a group of brothers or a group of sisters) are classed as equivalent in the reckoning of kin relationships. Thus my father's brothers are classed as one with my father and are called 'father' by me; likewise, all women my mother calls 'sister' are my 'mothers'. Following this logic, the children of all people I call 'father' or 'mother' will be classed as my 'brothers' and 'sisters'. Second, in theory this social web can be extended to embrace all other people with whom one comes into contact in a lifetime. Strangers are rarely encountered in the desert but when they are, particularly at the time of big meetings, it is the job of knowledgeable elders to decide their kinship status. A single kin relationship between a stranger and a member of the encountering group is all that needs to be found, then all others present can work out their relationship to the stranger. If the stranger turns out to be a 'brother' of my 'mother's brother' then, following the first classifying principle, I will call him 'mother's brother'. In the etiquette of desert encounters, incoming stranger groups always camp at first some distance from the host group, until representative elders have met to work out their kin relationship. A formal introduction is then held before any mingling can take place between members of the two groups. Once all the correct kin relationships are established, people can adopt the appropriate behaviour — avoidance, joking, restraint — towards their new-found relatives.

Because kinship underlies virtually all social interaction, the Mardujarra frequently use kinship terms rather than names in addressing or referring to someone. The kinship system eliminates the need to negotiate or test how they will interact when they meet. The use of a kinship term carries with it the obligation to observe certain behavioural rules known to all, and this makes it easy for interaction to proceed along well-defined lines, regardless of whether the person encountered is loved or hated, admired or feared.

Education in kinship begins early in life, although children are not expected to obey the behavioural rules until they reach their teens and become self-conscious about them. Despite the great freedom small children enjoy, they are constantly being instructed about how to behave correctly towards their kin. They are born into a world of kinship and they hear kin terms being applied to themselves and others all the time. Without effort they learn both ideal and actual patterns of social relationships in preparation for the time when, unbidden by their elders, they will begin to conform to the behavioural codes.

All Mardujarra groups share the same basic system of kinship, despite some differences in the names for particular terms. Many of the terms are commonly used throughout the entire Western Desert region. The table gives by way of example the terminology used by members of the Gardujarra linguistic group.

MAN SPEAKING			WOMAN SPEAKING		
English	Gardujarra	Reciprocal	English	Gardujarra	Reciprocal
spouse	*mardungu*	*mardungu*	spouse	*mardungu*	*mardungu*
EB; FBS; MZS	*gurda*	*marlangu*	EB; FBS; MZS	*gurda*	*marlangu*
EZ; FBD; MZD	*jurdu*	*marlangu*	EZ; FBD; MZD	*jurdu*	*marlangu*
F; FB	*mama*	*gaja*	F; FB	*mama*	*yurndal*
M; MZ; WFZ	*yagurdi*	*gaja*	M; MZ	*yagurdi*	*yurndal*
S; DH; ZS; ZDH; BS	*gaja*	*mama; gaga*	S; BS; ZS	*gaja*	*yagurdi; gurndili*
D; ZSW; BD	*yurndal*	*mama*	D; BD; ZD	*yurndal*	*yagurdi; gurndili*
FZ	*gurndili*	*gaja*	FZ; HM	*gurndili;*	
				ngunyarri	*yurndal; ngunyarri*
MB; WF; MMBS	*gaga*	*gaja*	MB	*gaga*	*yurndal; ngunyarri*
WM and some					
FZ; MBW	*umari*	*umari*	DH	*umari*	*umari*
WB; ZH; MBS; FZS	*yungguri*	*yungguri*	BW; ZH; MBD; FZD	*juwari*	*juwari*
some MBS; FZS	*wajirra*	*wajirra*	some MBD; FZD	*wajirra*	*wajirra*
some MBD; FZD	*yingarni*	*yingarni*	some MBS; FZS	*yingarni*	*yingarni*
ZD	*ngunyarri*	*gaga*			
FF; MF; SS; DS and			FF; MF; SS; DS and		
ZDS; FMB; MMB	*nyamu*	*nyamu*	BDS; FMB; MMB	*nyamu*	*nyami*
FM; MM; SD; DD and			FM; MM; SD; DD and		
ZDD; FMZ; MFZ	*nyami*	*nyamu*	BDD; FMZ; MFZ	*nyami*	*nyami*
some MBDS; FZDS			some MMBS; MMBD		
and MBDD; FZDD	*bunyayi*	*bunyayi*	and MFZS; MFZD	*bunyayi*	*bunyayi*

Gardujarra terms of address; kin categories to which each term refers; reciprocal terms used by whoever is being addressed. The shorthand kin term designations mean the following: F = father; M = mother; B = brother; Z = sister; D = daughter; S = son, W = wife; H = husband; E = elder. Thus FZD means 'father's sister's daughter'; MMBS means 'mother's mother's brother's son'; HM means 'husband's mother', and so on.

Males and females often share the same terms. Members of each sex use seventeen kin terms; only the term *umari* is not used in address, because men and women so related must completely avoid one another most of the time. Several different categories of kin are normally lumped together under the one term. For example, all one's grandparent and grandchildren generations are condensed to two terms, which differ only for the sex of the person being addressed. Thus one's father's mother, mother's mother, daughter's daughter and son's daughter are all called *nyami*, and all male relatives in those two generations are called *nyamu*.

Likely behaviour patterns are suggested by whether or not pairs of individuals use identical reciprocal kin terms to address each other (for example, 'spouse'–'spouse' or 'cousin'–'cousin' are identical whereas 'father'–'daughter' or 'nephew'–'uncle' are not). Identical reciprocal terms, such as those used between most members of the same generation and their grandparents, indicate that there will be a fair degree of equality in expected behaviour. But when reciprocal terms are not identical, as between parents and children or older and younger siblings, this suggests status differences, with one member of the pair being expected to defer to the other. Older siblings share an obligation to discipline younger ones who misbehave, but they should also nurture them and defend them against unwarranted verbal or physical attack.

Kinship behaviour varies from complete avoidance at one extreme to special joking relationships at the other. These extremes are easy for an outsider to detect. With joking relationships, for example, the two people are expected to engage in uninhibited horseplay and loud verbal jousting, much of it rude and designed to delight the audience. A range of variation in actual behaviour is tolerated by the society at large, so people have more latitude in their relationships than any formal description of relationships could cover. Women enjoy a greater number of relatively uninhibited relationships with one another than do men. They may talk and interact freely with most other female kin, perhaps because they spend more time than men together in groups.

In relationships involving restraint of some kind, there is an underlying element of shame or embarrassment. Restrained behaviour suggests an inequality of status in which one of the pair should show deference, obedience, respect or submission to the other. Such unequal relationships are marked by restrictions of various kinds which prohibit touching, joking, calling by name, direct eye contact, the passing of objects from hand to hand, visiting the other person's camp, argument, sexual innuendo or physical assault. Among the Mardujarra, a man's behaviour towards most of his close adult blood relatives is characterized by various degrees of restraint. With fairly unrestrained behaviour, as between spouses, it is up to the pairs of individuals concerned to decide on a mutually satisfying level of familiarity and intimacy. Relative age, personality, individual inclination and emotional state play larger roles in these more open relationships.

The Mardujarra draw their marriage partners from the kin categories of cross-cousin; that is, people classed as mother's brother's children or father's sister's children. But some cross-cousins — some mother's brother's children and some father's sister's children — are classed as if they are siblings, and are not marriageable. People enjoy warm, close relationships with 'sibling' cross-cousins of the same sex (*wajirra*), but must show great restraint in their behaviour towards those of the opposite sex (*yingarni*). The Mardujarra prefer to select their actual spouses from other more distant and remotely related groups. So, although most people related by blood as cross-cousins call each other 'spouse', they do not often marry.

Because second cross-cousins (those whose parents are related as cross-cousins) are also classed as people whom one may marry, a wide selection of spouses is available. This is perhaps a major reason why there are so few incorrect marriages; that is, unions between pairs of people not related to each other as 'spouse'. The classificatory system defines all such wrong unions as incestuous, regardless of whether or not any blood relatedness is involved. A 'daughter' is a daughter, whether by blood link or classification, and must therefore be treated with a restraint devoid of sexual overtones; the same applies to all 'mothers' and 'sisters'.

The Ideal and the Actual

All over Australia, kinship is undeniably the most important single factor in structuring Aboriginal social relationships. It sets ideal or broad limits within which people are encouraged to behave. Harmony and order are maintained in this way, but what actually happens when people meet is more complicated than any ideal system. Within the varying limits set by kinship rules, there is much flexibility. Nobody is so imprisoned by the kinship system that he or she feels unable to give vent to feelings and emotions when the urge comes on. There is room for differences in individual temperament and personality, and allowances are made for the distorting effects of emotional outbursts and extreme anger.

In some respects, kin categories are imprecise. They make no distinction between distant kin and close blood relatives, nor do they offer clues about the emotional content of relationships. Although a person treats all women whom he or she calls 'mother' in much the same general way, the emotional component in the behaviour will vary according to whether the 'mother' is a close or distant relative. Apart from the few terms that distinguish older from younger siblings, the classificatory system ignores relative age, and in every kinship category there are people of all ages. Obviously, a person's behaviour towards an infant 'daughter' will differ markedly from that towards a 'daughter' who is an old woman.

Kinship is also modified by friendship. During childhood, friendships are made with many others of about the same age; so when the time comes to observe the rules of kinship behaviour, some people will bend them towards a more relaxed relationship, even if the system calls for restraint. Those who modify their behaviour in this way do so without fear of retribution. The system is not policed, but relies on inbuilt feelings of shame and embarrassment to inhibit people from breaking its rules.

Viewed as a community, the Mardujarra are a small population whose members encounter one another periodically throughout their lives. Even when they are not in actual contact, people hear news and gossip about others every time two bands meet. Despite their isolation for most of the year, people maintain a lively interest in the affairs of others. Everyone builds up a mental dossier on the personalities and behaviour of other members of the community. This gives them a fairly reliable guide to the likely actions and responses of many of their fellows in particular contexts — regardless, in some cases, of the kin relationships involved. As in all human societies, the decision to initiate or avoid contact is partly based on personal likes and dislikes. The physical setting, the weather and many other factors can influence a person's emotional state, general disposition and needs. People thus sometimes act with scant regard for the rules of kinship. An outsider, knowing only the kin categories involved, should have some success in predicting the kind of behaviour that results when two people meet. But unless the rules of behaviour demand complete avoidance, many other factors would have to be taken into account in order to be sure what will happen.

When life is proceeding normally for the Mardujarra, the gap between the ideal and reality in terms of kinship patterning and social interaction is small. But when things go wrong and emotions run high, people at times lose their normal inhibitions and ignore the rules governing proper conduct towards kin. What seems at first to be a minor upset can suddenly inflame tempers and erupt into angry confrontations, with threats or acts of violence resulting. Fortunately for law and order, the passions that can be aroused so quickly tend to die down rapidly, and people do not as a rule hold grudges.

Madujarra adults are usually pleasantly disposed, have a keen sense of humour and are not egotistical. When excessive or antisocial behaviour occurs, as it must do at times in all societies, the culprit is said to have become *ngagumba*, which translates variously as 'mad', 'unknowing' or 'forgetful', and others try to restore equilibrium. Those who overstep the mark and ignore the restraints of correct kin behaviour are accused by others of being *gurndabarni*, 'without shame', and are exhorted to act *yurlubidingga*, 'according to the law'.

There are acceptable means of drawing attention to one's grievances without resort to disapproved behaviour. One such strategy is *yurndiri*, 'aggressive sulking', which involves drawing the attention of others to one's unhappiness. This forces them to enquire about the problem and thus enables the person to air his or her grievance in response, spared the embarrassment of having to initiate such action. Most people find it difficult to assert themselves forcefully in front of an audience of their peers. As confident oratory suggests egotism, the appropriate Mardujarra public speaking style is self-effacing and apologetic. This is why disputes are so often aired under cover of darkness, when families are sitting by their campfires. People in this situation are less inhibited about speaking their minds, and in the dark strong words are unlikely to lead to weapon-throwing.

The eruption of violent conflict within the band would cause severe damage to the fabric of everyday life, so there are strong sanctions against it. Within the family, however, wife-beating is treated as a private affair and other band members interfere only in protracted fights where serious injury seems likely. Conflicts among men are hedged about with conventions that permit them to give full rein to their anger in an atmosphere of drama and menace, but with a minimum of physical violence. Usually words rather than blows are exchanged and in such a way that honour is seen to be satisfied. Afterwards both parties may claim victory.

When the equilibrium of daily life is upset, people are likely to ignore the rules of kinship; yet the kinship system then comes into full play to control the situation and to restore order. Aboriginal society has no chiefs or law enforcement specialists. Apart from generalized status distinctions that favour older people over younger ones and men over women, social life is based on broadly egalitarian values. Conformity is maintained through individual self-regulation rather than through fear of external authority or the wrath of gods. There are no leaders of the kind who stand above their fellows and direct their activities or admonish offenders, regardless of circumstance or content. Leadership among the Mardujarra depends upon the particular situation. It is most often exercised in the realm of religious activity, but the leaders change according to the ritual that is being organized and performed. As the basic social unit is the band, leadership of the directorial kind is not needed, since most decisions are taken by family heads in consultation with other adult members of the group. People who disagree strongly with such decisions are free to leave the band and join another.

When disputes do break out, at whatever level, a group needs effective ways to resolve them, or at least to restore order. Kinship comes to the fore at such times as the means by which people decide what action is required. Depending on their kin relationship to those who are in conflict, other individuals will adopt one of several roles: to restrain, chastise, defend, substitute for, inflame and condemn, appeal to reason, disarm or weep and inflict injury on oneself, and so on. When conflict occurs within the band, close kin are generally involved, so most effort is directed towards resolving the problem as quickly as possible and with a minimum of bloodshed. The guiding structure is that of the kinship system.

The norms of kinship are indispensable guides in a wide variety of situations when decisions must be taken and action initiated by groups of people. This is particularly so in the organization and execution of many different religious activities. Middle-aged and older men make most of the decisions. They operate on the basis of consultation and consensus, but even in the complex organization of rituals, kinship considerations are never ignored or overridden by other factors. Even when men are called upon to direct, perhaps in the mounting of a major ritual, they never give commands to others whose kin relationship to them precludes such behaviour; instead, they use intermediaries or frame their commands as polite requests.

Although the kinship system may appear to constrain Aborigines unduly, they do not chafe under it. Its crucial role as a guide to behaviour and its law-like status, derived from the Dreaming, ensure that it is accepted without question. Kinship provides a useful yardstick both for one's own behaviour and for predicting the likely behaviour of others. People derive a strong sense of well-being from living within a network of kin that extends to the outer limits of their social world. The knowledge that everyone is related through kinship is a source of comfort and security, especially when people travel beyond their home territories.

The system of kin relatedness is bolstered by strongly held values that have their basis in religion. People are judged as worthy by others largely in terms of modesty, generosity and the willing fulfilment of kinship and ritual obligations. People are strongly obliged to care for and support those whose kin relationship demands it. When people grow old, they in turn can demand and expect to receive the same support from their younger kin. Young people are also obliged to reciprocate because of the store of knowledge that is entrusted to them by the older generation of men and women.

Social Categories

All Mardujarra are born into one of four named categories, or sections. These sections are never seen as actual gatherings, although there are times when members of paired sections congregate in one group; rather, they locate people within the social structure and have their greatest use among the Mardujarra as labels of address or reference. Personal names are not commonly used and people never refer by name to anyone with whom they have a relationship of restraint or avoidance. Within families and bands, kinship terms are commonly used, but beyond the range of close kin people make frequent use of section names when speaking to or about others. They do this despite there being only four terms, with the same term in use for male and female members of a section. This is not a very precise way of identifying others, yet people never seem to be in doubt as to who is being spoken to or referred to.

The section system is based on a few simple principles. The diagram gives the Mardujarra terminology, shared by all groups in this part of the Western Desert:

$$\text{BANAGA} \quad = \quad \text{GARIMARRA}$$
$$\text{BURUNGU} \quad = \quad \text{MILANGGA}$$

The equal signs indicate intermarrying pairs of sections, and each pair connects a generation. Thus a Banaga man marries a Garimarra woman he calls 'spouse', and their children are all members of the Milangga section; a Milangga man marries a Burungu 'spouse', and their children are all Banaga, and so on. A man, his wife and their children are always members of three different sections. This system cuts across not only the family, but also local groups such as the band and the estate group, as well as the kinship system.

Sections are of a different order from kinship, which is a network of relationships that spreads out from each individual in such a way that no two people share precisely the same kin relationships to all others in their social field. Sections are sociocentrically ordered; that is, they exist 'out there' to be seen from a similar perspective by everyone and referred to in the same way, by name. In daily life the section system matters much less than kinship, yet there are important parallels between the two ways of ordering relationships in Mardujarra society. The sections lump together sets of kin (for example, in any person's section are his or her actual and classificatory brothers, sisters, parallel cousins, father's father, mother's mother, mother's mother's brother, father's father's sister, son's son, son's daughter, and so on). The sections give people clues to the general kind of behaviour they should observe towards others. For example, when a band encounters a small group of strangers, it may occasionally happen that no connecting kinship link can be established. The strangers then identify themselves by their section name, which immediately reduces the range of possible kin relationships. A member of the band may then decide that one of the stranger elders whose section is the same as his should be designated as 'brother' or, if the stranger is a very old man, as 'father's father'. As soon as this one link is decided on, all the kin relationships of members of both groups can quickly be worked out.

It is impossible to change categories, because membership is ascribed by birth. Although they do indicate both intermarrying categories and those categories between whose members marriage is forbidden, sections do not regulate marriage. As sections are too broad a method of classifying people, the kinship system provides the necessary precision in designating who can marry whom. For example, a woman's intermarrying section contains not only men she calls by the term for 'spouse', but also certain cross-cousin 'brothers' as well as 'mother's fathers' and 'son's sons', none of whom is marriageable.

Groups sometimes form on the basis of pairs of combined sections. At big meetings, for instance, the Mardujarra group their camps into two sides, with the sections of fathers and sons combining on each. The same kind of division is seen also in the seating arrangements for certain male rituals and during ceremonial gift exchanges between groups. The most common division, however, is formed by intermarrying pairs of sections; it figures prominently in many rituals and is seen not only in seating arrangements but in the entire organization of activities.

Both the father–son pairs and the intermarrying pairs are useful divisions. They separate into opposite groups many kin categories whose members must observe restraint or avoidance behaviour in their everyday inter-action. In rituals involving such dual division of the participants, members of both groups commonly exchange mild insults and engage in verbal jousts. The targets for such light-hearted attacks are members of particular kin categories, especially those related as wife-givers or wife-receivers, who dwell on alleged shortcomings in reciprocity. People offer or demand gifts of vegetable foods (owed by wife-givers) or meat (expected from wife-receivers), or of women as wives or infants in betrothal. These shouted exchanges of offers, insults and accusations of stinginess generate a great deal of humour among all present.

The expression of ritual opposition between the assembled sides allows for a harmless easing of tensions in the society. Some rituals even include mild physical aggression between certain kin who in everyday life would never normally engage in such activity. As the rules of ritual conduct demand that such exchanges never become acrimonious, the aggression remains good-natured. It adds zest to an already exciting and dramatic atmosphere, which is the mark of large ritual gatherings. The ritual con-text thus provides a controlled arena for the relaxation of conventions. In being able to say the normally unsayable, people forcibly remind each other that kinship is about obligations and responsibilities fundamental to an orderly existence.

Another kind of dual division, similar to the sides formed by intermarrying pairs of sections, features prominently in certain religious activities. It occurs particularly during male initiation and during death and burial ceremonies. When novices are seized — according to prescribed ritual — before the initiation rite of circumcision, hostile accusations may erupt between members of the two groups, usually centring on claims that there has been insufficient prior consultation and that things are being rushed. Even though these protests are ritualized and expected, men are some-times carried away and must be forcibly prevented from hurling boomerangs and spears.

Most of the time, no matter what kind of division is operating, there is a strong and overriding emphasis on unity. The Mardujarra frequently stress that they all share the one 'law', originating in the same Dreaming. They are convinced that rituals can succeed only when conflict is absent and all participants have good feelings in their stomachs; according to Mardujarra belief, the stomach is the seat of the emotions. This is why, when big meetings are held, the first order of business is always the public settlement of disputes. These must all be resolved to the satisfac-tion of the assembly before any religious activity can begin.

In the everyday life of the band, kinship rather than social categories dominates as the mechanism through which people conduct their social relationships. But whenever larger groupings occur in desert society, and especially in the organization of the all-important religious life, social categories and dual groupings play a major role in structuring the proceedings.

When compared to other hunter–gatherer peoples of the world, Australian Aborigines stand out because of the complexity of their social organiz- ation. Their lives seem to be burdened by a bewildering number of classifying and ordering systems or principles, which group people for certain purposes and differentiate them for others. Why is Aboriginal cul- ture in this respect so complex? Of course, the Aborigines who live enmeshed in these webs of belonging and relatedness do not consider them to be a burden. They regard them as natural and vital aspects of their social identity. Some scholars have suggested that this complexity, especially in the elaboration of social categories, is a kind of game, but there is more to it than that. These multiple sets of memberships and conventions clearly contribute to the integration of societies that lack centralized institutions of authority and control.

According to the anthropologist K. O. L. Burridge, who has proposed the most satisfying explanation to date, the strong elaboration of classi- ficatory schemes relates to two major aspects of Aboriginal social organization. First, each form of category or grouping brings together people who in other situations and other systems of categorization will be differently combined. This crosscutting is so thorough that no category grouping people for a particular purpose contains persons who belong only to that group and to no other. All are members of many other groupings and categories as well. Rivalry in some contexts is offset by co-operation in others, resulting in what Burridge calls 'a complete integration and union of the self with otherness'. In desert areas of Australia particularly, the unifying aspect of complex classifications assumes great social importance. Through them every individual can identify and use linkages with people who are located far beyond the limits of the band, estate group or dialect unit.

The second aspect of this cultural elaboration, Burridge suggests, is the way in which the classifying schemes enhance the personal identity of individual Aborigines, even while binding individuals into a wider social whole. No two people, even full siblings of the same sex, share exactly the same constellation of memberships. The individual thus assumes a unique position in relation to all the different groups within the society, and is thereby endowed with as strong a sense of individuality as of belonging.

Throughout the continent, different groups of Aborigines have evolved different mixtures of these two central tendencies, present in all societies: the centripetal kind that favours local, parochial interests and concerns at the expense of wider unities, and the centrifugal kind that opposes atomization in favour of promoting the widest possible sense of com- munity. The Mardujarra strongly favour the second kind, for good environ- mental and social reasons. The Western Desert, on the available evidence, shows a remarkable cultural continuity extending back in time at least

10 000 years. This strongly suggests that the desert Aborigines have long since solved the problem foreshadowed earlier; namely, how to maintain coherence in a society whose component parts are small groups which nearly all the time are widely dispersed.

This discussion has focused on kinship as a major component in binding together the Mardujarra and their desert neighbours into a larger social whole than that encompassed by the band, estate group or linguistic unit. The most important cohesive element, however, is religion. It links people, places, objects and past events (the creative marvels of the Dreaming) to both spiritual and natural realms in such a way as to provide the widest cultural horizons experienced by the desert Aborigines. Through their religion, they come to know about places they will never physically see and feel spiritual kinship with groups far beyond the margins of their social universe.

This expansive world view derives from the extensive wanderings and creative activities of the many beings of the Dreaming, whose ancestral tracks crisscross vast stretches of the Western Desert. Cultural pressures to pass on to other groups the rituals that each group borrows or composes have resulted in a remarkable diffusion of religious lore throughout the entire region. Two groups more than 1000 kilometres apart may be performing the same ritual at the same time, singing the same songs and using some of the same types of objects that have been handed on as an integral part of the ritual concerned.

Even at the time of the big meeting, when the many component bands of Mardujarra society are integrated, people are linked so extensively and share so many of their basic values and understandings that little negotiation is necessary. An elaborate host–visitor etiquette dominates the initial proceedings, and usually allows for a smooth transition into the main business of the gathering. Thanks to the operation of kinship and many other systems of classification, different activities occur without prolonged debates over status or roles.

These brief periods of intense social activity demonstrate the immense practical value of such complex networks. The Mardujarra take for granted the skills needed to get a living from the land. What they work hard at and consider vital to the survival of their culture are their relationships with each other and with the spiritual forces of the Dreaming on which they believe their ultimate destiny depends.

10
Leadership in Aboriginal Society

W. H. EDWARDS

Part 1: The Nineteenth Century

During the nineteenth-century era of exploration and settlement in Australia a number of explorers, settlers, government officials, missionaries and scholars recorded their observations of the Aboriginal inhabitants. Their comments reflected changing approaches which were dominating Western philosophy and science, and in turn contributed, to some degree, to the emerging Science of Man, as they provided European scholars with the opportunity to take account of reports based on observations of groups of people whom they considered to be living still at the earliest stage of the evolution of human social life. 'Thought to exemplify the earliest and most primitive condition of mankind, Aborigines and their cultures lent themselves to evolutionary studies.' (Burridge 1973:47). In his article 'The Australian Aborigines, Opinion and Fieldwork, 1606–1929', D. J. Mulvaney has provided a sketch of the development of this research (Mulvaney 1964). The observations of early explorers were restricted to physical characteristics and material culture. Mulvaney suggests that popular caricatures based on those observations and reflecting the current opinion that such people were a link between man and the monkey tribe, explains the diminished interest in Aboriginal life in the early decades of the century. He commends the works of Edward John Eyre and George Grey, two explorers, who during this period 'made the most positive contribution to aboriginal studies' (Mulvaney 1964:23).

In summarizing the references in the nineteenth century I will survey a range of opinions from those who asserted that there was no form of government, through those who claimed that Headmen or Councils of Elders had authority, both religious and secular, to those who asserted that there were centralized chiefs in the tribes. While an historical study of the references would indicate a general tendency to deny the existence of forms of government in the early decades of the century, to indentify the presence of chiefs in the middle decades and to assert the existence of Headmen and Councils towards the end of the century, there are exceptions to this model and I will follow a thematic approach.

Unpublished dissertation (1975).

No government

The most extreme position under this general theme was taken by Flanagan who wrote articles in the *Sydney Empire* in 1853–54. He stated that 'among the aborigines authority of a fixed and definite character, whether centred in individuals of the body or contained in some well-known and well-established laws, is altogether wanting. The mere suggestion of instinct and the most palpable laws of nature seem to have weight with them.' (Flanagan 1888:17). Other writers placed less emphasis on the role of instinct than on the role of custom, family organization or kinship in maintaining social control. Following Eyre's explorations in South and Western Australia, Grey appointed him as Resident Magistrate at Moorundie on the River Murray. In his *Journals* he wrote:

> There can hardly be said to be any form of government existing among a people who recognize no authority, and where every member of the community is at liberty to act as he likes, except in so far as he may be influenced by the general opinions and wishes of the tribe. (Eyre 1845:315)

He stated that none of the tribes had been known to have a chief although there were always men who would take the lead and whose opinions were respected. Fathers had absolute power in families and when tribes assembled the elders met and made decisions. He reported that age produced influence although the leading men were those in the 45 to 60 age bracket, rather than the very elderly. Respect and deference increased when a man possessed the attributes of strength, courage, energy, prudence and skill, and collaterally by his family connections. However, although such men may address the tribe, 'after this the various members are left to form their own judgments, and to act as they think proper.' (Eyre 1845:317). Thus Eyre's emphasis is on authority within the family, with a vague influence only beyond it, with this being dependent on personal attributes and age.

Another early observer in South Australia, the German missionary C. G. Tiechelmann, supported Eyre's general position. In his *Notes* he reported that no chieftainship is recognized and that they could not give a term equivalent to that of Governor other than *tauara neuu* or bigman (cf. Berndt 1965:176). They lived as large family groups protected by the fathers. Elders were the leaders but the only subordination was that of women to men. They were accustomed 'to live independently and to be their own masters'. (Tiechelmann 1841:6). George Fife Angas, one of the architects of the South Australian settlement, accompanied Grey on one expedition, and on other journeys recorded his impressions in words and paintings. Although claiming to have made constant search and inquiry into their history and customs his remarks are very general. He wrote that 'The native tribes have no distinct form of government, each man joins in the common hostility against his opposite tribe, and the men of most influence in matters of importance are the old and successful warriors.' (Angas 1847:2.88).

The Rev. John Mathew in writing about the Aborigines of New South Wales stressed the power of rules which prescribed conduct and which were supported by the threat of severe penalties: 'The cohesion of a community depends entirely upon consanguity and derives no strength at all from governmental authority.' (Mathew 1889:398). There were no recognized chiefs or kings, nor any elective or hereditary ruling body. The use of the name chief or king was an 'unwarrantable imposition of foreign ideas into descriptions of Australian life' (Mathew 1889:398). The older men have a certain amount of control and other men of strength and courage in conjunction with them, advise the rest, settle disputes and enforce obedience to traditional law. His definition of governmental authority is not broad enough to embrace such control and thus his emphasis is on the cohesion established and maintained by kinship. Writing of the tribes of the Gulf of Carpentaria region in 1893, W. G. Stretton stated that they have no definite forms of government and that chiefs have little power beyond directing wars or conducting ceremonies (Stretton 1893:242). He did not define his use of the term chief.

Another German missionary, W. Schurmann, writing of the people in the Port Lincoln area, emphasized the egalitarian nature of Aboriginal society. To him the fact that they had no chiefs or persons of acknowledged authority was a strong proof of their degraded social condition. According to him 'All grown-up men are perfectly equal' (Schurmann 1879:226) although considerable deference is shown to the old men, a natural respect for age being increased by the superstitious awe of certain mysterious rites.

George Grey does not fit neatly into any of the three categories of opinion which I am identifying but as his emphasis is on the power of custom rather than of centralized human authority, and his views on equality differ from those of Schurmann, I am including him at this point. He had contact with the Aborigines during his explorations in the north-west and western coastal areas of Western Australia, and as Governor of South Australia. He recognized the strength of social life and the force of custom, the latter 'ingeniously devised as to have a direct tendency to annihilate any effort that is made to overthrow them.' (Grey 1841:2.218). He observed: 'They appear to live in tribes, subject perhaps, to some individual authority.' (1841:1.252). During a skirmish in the north-west he observed two men who appeared to direct the general movements (1841:1.145). Grey had a somewhat prejudiced view of the equality of opportunity in Western societies and contrasted this with the influence of superstitions and customs in Aboriginal society which deprived certain classes of benefits which are enjoyed by others.

> This people reject, in practice, all idea of the equality of persons or classes, they make indeed no verbal distinctions upon this point, and if asked, were all men equal? they would be unable to comprehend the question; but there is no race that imposes such irksome restraints upon certain classes of the community. (Grey 1841:2.218)

The female sex, the young, and the weak were condemned to a hopeless state of degradation. This was attributed to fixed and unalterable laws which could not have changed until 'contact with a civilized community exercised a new influence which might sweep away the ancient system.' (Grey 1941:2.223). He neglected to make the point that the young males at least would rise to a higher status. Grey admits the presence of leaders during times of warfare but his emphasis is on the power of custom and its influence in preserving inequalities based on sex, age and physical characteristics.

E. W. Curr belongs under this heading but as he criticized the views of others whose views are to be considered later I will outline his opinions then.

Chiefs

The most extreme statement suggesting the presence of chiefs was expressed by James Dawson, a pastoralist, who wrote about the people of western Victoria. He claimed to have obtained information from the Aborigines themselves in their own languages, and that he was not dependent on the words of other whites. He wrote:

> Every tribe has its chief, who is looked upon in the light of a father, and whose authority is supreme. He consults with the best men of the tribe, but when he announces his decision, they dare not contradict or disobey him. (Dawson 1881:5)

He stated that the chiefs and their families were waited upon by others, received services and gifts, and preceded the other members of the tribe on journeys. 'The succession to the chiefdom is by inheritance.' (1881:6). In using terms such as chiefdom and regent Dawson was an example of those who, according to Mathew, imposed foreign ideas. Although Dawson stated that 'it is of the utmost importance to be able to converse freely with them in their own language' (1881:iii), he gives little evidence of his ability to do this, a shortcoming of many researchers in Aboriginal life.

The terms chief and king were used loosely by some writers whose contact with the Aboriginal people was limited. Edward Stephens, writing about the Adelaide Plains in 1889, stated that as late as 1879 he knew one brave old chief or king, and also wrote of the people burying their queen near the River Torrens (Stephen 1889:480, 495). Biskup refers to an attempt in Western Australia in 1852 to maintain order by recognizing the appointment of Aboriginal 'kings' or 'governors' but notes that this attempt was due to failure because of the acephalous structure of the societies and the attitude of the settlers (Biskup 1973:10).

One man who had long contact with Aboriginal people, and who used the term chief and even that of king, was George Taplin, the first missionary at Point Macleay in South Australia. Writing of the Narrinyeri in 1879, he stated that each of the tribes of the Narrinyeri has its chief, whose title is Rupelle, which means landowner. The Rupelle was a leader in war, a negotiator, spokesman and an adviser. His authority is supported by the heads of families. According to Taplin he formerly divided the animals taken in hunting. This assertion gives rise to suspicion as to the accuracy of his information in view of the widespread practice of dividing meat according to kinship. In contrast to Dawson he wrote that 'The chieftainship is not hereditary, but elective.' (Taplin

1879:1.32). He referred to the Rupelle of Port Malcolm, Peter, and in a description of a meeting between two clans referred to him as King Peter (1879:1.35). Taplin also referred to the Tendi, as 'a form of government among the Narrinyeri [which] was much more complete and regular than would have been expected amongst such a barbarous people.' (1879:1.34). He compared this as an institution to trial by jury. It was a council of elders of the clans and was presided over by the Rupelle. Reference will be made later to Curr's criticism of Taplin's assertions.

Taplin edited a volume on the folklore, manners, customs and languages of the South Australian Aborigines, and the book is an example of the methodology of recording such information in that period. The government sponsored the publication and questions were sent out to various settlers, police officers, Crown Lands rangers, telegraph station masters and others who had the opportunity to observe Aboriginal life. One question related to government and while most informants answered that there was no form of government, some referred to government by old men, others to an old man as chief, and one stated that they had formerly been ruled by a chief. The unsatisfactory nature of much of this research was illustrated by the correspondent from Fowlers Bay who reported that there was no government, no totems, no legends and no sorcery (Taplin 1879:2.94).

Headmen and councils

The writers who emphasize the role of clan headmen and tribal councils can be considered under the one heading as most of those who referred to headmen also note that they met in councils. R. H. Mathews, recognized by Elkin as one of the amateur founders of social anthropology in Australia (Elkin 1975:1), claimed as his authority for writing on the Aborigines that he was born in the bush, played with black children as his earliest playmates, and while a station worker and surveyor enjoyed the confidence of their chief men and understood their languages. Writing about an initiation ceremony in New South Wales he referred to the head men of the different tribes (Mathews 1894:106), and writing of similar ceremonies in Victoria he referred to the arrangements being made by the council of old men and the chief men of each contingent (Mathews 1904:327–8).

John Fraser, writing of the Aborigines of New South Wales in 1892, stated that there was no kingly rule or over-chief for the whole tribe, but that 'the affairs of each section of a tribe are administered by a number of elders, among whom one man is considered the leader or chief, because of his superior wisdom and influence' (Fraser 1892:38). This person received deference and, with his assessors, regulated all matters referred to them, as well as settling disputes, allotting punishments, decreeing war or peace and conducting the ceremonies. The succession was neither hereditary nor elective. He referred to a council which sat in a circle at a distance from the camp and decreed punishments and decided causes brought before it (1892:39).

More recent debates about the existence of councils were fore-shadowed in the works of Brough Smyth and E. W. Curr. The former served as Secretary of the Board for the Protection of Aborigines in Victoria. He claimed that the information provided in his large two volume work was founded on reports given by men who had frequent opportunities to observe the habits of the natives, for example A. W. Howitt, and several missionaries. Brough Smyth referred to the head of a tribe who was advised by the council of old men (1876:1.123). He wrote that 'The government of Aboriginal tribes is not a democracy' (1876:1.126), but that at various times power is in the hands of sorcerers, warriors, dreamers and the old men or councillors. He was perhaps unique at that time in observing that the old women could also exert some influence, although he gave no specific evidence on this aspect. He referred to one man as King Benbow, and stated that he was well known in Melbourne in 1848. His volumes have an Appendix by A. Le Souef, who had some experience with the Aborigines of the Murray and Goulburn tribes. He asserted that there was no chieftainship as amongst the American Indians but that a few men — 'generally the boldest and strongest and very often the most mischievous' (Smyth 1876:2.295) — gained some ascendancy.

Nineteenth-century ethnographical research in Australia reached its peak towards the turn of the century with the contributions of A. W. Howitt and Professor Baldwin Spencer and F. J. Gillen, with the fame of the latter pair obscuring the achievement of Howitt (Mulvaney 1964:44). Following his contacts with Aboriginal people as an explorer and as a Magistrate in Victoria, Howitt corresponded with Lewis Morgan and the latter's theories on stages of evolutionary development of cultures and social forms were reflected in Howitt's work. Howitt concluded that while it may appear to an ordinary observer that there is no recognized form of government, that no person or group has the right to command, a more intimate acquaintance shows that there must be some authority beyond what Curr referred to as an impersonal power. 'I have shown that there are, and were, men recognized as having control over the tribal people, and whose directions are obeyed. Such men receive designations which in some cases, may be translated "Elder" or "Great man".' (Howitt 1904:319). However he found that in most cases the headmen exercised less power than that described by Spencer and Gillen as being exercised by Aranta leaders. Howitt referred to tribal councils:

> I have constantly observed in those tribes with which I have had personal acquaintance that the old men met at some distance apart from the camp and discussed matters of importance such as arrangements to be made for hunting game, for future or ceremonial meetings, or indeed any other important matter. (Howitt 1904:320)

In writing of the Kurnai he associated authority with both age and exceptional qualifications such as intelligence, cunning and bravery. There was no hereditary authority (Howitt 1880:211–12). Mr G. W. Rusden provided him with information on the Grawe-Gal tribe of the Hunter River in New South Wales. Rusden referred to headmen acting with the consent of the elders, and being only *primus inter pares* (Howitt 1880:281).

Two further points should be made in relation to Howitt's contribution. First, he concluded that social organization was influenced by ecological conditions and that increased rainfall enabled an easier life in the southeast and aided the process of social advancement in that region.

> This comparison will not fall in line with previous conclusions, namely, that the tribes of the Lake Eyre basin have remained in a far more pristine condition socially than those of the south-east of Australia. If so it would point to conditions of better climate, and more abundant and regular food supply, as potent causes in the advancement of the social condition of the south-east tribes. (Howitt 1904:155).

He supports this by reference to family arrangements rather than to political forms, possibly influenced in this emphasis in research by his correspondence with Morgan.

Secondly, while most observers provided us with generalized comments about headmen, Howitt refers at some length to at least two of these men. Writing of the Dieri people of the Lake Eyre region he noted that 'the oldest man of a totem is its Pinnaru, or head. In each horde there is also a Pinnaru who may happen also to be the head of a totem ... The Pinnaru are collectively the Headmen of the tribe'. (Howitt 1904:297). He wrote that when he knew the tribe in 1862–63, 'the principal Headman was one Jalina Piramurana, the head of the Kunaura totem, and he was recognized as head of the Dieri tribe.' (1904:297). Howitt referred to his oratorical powers, his authority in settling disputes, arranging ceremonies, sending messengers and receiving gifts and respect from his own tribe and from others, arranging marriages, and presiding at meetings of the Pinnarus. He was the son of a previous headman and was recognized as a medicine man. However this person should not be taken as typical of Aboriginal headmen. Howitt admitted that he was exceptionally able and an unusually influential man (1904:300). Also Howitt may have been dependent on information supplied by Mr Samuel Gason who in another work wrote that 'a more treacherous race I do not believe exists.' (Curr 1886:2.45). Howitt had closer knowledge of the Kurnai and neighbouring groups and he referred to Bruthen Munji as 'a leader in war and council' amongst the Brabrolung (Howitt 1880:212). Other descriptions of headmen during the earlier contact period were given by H. Simpson Newland, a South Australian pastoralist (Reynolds 1972:35).

In their monumental works on the tribes of central and northern Australia, Spencer and Gillen described several local groups and referred to their headmen. 'Every local group has its headman, usually called Inkata, though at Alice Springs he is known as Alatunja.' (Spencer & Gillen 1928:1.313). Authority depended on both age and ability and the authority of the Inkata is of a vague nature. 'Within the narrow limits of his own age group no head man has of necessity any special power ... There is no such thing as a chief of the tribe.' (Spencer & Gillen 1927:1.9). The post of Inkata is, within certain limits, hereditary. Spencer and Gillen asserted that the fact that they were not aware of anything quite equivalent to this position in other tribes pointed to the association of this position with the strong development of the local groups in the area (1928:11). The headman consults with other elders to arrange ceremonies and to impose punishments. Thus any man breaking the codes must face more than Curr's impersonal power. The most important function of the Alatunja is to take charge of the sacred storehouse where the sacred objects of the group are kept. Spencer and Gillen recognized the power of custom but also that this gave authority to the custodians of the traditions. Thus writing of a ceremonial occasion they stated:

> Everything in native camps is governed by custom and, on this occasion, the supreme control lay in the hands of one man, who apparently, without any trouble, or the slightest hitch, governed the whole camp, comprising more than one hundred fullgrown men. (Spencer & Gillen 1928:1.317)

Although the final decision in all matters was in his hands he met with other headmen in a secluded spot to discuss matters of procedure.

Although Spencer and Gillen stated that there were no chiefs, 'every now and then a man arises of superior ability to his fellows' (Spencer & Gillen 1927:1.11–12). They deduced that any changes of custom arise from the influence of such men. Although they cannot give actual illustrations of this they had noted changes which had occurred and in view of the rigid conservatism assume that those changes could only come about as the old men agreed to the suggestion of a man who commanded considerable respect.

I will conclude this summary of the views of the early observers by referring to one who criticized the conclusions reached by others and who in turn was criticized by later writers. E. W. Curr was a Victorian squatter who compiled a four volume work called *The Australian Race*. Despite Brough Smyth's claim to have founded his work on reliable information, he is dismissed by Curr as having no personal knowledge of the blacks: 'The truth is that a fancy picture has taken the place of a statement of facts.' (Curr 1886:152). Curr asserted that while heads of families exercised authority over their wives and children there was nothing akin to government. Outside the family, custom was enforced for the most part by an impersonal power. The influence of evolutionary theory on Curr is illustrated by his remark that 'the delegation of authority to chief or council belongs notoriously to a stage of progress which the Australian race has not reached' (Curr 1886:1.52). If any persons had such authority they would have claimed it in contacts with whites. The mode of life, with movement in small parties, rendered impossible the interference of a council of old men. Curr also criticized Dawson on the grounds that there were insufficient numbers in the groups to provide the attendants on chiefs and their families as enumerated by Dawson. He attacked Taplin's reference to the Tendi or council on the grounds that it was strange that it took Taplin twenty years to discover the existence of such a government. One of the writers commended by Curr was Morgan who had written *The Life and Adventures of William Buckley*, an escaped convict who lived with the Aborigines in Victoria for 32 years. Buckley had stated that the tribes 'acknowledge no particular chief as being superior to the rest.' (Curr 1886:1.65.)

In summarizing the views of those who observed Aboriginal societies during the nineteenth century I have been dependent on a variety of sources of varying worth. There was a wide spectrum of opinions ranging from assertions that there was no form of government to those who stated that there were chiefs of tribes. While the extreme positions have been repudiated, the debate between those who take less extreme positions continues. Curr's arguments against Dawson and the later views of Taplin were supported by evidence from Howitt, and Spencer and Gillen. However in advocating the influence of an impersonal power he did not take sufficient account of the authority exercised by men who upheld the customs and who, according to Spencer and Gillen, were responsible for changes in the traditions. The current debate centres on the question as to whether social control was maintained by kinship ties and obligations, religious observances and traditional laws or whether individuals and groups played a significant role in maintaining this control, extending their religious influence into secular affairs.

A variety of factors limited the worth of much of this early material. Some reports were not based on an adequate methodology or scientific purpose. Concepts which did not fit the Aboriginal structures were imposed upon them. Social Darwinism gave some scientific direction but its assumptions imposed their own bias on the conclusions. However the main positions taken in more recent debates were foreshadowed in the remarks of these earlier observers. For example, we can compare the statements of Schurmann, 'All grown-up men are perfectly equal', and of Eyre, 'The various members are left to form their own judgment, and to act as they think proper', with those of Meggitt: 'the tribal communities ... were egalitarian', and 'in a real sense, the Aborigines exercised self-government.' (Meggitt 1966:67, 74). John Mathew wrote: 'The cohesion of a community depends entirely upon consanguity,' (Mathew 1889:398) and Sharp later agreed that 'all of this is simply kinship' (Sharp 1958:7). Some of Howitt's comments foreshadowed Elkin's references to elders and councils. Some of Berndt's statements and the examples he gives of local groups, leaders and the influence of religion and kinship are reminiscent of Spencer and Gillen, Brough Smyth, and Howitt. These comparisons will provide a link as I review more recent literature on the subject of leadership and authority in Aboriginal societies.

Part 2: 1900–1950

Just as the reports on Aboriginal societies in the nineteenth century reflected, and contributed to, the influence of evolutionary theory on anthropology, so the research in the early decades of the twentieth century reflected, and contributed to, the development of Functionalist and Structuralist approaches. Two pioneers in applying these approaches to the study of small-scale societies, Malinowski and Radcliffe-Brown, used observations of Aboriginal societies in developing their models of social systems; Malinowski having written a dissertation on the Aboriginal family and Radcliffe-Brown undertaking fieldwork in Western Australia.

Whereas during the earlier period the ethnographers such as Howitt, and Spencer and Gillen were dependent on the advice of ethnologists such as Morgan and Fraser and their findings were at times shaped by the kind of questions suggested by them, during the period now under review the roles of ethnographer and ethnologist tended to be combined in the same person. During this period the fieldwork approach developed by Spencer and Gillen was extended and refined by researchers such as Warner, Hart and Kaberry. At the same time the emphasis on the study of kinship organization tended to divert attention from the problems of government and political organization. However there were some references to the subject and as no writers asserted seriously during this period that there were chiefs over whole tribes, the references can be summarized under two main headings, those who denied the existence of government and those who emphasized the role of headmen and councils. It should be noted that this classification is not entirely satisfactory as the difference between two people who are placed in opposing classifications may be one of emphasis and definition.

No government

Radcliffe-Brown wrote the Preface to the book *African Political Systems*, a collection of papers published in 1940. The authors attempted to determine whether there are societies which could be said to have no political system. Much depended on definition. Mair interprets their conclusion as being that 'though all societies have political systems, some, they said, do not have governments' (Mair 1962:16). In the Preface Radcliffe-Brown wrote: 'In studying political organization, we have to deal with the maintenance or establishment of social order, within a territorial framework, by the organized exercise of coercive authority through the use, or the possibility of use, of physical force.' (Fortes & Evans-Pritchard 1970:xiv). He concluded that because of the powerful influence of public sentiment and ritual sanctions in small-scale communities the political and legal systems were present in rudimentary form only. One of the editors of that volume noted (in a later work) that early travellers amongst the Nuer did not refer to their leaders as having any great authority and that therefore 'We might say they have no government.' (Evans-Pritchard 1974:172).

Radcliffe-Brown (1930) focused attention on the local land-occupying group which he referred to as the horde. He found past accounts unsatisfactory because of the loose use of terms such as tribe and family. He wrote that 'The Australian tribe has usually, if not always, no political unity. There is no central authority for the tribe as a whole, nor does the tribe act as a unit in warfare. The political unit, if it can be properly called such, and normally the war-making unit, is the horde.' (Radcliffe-Brown 1930:37). He does not refer to headmen or councils but emphasizes the role of kinship in the social structure. 'The study of kinship terminology ... is the only way to any real understanding of Australian social organization.' (Radcliffe-Brown 1930:43). His definition of the horde as being patrilineal, patrilocal and exogamous was accepted as the norm until more extensive fieldwork over the past two decades has produced evidence of many exceptions to this model (Hiatt 1968:99).

Lauriston Sharp sought to answer the question raised in the book *African Political Systems* on the basis of his fieldwork amongst the Yir-Yoront of Cape York in north Queensland. He noted that terms such as tribe, chief, headman, gerontocracy and council have seeped into and seriously rigidified much of the discussion and given to Aboriginal groups an appearance of political organization and government, 'yet in all north Queensland none of the foregoing paraphernalia of government and politics is found.' (Sharp 1958:2). According to Sharp kinship defined role behaviour and without a radical change in the entire kinship structure the Yir-Yoront could not even tolerate mild chiefs or headmen. The avoidance of communication with certain in-laws would make the existence of councils made up of in-laws a practical impossibility. Certain men in their prime act as a kind of a head of the family but their authority is severely limited (Sharp 1958:6). These heads acknowledged no higher political authority. Behaviour is organized around kinship roles and rules based on a system of law and Sharp concluded that 'all of this is simply kinship ... The Yir-Yoront are a people without sovereignty, without hierarchy outside the family, whose whole life operates through the familial institution — they are a people without politics.' (Sharp 1958:7).

W. L. Warner engaged in fieldwork in the 1930s amongst a group in Arnhem Land whom he identified as the Murngin. He also noted that the social organization is built on the pattern of kinship and that 'A man's or woman's place in Murngin society is fixed by his or her position in the kinship structure.' (Warner 1958:7). In the extended family group the older brother or Wawa is the head but all the brothers confer on an almost equal basis on ceremonial matters. Each clan has ceremonial leaders and this authority is inherited by the oldest son or the next brother. This person is a kind of clan headman. However Warner stated:

> Politically the clan is almost impotent when it comes to positive action ... The ceremonial leader is considered headman, and if physically able and of sufficient talent, he is also war leader, but his power is at an absolute minimum except as a ritual leader; it is in the field of ritual and not of government that he exercises his leadership. (Warner 1958:389).

He stressed the determining influence of position in the social structure.

> The totality of his behaviour toward all the people in his community and of their behaviour in relation to him, with all the concomitant obligations, duties, and privileges, is determined by his being placed exactly in this social structure through the operation of certain mechanisms. (Warner 1958:7)

Whereas the women's group remains relatively undifferentiated, age-gradings differentiate the status of men. By virtue of their knowledge of the religious mysteries the older men control the younger. Thus, 'like other Australian tribes, this people's "political" control might be termed a gerontocracy, but it is more than merely the rule of old men' (Warner 1958:396), the qualification probably arising from the fact that the old men were subject to tradition.

Other writers who used the term gerontocracy with a qualification were Hart and Pilling, whose work I place in this period although published in 1960, as Hart's fieldwork amongst the Tiwi was carried out in 1928–29, and Pilling's in the early 1950s. They stated categorically that 'There was no tribal government' (Hart & Pilling 1960:11). They also emphasized the importance of the horde as a unit of social organization. They gave details about one old man, Tu'untalumi, who was widely respected as a big man but noted that although he travelled widely to attend ceremonies and deference was paid to his decisions at them, most of his time was spent with his own household group, thus with authority usually over his wives and children only. They recorded that such influence as was attained by older men was built up by slow and devious manoeuvring during adult years. Women were the main currency in the influence struggle and to hinder the advance of men junior to them the old men tried to pass on their influence to those twenty years or so their junior. 'Thus the Tiwi system actually deserves to be called a primitive oligarchy as much as it deserves to be called a gerontocracy.' (Hart & Pilling 1960:77). They also commented on the isolation of this island group which made it more difficult for offenders to seek refuge with other groups. 'The isolation of the Tiwi made the rule of the gerontocracy much more absolute and the enforcement of it much more effective than was possible for any of the mainland tribes.' (Hart & Pilling 1960:80). They attributed the presence of distinctive features within Tiwi culture which modified mainland patterns not only to the absence of neighbours but also to the relatively favourable food and rainfall situation on Melville Island.

Headman and councils

Phyllis Kaberry, following fieldwork in the Kimberley region of Western Australia in the 1930s, wrote of the authority of headmen and elders of local groups. They were responsible for arranging ceremonies and dealing with cases of death by sorcery. The office tended to be hereditary. The political organization is described as 'an aristocracy, a government by the best, by those who are fitted for the task by their knowledge, experience and personality' (Kaberry 1939:178).

The most definite statements about the role of headmen and councils during this period were those of Malinowski. Whereas his contemporary Radcliffe-Brown had limited the use of the terms law and politics to those situations in which there were institutions which maintained control through the use of coercive power and force, Malinowski's functionalist definitions were broader and allowed for the presence of law and government in all societies as all had certain institutions operating for the functioning of the totality of social life. As in Aboriginal societies there were norms, and sanctions upholding these norms, 'we may generally point to the existence of tribal government. That a kind of centralized authority exists in Australia and that it has well-determined functions has been shown at full length by Howitt.' (Malinowski 1969:11). He went on to assert that this government consists of headmen and a tribal council composed of old men, skilled magicians and experienced warriors. 'The influence of old men, magicians and "doctors", is almost universally reported, and the council made up of them seems to wield the real power in the tribe.' (1969:12. fn. 1). The council acted as both legislator and judge as the old men who were the custodians of tribal lore discussed important matters and decided difficult cases brought before them. They also possessed executive power and arranged for armed parties and controlled punishments by magic. It should be noted that the work containing these statements was written before Malinowski had visited Australia and that he was dependent on the reports of Howitt and others.

In view of his roles as Professor of Anthropology at the University of Sydney, and Editor of *Oceania*, during the last two decades of this period, A. P. Elkin was influential during the period. Whereas some writers had minimized the importance of tribal organization and stressed the role of the horde, Elkin continued to place some emphasis on the importance of the tribe while recognizing that the local subdivision had more important functions. He stated that the male elders exercised authority in the local groups and that usually one headman presided at meetings of these groups at which disputes were settled and decisions made bearing on the group's economic, social and ceremonial activities (Elkin 1956:82). Writing of the tribes of the Lake Eyre region he reported that 'Each of these ceremonial clans has a headman. The office is hereditary from father to son, provided that the latter be old enough, fully initiated and sufficiently well-versed in the myth and ritual.' (Elkin 1931–32:58). Elkin supported the idea that a council existed and was important in tribal matters in that it linked the different local groups.

> The headmen of the various groups of a tribe constitute a council — informal in nature — who talk over matters of common interest and make decisions, when several local groups are together. Their authority depends on knowledge, position in the secret life and personal respect. (Elkin 1956:44)

This became the definitive statement for those who accepted that such councils existed. The link between the groups was not so much one of political organization but based on the sentiments of family and kinship. Elkin held that meetings of the headmen were essential for the acceptance and dissemination of any modifications to the social rules.

In closing this Part we may note that while the extreme positions had been repudiated and that there was general agreement as to the centrality of ceremonial knowledge, the importance of the local group and the role of kinship in maintaining cohesion and control, there was disagreement as to the extent to which the authority of ceremonial leaders extended into the secular sphere and the degree to which a local group was subject to the authority of a tribal council.

Part 3: 1951–1975

During the next quarter century there was a marked increase in the amount of fieldwork by anthropologists in Aboriginal communities. Those who have engaged in this fieldwork have tended to support the findings of their predecessors who had denied that leaders or councils had authority beyond the religious and ceremonial sphere. Some have questioned these conclusions on the grounds that it was impossible to gain reliable information relating to traditional life. However Hiatt claimed that the more recent researchers in remote areas were as close as, or closer to, the traditional patterns than were earlier observers, who had also worked in post-contact situations (Hiatt 1968:147). This position was challenged by two men who had engaged in extensive fieldwork, Strehlow and Berndt. The two main positions taken in the debate during this period were typified by the works of Meggitt and Berndt.

No government

For the sake of continuity I am using the same headings as in the earlier Parts although Meggitt's definition of government is sufficiently broad to include his position. 'By government I mean the ways in which a group or association of people runs its affairs.' (Meggitt 1966:57). However in Aboriginal societies he found 'no formal apparatus of government' (1966:74). Meggitt did his fieldwork amongst the Walbiri people of Central Australia in the 1950s and in his book *Desert People* he stated that 'There were no tribal leaders, headmen, or chiefs; nor was there any controlling or ruling class of old or important men whose power extended through society.' (Meggitt 1974:242). Amongst the Walbiri the norms relating to the religious and kinship systems constituted an enduring and comprehensive master-plan to guide action and 'There was, therefore, little need for secular leaders in the community.' (1974:248). The only approximation to institutionalized leadership lay in the ritual and religious field. Meggitt denied that any group could exercise control over the actions of others and although there were age-gradings associated with ritual this did not entail a gerontocracy. 'In short, the community had no recognized political leaders, no formal hierarchy of government.' (Meggitt 1974:250). The definitive statement of this position was contained in his earlier article, in which he took issue with earlier writers who had assumed that tribal government rested in the hands of the old men. He emphasized the importance of the local groups, the egalitarian nature of tribal communities and that the norms of kinship and religious systems provided 'timeless and ubiquitous guides to actions which, the people believed, had met all contingencies in the past and would continue to do so in the future.' (Meggitt 1966:70). He analysed the roles of ritual experts, medicine-men, elders and fighting men and found that none of them provided extensive or permanent leadership. The authority of the ritual leader did not extend into the secular sphere. When an event demanded action such as revenge or punishment, relationship to the principal actors determined who would carry out the role. Meggitt's conclusion was that:

> although the local communities that made up the Australian tribes were the significant political and administrative units, they had no formal apparatus of government, no enduring hierarchy of authority, no recognized political leaders. In a real sense, the aborigines exercised self-government.' (Meggitt 1966:74)

Hiatt, following fieldwork among the Gidjingali people of Arnhem Land, applied a conflict model to the analysis of government. He agreed with the general lines of Meggitt's approach. In each patrilineal group there were men known as *bunngoa*, or bosses. A *bunngoa* 'is a dignitary in the religious sphere and not obviously a man of special importance in secular matters' (Hiatt 1959:192). If these men became involved in disputes it was not as adjudicators but in the same way as any other person was involved — as kinsman. He concluded that 'among these people quarrels are settled neither by headmen nor councils of elders' (Hiatt 1959:192). Most quarrels related to problems over women. 'There was no institution with authority to deal with such disputes; but there was a community of people with a set of common values and a system of formally defined rights and obligations.' (Hiatt 1965:146).

Tonkinson, who did his fieldwork with the Mardudjara people at Jigalong Mission in Western Australia, supported Meggitt's conclusions by stating that at Jigalong, Aboriginal leadership accorded closely with that of the Walbiri. In the traditional culture authority was largely a function of sex and age. 'Leadership and authority, in the sense of individuals telling others to do things, were confined largely to religious contexts and were always defined situationally.' (Tonkinson 1974:63). During rituals, various men had authority according to their 'ownership' of the particular ritual. In secular life there was no leadership structure outside the family. Gould, who had also studied a Western Desert group during the 1960s, also recorded that 'in daily life there were no official leaders of privileged groups, hereditary or elected, among the Aborigines. The emphasis instead is on equality and sharing' (Gould 1969:90). He noted that the egalitarian tendency was also evident during ritual. 'No one is in a position of authority to start the ceremony.' (1969:114). Since no one wants to appear 'bossy' all wait until one person feels that he has the approval of all to act. 'Since there is no official leader or governing body in Aboriginal society, it takes a while for the matter to be decided.' (1969:114). Gould referred to the structure as a kind of ideal communism.

Maddock also saw Aboriginal society as exhibiting some of the characteristics of a communist society as envisaged by Marx and Engels. He wrote: 'If the state is taken to mean an institution monopolizing force within a territory, then Aboriginal society is stateless.' (Maddock 1973:182). But this condition of anarchy does not mean that there was no authority present in the society. The authority is of a religious nature and is distributed amongst the various clans through the initiated males. 'Egalitarian mutuality is the governing principle.' (Maddock 1973:184).

Thus we find once again that religion and kinship are viewed as determinative for social control. Kolig, writing of the Wolmadjeri of northwest Australia, also related authority to religious knowledge. 'The traditional ''bosses'', individuals outstanding because of their religious knowledge, had a primus-inter-pares position.' (Kolig 1972:10).

Headmen and councils

Berndt (1965) took issue with some of these writers and sought to support some of the points made by Elkin and Radcliffe-Brown. In reports on his earlier fieldwork at Ooldea, he referred to the camp headman or 'boss'. 'He holds this position by virtue of full membership in his cult lodge, his amiability to all camp fellows, his having the welfare of the camp at heart, and his erudite knowledge of totemic law and mythology.' (Berndt & Berndt 1942:156). He had some responsibility for keeping the peace although must not interfere unwarrantably. Other old men met informally under the headman to discuss both sacred and secular matters. Berndt accuses Sharp, Hiatt and Meggitt of generalizing on the basis of the materials they have gathered from the Yir-Yoront, Gidjingali and the Walbiri. He argued that their approaches were defective in that they evaded significant aspects such as (1) the concept of authority in the Aboriginal sense; (2) the place of the elder or leader in Aboriginal society; and (3) the many examples of institutionalized procedures designed to maintain the peace (Berndt 1965: 169). He acknowledged the importance of kinship in articulating social relationships but denied that it was all simply a matter of kinship. While minor breaches of the norms were dealt with according to kin obligations, there were major offences which required the intervention of a higher authority. He recognized the importance of tradition and the value placed on maintaining the status quo but this enabled the religious leader to exercise a wider influence. He acknowledged that the Aboriginal view of the world was a religious one, and that the authority of the leaders derived from their religious life and involvement in sacred affairs. However, this status was enhanced through other activities such as hunting, healing, craftmanship, dancing and fighting.

Berndt questioned Meggitt's use of the term egalitarian and wrote that the idea 'that Aboriginal society is egalitarian is often no more than a social fiction' (Berndt 1965:175). Potentially there were equal opportunities but not all achieve prominence and status as leaders. There was a hierarchy of gradings in religious experiences and although position was partly ascribed it depended partly on interest and proficiency. Kin ties could be manipulated to gain more prominence. Berndt claimed that the religious leaders could take action in affairs other than those of a strictly sacred nature, although it is difficult to draw a sharp distinction between the sphere of the sacred and that of the mundane.

> These religious leaders have a considerable say in everyday affairs, much more
> so than is acknowledged by some writers who have worked in regions where
> traditional sanctions are no longer in force, and where the authority of the

leaders is undermined and negated by introduced forms of control. (Berndt 1965:204)

He asserted that these leaders were concerned with maintaining the law and that although there was no centralized authority, and authority was limited, there was evidence in the writings of Howitt, Spencer and Gillen and others that some institutions had existed for the settlement of disputes (1965:181). Berndt referred to the system as nominally geron-tocratic, the qualification being necessary because men became leaders not only because of age but also because they had something to offer. Berndt accepted that men met together in some form of council. 'Such councils of elders or men of importance, or leaders (tribal, clan, local group, ritual) seem to have been, traditionally, fairly common.' (Berndt & Berndt 1968:292).

T. G. H. Strehlow took up some of the ideas presented by Berndt and elaborated on them from his own studies of Aranda totemic sites and mythology. He referred to the leaders of the local groups which formed religious and political units. Each totemic centre of the Arandas had a ceremonial chief whose duties were not merely religious: 'he was a person of very real secular authority' (Strehlow 1970:110), an authority which stemmed from some of his religious functions. These chiefs held, in a sense, the status of a head of a food producing unit and the chief with his council of elders exercised economic functions. He gave examples from this ar :a of the use of their authority in imposing punishments and sanctions. Reports of his informants concerning their fear in earlier times when they saw a group of old men sitting together outside the camp area, indicated that some form of 'council' meeting had authority in the local groups. Strehlow also commented on authority in the Western Desert area and questioned the validity of Meggitt's assumptions on the grounds that the traditional structures had been undermined by the time of Meggitt's research. This was due to the efforts of police officers, station owners and missionaries, the effects of the government's assimilation policy and the influence of schools, and the fact that many of the Walbiri people were then living in a near-refugee situation as a result of earlier punitive expeditions and their dispersal to government settlements away from their totemic centres. Strehlow gave examples of individual leaders in various Western Desert groups and stated that the ritual leadership of these men over their own group and over others who had joined them on their own sites, provided them with an authority which, 'at other times ... carried over, to a greater or lesser extent, into the secular lives of the people who had personal ties with the areas surrounding the totemic sites of which these leaders were the main guardians' (Strehlow 1970:109).

Referring to Hiatt's conclusion that although the people organized and controlled their activities, he and Meggitt had found no government institutions, Strehlow observed that the confusion among anthropologi-cal observers was caused by the fact that they approached the problem of authority from insights gained in European or non-Australian com-munities. He agreed that there were no centralized authorities such as chiefs or councils with power to make religious or legal decisions for the whole tribal area but saw authority based not on religion alone but as 'resting on religion and on geography' (Strehlow 1970:128). He too saw the system as comparable to an ideal state of communism as envisaged by Marx, but took issue with others on the grounds that they have not taken sufficient account of the fact that 'because all men in these localized permanent Aboriginal communities belonged to totemic clans, there was no sharp division between religious and secular authority' (1970:133). The precedents which dictated action in 'secular' offences were related to the ancestral beings in much the same way as the ritual activities. He thus points to 'the vital tie which bound up the social, political and religious institutions of the Aboriginal Central Australians with the economic facts of their geographical environment and the details of their totemic landscape' (Strehlow 1970: 133). The relationship to the totemic sites made questions of hereditary succession superfluous. Authority is not derived from relationship to other humans but from the relationship to the totem.

> There was no need of hereditary ruling families: the major totemic sites continuously sent out sparks of the life from which future elders and cer-emonial chiefs could become reincarnated; each major site was the geographic fountain of authority for the territory surrounding it. (1970:134)

Strehlow's approach to the problem of authority is in line with the suggestion of Burridge that 'although very little has as yet been done on the relation of myths and dreams to Aboriginal political life, the internal evidence points to a rich vein' (Burridge 1973:81). Burridge referred to the communities as gerontocracies which were managed by the capable older middle-aged men who had added to their religious experience their own personal and pragmatic experience of life. There was therefore some room for the achievement of influence and prestige. 'The men who managed affairs were generally those with well-rounded characters, shrewd men whose intellectual and imaginative capacities were balanced by political acumen, economic and domestic skills.' (Burridge 1973:70).

This position is also supported by Rose who engaged in fieldwork in both Arnhem Land and Central Australia. He stated that in the local groups, which were the important political units, one or two elders wielded authority by reason of their knowledge of custom, their ability as hunters and the respect they enjoyed. When a number of groups met together, a loosely constituted council of elders was set up to discuss inter-group matters such as marriages and disputes (Rose 1968:166).

From this review of references to leadership and authority in literature relating to the Australian Aborigines it is obvious that points which were a matter of dispute in earlier reports remain unresolved. Towards the end of the nineteenth century Curr, referring to Brough Smyth, wrote: 'The truth is that a fancy picture has taken the place of a statement of fact.' (Curr 1886:1.52). More recently Berndt, commenting on Meggitt's state-ment that the Aboriginal communities were egalitarian, wrote that the idea 'that Aboriginal society is egalitarian is often no more than a social fiction.' (Berndt 1965:175). While there is general agreement as to the religious basis of authority, the determining role of kinship in regulating behaviour and a strong emphasis on the maintenance of the status quo and custom, there is disagreement as to the amount of freedom and flexibility allowed to individuals to act independently, or for some individuals to impose their wills upon others.

As it is now impossible to observe the traditional structures it is unlikely that this debate will reach a satisfying conclusion. I suggest that as it proceeds the following points should be noted as they may assist in clarifying some aspects of the debate. First, as some observers have commented in the past, the debate has been confused by the use of terms introduced from Western political structures but which do not fit the Aboriginal situation. More attention should be paid to the analysis of terms used in Aboriginal languages and of English words which Aboriginal groups have assimilated into their languages during the contact period.

Secondly, English words have been used frequently in the debate without adequate definition. Much of the recent debate has hinged on the use of the term egalitarian and Sahlins has defined an egalitarian society as one in which the universals of age, sex and personal characteristics, are the only qualifications for higher status (Sahlins 1958:1–2). Can the skills and knowledge which according to Berndt and Strehlow enhanced status be subsumed under the personal characteristics of this definition? Thirdly, has sufficient attention been given to regional differences? Differing emphases in the debate may arise in part from the varying ecological and demographic factors relating to the groups under discussion. For example, I first read Meggitt's article when working in the northwest of South Australia with Pitjantjatjara people and it seemed to shed light on the situation in which I lived. I later spent a year in the northwest of Western Australia and I sensed that in that area individuals could attain greater prominence and exert more influence. Lastly, too little attention has been given to comparative studies with non-Australian societies. Comparisons with Polynesian and Melanesian societies would seem to highlight the egalitarian nature of Aboriginal societies.

It may be asked whether it is worthwhile pursuing a debate which is unlikely to reach a satisfactory conclusion. However as Aboriginal people are today involved in attempts to develop political structures which will enable them to interact with other Australian political structures, administer resources which are being made available to them and to exercise some control over their communities, some understanding of the traditional structures is essential if they are to be assisted in these processes. Attempts have been made to impose structures which are in conflict with the traditional structures and insufficient time given for them to develop new structures which reflect the traditional patterns.

References

ANGAS, C. F. (1847), *Savage Life and Scenes in Australia and New Zealand*, Two Volumes, London: Smith, Elder & Co.

BERNDT, R. M. (1965), Law and Order in Aboriginal Australia, in R. M. & C. H. Berndt (eds), *Aboriginal Man in Australia*, Sydney: Angus & Robertson.

BERNDT, R. M. & C. H. BERNDT (1942), 'Fieldwork in Western South Australia', *Oceania*, **13**(2).

—— (1968), *The World of the First Australians*, Sydney: Ure Smith.

BISKUP, PETER (1973), *Not Slaves Not Citizens*, St Lucia: University of Queensland Press.

BURRIDGE, KENELM (1973), *Encountering Aborigines*, New York: Pergamon Press.

CURR, E. W. (1886), *The Australian Race*, Four Volumes, Melbourne: Government Printer.

DAWSON, JAMES (1881), *Australian Aborigines*, Melbourne: George Robertson.

ELKIN, A. P. (1931–32), 'The Social Organization of South Australian Tribes', *Oceania*, Vol. **2**.

—— (1956), *The Australian Aborigines*, Sydney: Angus & Robertson.

—— (1975), 'R. H. Mathews: His Contribution to Aboriginal Studies', *Oceania*, **44**(1).

EVANS-PRITCHARD, E. E. (1974), *The Nuer*, Oxford: Oxford University Press.

EYRE, E. J. (1845), *Journals of Expeditions of Discovery into Central Australia and Overland from Adelaide to King George's Sound*, London: T. & W. Boone.

FLANAGAN, R. (1888), *The Aborigines of Australia*, Sydney.

FORTES, M & EVANS-PRITCHARD, E.E. (eds) (1970), *African Political Systems*, Oxford: Oxford University Press.

FRASER, JOHN (1892), *The Aborigines of New South Wales*, Sydney: Government Printer.

GOULD, R. A. (1969), *Yiwara*, London: Collins.

GREY, GEORGE (1841), *Journals of Two Expeditions of Discovery in North-West and Western Australia*, Two Volumes, London: T. & W. Boone.

HART, C. W. & PILLING, A. R. (1960), *The Tiwi of North Australia*, New York: Holt.

HIATT, L. R. (1959), 'Social Control in Arnhem Land', *South Pacific*, **10**(7).

—— (1965), *Kinship and Conflict*, Canberra: Australian National University Press.

—— (1968), 'Ownership and Use of Land Among the Australian Aborigines', in R. B. Lee & Irvin De Vore, *Man The Hunter*, Chicago: Aldine.

HOWITT, A. W. (1880), *Kamilaroi and Kurnai*, The Netherlands: Anthropological Publications (1967 facsimile).

—— (1904), *The Native Tribes of South-East Australia*, London: Macmillan and Co.

KABERRY, P. (1939), *Aboriginal Women; Sacred and Profane*, London: Routledge.

KOLIG, E. (1972), 'Bi:n and Gadeja', *Oceania*, **43**(1).

MADDOCK, K. (1973), *The Australian Aborigines*, London: Allen Lane.

MAIR, LUCY (1962), *Primitive Government*, Harmondsworth: Penguin Books.

MALINOWSKI, B. (1969), *The Family Among the Australian Aborigines*, New York: Schocken Books.

MATHEW, J. (1889), 'The Australian Aborigines', *Journal and Proceedings of the Royal Society of New South Wales*, Vol. XXIII.

MATHEWS, R. H. (1894), 'Aboriginal Bora Held at Gundabloui', *Journal and Proceedings of the Royal Society of New South Wales*, Vol. XXVIII.

—— (1904), 'Ethnological Notes on the Aboriginal Tribes of New South Wales and Victoria', *Journal and Proceedings of the Royal Society of New South Wales*, Vol. XXXVIII.

MEGGITT, M. J. (1966), 'Indigenous Forms of Government Among the Australian Aborigines', in Ian Hogbin & L. R. Hiatt (eds) *Readings in Australian and Pacific Anthropology*, Melbourne: Melbourne University Press.

—— (1974), *Desert People*, Sydney: Angus & Robertson.

MULVANEY, D. J. (1964), 'The Australian Aborigines, Opinion and Fieldwork. 1606–1929', in *Historical Studies; Selected Articles*, Melbourne: Melbourne University Press.

RADCLIFFE-BROWN, A. (1930), 'The Social Organization of Australian Tribes', *Oceania*, 1.

REYNOLDS, HENRY (1972), *Aborigines and Settlers*, Melbourne: Cassell Australia.

ROTH, W. E. (1897), *Ethnological Studies Among the North-West-Central Queensland Aborigines*, Brisbane: Government Printer.

ROSE, F. (1968), *Australia Revisited*, Berlin: Seven Seas.

SAHLINS, M. D. (1958), *Social Stratification in Polynesia*, Seattle: University of Washington Press.

SCHURMANN, C. W. (1879), 'The Port Lincoln Tribes' in J. D. Woods (ed.), *The Native Tribes of South Australia*, Adelaide: E. S. Wigg & Sons.

SHARP, L. (1958), 'People Without Politics', in V. F. Ray (ed.), *Systems of Political Control and Bureaucracy*, Seattle: University of Washington Press.

SMYTH, R. Brough (1876), *The Aborigines of Victoria*, Two Volumes, Melbourne: John Currey, O'Neil.

SPENCER, BALDWIN & GILLEN, F. J. (1927), *The Aranta,* Two Volumes, London: Macmillan and Co.

—— (1928), *Wanderings in Wild Australia*, London: Macmillan and Co.

—— (1968), *The Native Tribes of Central Australia*, New York: Dover.

STEPHENS, , E. (1889), 'The Aborigines of Australia', *Journal and Proceedings of the Royal Society of New South Wales*. Vol. XXIII.

STREHLOW, T. G. H. (1970), 'Geography and the Totemic Landscape in Central Australia', in R. M. Berndt (ed.), *Australian Aboriginal Anthropology*, Perth: University of Western Australia Press.

STRETTON, W. G. (1893), 'Aboriginal Tribes of the Gulf of Carpentaria', *Transactions and Proceedings and Reports of the Royal Society of South Australia*, Adelaide.

TAPLIN, G. (1879), 1. The Narrinyeri, in J. D. Woods (ed.), *The Native Tribes of South Australia*, Adelaide: E. S. Wigg & Son.

2. *The Folklore, Manners, Customs, and Languages of the South Australian Aborigines*, Adelaide: Government Printer.

TIECHELMANN, C. G. (1841), *Illustrative and Explanatory Notes of the Manners, Customs, Habits, and Superstitions of the Natives of South Australia*, Adelaide.

TONKINSON, R. (1974), *The Jigalong Mob: Aboriginal Victors of the Desert Crusade*, California: Cummings Publishing Co.

WARNER, W. L. (1958), *A Black Civilization*, New York: Harper Bros.

11
Aboriginal Political Life

L. R. HIATT[1]

In 1841 Edward John Eyre took up a selection on the Murray River at Moorundie, a few kilometres south of what is now Blanchetown. He was 26 years of age and had just returned from his heroic journey from Adelaide to Albany. In acknowledgment of his achievement, the Governor of South Australia appointed him Resident Magistrate and Protector of Aborigines on the Murray River.

At Moorundie Eyre found himself in a region 'more densely populated by natives than any in [the] colony, where no settler had ventured to locate, and where, prior to my arrival ... frightful scenes of bloodshed, rapine, and hostility between the natives and parties coming overland with stock, had been of frequent and very recent occurrence' (1845:148). Over the next three years Eyre travelled widely among the Murray and Darling tribes and evidently established a humane and peaceful relationship with them. He resigned as Protector late in 1844 and soon afterwards returned to England. On the voyage home he drafted an account of his expeditions of discovery, together with a description of the manners and customs of the Aborigines. The work was published in two volumes in 1845.

On the question of indigenous government, Eyre's view was that there was none. The natives of Australia, he thought, recognize no authority apart from time-honoured traditions: 'Through custom's irresistible sway has been forged the chain that binds in fetters a people, who might otherwise be said to be without government or restraint' (1945:384). Admittedly men of influence exist; they are typically individuals from 45 to 60 years of age, possessing strength, courage, energy, prudence, skill, and so on, and often belonging to powerful families (1845:317). Male elders discuss and decide upon matters of importance, and influential men may address the community. But '... though at such times a loud tone and strong expressions are made use of, there is rarely anything amounting to an order or command; the subject is explained, reasons are given for what is advanced, and the result of an opposite course to that suggested fully pointed out' (1845:318). After that, people are left to form their own judgements, and to act as they think proper.

In Eyre's opinion, then, talking things over and offering advice do

First given as the Wentworth Lecture, 1984. Reprinted by permission of the Australian Institute of Aboriginal Studies.

not amount to government. Government means the power to give orders and have them obeyed. Years later, as Governor of Jamaica, Eyre demonstrated executive powers in their most awesome form. Following a massacre of whites at Morant Bay in 1865, he declared a period of martial law in the course of which 439 people were executed and 600 flogged. I put the matter curtly to make an analytical point, not a moral judgment — many of you will be familiar with Geoffrey Dutton's sympathetic account of Eyre, *The Hero as Murderer*.

Some years ago John Mulvaney praised Eyre's contribution to Aboriginal studies and expressed regret that it had 'never emerged from its oblivion as an appendage to his exploration memoirs' (1958:146). That was in 1958, in the journal *Historical Studies*. By then Eyre's description of government had been superseded by formulations attributing to Aboriginal social organization a greater degree of hierarchy and centralization of power than Eyre had been able to discern at Moorundie. However, in that same year (1958), in a symposium entitled 'Systems of political control and bureaucracy in human societies' organized by the American Ethnological Society, Lauriston Sharp gave a paper on the Yir-Yoront of western Cape York Peninsula that Eyre, had he been present, would certainly have applauded (even if he might not have been able to understand all of it). Sharp, who had carried out fieldwork in the Mitchell River area in the early 1930s, referred to a number of concepts that had, as he put it, 'seeped into and seriously rigidified much of the discussion of Australian Aboriginal social structure' (1958:2); concepts such as 'chief', 'headman', 'council of elders', and 'gerontocracy'. Yet, he went on, in the whole of north Queensland no such institutions or structures are to be found.

To the European mind, accustomed as it is to positions of authority and hierarchies of command, a state of ordered anarchy poses a set of intellectual and emotional problems: how do people know what to do? who punishes wrong-doers? how are the weak protected from the strong? who organizes the community's defence against its enemies? who takes responsibility for the society's religious life? and so on. Eyre, as we have seen, attributed the performance of such civic tasks to the invisible hand of custom. Sharp, with the benefit of a century of ethnography, sought to give flesh to this notion by locating it in the domain of kinship:

> As an orderly organization of a very limited number of highly standardized roles which an individual plays over and over again in almost all his interactions with others, the Yir-Yoront or any other Australian kinship system constitutes an extremely simple but almost complete social system. (1958:4)

What Sharp meant was something like this. In accordance with well understood principles of classification, each individual in an Aboriginal community stands to every other individual in one or other of a limited number of relationships stated in the idiom of kinship. For example, approximately one-eighth of the males in my social universe may be classified as my 'father', one-eighth of the females as my 'mother', and so on. All my rights, privileges, and obligations are defined on the basis of kinship, either actual or classificatory; and, as I grow up, I also learn rules of etiquette which constrain or shape my behaviour towards others according to my predetermined relationship with them. In short, kinship rules provide a total framework for social interaction.

So far the formulation is more or less classical Radcliffe-Brown (e.g. 1952:79). Sharp, however, made these two interesting additions. First, all kinship relations among the Yir-Yoront (or, at any rate, Yir-Yoront males) are characterized by an imbalance of status; that is to say, one party to the relationship is superior or superordinate, the other is inferior or subordinate. The basis of this asymmetry has to do either with the giving and receiving of women in marriage (i.e. the gift of a bride and its attendant obligations) or with relative age. The important point is that, while no man has dealings with any other man on exactly equal terms, in half of his relationships he is superior and in the other half inferior. In such circumstances, Sharp argues, no one can be absolutely strong or absolutely weak. A fixed hierarchy of authority is an impossibility. In point of fact, 'the Yir-Yoront cannot even tolerate mild chiefs or head-men, while a leader with absolute authority over the whole group would be unthinkable' (1958:5). if authority above the level of the family is a necessary criterion for true political organization, then the Yir-Yoront are 'a people without politics' (1958:7).

Sharp's second point was that kinship roles have an aggressive or punitive aspect as well as a benevolent one. Normally the altruistic or supportive aspect is uppermost. But kinsmen also exercise some surveillance over each other's behaviour, and they may take measures against neglect of duty, breach of promise, or other delinquencies. Although there is no judiciary or police force as such in Aboriginal societies, these surveillance and disciplinary components in kinship roles serve a quasi-legal function (1958:7).

Sharp concluded, then, that Aboriginal society lacks special institutions or organizations existing for the purpose of government (1958:7). A few years later, M. J. Meggitt independently advanced a similar viewpoint. In a paper entitled 'Indigenous forms of government among the Australian Aborigines', he described Aboriginal society as 'intensely egalitarian' (1964:176) and maintained that 'although the local communities that made up the Australian tribes were the significant political and administrative units, they had no formal apparatus of government, no enduring hierarchy of authority, no recognized political leaders' (1964:178). In support of this proposition he made three main points. First, religious precedent as conceptualized and articulated within the framework of the Dreamtime provided a moral master-plan for behaviour that largely obviated the need for chiefs or headmen (1964:174). Second, although men gained ritual knowledge and ceremonial status as they grew older, the authority and prestige of male elders in the sacred sphere did not carry over into the secular sphere (1964:176). Third, the organization of co-operative undertakings such as initiation rites, death rites, or revenge expeditions was not the preroga-tive of a chief, headman, or council of elders, but (depending on the circumstances) of any and every man of mature age in the community (1964:178).

Meggitt's paper was published in 1964. In the following year, in my book *Kinship and Conflict*, I supported Meggitt's proposition on the basis both of a critical appraisal of the previous literature and of my own research among the Gidjingali. In speaking of the latter, I gave details of an ethic of generosity regulating access to resources; and I tried to bring out the importance of a set of common values and formally-defined rights and obligations operating within a political system lacking institutionalized authority. In 1972 Maddock in his general work on the Australian Aborigines described the traditional polity, with its freedom from institutions of enforcement and its stress on self-reliance and mutual aid, as a 'kind of anarchy, in which it was open to active and enterprising men to obtain some degree of influence with age, but in which none were sovereign' (1972:44).

One aspect of Meggitt's formulation I had some reservations about was the significance he attached to the notion of a transcendental master-plan. Undoubtedly, Aboriginal conceptions of correct behaviour have a basis in those cosmological and metaphysical speculations that have come to be known collectively as the Dreaming; furthermore, sanctions are certainly believed to issue from the transcendental here and now. But the existence of a supernaturally-sanctioned moral code does not imply the non-existence of governmental authority; indeed, there are innumerable instances in which the two flourish side by side. A second point is that Dreamtime heroes, like those in many other mythologies, are not always heroic; nor are they always punished for setting a bad example. As the late Professor Strehlow once commented: 'the lives of the totemic ancestors are deeply stained with deeds of treachery and violence and lust and cruelty: their "morals" are definitely inferior to those of the natives of today' (1947:38).

In short, Aboriginal religious beliefs are not so explicit and unequivocal, nor sanctions so unerring, as to constitute a set of instructions which people follow automatically. Indeed, Dreamtime formulations often manifest a deeper concern with understanding what man is than with prescribing how he ought to behave. If traditional Aboriginal society truly lacked government, the reason is unlikely to be found in the content of the traditional religion (see Sackett 1978:42; Hiatt 1975, 1983).

Putting this particular issue to one side, the common ground between me and Meggitt, and between us and Sharp, is clear enough: Aboriginal political life is characterized by a uniform distribution of rights, privileges, and duties throughout a social order based on kinship and suffused by an egalitarian ideology. In recent years this position has been assailed from two directions; on the one hand, there has been what we can refer to as 'class-oriented' Marxist critique; and, on the other, a kind of Hobbesian individualism. Let us begin with the second.

After Sharp left Mitchell River in 1935, no further anthropological research was carried out in western Cape York until 1968, following the establishment of a chair of anthropology at the University of Queensland. John von Sturmer and Peter Sutton, who worked at

Aurukun and Cape Keerweer respectively and who submitted important doctoral theses in 1978, have both explicitly challenged Sharp's formulation. Sutton underscores the point by referring to Aborigines as 'people *with* politicks'. In his thesis on Cape Keerweer he reported that each clan usually has a senior man or woman who is unambiguously the spokesperson for that clan's country; that 'big men' or 'bosses' occur at a regional level, encompassing numerous clans; and that the success of such leaders depends on qualities such as political astuteness, skill in argument, fighting prowess, and the ability to mobilize large numbers of kinsmen and kinswomen as supporters. In a recent paper (1982), written in collaboration with Bruce Rigsby, he argues that traditional Aboriginal political life has been misrepresented because anthropologists have preferred to believe that Aborigines lack the competitiveness and shrewdness of urban industrial peoples.

Political life among the Kugu-Nganychara, as described by von Sturmer (1978), revolves around the pursuit of pre-eminence as a ceremonial 'big man' or 'boss'. Two vital ingredients for success are (1) an aptitude for ritual discipline, and (2) control of an important totemic site. While all men of normal intelligence and ability graduate to the status of *pama manu thaiyan* (meaning a man of thick or strong neck), only some are singled out for the special training necessary for big-man status (*pama kathawawa*). This involves periods of celibacy and fasting, undergoing various other mental ordeals and indignities, as well as instruction in the performing arts. But talent and special training, while necessary for pre-eminence, are not sufficient. Ceremonies focus on particular sites, and to be boss of a big ceremony, one has to control a big site. Ownership is normally transmitted from father to eldest son; but unless an inheritance is actively protected and reaffirmed, it may be lost to more forceful rivals. In short, land tenure is subject to competition; and von Sturmer surmises that, over time, the most powerful individuals and their supporters will gravitate towards the most important sites.

Important ritual sites are often located at or near favoured camp locations (e.g. at the mouth of a river, offering ready access to ample water and food resources). They constituted the premium ecological vantage points along the coast; and, in von Sturmer's judgement, there would have been a tendency in pre-European times for the boss of such a focal site to have become the focal male for a whole riverine community. There can be no question, he says, 'that certain individuals . . . achieved a level of eminence and prestige beyond that enjoyed by their peers (sic), and wielded authority at a supra-familial level' (1978:421). The nature of this authority is a question I shall return to.

In 1974 John Bern advanced a similar analysis of the relationship between land, ritual, and politics in his thesis on political struggle and competition in southeastern Arnhem Land. According to Bern:

> Control of the major rites is based on the custody of the ritual estates, and both are subject to competition. Success in this competition confers prestige on the victor, a prestige whose relevance is largely restricted to ritual performances and associated activities. The competition for prestige is a major interest in the holding of the ceremonies. (1974:217)

Subsequently Bern was led to consider whether Aboriginal political life is amenable to analysis within a 'Marxist problematic'. And in *Oceania* 1979 he published a critique of the Sharp/Meggitt/Hiatt position in which he asserted that not only were the conclusions false but the wrong questions were being asked. According to Bern, the representation of Aboriginal politics as an embodiment of ordered anarchy and equality can be sustained only by pretending that the female sex and the junior half of the male population do not exist. In addition, we have to assent to an analytic division of the social milieu into secular and ceremonial activities as though they constitute two separate and unconnected domains. On the contrary, Bern argues, religion is the ruling ideology where the relations of domination in the Aboriginal social formation are articulated and justified. The dominant category in traditional society is made up of senior males. It is they who control the secret religious cults, from which women are excluded and into which junior males are inducted through elaborate initiation procedures. And it is they who control female reproductivity through the institution of bestowal. Typically, young women marry senior males, who not uncommonly acquire a plurality of wives as they grow older. Young men are thus deprived of wives and, moreover, are officially expected to remain celibate throughout their bachelorhood (which roughly coincides with the period of their induction into religious mysteries).

Now the immediate question is whether these three formulations represent contradictory viewpoints or whether in fact they are mutually compatible statements about different aspects of a complex field of inquiry. I want to argue for the second alternative, but let me straightaway dipose of what I consider to be a non-issue, viz. the question whether Aborigines have, or do not have, politics (spelt with a 'k' or without one). We could agree about the facts of Aboriginal social life, yet continue to disagree as to whether or not Aborigines have politics simply because we disagree about the definition of politics. I do not intend to get into an argument about terminology. I see no special virtue in the evolutionist taxonomy accepted by Sharp for the purposes of his discussion in 1958, and I am perfectly happy with the broad usage advocated by Sutton and von Sturmer. Indeed, from 1962 onwards, following Hart and Pilling in their book on *The Tiwi*, I have regularly used the expression 'politics of bestowal' to refer to strategies used by bestowers and seekers of wives to advance their interests in a context of scarcity. In short, I do not argue, and never have argued, that Aborigines are 'people without politics'.

In making a retrospective evaluation of Meggitt's paper on Aboriginal government, we should remember that its objectives were largely set by programmes established within the British structuralist school of social anthropology, then still flourishing. Meggitt refers at the beginning to two exemplary collections of essays on African political systems, one edited by Fortes and Evans-Pritchard (1940), and the other by Middleton and Tait (1958); and his own paper can be fairly described as a contribution to what Radcliffe-Brown called 'comparative morphology'

(1952:195). 'In the political structure of the United States', Radcliffe-Brown wrote, 'there must always be a President; at one time it is Herbert Hoover, at another time Franklin Roosevelt, but the structure as an arrangement remains continuous' (1952:10). The question Meggitt therefore asked himself was whether in traditional Aboriginal society there is a structure of government which can be described independently of the individuals who, as it were, pass through it.

Against this background it is clear that when Meggitt concludes that Aboriginal communities have no enduring hierarchy of authority, the critical word is 'enduring'. With respect to the administration of public affairs, he is asserting that there is no single articulated set of super-ordinate and subordinate statuses which operates from one situation to another and which persists as a system over time in accordance with acknowledged rules of recruitment. In these terms, the Aboriginal polity would seem to be morphologically distinct from, say, a Polynesian chiefdom which comprises a pyramidal structure of positions filled by a formal process of installation, designated by titles, and carrying with them authority over a wide range of public matters as an inherent feature.

From such a viewpoint, statements about relations of domination and subordination on the basis of age and sex differences, as well as about individual differences in achievement and prestige, might be regarded as true but irrelevant. To make a simple analogy, the author of an essay on school government might consider it important to describe the prefect system (the duties and privileges of office, method of appointment, powers of the head prefect, etc.) but regard it as outside the scope of the analysis to investigate bullying and bastardization of juniors by seniors, or competition for success in various spheres of activity such as scholarship, sport, performing arts, and so on.

For my own part, I see no logical difficulty in maintaining simultaneously that traditional Aboriginal communities lack enduring hierarchies of authority for the administration of public affairs; that individuals, especially senior males, compete for control of scarce natural and metaphysical resources in order to gain or enhance reputations as ceremonial big-men; and that, collectively, senior males exercise a degree of domination over junior males and females, especially in the sphere of religion. Furthermore, I believe that all three propositions are substantially true. In that case, however, what do we make of Meggitt's description of Aboriginal society as 'intensely egalitarian'? Was he mistaken?; or are we confronted here, in this Wentworth Lecture of 1984, with a version of Orwell s paradox 'all [men] are equal, but some are more equal than others'?

Now, as it happens, Fred Myers has argued in a recent series of papers (1980a, 1980b, 1982) that a central paradox of Pintupi political life is the coexistence of hierarchy and egalitarianism; furthermore, the traditional resolution of this problematic, as Myers phrases it, comes remarkably close to the Orwellian formula. He says: 'The content of this mediation might be summarised as the statement that while all men are ... equal because all are subordinate to the same moral imperative, those who came before (viz. the elders) hold and represent The Dreaming for those who come after' (1980b:312). What the elders hold in trust is esoteric knowledge, deemed necessary for the attainment of full manhood. The only legitimate way to procure it is through initiation. Therefore, to put the matter somewhat more bluntly, while all men are subordinate to the transcendental, those who need the word are subordinate to those who have it (see Kolig 1982).

The disciplines imposed by Pintubi men are sustained and severe. They include tooth avulsion, nose-piercing, circumcision, subincision, fire ordeals, and the removal of finger-nails. Novices may be beaten for too much talking, inattention, or insolence. They may be awakened at any hour of the night and chased with bullroarers. From time to time they stand in a line with heads bowed, signifying subordination; and during ritual performances, senior men shout orders at them and threaten them with violence. Indeed, according to Strehlow (1970:120) 'Executions of younger males, especially of those who were considered to be disrespectful to the authority of their own elders, on charges of sacrilege were ... a feature of the accepted penal systems of all ... tribes in the Centre'.

This may seem a harsh regime. Yet, by focusing upon the Pintubi concept of 'holding' or 'looking after', Myers is able to show how the conservation and transmission of transcendental knowledge is represented as a kind of nurture. Within the context of the secret cult, initiated men act symbolically as 'male mothers' who pass on to neophytes the wherewithal for spiritual development. The subordination of young men and their maintenance in a protracted state of immaturity and bachelorhood is conceived as a necessary condition for the discharge of a sacred duty: the custodians of esoteric knowledge act out of a loving responsibility for succeeding generations and for the cosmos itself.

This profound and pervasive paternalism would hardly seem to provide a fertile ground for the development of egalitarianism. Yet, according to Myers, egalitarianism is a central value in Pintupi culture. He speaks of 'the contemporary community at Yayayi with its egalitarian ethos' (1980b:313), of the Pintupi as a 'society of autonomous, egalitarian actors' (1980b:311), of 'the over-riding concern of individuals with "egalitarianism"' (1980b:315), and so on. In essence, Pintupi egalitarianism means 'no one is better than me'; and it is common for men to say such things as 'he's only a man like me'. From Myers' account, it would seem that the concept embraces both a sentiment of equal intrinsic worth and a notion of an equality of rights and privileges (cf. Jayawardena 1968). The question is, how can it flourish side by side with religious authoritarianism?

Meggitt's answer, as we have seen, is that religious authority is non-portable. To quote his precise words:

> ... no matter how much authority people conceded to a ritual leader in the sacred sphere, it did not as a rule extend at all into secular affairs ...; the religious expert did not on this account derive any special freedom from social conventions in the secular world: he had no immunity from criticism or from open violence in everyday disputes. Away from the ceremonial ground he was but another member of an intensely egalitarian society ... (1964:176)

Strehlow (1970) has challenged this formulation on empirical grounds, asserting that in pre-European times ceremonial leaders and old men of authority terrorized whole communities through their monopoly of cult-based power. However that may be, Meggitt's final sentence now seems unsatisfactory to me on logical grounds, since it leaves the existential status of the ceremonial ground completely obscure: is it part of Aboriginal society or not? Assuming that it is, and that the values in force there are non-egalitarian, the description of Aboriginal society as intensely egalitarian is clearly in need of some correction.

Myers' argument, so far as I can follow it, is not merely that hierarchy and egalitarianism flourish together in Pintubi society but that, in some sense or in some degree, the latter is actually a product of the former. Like others before him, he contrasts the severity of initiation procedures with the lack of discipline in childhood. To an American observer, he says, the freedom enjoyed by Aboriginal children is truly remarkable. Nowadays Pintubi youths refer to the period of seclusion for initiation as 'high school', thereby alluding to its educational content, but also as 'prison'. The newly-initiated are said to be 'free men'. What we have, then, is a transition from the irresponsible freedom of childhood to the responsible freedom of adulthood, mediated by a period of humiliation, suffering, and subordination. The experience certainly induces an abiding respect for seniority, and for years to come the initiates will be inhibited and unassertive in the presence of their male elders. But, according to Myers, through the laying on of hands and the gift of the spirit, it also provides a foundation for the development of personal autonomy and self-respect.

As it is only a year since we celebrated the 500th anniversary of the birth of Luther, there is no need for me to remind you that the mediation of man's relation to God by religious hierarchies has a long and complex history. Much as I am impressed by Myers' empathy with Pintubi culture, I am not convinced that Aboriginal egalitarianism depends on paternalism and graded access to the transcendental. If personal autonomy means independence, as I should suppose it does, it is hard to understand how it is promoted by cultivating in grown men a spirit of dependence upon authority. Unless, of course, authoritarianism has a tendency to create its opposite. Perhaps this is the clue. After the indulgence of a mother-focused infancy followed by a permissive boyhood, Aboriginal youths are suddenly confronted by father-figures in whom threat is dramatically magnified, at the same time as benevolent paternalism is proffered in return for obedience. Within the context of the cult, the only option consistent with survival is submission. Outside the cult, however — back in the general community — a compensatory anti-authoritarianism takes hold. Egalitarianism becomes 'intense' (Meggitt), the notion of a chief 'intolerable' (Sharp).

I place no great weight on this speculation. The essential point is that the indigenous Australian polity was neither wholly authoritarian, nor wholly egalitarian. Rather, both elements coexisted in strong measure. It may be (and here I offer a further speculation) that the tension between them helps to explain some of the characteristic adaptations of

Aboriginal society to European hegemony. On the one hand, traditional egalitarianism militates against the emergence of black political leaders. According to Myers, rank-and-file Pintupi regard decisions by the village council not only as having no authority but as lacking respect for the autonomy of others; as one man said after the announcement of a no-liquor law, 'it's only their idea; they are just men like me' (1982:7; cf. Sackett 1978). On the other hand, traditional religious authoritarianism may perhaps pave the way for a ready acceptance of paternalism emanating from an external source. A white 'boss' is conceived as a person who 'looks after' Aborigines in return for deference and obedience. As Chris Anderson notes: 'Aboriginal people today in south-eastern Cape York Peninsula speak of "my old boss", often with a great deal of humour and affection, sometimes even when he had been "hard" or "cheeky"' (1984:228). One man said sorrowfully of another: 'Poor old fella, he got no boss' (1984:228).

Let us move from the corporate power of senior males to the question of individual 'bigmanship'. At the outset I should make it clear that when I refer to egalitarianism in Aboriginal society, I do not in any sense imply that individuals are endowed with a natural disinclination to excel or to be admired or to gain ascendancy over others; any more than I imply that Aborigines are by nature unselfish when I draw attention to the importance they attach to generosity. It would be more accurate to say that in both instances we are dealing with cultural values directed *against* natural tendencies. Traditionally, public disapproval of selfishness and self-importance reinforced the distributive effects of the laws governing land tenure and marriage, and inhibited the emergence of marked differences in wealth, status, and power. To inhibit ambition is not, however, to remove it; and, as Eyre acknowledged when he spoke of 'powerful families', the status profile of an Aboriginal community is not entirely flat. Probably everywhere, through a combination of genealogical good luck, enterprise, and energy, some men acquired more wives than others and raised more children. Ian Keen (1982) has argued that, on this basis, certain kinship systems may generate a higher degree of social inequality than others. Some Yolngu men, for instance, are able to acquire unusually large harems (Berndt & Berndt 1964:172). Such achievements tend to produce fast-growing clans through positive feedback (i.e. success tends to breed success); and flourishing clans may acquire the estates of dying clans through a process, well-described by Howard Morphy (1977), of ritual custodianship and accretion. The senior men of such clans, with their ample resources in land, wives, and warriors, are well-placed to become citizens of note; and, not uncommonly, they embellish their reputations by becoming patrons and practitioners of the religious arts.

A long-standing problem in the study of Aboriginal religion is why certain totems become more important than others. Let me give an example. In their great work of 1899, Spencer and Gillen described the Engwura ceremony, the final and most important of the four rituals constituting the male initiation complex among the Aranda. It lasts about four months and consists of a long series of totemic rituals culminating in the revelation of a particularly sacred icon, symbolising female generative powers. The totems represented vary from one Engwura ceremony to another, depending on which local groups happen to be present. But one totem, the ancestral Wild Cat, is always pre-eminent. According to Aranda mythology, all totems and totemic sites were created in the Dreamtime by a supreme superhuman ancestor called Numbakulla. Numbakulla's first creation was Wild Cat. Before disappearing forever, Numbakulla gave the sacred icon to the first Wild Cat man; the Engwura ceremony as performed today is said to reproduce in all essentials the Engwura ceremony performed by the Wild Cat ancestors in the Dreamtime.

Spencer and Gillen describe the Engwura as the 'great central ceremony of the whole tribe'. When Durkheim wrote *The Elementary Forms of the Religious Life* not long afterwards, he viewed rituals like the Engwura as constituting an evolutionary step towards a higher level of social integration: initially, so the argument goes, there were totems symbolizing the unity of the individual clans; subsequently, one of these totems came to symbolize the unity of the whole tribe (1961:320–1). What is unexplained, however, is why it was this one rather than that one (i.e. why Wild Cat rather than Kangaroo, or Eaglehawk, etc?). Spencer and Gillen indicate that the Engwura, though performed by all initiated Aranda men, belongs primarily to the people of the Wild Cat totemic group, who officially control the ceremony (1899:233). Although the authors give the mythological ratification for Wild Cat supremacy, they are unable to provide any sociological clues as to how this may have come about historically. No doubt any such clues are lost forever in the case of the Aranda. But the trend of recent research suggests that, whatever integrative function Aboriginal religion may have, it also constitutes a major domain in which men compete for prestige. It is a reasonable speculation that, within this arena, the pre-eminence of particular rituals and supernatural conceptions may represent the success of particular mortal aspirations and energies.

Although a man may try to become a 'big name' through the deployment of artistic, administrative, and political talents in the religious life, we should note that the religious and artistic forms as such do not glorify individual human achievement or reputation. Men may become great singers, but singers do not sing the praises of great men. Furthermore, the extent to which individual achievement in ceremonial matters confers authority over other mature men in non-ceremonial contexts remains a vexed and unresolved issue. Von Sturmer says that 'the "big man" is not only the major decision-maker and instructor in matters of ceremony, he is also the arbiter of what constitutes correct or incorrect knowledge. While every individual has the right to air his or her views on all issues of moment, the "big man" speaks only after all others have spoken. His is literally the final word. While others speak, he is heard' (1978:450). But, having heard, do people obey; or, to recall Eyre's words, do they 'form their own judgments, and ... act as they think proper' (1845:318)? And if actions regularly conform to the "big man's" prescriptions, is it because of his position and power, or is it because, having listened to everyone, he articulates a consensus that has already been reached? Or a combination of both? Unfortunately we know little more about the forms and effects of traditional oratory and debate than Eyre did (cf. Thomson 1956:91), and I sincerely hope that this aspect of Aboriginal political life will attract the attention it deserves in the future as a matter of urgency.

Years ago my colleague Frank Gurrmanamana explained to me how, in northern Arnhem Land in pre-European times, an assembly of men might reach a decision to execute an individual whose violence had become a matter of deep public concern. Gurrmanamana invented a scenario in which a man he described as 'the oldest brother, an old man, a really important man' opens the meeting with these words (I translate from the Gidjingali): 'You who are assembled here, I speak to you all. Perhaps you will agree with me.' Someone replies: 'Tell us what you have to say. Then we will tell you whether we agree with you.' The senior man speaks of two killers whose violence has terrorized the whole community; and he suggests that they should be assassinated. 'Talk it over among yourselves', he says, 'and if you decide to do it, we must not say a word about it.' Two men volunteer, and with the moral backing of the meeting, carry out a surprise night attack, and the deed is done.

Although I realize that such a slender piece of evidence proves nothing, I offer it as an example of a style of 'big man' oratory more in keeping with a secular polity structured around consensus than with a system geared to a hierarchy of command. It may well be that in western Cape York the style is more authoritarian, and consensus less important. In a recent paper, Athol Chase states that at Lockhart River in eastern Cape York, 'There can be a "big man" for ceremonies, and a "boss" for sites and country, but rarely a "boss" for people ... The ethos is that to set oneself up as a spokesperson or a leader of people against others is an act of foolhardiness, and one which will lead to public humiliation ... Leadership, if it occurs, is covert' (1984:117).

Chase suggests that the uniform spread of natural resources along the east coast inhibits the emergence of economic and political inequality, whereas the special importance of estuarine sites on the west coast facilitates it. This close-grained analysis of the role of ecological factors in determining cultural variation is obviously important and deserves to be pursued further. But a similar point also needs to be made about historical factors, viz. that some of the forces emanating from white Australia may inhibit 'big man' tendencies, while others may strengthen them. As Rolf Gerritsen has argued in two recent papers (1984a & b), a combination of white patronage, ceremonial prominence, and 'traditional owner' status under the Northern Territory Land Rights Act of 1976 is producing a category of (to use his words) 'dominant men' in Aboriginal communities who are able to magnify their importance by controlling the distribution of new wealth. It would appear that in some instances such individuals have consolidated their positions to the extent that they are no longer susceptible to constraining or levelling forces inherent in the traditional polity (Smith 1984).

In this review of perceptions of Aboriginal political life, I have spent my allotted time talking about issues of egalitarianism, authoritarianism, and careerism among men. I regret that I have said nothing about women, apart from alluding to their alleged subordination. Although individual women display leadership and initiative in the organization and performance of women's secret ceremonies (see, for example, Kaberry 1939:253–68), no one yet has spoken of ceremonial 'big womanship'. Nor has anyone reported that induction into women's cults is accompanied by disciplines of the sort that characterize male initiation. In many parts of Australia, women are expected to act as junior partners to their menfolk (White 1970:26); and often their labour and ideologically-cultivated nurturing responsibilities are exploited for the purpose of sustaining male cults (Hamilton 1975:170). The reverse seems not to occur. Indeed, from the viewpoint of gerontocratic polygynists, women's so-called 'love magic' rituals may seem more like hotbeds of subversion than adjuncts to orthodox religion, in so far as they glamorize inclinations towards sexual infidelity (Kaberry 1939:267; Berndt 1965:245; Reay 1970). For the most part, women are not in the business of domination but of resistance (Cowlishaw 1978; 1979), through which in favourable circumstances they may achieve the kind of collective autonomy so well-described in the recent work of Annette Hamilton (1980) and Diane Bell (1983). I see women, therefore, as contributing more to the egalitarian and anarchistic tendencies in Aboriginal society than to its authoritarian components, though it should be acknowledged that they may also feel obliged to support the ambitions of their menfolk.

As John Bern (1979) has remarked, Meggitt's paper for a time was regarded as the definitive statement on traditional Aboriginal political life. Its publication coincided with the formal establishment of the Australian Institute of Aboriginal Studies. Practically all the work I have surveyed in the second part of my paper has been carried out under the Institute's auspices; and, if I have done nothing else, I hope I have demonstrated that our understanding of Aboriginal political life has been considerably advanced as a result of it. Far from being settled, the topic is in a state of ferment. That in itself must be a source of satisfaction to the man in whose honour this lecture is named, since intellectual ferment is the state he probably relishes most.

Note

1. For comments and suggestions I am particularly grateful to Margaret Clunies Ross, Jeremy Beckett, Gillian Cowlishaw, Diane Bell, John Bern, Jan Larbalestier, John von Sturmer, Peter Sutton, and Fred Myers.

References

ANDERSON, C. (1984), The political and economical basis of Kuku-Yalanji social history, unpublished PhD thesis, University of Queensland.

BELL, D. (1983), *Daughters of the Dreaming*, Melbourne: McPhee Gribble.

BERN, J. (1974), Blackfella business, whitefella law, unpublished PhD thesis, Macquarie University.

—— (1979), 'Ideology and domination: toward a reconstruction of Australian Aboriginal social formation', *Oceania*, **50**, 2, 118–32.

BERNDT, C. (1965), 'Women and the "secret life"', in R. & C. Berndt (eds), *Aboriginal Man in Australia*, Sydney: Angus & Robertson.

BERNDT, R. and C. (1964), *The World of the First Australians*, Sydney: Ure Smith.

CHASE, A. K. (1984), 'Belonging to country: territory, identity and environment in Cape York Peninsula, Northern Australia', in L. R. Hiatt (ed.), *Aboriginal Landowners*, Oceania Monograph No. 27, Sydney University.

COWLISHAW, G. (1978), 'Infanticide in Aboriginal Australia', *Oceania*, **48**, 262–83.

—— (1979), Women's realm: a study of socialization, sexuality, and reproduction among Australian Aborigines, unpublished PhD thesis, University of Sydney.

DURKHEIM, E. (1961). *The Elementary Forms of the Religious Life*, New York: Collier Books.

DUTTON, G. (1967), *The Hero as Murderer*, Sydney: Collins.

EYRE, E. J. (1845), *Journals of Expeditions of Discovery into Central Australia and Overland from Adelaide to King George's Sound 1840–1*, Vol. 2, London: Boone.

FORTES, M. & Evans-Pritchard, E. E. (eds) (1940), *African Political Systems*, London: Oxford University Press.

GERRITSEN, R. (1981a), 'Thoughts on Camelot: from Herodians and zealots to the contemporary politics of remote Aboriginal settlement in the Northern Territory', Paper presented to the Australian Political Studies Association, 23rd Annual Conference, Canberra.

—— (1981b), 'Blackfellas and Whitefellas: the politics of service delivery to remote Aboriginal communities in the Katherine region, N.T.', Paper presented at North Australian Research Unit, Darwin.

Hamilton, A. (1975), 'Aboriginal women: the means of production', in J. Mercer (ed.), *The Other Half*, Harmondsworth: Penguin.

—— (1980), 'Dual social systems: technology, labour and women's secret rites in the eastern Western Desert of Australia', *Oceania,* **51**(1), 4–19.

HART, C. & A. Pilling (1960), *The Tiwi*, New York: Holt, Rinehart & Winston.

HIATT, L. (1965), *Kinship and Conflict; A Study of an Aboriginal Community in Northern Arnhem Land*, Canberra: ANU Press.

—— (1975), *Australian Aboriginal Mythology*, Canberra: Australian Institute of Aboriginal Studies.

—— (1983), 'The relationship between Aboriginal religion and Aboriginal customary law', *Law Reform Commission Report* (*Aboriginal Customary Law*), Sydney: Australian Law Reform Commission.

JAYAWARDENA, C. (1968), 'Ideology and conflict in lower class communities', *Comparative Studies in Society and History*, **10**(4), 413–46.

KABERRY, P. (1939), *Aboriginal Woman: Sacred and Profane*, London: Routledge.

KEEN, I. (1982), 'How some Murngin men marry ten wives: the marital implications of matrilateral cross-cousin structures', *Man*, **17**(4) 620–42.

KOLIG, E. (1982), 'An obituary for ritual power', in M. Howard (ed.), *Aboriginal Power in Australian Society*, St Lucia: University of Queensland Press.

MADDOCK, K. (1972), *The Australian Aborigines*, London: Allen Lane.

MEGGITT, M. J. (1964), 'Indigenous forms of government among the Australian Aborigines', *Bijdragen tot de Taal-, Land- en Volkenkunde*, **120**, 163–78.

MIDDLETON, J. & D. TAIT (eds) (1958), *Tribes without Rulers*, London: Routledge & Kegan Paul.

MORPHY, H. (1977), Too many meanings: an analysis of the artistic system of the Yolngu of north-east Arnhem Land, PhD thesis, Australian National University.

MULVANEY, D. J. (1958), 'The Australian Aborigines 1606–1929: Opinion and Fieldwork', *Historical Studies*, **8**, Part I, 131–51.

MYERS, F. (1980a), 'The cultural basis of politics in Pintupi life', *Mankind*, **12**(3), 197–214.

—— (1980b), 'A broken code: Pintupi political theory and contemporary social life', *Mankind*, **12**(4), 311–26.

—— (1982), 'Ethnography, language, and social value among Pintupi Aborigines', Paper prsented in honour of Mervyn Meggitt, American Anthropological Association Meeting.

RADCLIFFE-BROWN, A. R. (1952), *Structure and Function in Primitive Society*, London: Cohen & West.

REAY, M. (1970), 'Decision as narrative', in R. Berndt (ed.), *Australian Aboriginal Anthropology*, Perth: University of WA Press.

SACKETT, L. (1978), 'Clinging to the Law: leadership at Wiluna', in M. Howard (ed.), '*Whitefella Business*': *Aborigines in Australian Politics*, Philadelphia: Institute for the Study of Human Issues.

SHARP, L. (1958), 'People without politics', in V. Ray (ed.), *Systems of Political Control and Bureaucracy in Human Societies*, Seattle: University of Washington Press.

SMITH, D. (1984), '"That Register business": the role of the Land Councils in determining traditional Aboriginal owners', in L. R. Hiatt (ed.), *Aboriginal Landowners*, Oceania Monograph No. 27, Sydney University.

SPENCER, B. & GILLEN, F. (1899), *The Native Tribes of Central Australia*, London: Macmillan.

STREHLOW, T. G. H. (1947), *Aranda Traditions*, Melbourne: Melbourne University Press.

—— (1970), 'Geography and the totemic landscape in Central Australia: a functional study', in R. M. Berndt (ed.), *Australian Aboriginal Anthropology*, Perth: University of WA Press.

SUTTON, P. (1978), Wik: Aboriginal society, territory and language at Cape Keerweer, Cape York Peninsula, Australia, unpublished PhD thesis, University of Queensland.

—— & RIGSBY, B. (1982), 'People with 'politicks': management of land and personnel on Australia's Cape York Peninsula', in N. Williams & E. Hunn (eds), *Resource Managers: North American and Australian Hunter-gatherers*, Colorado: Westview Press.

THOMSON, D. F. (1956), 'The Aborigines of Australia', in *The Australian Junior Encyclopaedia*, Sydney: Australian Educational Foundation.

VON STURMER, J. (1978), The Wik region: economy, territoriality and totemism in western Cape York Peninsula, North Queensland, unpublished PhD thesis, University of Queensland.

WHITE, I. (1970), 'Aboriginal women's status: a paradox resolved', in F. Gale (ed.) *Woman's Role in Aboriginal Society*, Canberra: Australian Institute of Aboriginal Studies.

12
All Bosses Are Not Created Equal

CHRISTOPHER ANDERSON

Introduction

It is generally agreed in the literature that older men in most if not all Australian Aboriginal societies had considerable formal power and constituted a structurally dominant category. However, some studies, focusing primarily on traditional systems and settings, have shown that certain individuals within that general category had considerably more power and authority than others. These positions have been variously termed boss, big man, head man and so on. I want to show, in a case study from south-east Cape York Peninsula, north Queensland, the continuity of this phenomenon in the move from traditional to neo-traditional camps and to centralized community living. Given the widespread usage of the term 'boss' in discussions of Aboriginal systems, it is an appropriate time to begin thinking in more theoretical terms about the notion. Accordingly, I attempt to lay some groundwork for understanding the relationship between individuals and the structural frameworks within which they operate. I should point out that this paper is part of a larger study (Anderson 1984) which examines Aboriginal bosses within a historical materialist perspective. In that work I deal much more fully with the structures within which action occurs.

Aborigines, Status and the Individual

Egalitarianism is accepted as fact in most historical and anthropological accounts of Aboriginal society. Yet in many of these same accounts, particular Aboriginal individuals stand out time and time again. We can see this in the records dating from the first phase of settlement as well as in those referring to recent times: for the Sydney area there is Bungaree (Collins 1802) and Colby (White 1790); Davey in the Port Stephens area (Reece 1974); Magill at Port Macquarie (Threlkeld 1974); Wongo (Thomson 1983), Mahkarolla (Warner 1958), Buramara (R. M. Berndt 1962) and Mawalan (Mountford 1956, 1967; Macknight 1976) from Arnhem Land; Durmugam from Daly River (Stanner 1959); and Nosepeg from Central Australia (Tindale 1974) to mention a few. Debates may rage over whether Aboriginal

First published in *Anthropological Forum*, **V**(4), 1988.

societies had gerontocracy or anarchy, government or no government, but who are these men and why do similar individuals constantly appear in the literature?

Similarly, one notices in Aboriginal Australia generally the strong association of particular individuals with particular places. Invariably, anthropologists and others familiar with Aboriginal communities, outstations and camps give unequivocal answers to questions concerning the Aboriginal 'powers that be' in a given place. In 1985 driving along the road from Fregon to Ernabella in northern South Australia, Peter Sutton and I saw half a dozen or more turnoff signs which said things like 'Katjikatji Horace' and 'Tjatja Bore Jimmy'. Subsequent enquiries revealed that these signs were composed of the names of homeland centres (Katjikatji, Tjatja, etc.) followed by the names of their respective focal people (Horace, Jimmy, etc.). Now this does not say anything necessarily about relative power, but neither does it fit the usual picture of an Aboriginal pantisocracy — a utopian community in which all are equal and all rule. It is interesting enough that residential sites are labelled by use of a single individual's name, but why those individuals and not others?

The notion of status has not been used extensively to analyse Aboriginal societies. This is probably because most studies of status go on to look at social stratification and people seem to have found it difficult to cope with the idea of stratification and Aboriginal society. Yet while status in Linton's (1936) sense involves an identity position in a social system, it also implies differential rights and obligations to others: in other words, inequalities. In this sense there appear to have been three primary sets of attributes associated with status positions in Aboriginal society: biological, structural, and what we might term informal or political ones. The biological comprises what Balandier (1970:79) calls 'the so-called "natural" inequalities'. These are 'based on differences of sex and age, but "treated" by the cultural environment in which they are expressed, [and] are revealed in a hierarchy of individual positions placing men in relation to women and each individual within the sex group according to age'. By structural attributes of status positions I refer to those formal attributes which are particular combinations of the biological (age and sex) and of kinship. Along with kinship, other factors which can be involved include territorial and totemic affiliation and descent. The 'political' attributes of status in Aboriginal society, on the other hand, refer to *achieved status*: positions obtained via qualities different from or over and above the *ascribed status* arising from biological and structural factors (cf. Linton 1936). These three sets of attributes are clearly interrelated in a complex yet hierarchical manner: for example, in some systems it may be impossible to attain a position of high structural status (e.g. clan head) without a 'high' biological status (e.g. old age), and similarly, impossible to attain political status at all without the other two (cf. Sutton 1982:183–6).

Inequalities are implied in all three of the above attribute sets. Yet most writers, in discussing, for instance, differential power and authority in Aboriginal societies, have stressed almost exclusively the biological and structural aspects. In other words, they maintain that power differences are due only to factors such as age, sex and kinship. I suggest that these were only prerequisites and that there existed in Aboriginal societies positions of achieved status which had roles of great significance. Because they have not made the distinction between ascribed and achieved status in analysing Aboriginal societies, most writers have underestimated the importance of achieved status positions. It is the people in these roles who were the 'leaders' in Aboriginal life. The focus on achieved status allows us to resolve certain of the difficulties with discussions about Aboriginal 'government' and politics. It also adds a new dimension to the debate on Australian local organization. This paper proposes that a primary determinant of camp and, in centralized communities, 'mob' or group composition was the existence of 'bosses' who have status, power and authority over and above that of persons of equivalent biological and structural status.

Power and Authority at Bloomfield River

Previous work on reconstruction of Aboriginal land and political systems in Cape York Peninsula demonstrates a distinction between status and authority arising from structural position and that stemming from other sources. The power of particular individuals in dispute settlement and in discussion of matters affecting the group is mentioned by Thomson (1933:495, 1935:463) who uses the notion of 'big man'. Chase (1980, 1984), working later in the same area of Cape York Peninsula, also uses this term and describes some of the attributes on which the position is based. In western Cape York Peninsula, Sharp — although later (1958) denying the existence of any 'chiefs' or 'headmen' — in his 1934 paper talks about various Yir-Yoront clans as being ranked to a degree, with 'their prestige depending on the tribal importance of the clan's ancestors ... [and] on the importance of the men in the living clan ...' (1934:20). Sharp also mentions that diffuse moral sanctions among the Yir-Yoront derive from 'the effect of the example of the "great men", living and dead, who epitomize the social standards of conduct and belief and who are greatly admired ...' (ibid.:39). More recently, Sutton (1978, 1982) and von Sturmer (1978) present important data documenting the role of particular individuals in western Cape York Aboriginal political life and especially their role as focal points for household, larger residential groupings and regional entities. Von Sturmer describes how 'the "big man" becomes the pivotal member of a network which embraces, and, through the character of its linkages, defines the resident and exploiting population' in the vicinity of important residential and ceremonial sites (1978:451). (See Hiatt (1982, 1984) for a summary of this work.)

I want to add to the above picture by describing something of the nature of power and domination among the Kuku-Yalanji of Bloomfield River in south-eastern Cape York Peninsula. I also want to demonstrate, though, continuity in the nature of certain political positions and relationships within Kuku-Yalanji society despite the shift from bush camps to a mission setting.

Formal system and practice around 1880

The term *Ngujakura* describes an ideological system seen as governing
the interaction between Kuku-Yalanji and the environment and between
members of the Kuku-Yalanji. As such, it reflected the social relations of
production in Kuku-Yalanji society. It ensured the supply of necessary
resources, and it secured the distribution and channelling of resources in
particular directions. *Ngujakura* also defined in a general way the form of
social relationships. The Kuku-Yalanji world order was seen largely to be
dependent on fulfilment of this law.

Bingabinga, adult and older men, were viewed as the cornerstones of
Ngujakura through their connections with the spiritual world. The upholding of the law — as defined by the *bingabinga*, of course — protected
humans from spirit mal-intent. In addition, it ensured continuance of the
Kuku-Yalanji world order. However, it also helped maintain the relations
of production and, specifically, the dominant position of the *bingabinga*.

There is a range of situations in which can be seen the exercise of this
domination and its justification in *Ngujakura*. I describe these in detail
elsewhere (Anderson 1984). To summarize them:

1. Kuku-Yalanji relations of production enabled *bingabinga* to effect a
   direct and indirect appropriation of certain food items (particularly
   high protein ones) as well as the most desired parts of other food items
   by: (a) reserving items obtained by young men for themselves; (b)
   prohibiting certain foods to categories of people other than themselves
   (women, initiates, temporary prohibitions on younger men); (c)
   prohibiting food of any kind from certain areas to anyone other than
   themselves; and (d) controlling the redistribution of food generally.
2. The betrothal system reserved young women for the *bingabinga*, who
   were then able to have multiple wives, thereby increasing their political
   power and the economic output of their domestic groups. Augury
   ceremonies such as tooth evulsion allowed for further manipulation of
   marriage patterns of both young men and women by older men.
3. *Nganja*, the Kuku-Yalanji initiation ceremony, marked the dramatic
   transition of young men from powerless non-responsibility to a state of
   at least being formally aware of a new sphere of knowledge, and thereby
   into a position of potential power — i.e. they were co-opted. The ceremony
   was training in the acceptance of power, if not in its actual exercise. It
   also served, for others, to foster the continued mystification and enhance-
   ment of power, while for the young men, the ceremony acted to a large
   extent to demystify power. Kuku-Yalanji women had no equivalent
   transition ceremony.
4. Women in general were excluded from what was seen by both men and
   women as the sphere of significant knowledge. As such, they had little
   formal power, and as a consequence their status was an unabashedly
   subordinate one.[1]
5. *Bingabinga* were in judicial control in that it was in their power to
   determine whether transgressions of various laws had occurred and if
   so, to legitimate (or not) retributive action. The power thus lay in their
   ability to determine 'guilt'. They played fundamentally important roles
   in the management of grievances and in the settling of disputes.

6. *Bingabinga* were the major figures in decisions to be made concerning the camp as a whole.

Bingabinga, then, in the above summary, constituted a structural category and I have described aspects of their status and power which stemmed from their position. However, the relations of production in pre-contact Kuku-Yalanji society cannot be wholly defined in this way. *Bingabinga* status and power were not undifferentiated, and it seems clear that certain individuals within this group had high levels of achieved status, and thus greater power and authority, while others had very little. In order to look at this we must examine in general the individual and status.

Apart from the status differences mentioned already for Kuku-Yalanji society, status position also varied over the course of the lifetime of an individual. Several points can be made about the formal status positions in Kuku-Yalanji society and how they changed over time:

1. In the case of men and women of equivalent age, men almost always had more power and authority than women. The only possible exception was after a young woman's marriage, when young men of an equivalent age were still considered children.
2. There was a steady increase in both female and male power and authority with age, but the rate of increase for males was greater than that for females (although this may not always have been so).
3. Female power declined earlier than that of males, but male power also declined as very old age set in.
4. The power and authority of deceased males (via their spirits) remained viable for longer than that of females.

The power and authority of *bingabinga* as a social category was not totally general and undifferentiated. Above and beyond the power attributed to a person by virtue of his or her gender and age, there was considerable scope for difference in individual male (and to a lesser extent, female) power and influence. There exists a host of Kuku-Yalanji terms indicating a general recognition of exceptional personal qualities in individuals (see Anderson 1984:154). A number of early sources for the south-eastern Cape York Peninsula demonstrate this recognition. For example, W. E. Roth notes:

> The Bloomfield River natives make a distinction in the final obsequies between those males who have passed their days in comparative peace and quiet and those who have rendered themselves unusually prominent ... In the case of any male who happens to have no powerful relatives, or who was never made conspicuous by any deeds of valour or prowess ... [burial is simple and there is no question of sorcery] ... When an aboriginal who has had plenty of friends or who has made a name for himself, at last closes his eyes in death, there is a greater amount of mourning, and steps are taken to discover the murderer who doomed him, then to punish him ... (Roth 1907:385–6)

There were other individuals too who had special powers by virtue of certain personal qualities, experience and training. These were the *runyuji* or Aboriginal 'doctors', who specialized in the use of spiritual and natural powers for socio-medicinal purposes.

More generally, though, there were powerful individuals within the *bingabinga* category who were termed *maja*.[2] Such a distinction corresponds to Pareto's (1935 [1915–19]) notion of a governing elite within an overall elite. This is not to imply that *majamaja* (the plural form of *maja*) governed in any co-operative sense. (I return to this point below.) The unity implied in the notion of the so-called council of elders mentioned in the early literature for Aboriginal Australia is much overstated. *Bingabinga*, being a social category and not an actual group, would have rarely acted in concert. The distinguishing quality of *majamaja* was achieved status, and this necessarily derived from competition between individuals which must have militated against too many co-operative endeavours, particularly political ones. A comment of Roth's supports this. He notes that in an 'assembly of elders' at Bloomfield:

> Care is taken that no one of any importance is neglected for, should such a one consider himself slighted, he might turn sulky and cause trouble. Age by itself is not necessarily deemed sufficient to raise an individual to the degree of importance necessary to give his opinions weight: fighting qualities, but especially social rank ... have a very great deal to do with it. The possession of many wives also gives a man social importance; more wives mean more relatives, and so a larger following. (Roth 1906:5; see also Hodgkinson 1886:4)

In general, Roth (1906:6) notes: 'Natives regard the man according as he can hold his own in fighting and in hunting — *i.e.* in proportion to the possession of those qualifications which enable him to overcome an adversary and ensure his success in the search for food.' People at Bloomfield today speak of certain legendary — although real — men who were able to flout rules with impunity, particularly those relating to sexual matters. As one man said: '*Bama* couldn't help it. [i.e. there was nothing people could do about the transgressions.] That fella too strong. *Nyulu maja!*' ['He was a boss!'] (see also Chase 1980:187; Sutton 1982).

On the other side, Roth (1907:386) mentions that some Aboriginal men 'who happen to have no powerful friends' were the butt of sorcery accusations. And he notes that 'some poor wretch, who has comparatively few friends' (1903:33) would be blamed for someone's death, noting that in the Bloomfield district 'some one must die, *must* be killed for the death of every "important" male aboriginal' (1907:386, his emphasis). In Kuku-Yalanji, the term *kurrbarbuyun* refers to a powerless person, one with no allies or friends. Roth notes too that 'powerful friends' at Bloomfield would prevent offenders against the law from being killed (1906:9).

The power of individuals also varied according to where they were camped. Older men were usually at their most powerful on the estate of which they were the primary and senior patrilineal descendants. One of the first reports sent by the Lutheran missionaries at Bloomfield in 1887 demonstrates this:

> They are polygamous here ... the headman for instance, has 6 wives ... He does not join in [with the other Aborigines'] labours. He claims that all this land is his but he is agreeable to let us work it, as long as he gets meals ... his word seems to carry a lot of weight amongst them. (Meyer 1887)[3]

Beyond status determined only by formal attributes, the historical record thus suggests the existence of individuals within the *bingabinga* category who had not only structural power, but also achieved status. We shall see more clearly these *majamaja* and their status by looking at the camps in which Kuku-Yalanji lived from at least the 1880s until the late 1960s.

Bosses and comps, post-1880

Kuku-Yalanji residence patterns in south-eastern Cape York Peninsula over at least the last 100 years have been characterized by a series of relatively large, permanent camps: six in the Bloomfield valley and seven in the neighbouring Annan River valley. From my reconstructions, there were usually between 20 and 30 people in these camps, but at times there were up to 60. With respect to clan/estate ties of residents, the composition of the camps was almost always mixed. The major camps were sited on a single estate and the residents had ties with most of the other estates clustered in the immediate river valley. However, the camps always had a core group from the estate on which the camp was situated, and very often a focal person in the camp was one of its senior owners. In some cases the camps were known by the name of the surrounding estate. Mostly, though, they were labelled according to the name of the focal person for the camp or by the site they were on and, in fact, these were generally the same. While the camp composition was fluid and mobility was high for some people, the continuity and identity of the camp was maintained by existence of *majamaja* as focal or core elements.

Dikarr, for example, the camp near the mouth of Thompson Creek on the Bloomfield River, was the largest of the Kuku-Yalanji camps at Bloomfield for most of this century. Residential groupings were based on estate cluster affiliation, and the three major subcamps in the 1950s and early 1960s were focused on three different men. One of the most renowned of these was Kalkamanangu, or 'King Billy' as he was known to Europeans. He was the senior male owner of a central estate in the cluster on which the group was based and he had influence over a large number of people associated with that area. He had three wives more or less simultaneously (one of only eight or nine recorded cases of Kuku-Yalanji polygyny in over 100 years). One of these wives was the senior owner of Dikarr, the site of the Thompson Creek camp. According to people who lived there at the time, Kalkamanangu's temper and quickness to fight had been remarkable. Also his word was considered absolute. Lutheran missionaries in the area at the time report that when Kalkamanangu died, the wailing of the women at Thompson Creek went on for much longer than usual and mourners came from all over south-eastern Cape York Peninsula. Long after his death, Kalkamanangu remained as a focal point for the largest residential grouping at Dikarr.

There were similar situations in most of the other Bloomfield and Annan River camps: Wawu Romeo, the *maja* at Wayalwayal, the camp on Wyalla Station in the late 1890s; Wulbar at Banabila near the Bloomfield River mouth in the 1920s; Yanban and Big Jack at China Camp around the turn of the century; Bluja King at Kuna on Shipton's Flat and so on (see Anderson 1983, 1984).

Kuku-Yalanji today speak of these camps and these individuals synonymously. A particular camp is defined by the identity of its focal individual, and to a lesser extent by members of his immediate family who were also co-resident. In looking at these focal individuals more closely, certain common traits become evident. They were all men. They had influence over marriage choice of persons other than their own children, and they sometimes had more than one wife themselves. They often settled disputes and their decisions regarding these and other matters were (at least reportedly) incontrovertible. They had reputations over wide areas and were able to muster supporters widely for events such as fights or ceremonies. They often influenced cultural innovation (including song and dance styles, material culture, etc.) These individuals also often made decisions concerning dealings with Europeans by camp members (although this did not mean that they necessarily dealt directly with Europeans). The deaths and funeral ceremonies of these men were occasions of note, and a camp would sometimes dissolve on the death of its focal person.

Majamaja could attract followers for various purposes and they were definers of 'tradition'. Most importantly, they were nuclei around whom residential camps formed. These camps were social groups and not merely physical ones, but membership was not by reference to *common* descent, but rather by reference to the *maja* and *his* descent. These residential entities must thus be examined not by reference to descent or clans, but rather from an ego-centred point of view. The groups were ones of kindred, but anyone else could also be absorbed as determined by the *maja* or his immediate family. These camps were the economic, the reproducing and the political units of Kuku-Yalanji society during at least this era. The status of the various *majamaja* arose largely within the camp domain, but there was also a polity of competing *majamaja* from camps within the same estate cluster. It was these men, the *majamaja*, not *bingabinga* in general, who acted as social reference points and as mediators between their camp residents and the broader 'world order'.

These individuals, who lived in the post-contact camps, were *majamaja* in the traditional sense. Their positions had direct continuity from precontact times. Politicking between potential *majamaja* within the same large camp (and occasionally, the competition between *majamaja* from different camps if the context was appropriate) was a major dynamic in determining, for example, Kuku-Yalanji residence, overall demographic patterns, conflict and fission and fusion patterns in the contact era and before. It is a basic proposition here that the existence of such positions in Aboriginal society meant that an inequality of individuals (on other than structural grounds), of a kind rarely dealt with in the literature, was basic to Aboriginal politics. And because the fortunes of a camp varied with the status and power of its *maja*, groups were also unequal. This is a crucial consideration when looking at Aboriginal–European relations; examination of the role of these *majamaja* is vital in order to account for the maintenance and reproduction of some groups and the utter extinction of others (see Anderson 1983).

Focal individuals, bosses and mobs at Wujalwujal Mission: 1977–1980

Not surprisingly, the groups from the major camps maintained separate identities after coming in to live at Wujalwujal, the new Lutheran mission at Bloomfield, in the 1970s. A major part of their identity was their association with particular individuals. In the period 1977 to 1980, Wujalwujal Mission contained eight distinct groups or mobs. These mobs were all associated with the Kuku-Yalanji camps from the earlier era. I discuss the composition of the mobs in another work (Anderson 1984). Here I will discuss primarily only the position and role of particular individuals with respect to them.

Kuku-Yalanji mobs in the mission were kindred clusters crystallizing about one or two central figures. It was usually only the descent line of these latter that was significant in any notion of the mob as a clan — that is, they had a clan-like 'ideal', but in reality mobs were kindreds. There were differences, however, between what we could term focal individuals and *majamaja* or bosses. While a boss was always a focal individual, the reverse was not necessarily true. While a focal person was essential for the very existence of a mob, having a boss in a mob currently or in the recent past had a powerful unifying effect on a mob and more or less ensured for it a powerful position. I want to examine briefly characteristics of the two categories.[4]

The focal individual was normally a man of at least middle age or older, yet not old enough to be physically or mentally debilitated. As I have shown elsewhere (Anderson 1984), the status of women in Kuku-Yalanji society traditionally meant that only exceptional women gained positions of real power and focus. This was still true in mission times. Focal individuals were normally married, lived with their spouses and had numerous children and grandchildren, some of whom were normally resident with them. In order words, a focal individual headed a residence unit which consisted of one or more households. They also headed economic units in which they exerted some degree of control over production and distribution of both bush resources cash income. Their decisions on a range of matters including mob moves and general activities affected a number of people (c. 10–15). Focal individuals were the persons whom people in the mob generally used as a reference point for each other. These persons were also reference points for the group used by outside, non-mob members. A focal individual's name was generally used for the mob itself (e.g. 'Walker mob') and such a name was also often used for a bush camp associated with the mob (e.g. 'Walker camp'). If someone said, for example, that 'Old Man Walker is camping down Thompson Creek', then it was taken for granted that this meant that his mob was there, and it was relatively easy to predict who at least the core residential group might be (cf. Sutton 1978).

The term boss[5] had a number of meanings at Bloomfield. Anyone could take on a boss-like role in specific situations. For example, a young woman might be 'boss' for a tape recorder or similar item for which her money had paid. Yet this usually meant little in practical terms as to other people's use of it. People also used 'boss' as a term of address for people from whom they were trying to obtain money or other goods.

To *be* a boss was generally quite different.[6] It depended on an ability to influence people, either positively or negatively. The amount and extent of this influence is where we can see the difference between the focal individual of a mob and a proper boss. Bosses' decisions affected a far greater number of people, including those in other mobs. On the other side, many decisions, even about fairly minor matters, could not be made in the absence of a boss. Such influence was a complex interaction between structural position (age, sex and clan membership and affinity), personal qualities and mob status and prestige.

In the case of structural qualities, I noted that it was impossible for a younger person (*c.* 20s or 30s)[7] or a woman to be a boss. It was also difficult for a man with all the other requirements but who was from a foreign or non-Kuku-Yalanji clan to be a boss. A young man, a woman or an outsider could be focal individuals for a mob and be influential people, but they would not be real bosses.

Thus bosses had to fulfil the structural principles on which the pre-1880 Kuku-Yalanji system operated. Yet other qualities were necessary. These included, as with the bosses of old, forcefulness, determination, articulateness and an ability to resolve issues for people, intelligence, political acumen, willingness to be aggressive and, perhaps most importantly, a *self*-conscious or a righteous belief in one's own importance. Two other significant factors were a personal history which meant that one had a combination of solid knowledge and skills in the traditional Kuku-Yalanji sphere and, at the same time, an ability to deal successfully (even if indirectly) with Europeans. This generally meant that such individuals had not left or been removed from south-eastern Cape York Peninsula for any significant time during their lives, and that they had had dealings with Europeans earlier at one of the major camps.

Structural and individual characteristics were linked with mob status and prestige in a reciprocal fashion. The stronger mobs tended to have strong focal individuals, who may or may not have been bosses (and this latter in turn depended on the status of their mobs). The weaker mobs inevitably had weaker focal individuals. Mob and individual prestige and authority were inextricably linked. It was almost impossible in the long run for a strong individual not to have a strong mob, unless some other condition was not met — for example, that he chose not to, or that he was an outsider or a traveller. In order for a mob to be powerful and to have a prestigious reputation, it had to have a strong individual and preferably a full-blown boss, if not in the present then at least somewhere in its recent past. It is doubtful whether the force for unity provided by a dead boss could survive for long without a new, living boss.

The importance of mobs and bosses can be seen by the fact that those without affiliation to a mob were quite literally without any power or influence. They missed out on getting new houses at the mission, they got little or no access to mission resources such as vehicles, they were rarely represented on the community council and so on. Without a boss, they were considered 'poor-fellas', marginal to real life on the mission.

There are other conditions which also had to be met before a mob could attain a powerful position and before a focal individual could fulfil his potential as a boss. The latter himself or his sisters had to have lots of children. This was a most important factor and Kuku-Yalanji explicitly discussed the political and economic advantages which having a lot of children gave one's family. The mob itself also had to be viable enough to keep children affiliated with it once they had married. Also, the mob (though not necessarily the boss) had to have solid descent ties with currently significant country (i.e. areas such as the mission reserve land or land that was used frequently for camping or for hunting). Often related to this was the need for a mob to have a direct descent link to one of the old camp bosses. Access to and control of a major residential site outside of the mission was also essential. Having met these conditions, a mob had to have an individual with the structural and personal characteristics necessary to take advantage of them. Most importantly, this person had to be willing and able to control the actions of mob members, especially young adults. His authority had to be respected and his arguments listened to. This was particularly so in the case of economic activities, sexual behaviour, marriage and young male agonistic behaviour (both to be able to stop and to instigate the latter).

Given a number of people of the same generation in the same mob, it was also necessary for them, for reasons of choice or of personality, not all to want the sort of responsibilities required of a boss. In other words, most of the adults in a mob had, for most of the time, to be willing to follow the lead of a boss, rather than be his rivals. Male sibling rivalry, in particular, always had the potential to be a major cause of mob fission.

In summary, Kuku-Yalanji mobs at Wujalwujal in the late 1970s were defined to a large extent by certain individuals within them. I have made a distinction between focal individuals and bosses, both as focal or reference points for groups and as controllers of actions within them. However, the difference between the two was one of degree rather than category and the difference is basically between structural characteristics and informal or political/personal ones. The outcome was different amounts and ranges of influence. The status and prestige of the mob were also significant here for determining the relative power of their focal individuals or bosses.

Bosses, Elites and Structural Domination

The general picture which emerges is one of a status position with a great deal of significance in Aboriginal life. Yet, the position is one which is not immediately visible given an exclusive focus on biological and structural status. It is one which, following contemporary Aboriginal usage, I have termed 'boss'. Yet I have chosen to reserve my use of the term for particular status positions only. 'Boss-ness' exists at different levels and in different contexts and is based on structural power, in so far as without that form of advantage such a position would be difficult to attain. Yet the important aspect is that there exist attributes which bring about achieved status — position obtained over and above structural factors. It is these attributes which define 'boss-ship' in real terms. These achieved status positions were clearly not filled by men exclusively. To varying degrees, women were able to attain considerable prestige and power and to fulfil certain of the boss-like roles in other parts of Australia. Yet women's generally low (ascribed) status position across most of the continent ultimately severely limited their success in the struggle for achieved status (C. H. Berndt (1970), Kaberry (1939) and White (1970) would maintain, on the other hand, that women did not seek 'boss-ness' in the same sense as men).

The attributes and roles of bosses which I have described above can be distilled into four related features: (1) a willingness and ability to gauge opinions, to be able to make decisions based on these and, most importantly, to take responsibility for those decisions; (2) a capacity (beyond that stemming from structural position) to make people dependent upon one, so that they let one make decisions or have opinions for them; (3) instantiation or embodiment of the group in the individual; (4) an ability to 'look after' people in a variety of ways including physical protection, providing an economic niche and a social identity through membership of a mob, as well as providing access to 'spiritual' protection through intermediary action. This fourth characteristic, 'looking after', is perhaps the most important in that it underlies the others to some extent and seems basic to Aboriginal culture (see Myers 1980a, 1980b, 1986).

Bosses were thus persons of high achieved status who — at least in Cape York Peninsula, although probably elsewhere too — played significant roles in Aboriginal life. We can see this in patterns of changing tradition where forces for change occur and operate primarily via such individuals. They are the reinterpreters of tradition and the 'editors' of history. These people also play an active role in altering or emphasizing different aspects of land tenure principles, in affecting patterns of succession (including active takeover), and in determining on-the-ground usage of land and resources, particularly the location, composition, size and resource base of camps (see Anderson 1983, 1984; Chase 1980; Sutton 1978; Sutton & Rigsby 1982; von Sturmer 1978 for examples). All these are areas where bosses play decisive if not primary roles.

I have argued that this status position, boss, which was integral to pre-contact Kuku-Yalanji life, continued to be a significant one in the post-contact semi-traditional camps, and in the centralized mission community setting. In all of these contexts bosses ruled in a sense. Yet they did not constitute a ruling class. For one thing, bosses were not often able to transfer perfectly their power and prestige to the next generation. There were simply too many variables not within the control of a given individual. Yet it did happen sometimes. The most important mobs at Wujalwujal all have either a boss or a focal individual descended from a camp *maja*. However, it is doubtful that the line would often go beyond two generations. In fact it is likely that a *maja* would sometimes be in competition with his own sons for power.

In addition, *majamaja* did not constitute a ruling class because of their lack of common interests and their separate spheres of influence. The power of a *maja* was usually constrained by his rights in land — that is, his authority and influence were limited to the sites and areas on which he lived and with which he was affiliated. As other *majamaja* were, by definition, operating in their own domains, the areas of common interest would generally have been seen as few. More often than not, as I have noted, competition for followers, the desire to keep resident married children, etc. would have all worked against much co-operation.

The best way to consider Aboriginal bosses, in my view, is as a horizontal series of independent and circumscribed elites. The analogy which Sampson (1962:624) draws in a very different setting is an apt one: '. . . the rulers are not at all close-knit or united. They are not so much in the centre of a solar system, as in a cluster of interlocking circles, each one largely preoccupied with its own [affairs] and expertise, and touching others only at one edge ... they are not a single Establishment but a ring of Establishments, with slender connexions' (see also Sharp 1968:159; Sutton 1978 *passim*). It was possibly the frictions and balances between these different circles which were primary limiting factors for change towards concentration of political power in larger units in Aboriginal Australia.

I do not see a focus on individual action, on political process, on bosses, as all there is to understanding Aboriginal politics. As I have shown, *majamaja* are important, but they are only part of the picture. There is also the structural framework within which they operate. Hence I have very briefly described *Ngujakura* and Kuku-Yalanji relations of production. More generally though, as Bern (1979) points out, religion is 'where the structure of dominance was located in the Aboriginal social formation' (p. 126), and it was 'the dominant category of mature men who had legitimate control over the organization of society' (p. 127) through their control of religion. *Majamaja* were also *bingabinga*.

The analytical separation of structural status and power from processual or everyday status would seem to be useful in resolving the debate over the existence of 'chiefs' in Aboriginal Australia. It also throws new light on the question of whether or not religious leaders had secular powers. The point is that *some* religious leaders were powerful in mundane affairs, but not exclusively by virtue of their religious knowledge and ritual status (cf. Strehlow 1970). As Berndt (1965:205) has suggested, the latter must be combined with certain personal attributes. Although all mature males were structurally and therefore potentially powerful, they did not all achieve this power. Those men who had both religious authority by virtue of their biological and structural attributes *and* secular influence by virtue of other attributes,[8] were no doubt those labelled as 'chiefs', 'headmen' and 'kings' by early writers on Aboriginal societies. They occurred among different groups at different times and with varying degrees of influence. It is these individuals who in all likelihood are those who stand out so often in the literature too. The important thing is that their existence did not stem only from the structural form of Australian society. What made the difference between the potentially and the actually powerful were the attributes which contributed to achieved status.

Acknowledgements

Fieldwork at Bloomfield River was funded by the Australian Institute of Aboriginal Studies and the Department of Anthropology and Sociology, University of Queensland. I have benefited from discussions with Peter Sutton, John von Sturmer and Françoise Dussart on the topic of this paper.

Notes

1. I must stress here that this statement only applies to south-eastern Cape York Peninsula. I think in many ways Bloomfield is atypical in this respect, certainly

in comparison with western Cape York where women were accorded greater status and had more formal and informal political power.

2. Hershberger & Hershberger (1982) believe this term may be a derivative from the English 'master'. They also note though the use of the term *dukul* ('head') for 'boss' in similar contexts.

3. This mission was situated — as it is today — on the Kuku-Yalanji estate, Wujalwujal, and the man mentioned was a senior male of the clan who owned the estate. The first Lutheran mission operated from 1887 to 1902. Missionaries arrived again in the late 1950s and set up the present community on the old site in the 1960s.

4. Gerritsen's (1982) concepts of 'dominant men'/'prominent men' and Sansom's (1980) term 'masterful men' are relevant here, but I feel that both writers ignore tradition-oriented Aboriginal sociocultural factors as bases for power and position.

5. It is interesting that this term seems to have been quickly and readily adopted by Aborigines all over Australia regardless of their varying situations with respect to Europeans. This is so because the term had a traditional referent and did not arise solely from Aborigines being in a capitalist labour situation (sèe Hamilton 1972:43; and Myers 1980a:203, 1980b, 1986).

6. It is important to state that this does not mean that the term 'boss' was always necessarily used for such individuals. The overuse of the term by someone ('skiting') usually, in fact, indicated a lack of real power. I use the term more as a convenient label.

7. However, use of the term 'old man' in a case where a man is not of particularly advanced age refers explicitly to achieved status.

8. This is not to say that religious 'boss-ship' is not also achieved. Membership status may have a mainly bio/structural basis but religious authority is certainly worked for.

References

ANDERSON, C. (1983), 'Aborigines and tin mining in north Queensland: a case study in the anthropology of contact history', *Mankind*, **13**:473–98.

—— (1984), 'The political and economic basis of Kuku-Yalanji social history', Unpublished PhD thesis, University of Queensland.

BALANDIER, G. (1970), *Political Anthropology*, Middlesex: Penguin.

BERN, J. (1979), 'Ideology and domination: toward a reconstruction of Australian Aboriginal social formation', *Oceania*, **50**:118–32.

BERNDT, C. H. (1970), 'Digging sticks and spears, or, the two-sex model', in F. Gale (ed.), *Women's Role in Aboriginal Society*, Canberra: Australian Institute of Aboriginal Studies.

BERNDT, R. M. (1962), *An Adjustment Movement in Arnhem Land*, Paris: Mouton.

—— (1965), 'Law and order in Aboriginal Australia', in R. M. & C. H. Berndt (eds), *Aboriginal Man in Australia*, Sydney: Angus & Robertson.

CHASE, A. K. (1980), '"Which way now?" Tradition, continuity and change in a north Queensland Aboriginal community', Unpublished PhD thesis, University of Queensland.

—— (1984), 'Belonging to country: territory, identity and environment in Cape York Peninsula, northern Australia', in L. R. Hiatt (ed.), *Aboriginal Landowners, Oceania* Monograph No. 27:104–22.

COLLINS, D. (1802) [1971], *An Account of the English Colony in New South Wales*, Vol. II (facsimile edition), Adelaide: Libraries Board of South Australia.

GERRITSEN, R. (1982), 'Outstations, differing interpretations and policy implications', in P. Loveday (ed.), *Service Delivery to Outstations*, Darwin: Northern Australia Research Unit.

HAMILTON, A. (1972), 'Blacks and Whites: the relationships of change', *Arena*, **30**:34–48.

HERSHBERGER, H. & HERSHBERGER, R. (1982), *Kuku-Yalanji Dictionary*, Work Papers of Summer Institute of Linguistics, AAB Series B, Vol. 7, Darwin: Summer Institute of Linguistics.

HIATT, L. R. (1982), 'New research perspectives on Aboriginal land tenure: 1971–1980', *Newsletter, Australian Anthropological Society*, **16**:15–26.

—— (1984), *Aboriginal Political Life*, Wentworth Lecture, Canberra: Australian Institute of Aboriginal Studies.

HODGKINSON, W. O. (1886), *Report re Visit of Inspection to Bloomfield River Mission Station, also Information re Habits of the Aborigines*, Report to Under Colonial Secretary, No. 8580 Col/A 481, Brisbane: Queensland State Archives.

KABERRY, P. (1939), *Aboriginal Woman: Sacred and Profane*, London: G. Routledge & Sons.

LINTON, R. (1936), *The Study of Man*, New York: Appleton-Century.

MACKNIGHT, C. C. (1976), *The Voyage to Marege*, Melbourne: Melbourne University Press.

MEYER, C. (1887), Letter to Pastor Rechner, April 1887, No. 56 in UELCAA File B833.

MOUNTFORD, C. P. (1956), *Art, Myth and Symbolism*, Records of the American–Australian Scientific Expedition to Arnhem Land, Melbourne: Melbourne University Press.

—— (1967), *Australian Aboriginal Portraits*, Melbourne: Melbourne University Press.

MYERS, F. R. (1980a), 'The cultural basis of politics in Pintupi life', *Mankind*, **12**:197–214.

—— (1980b), 'A broken code: Pintupi political theory and contemporary social life', *Mankind*, **12**:311–26.

—— (1986), *Pintupi Country, Pintupi Self: Sentiment, Place, and Politics among Western Desert Aborigines*, Washington DC: Smithsonian Institution Press.

PARETO, V. (1935) [1915–19], *The Mind and Society* (4 Vols), London: Jonathan Cape.

REECE, R. H. W. (1974), *Aborigines and Colonists: Aborigines and Colonial Society in N.S.W. in the 1830s and 1840s*, Sydney: Sydney University Press.

ROTH, W. E. (1903), Progress report to Home Secretary, 18/9/1903, No. 27642 [copy in possession of author].

—— (1906), *Notes on Government, Morals and Crime*, NQEB No. 8, Brisbane: Queensland Government Publisher.

—— (1907), *Burial Ceremonies and Disposal of the Dead*, NQEB No. 9, *Records of the Australian Museum*, **VI**:365–403.

SAMPSON, A. (1962), *Anatomy of Britain*, London: Hodder & Stoughton.

SANSOM, B. (1980), *The Camp at Wallaby Cross*, Canberra: Australian Institute of Aboriginal Studies.

SHARP, R. L. (1934), 'Ritual life and economics of the Yir-Yoront of Cape York Peninsula', *Oceania*, **5**:19–42.

—— (1958), 'People without politics', in V. F. Ray (ed.), *Systems of Political Control and Bureaucracy in Human Societies*, Proceedings of the American Ethnological Society.

—— (1968), 'Hunter social organization: some problems of method', in R. B. Lee & I. De Vore (eds), *Man the Hunter*, Chicago: Aldine.

STANNER, W. E. H. (1959), 'Durmugam: a Nangiomeri', in J. A. Cassagrande (ed.), *In the Company of Man: Twenty Portraits by Anthropologists*, New York: Harper Bros.

STREHLOW, T. G. H. (1970), 'Geography and the totemic landscape in Central Australia', in R. M. Berndt (ed.), *Australian Aboriginal Anthropology*, Perth: University of Western Australia Press.

VON STURMER, J. R. (1978), 'The Wik region: economy, territoriality and totemism in western Cape York Peninsula, North Queensland', Unpublished PhD thesis, University of Queensland.

SUTTON, P. J. (1978), 'Wik: Aboriginal society, territory and language at Cape Keerweer, Cape York Peninsula, Australia', Unpublished PhD thesis, University of Queensland.

—— (1982), 'Personal power, kin classification and speech etiquette in Aboriginal Australia', in J. Heath, F. Merlan & A. Rumsey (eds), *Languages of Kinship in Aboriginal Australia*, *Oceania* Linguistic Monograph No. 24:182–200.

—— & RIGSBY, B.(1982), 'People with 'politicks': management of land and personnel on Australia's Cape York Peninsula', in N. M. Williams & E. S. Hunn (eds), *Resource Managers: North American and Australian Hunter–Gatherers*, Boulder: Præger.

THOMSON, D. F. (1933), 'The hero cult, initiation and totemism on Cape York', *Journal of the Royal Anthropological Institute*, **63**:453–538.

—— (1935), 'The joking relationship and organized obscenity in north Queensland', *American Anthropologist*, **37**:460–90.

—— (1983), *Donald Thomson in Arnhem Land*, N. Peterson (Comp.) Currey O'Neil, South Yarra, Vic.

TINDALE, N. B. (1974), *Aboriginal Tribes of Australia*, Canberra: Australian National University Press.

THRELKELD, L. E. (1974), *Australian Reminiscences and Papers of L. E. Threlkeld*, 2 Vols, N. Gunson (ed.), Canberra: Australian Institute of Aboriginal Studies.

WARNER, W. L. (1964) [1958], *A Black Civilization*, New York: Harper (originally published 1937).

WHITE, I. M. (1970), 'Aboriginal women's status: a paradox resolved', in F. Gale (ed.), *Women's Role in Aboriginal Society*, Canberra: Australian Institute of Aboriginal Studies.

—— (1975), 'Sexual conquest and submission in the myths of central Australia', in L. R. Hiatt (ed.), *Australian Aboriginal Mythology*, Canberra: Australian Institute of Aboriginal Studies.

WHITE, J. (1790) [1962], *Journal of a Voyage to New South Wales*, London: Debrett (1962 reprint edition: Sydney: A. W. Chisholm).

13
Traditional Aboriginal Society and its Law

AUSTRALIAN LAW REFORM COMMISSION

Overview

To comprehend the nature of Aboriginal customary law it is necessary to have some understanding of how traditional Aboriginal society and law operated before the white settlement of Australia. Consideration can then be given to the manner and extent of operation of Aboriginal customary law in Australia today.

Its diversity

One of the common misconceptions of white Australians is that Aborigines are a homogeneous people of substantially the same stock. However, there is no one Aboriginal type, any more than there is any one Australian-European type. Significant physical differences existed and still exist between regional groups, say, between Aborigines from Arnhem Land and those from Central Australia. In addition, environmental differences throughout the Continent encouraged different ways of living, behaving and thinking, producing a cultural diversity (Berndt & Berndt 1977: 16). There was no lingua franca, no shared language by means of which a person could make himself or herself understood from one end of the Continent to the other. Even where one language covered a wide area, everyone in that area might need to speak or at least understand more than one dialect. It has been estimated that there were as many as 600 dialects when the white man arrived (Blainey 1980:63). The significance for the reference of these differences is that they, in turn, resulted in variations in the law from one region to another. There was not at any time a body of law of universal application throughout Aboriginal Australia.

Importance of religion

Throughout Aboriginal Australia religion was the mainstay of social existence. No distinction was drawn between the physical and spiritual

---

First published as Discussion Paper (no. 17, November 1980) on Aboriginal Customary Law by the Australian Law Reform Commission.

universes so that the whole of the Aboriginal world was under spiritual authority. There was no systematic belief in gods nor any institutions of priesthood, prayer or sacrifice (Stanner in Berndt & Berndt 1965:207 et seq). The mythical characters of the Dream Time provided the source of their religion which focused on every aspect of life. They laid down precepts or made suggestions of which people were expected to take notice (Berndt & Berndt 1977:337). They defined the broad roles to be played by both men and women in such matters as sacred ritual, economic affairs, marriage, child bearing and conduct at the death of relatives. They were the source of Aboriginal life and law. There was thus a religious sanction for the traditional dictates of right and wrong.

Sacred/secret matters

Although no priesthood existed, knowledge and control of certain special religious rites, mythology and songs, and possession of sacred objects was vested in a few men of each local group. This authority was not inherited. The men were chosen from initiated men, not necessarily medicine-men or sorcerers (see Elkin 1977), their knowledge of religion increasing with age as they deepened their experience of and expertise in the lore and ritual of their society (Maddock 1975:43). This special knowledge of religious matters was kept secret from all uninitiated persons, be they other men in the tribe or women or children. Not only that area of special knowledge confined to the selected few men in the band but also the more general knowledge of sacred information or matters pertaining to initiation and other rites or ceremonies could not be disclosed to the outsider. Today, the white enquirer will still find a curtain being drawn once questions touch on these matters. Women had their own secret-sacred religious knowledge and ritual which was complementary to that of the men.

Relationship with land

One instance of the union between the physical and spiritual is the relationship of the Aborigines with land. A spiritual linkage existed between a person and a specific site or part of the country by virtue of his birth or sometimes his conception.[1] There was thus a bond between the people and their land, which was profoundly religious and meant that certain sites were of special and sacred importance. In addition to the religious bond, there was the importance of land as a food collecting unit. The land was inalienable as no individual was entitled to or sought ownership, in the European sense, of any area. 'It would be as correct to speak of the land possessing men as of men possessing land' (Maddock 1975:27).

The question of government

Although it is agreed that there was no political entity nor any institutionalized forms of government at any level, controversy continues among anthropologists whether political authority was vested in elders or a council of elders of the tribe. Some attribute a governmental function to an informal council of elders whose influence depended on knowledge of sacred matters, ritual status and personal respect (Berndt in Berndt & Berndt 1965:167, 177; Elkin 1976:114). Others hold the view that the tribes had no formal apparatus of government and no recognized political leaders (Hiatt 1965:141–7; Meggitt 1976:248–50; Wilson 1961). The time has gone when the correct position can be ascertained. However, the issue may be relevant to a determination whether and, if so, how and in whom, authority to administer law, be it Aboriginal or Australian law, should be vested in any section of modern Aboriginal society.

Social Organization

The tribe or language unit

The term 'tribe' is often loosely used to describe the basic social group living and moving together. It has been estimated that at the time of the First Fleet there were as many as 500 tribes in Australia, all varying in size (Berndt & Berndt 1977:28). The Australian continent was divided into hundreds of tribal areas, representing different language units. Each tribe spoke its own language or dialect, tended to follow its own religious beliefs, ceremonies and customs, inhabited its own territory, and usually married within that territory (Blainey 1980:63). The tribe was not particularly important politically or economically. It usually consisted of a number of small units, attached to certain localities within its overall territory. These local groups, usually called 'bands', were the effective political and economic units, moving across the country hunting and food gathering, obtaining material for daily needs, participating in religious ceremonies, and moving from area to area as economic or other exigencies required. The maximum number in a band was about fifty but usually there were far fewer, and that is the position today (Berndt & Berndt 1977:43). The basic unit of everyday society, and the smallest, was the family — a man, his wife or wives and their children. Groups of families made up a band.

Other social divisions

Cutting across family units, bands and tribes are other divisions of social organization with a strong religious basis. In Aboriginal belief, all things in the physical and spiritual universes (and the difference between them seems not to be important) belong to one or the other of two classes or moieties. All natural phenomena, animate and inanimate, belonged to one or other of the moieties. Different social units, therefore, belonged to one moiety or another but never to both. Another important unit was the clan, which is a descent group. Every human being had his clan membership determined at birth. Descent in them was either patrilineal or matrilineal, that is, a person was affiliated at birth either with his father's male line or with his mother's female line. Sections and subsections added to an already complex social organisation. They established further rules which stipulated what is to be expected from one Aborigine to another and their position in the total Aboriginal society.

Kinship

One of the most important characteristics of the organization of Aboriginal society was the concept of kin relationships, which transcended both band and tribe. For most Australians, the kinship system usually denotes the immediate family and a limited range of other persons most closely related to it. It may be described as a family system of kinship. Although the nuclear family was the basic kinship and social unit for Aborigines, there also existed a most important classificatory system of kin relationships which operated throughout Aboriginal society (Elkin 1976:84). The system still operates among traditional Aborigines today and in modified forms among many non-traditional Aborigines. It can be summarized as follows. A classificatory system uses terms which primarily apply to lineal relatives to refer to persons who are collateral relatives. Thus, a father's brother is classified with and is called a father, the mother's sister is classified with the mother. Thus, 'uncle' is the mother's brother, not the father's brother, 'aunt' is the father's but not the mother's sister. As a father's brother is also a father, so his children are brothers and sisters. The details can be quite complex. It is sufficient for present purposes to know that kin relationships extend well beyond familial blood ties and are the basis of all social relationships, indicating the range of behaviour expected. 'It is the anatomy and physiology of Aboriginal society and must be understood if the behaviour of Aborigines as social beings is to be understood' (Elkin 1976:85). Thus, everyone in traditional Aboriginal society must be identified as part of a kin relationship so that the two persons concerned will know what their behaviour to one another should be. A person coming into a strange group for trading or ceremonial purposes is always allocated a kinship position, if one is not already held.

Kin relationships stipulate what a person should or should not do in respect of the people he calls relatives of one kind or another — which means everyone in his social perspective — in matters of everyday routine and in crises, major or minor, such as birth, initiation, marriage, sickness and death, quarrels and fights. Membership of a common moiety, section, social clan or local group intensifies or modifies these duties but does not override them (Elkin 1976:144). The grouping together by Aborigines under the heading of 'law' of what white Australians would consider to be both legal rules and norms of polite behaviour is perhaps best exemplified by the kinship rules. The obligations of kinship governed a person's behaviour from his earliest years to his death and affected life in all its aspects. They codified behaviour (Elkin 1976:142–4).

Kinship obligations

Kinship rules prescribed both what must be done and also what must not be done. Positive rules affected such matters as:
- marriage and betrothal arrangements;
- food gathering, distribution and sharing;
- sharing of other goods;
- certain trading relationships with people in other communities; and
- educational roles, involving not only parents but other kin as well.

Serious breaches of the rules will usually be punished but failure to meet minor kinship obligations need not attract more than expressions of disapproval. The position was flexible and it is unwise to attempt to crystallize rules. Detailed knowledge, like many areas of traditional life, is sketchy. 'We know something about what should happen in certain situations, and what people say does happen; but we are not so well informed about what actually happens' (Berndt in Stanner & Sheils 1963:401). It would be a mistake, furthermore, to attribute notions of the criminal law (breach and subsequent punishment) to departures from kinship rules and expected norms of behaviour. A breach may as easily result in remedies in the form of compensation. Thus, remedies and sanctions varied in range and the same breach would not necessarily attract the same remedy because remedies may also reflect the closeness of the relationship.

Kinship avoidance

One aspect of these kinship obligations is the rule whereby certain relatives must be avoided. Speaking generally (Elkin 1976:148–9):

(1) an individual is free to approach and talk to some relatives, but not others; he may joke with some, but on no account with others; he may refer to the names and totems of some but not of others;

(2) the restrictions vary in degree according to the type of relationship;

(3) the obligations apply to all classes of person not merely to actual blood and marriage relatives, imposing prohibitions and restrictions of various kinds and degrees of intensity. Sometimes the more distant the particular relationship, the less severe a prohibition becomes;

(4) the avoidances are not an expression of enmity. They are associated with mutual duties and gifts.

The strongest and most widely known is the prohibition, observed all over Australia, between a man and his mother-in-law (Elkin 1976:149). They are forbidden to utter each other's names. In some cases, there is a complete ban on speech between them or a third person may have to serve as an intermediary; in others a special vocabulary must be used; in others again, sign language is necessary. A woman may turn in her track and face the other way, or hide, if people shout to her that a man whom she calls her daughter's husband is approaching. The main thing is that two persons who stand in this relationship should avoid face to face contact, or any prolonged or familiar association. The prohibitions extend to certain other blood relations. For example, once childhood has passed, brothers and sisters, be they blood relations or tribal relations, must not converse freely. When they are talking, they must face in different directions. Brothers-in-law usually adopt a somewhat formal attitude towards one another, sitting a little distant apart and talking quietly. Thus, at meetings of traditional groups one may still find people facing different directions or speaking to another using another person as intermediary.

Social obligations

A person is expected to make gifts to specific relatives, often according to an order of precedence. This obligation arises from the principle of reciprocity which runs through all Aboriginal life, exemplified in the notion of 'sharing'. The individual concerned will have received gifts in the past from those with whom he now shares his pay, the results of the chase or of his industry, and he will be a recipient in the future. The obligation may also arise out of marriage, betrothal or initiation. A man is expected to make gifts including meat to his new wife's father, mother and brothers to compensate them for the loss of her services. He must make payments also to the men who initiate him. When there is an exchange of brothers and sisters in marriage, a tight network of co-operation exists between their respective family circles and what is given out in the form of payments and gifts to kin actually comes back in one form or another (Elkin 1976:81).

Aboriginal women

The position of women in traditional life and law is an important issue in the reference. In former times, Aboriginal women were not thought to play a significant role in the operation of customary law. It was thought that customary law and ritual life were primarily confined to men and that women were subject to the men's law rather than adhering to a separate system of their own. Officers of the Commission have been advised by male Aborigines that female Aborigines 'had separate ceremony, but no separate law' but it was suggested by white advisers in the field that women had considerable influence over their men in the making of decisions in a behind-the-scenes fashion (ALRC Field Report No. 2). However, recent research in Central and Northern Australia suggests that women, at least in those areas, are subject to an extensive and, at times, separate system of customary law from the law followed by the men (Bell & Ditton 1980; Land Claim 1979: para. 105). Some of the women's law is said to be solely the preserve of women, involving ceremonies and ritual solely for women with an important influence upon kinship ties, marriage arrangements, land-relationships, and other rights and duties. It also appears that in more ways than was previously thought, women share in certain areas of community law which may be of a secular rather than a ceremonial nature. Whatever may be the correct resolution of the controversial topic of the role and status of women in traditional Aboriginal society, it is clear that women performed a vital role. That role may now have changed but it is still vital and, in the context of this Reference, it it essential to note that women play an important role in the maintenance of order and resolution of disputes. The Commission will continue to examine this question.

Offences

Some rules identified

Anthropologists acknowledge that, except for a few specific areas, most of our information about traditional Aboriginal life is sketchy (Berndt in Stanner & Shiels 1963:394). Moreover, the task of identifying legal rules is made more difficult by local or regional variations. However, there are some rules of fairly common application. Some offences are breaches of traditional and supernaturally sanctioned laws, while other offences did not have this significance. For instance, in the context of incest, customary law said that a man must not cohabit with his sister, mother or wife's mother. The punishment was death. But if the degree of the relationship was not close, banishment from the corporate life of the tribe or else some other physical punishment might suffice. These matters would be decided by the elders, or more particularly by certain relatives, such as the 'uncle' and 'father-in-law', but a couple caught committing an act of serious incest would be speared on sight, because the person seeing them would be so shamed (Elkin 1976:144). The caution must again be sounded that it is not always possible to differentiate supernaturally sanctioned laws from others as Aboriginal customary law itself did not recognize such a distinction.

Breaches of sacred law

Women, children and uninitiated persons committed an offence against sacred law if they (even unintentionally) saw objects forbidden to them such as:
- certain Tjuringa (sacred objects);
- a sacred place; or
- a sacred ceremony or dance.

If a person privy to knowledge or custody of sacred matters were to disclose them to a person not entitled to that information, he too might be guilty of a breach against the law. Ritual leaders, meeting secretly, decided on the appropriate punishment, which in extreme cases usually was, and still is, death. In other cases, the offender might be speared which in turn might result in death. According to circumstances, two or more of the ritual leaders might take action themselves or delegate it to someone else. Those who carry out the punishment and those who ordered it would be regarded as criminals under Australian law.

Strict liability

In Australian law, while strict liability may exist in some areas, regard is usually had to the question whether an action is intentional or unintentional. Aboriginal customary law usually did not draw distinctions. Thus, where women or children may have inadvertently seen sacred objects or rites which were prohibited to them, the convention would be that they would be speared immediately without further deliberation.

Offences against property and persons

Although entitlements to the use of land existed, there was no ownership of land in the Anglo-Australian sense (ALRC Report 1973: para 28) and disputes did not seem to arise in relation to land. Small everyday items such as digging sticks, baskets, mats, wooden dishes, and fishing spears would not normally be stolen although they might be borrowed in accordance with kinship obligations. Thus, disputes over chattels were rare and usually trivial in traditional Aboriginal Australia. There are a number of striking differences between the two cultures in the context of interpersonal relationships. While killing (which included unauthorized use of sorcery) was forbidden, what amounted to sexual misconduct was sometimes quite different from and on occasions repugnant to Australian notions of proper moral conduct. Other offences against the person included usurpation of ritual privileges or duties, insults, swearing, and breach of name tabus such as using the names of dead persons.

Marriage laws

Rules permitted or encouraged marriage with certain relatives and prohibited marriage with others. Marriages were normally arranged by the two families concerned, usually between a young girl and a man many years older. The girl was sometimes promised before she was born. Affection and attraction were often subservient to kinship obligations and to the reciprocal obligations of families or large groups. Although the institution of arranged marriage is not unusual and is similar to the European institution of arranging marriages for political, national, family or economic motives, exception has been taken by white Australians to the custom whereby marriages were arranged between old men and young girls. The anthropological writing contains a number of rationalizations of this custom and points out that it has been modified by the institutions of elopement and capture. Although both elopement and capture may on occasion result in reprisal, compensation in the form of gifts, even another wife, would atone for either. Other customs connected with marriage may be considered objectionable by some white Australians. There were also customs permitting exchange or lending of wives (Elkin 1976:160). Berndt also notes (Berndt & Berndt 1977:90) that sexual relations could be used as a means of social control. A woman might be punished for 'too much running around' by forcing her to have sexual intercourse with a number of men one after another. Polygamy was legitimate but the majority of marriages were monogamous.

Meggitt's analysis

A convenient summary of the rules of customary law as practised by one Aboriginal people is contained in a study of the Walbiri tribe by Meggitt in 1962 (1976:251–63) which has categorized a number of offences which are commonly recognized by the Walbiri as unlawful forms of behaviour. He has ranked them in an approximate order of seriousness. The totality of the rules expresses the law, *djugaruru*, a term he translates as 'the line' or 'the straight or true way'. He continues (1976:252):

> The law not only embraces ritual, economic, residential and kinship rules and conventions but also what we would call natural laws and technological rules. The care of sacred objects by the men of one patrimoiety, the sexual division of labour, the avoidance of mothers-in-law, the mating of bandicoots, the rising of the sun, and the use of fire-ploughs are all forms of behaviour that is lawful and proper — they are all *djugaruru*.

Meggitt goes on to point out that, although in pre-contact times Aborigines were probably rarely required to distinguish between rules of law and norms of polite behaviour, contact has sharpened the distinction. Today, differences can be seen between an offence and poor taste. He is thus able to identify a set of legal rules (1976:256–7).

A. Offences of commission:

1. Unauthorized homicide (that is, not decreed as a punishment for another offence).
2. Sacrilege (that is, the unauthorized possession of sacred knowledge and objects and the unauthorized observation of sacred rituals).
3. Unauthorized sorcery (1. and 3. are not easily distinguished).
4. Incest (copulation with actual kin of certain categories).
5. Cohabitation with certain kin (usually classificatory relatives in the categories associated with 4.).
6. Abduction or enticement of women.
7. Adultery with certain kin (usually classificatory relatives in the categories associated with 5.).
8. Adultery with potential spouses (7. and 8. in effect cover all cases of fornication).
9. Unauthorized physical assault, not intended to be fatal.
10. Usurpation of ritual privileges or duties.
11. Theft and intentional destruction of another's property (exclusive of 2.).
12. Insult (including swearing, exposure of the genitals).

B. Offences of omission:

1. Physical neglect of certain relatives.
2. Refusal to make gifts to certain relatives.
3. Refusal to educate certain relatives.

Partly because most social behaviour conforms to a regular pattern, partly because of the limited number of possible offences, and partly because of the relative inability to offend without others knowing, it was rare that public opinion was divided on the question whether a person had broken the law. Such popular consensus of course does not always mean that he is guilty but it appears that miscarriages of justice were uncommon. Punishment was usually meted out in the public gaze. There was almost no privacy in any camp. The publicity may have been a significant factor determining the general conformity of the people to the more important rules.

Compliance with the law

The immediate family was largely responsible for maintaining discipline for minor offences and for children. Permissiveness was and is the theme of childhood. Children were told and shown what to do rather than receive or be subjected to a spate of injunctions. All this ceased for a boy with the onset of initiation and for a girl when she reached puberty when there was a shift in authority from the immediate family to the wider context of band or tribal group. Kin might still take disciplinary action but more people were entitled to intervene and actual parents might be overridden or perhaps not even consulted. Aborigines were encouraged to comply with the law by means of direct instructions and suggestion, conditioning acceptance of rules of behaviour as inevitable and impressing the need to conform. Outlets for socially harmful conduct were provided in popular stories, by which vicarious enjoyment in breaking tabus might be experienced, and in sexual matters by socially sanctioned extra-marital intercourse, which helped to provide some sexual flexibility without upsetting the institution of marriage. Rewards, such as ritual and secular leadership, were offered for conformity (Berndt & Berndt 1977:340–1).

Punishments

The range

Meggitt has prepared a table based on his studies of the Walbiri people indicating the penalties for the various offences noted in the table in para. 30 (Meggitt 1976:258–9).

1. Death — a. caused by a non-human agency (A2)
   b. caused by human sorcery (A1, possibly A3)
   c. caused by physical attack (A1, possibly A3).

2. Insanity — caused by a non-human agency (A2).
3. Illness — caused by human sorcery (A1, A2, A3, A5, A6, A7, A8; B1, B2).
4. Wounding — attack with a spear or knife, intending to draw blood (A5, A6, A7, A8, A9, A10, A11).
5. Battery — attack with a club or boomerang (A6, A7, A8, A9, A10, A11, A12; B1, B2, B3).
6. Oral abuse — this accompanies all human punishments.
7. Ridicule — this is directed mainly at offences of omission.

The range of penalties is as limited as the range of offences. Punishment options such as imprisonment and fines were plainly not available. There is some debate whether ostracism or exile were ever traditional punishments.[2] The stated penalties were in fact the maximum but it was possible for those sympathetic to the offender or his kin to plead for a lesser punishment. However, people (even close relatives) might seek the heaviest penalty possible. Other rules also determined who should carry out the punishment. These often were based on kin relationships but certain offences might result in others imposing punishment. For example, a religious offence might be punishable by certain persons at the direction of those elders in whom religious secrets were reposed. Some religious crimes attracted almost immediate retribution without the capacity for anyone to intervene on the offender's behalf. (Meggitt 1976:260)

For serious offences

In the case of more serious offences, which attracted a spearing as a penalty, for example, adultery, elopement or even physical injury, the offender is required to stand by while the aggrieved party or a close relative throws the spear. Usually the thigh is offered and the offender might be speared once or on a number of occasions. A careless or angry spearman may miss the thigh and strike a vital organ or the wound may become infected so that in the end the penalty may be more drastic than was conventionally anticipated. Murder or suspected murder could be dealt with in a number of ways. First, there might be open physical retaliation usually by a member of the family under a kinship obligation to the deceased, what has often been called 'pay back'. The kinship obligation would require a certain relative to avenge the death notwithstanding his own personal views. It could not be relied on to put an end to disputes. Blood feuds extending over many years and breaking out into open violence were not unknown (Berndt & Berndt 1977:346). Second, compensation in the form of goods may sometimes be offered, or demanded, for a death but acceptance was no guarantee that revenge would not be attempted. Third, where physical vengeance was not practicable the murderer would be identified to the satisfaction of the victim's relatives. One of them would then perform sorcery, or threaten to do so, or claim to have done so if that particular person became ill or died. A fourth method still used throughout Northern Arnhem Land was the *magarada*, a form of settlement by combat involving a ceremonial running of a gauntlet of spears, usually blunted.

Other methods of dispute resolution

Informal discussion was and still is sometimes used to settle disputes, with men and women voicing their views openly and noisily in the main camp. If an offence has just been committed and feeling is running high, words may lead to blows and fighting might break out in earnest. Otherwise talk and argument may go on at intervals for weeks or even longer. Older men and women usually have a controlling say in the long run. But angry people are in no humour to look at both sides of an issue, especially to begin with. If a man has a burning grievance against another, he directs a public harangue particularly against his antagonist, who may respond in kind or simply sit with averted face and downcast eyes ignoring him. The rest of the camp will probably go on with its ordinary activity, ostensibly taking no notice, but actually absorbing most of what is said. Long verbal battles between the disputants, with detailed monologues full of mythical allusions, may go on for night after night, or at intervals over long periods, until the matter is settled in one way or another (through compromise or bloodshed) or merely drifts off to be resumed later (Berndt & Berndt 1977:355).

No damages

Although gifts might be exchanged for certain privileges and in discharge of other obligations, a wronged person did not usually seek any kind of material compensation.

Summary

- Mechanisms for the maintenance of order and resolution of disputes, which might be called a system of law, existed among Aborigines.
- There were no formal institutions of government.
- There was no overall institutionalized law enforcing agency. Maintenance of order and resolution of disputes tended to be local and restricted to the band. Enforcement of sanctions was often effected by kin and on other occasions by tribal elders or others acting at their direction.
- Aboriginal customary law was not codified. Furthermore, it did not categorize legal rules so as to differentiate between mandatory rules which might be part of a separate legal system and rules of etiquette or standards of moral behaviour which in Australian law are generally seen to be quite separate.
- Kin relationships exercised a pervasive influence and regulated a considerable amount of behaviour.

- Many of the 'rules' do not in any way conflict with Australian law. A number of the obligations of kinship and the concept of sharing, for example, could be regarded as admirable. On the other hand, those 'rules' which require secrecy or result in harsh cruel punishments may raise difficulties for recognition.

A Dynamic Aboriginal Law?

The picture so far painted attempts to deal with the traditional customary law. As the communities were small, it was unlikely that disputes of any magnitude would occur with any frequency. The obligations were few and well known. In its field work, the Commission sometimes asked hypothetical questions endeavouring to ascertain what would be the position if a breach of a certain rule occurred. The response usually indicated that it would not be contemplated that a breach would occur. Being nomads, possessions were few and there was an absence of disputes about property. There was no sufficient intrusion of mercantile dealings to lead to disputes about commercial matters which occupies so much of modern law. Essentially, law was directed towards religious and social obligations. Hence the pervasive influence of religion and kinship. The extent to which these phenomena will continue when the society increases in numbers, changes its lifestyle, or when other influences are exerted may be doubtful.

Whereas western societies and their legal systems gradually evolved over many centuries from simple societies to their modern, sophisticated and complex forms, Aboriginal society was permitted no such opportunity. Traditional Aboriginal law did not remain static and was subject to change. But the sudden impact of Europeans, many of whom, albeit with the highest motives, solemnly believed in their duty and responsibility to 'civilize' Aborigines, severely curtailed any capacity for gradual development to accommodate the new order. The impact was perhaps even more drastic for those Aborigines living in more remote areas where contact with Europeans was postponed to the twentieth century. On one view, that may be a sufficient reason not to recognize Aboriginal customary law and practices. It may be contended that it is impracticable, if not futile, to give effect to a system which has been so abruptly confronted with another system which not only is entirely foreign but in a number of important instances contains inconsistent values and concepts. However, this view overlooks actual experience. In some areas of Australia, usually the more remote areas, certain aspects of Aboriginal customary law have demonstrated a capacity for survival and modification. For example, marriage rules, ceremony and initiation procedures still exist. The rules of kinship survive even among relatively urbanized Aborigines, albeit in a modified form. Aborigines today may light fires with matches, smooth boomerangs with metal rasps, and warm their bodies with clothing. Yet, although it is now unimportant whether a man acquires his meat by spearing a kangaroo or by collecting an issue of beef, Aboriginal opinion still demands that he be penalized if he refuses to share it with his father-in-law. Conventional ways of behaving may change as a result of European contact but the laws have altered little to meet new problems (Meggitt 1976:253–4). The extent to which Aboriginal customary law has exhibited a capacity for dynamism would be relevant when considering recognition.

Notes

1. With an increasing number of Aboriginal children being born in hospitals or nursing homes, this source of traditional links with land is being undermined.
2. Meggitt (1976:258) says that neither ostracism nor exile was practised by the Walbiri.

References

ALRC, *Field Report No. 2*, Pitjantjatjara, 11.

——, *First Report*, July 1973, Parliamentary Paper No. 138.

BELL, D. & DITTON, P. (1980), *Law: The Old and the New*, Canberra: Aboriginal History.

BERNDT, R. M. & BERNDT, C. H. (1977), *The World of the First Australians*, Sydney: Ure Smith.

—— (eds) (1965), *Aboriginal Man in Australia*, Sydney: Angus & Robertson.

BLAINEY, G. (1980), *A Land Half Won*, Melbourne: Macmillan.

ELKIN, A. P. (1976), *The Australian Aborigines*, Sydney: Angus & Robertson.

—— (1977), *Aboriginal Man of High Degree*, St Lucia: UQP.

HIATT, L. R. (1965), *Kinship and Conflict*, Canberra: ANU Press.

Land Claim by Alyawarra and Kaititja, Aboriginal Land Commissioner, 2nd edn, June 1979.

MADDOCK, K. (1975), *The Australian Aborigines*, London: Allen Lane.

MEGGITT, M. J. (1976), *Desert People*, Sydney: Angus & Robertson.

STANNER, W. E. H. & SHIELS, P. (eds) (1963), *Australian Aboriginal Studies*, Melbourne: OUP.

WILSON, J. (1961), Authority and Leadership in a 'New Style' Australian Aboriginal Community: Pindan, unpublished MA thesis, University of Western Australia.

14
The Dreaming

W. E. H. STANNER

I

The blackfellow's outlook on the universe and man is shaped by a remarkable conception, which Spencer and Gillen immortalized as 'the dream time' or *alcheringa* of the Arunta or Aranda tribe. Some anthropologists have called it The Eternal Dream Time. I prefer to call it what the blacks call it in English — The Dreaming, or just Dreaming.

A central meaning of The Dreaming *is* that of a sacred, heroic time long long ago when man and nature came to be as they are; but neither 'time' nor 'history' as we understand them is involved in this meaning. I have never been able to discover any Aboriginal word for *time* as an abstract concept. And the sense of 'history' is wholly alien here. We shall not understand The Dreaming fully except as a complex of meanings. A blackfellow may call his totem, or the place from which his spirit came, his Dreaming. He may also explain the existence of a custom, or a law of life, as causally due to The Dreaming.

A concept so impalpable and subtle naturally suffers badly by translation into our dry and abstract language. The blacks sense this difficulty. I can recall one intelligent old man who said to me, with a cadence almost as though he had been speaking verse:

> White man got no dreaming.
> Him go 'nother way.

First published in T. A. G. Hungerford (ed.), *Australian Signposts*, Melbourne: F. W. Cheshire, 1956.

Editor's note: Readers may find some of the language in this chapter offensive, for example the author's use of the term 'blackfellow'. The chapter is included in this book because of its importance in the development of the understanding of Aboriginal religion. The language reflects usage of the period in the mid-twentieth century in areas where the author was researching and writing the paper. Readers are encouraged to concentrate on the positive contribution he made in affirming the Aboriginal conception of their creative epoch as 'timeless', and in appreciating their 'metaphysical gift'. Because this seminal paper has influenced subsequent writings on Aboriginal religion it is included in this edition to make it readily available to students.

White man, him go different,
Him got road belong himself.

In their own dialects, they use terms like *alcheringa, mipuramibirina, boaradja* — often almost untranslatable, or meaning literally something like 'men of old'. It is as difficult to be sure of the objective effects of the idea on their lives as of its subjective implications for them.

Although, as I have said, The Dreaming conjures up the notion of a sacred, heroic time of the indefinitely remote past, such a time is also, in a sense, still part of the present. One cannot 'fix' The Dreaming *in* time: it was, and is, everywhen. We should be very wrong to try to read into it the idea of a Golden Age, or a Garden of Eden, though it was an Age of Heroes, when the ancestors did marvellous things that men can no longer do. The blacks are not at all insensitive to Mary Webb's 'wistfulness that is the past', but they do not, in aversion from present or future, look back on it with yearning and nostalgia. Yet it has for them an unchallengeably sacred authority.

Clearly, The Dreaming is many things in one. Among them, a kind of narrative of things that once happened; a kind of charter of things that still happen; and a kind of *logos* or principle of order transcending everything significant for Aboriginal man. If I am correct in saying so, it is much more complex philosophically than we have so far realized. I greatly hope that artists and men of letters who (it seems increasingly) find inspiration in Aboriginal Australia will use all their gifts of empathy, but avoid banal projection and subjectivism, if they seek to borrow the notion.

Why the blackfellow thinks of 'dreaming' as the nearest equivalent in English is a puzzle. It may be because it is by *the act* of dreaming, as reality and symbol, that the Aboriginal mind makes contact — thinks it makes contact — with whatever mystery it is that connects The Dreaming and the Here-and-Now.

II

How shall one deal with so subtle a conception? One has two options: educe its subjective logic and rationale from the 'elements' which the blackfellow stumblingly offers in trying to give an explanation; or relate, as best one may, to things familiar in our own intellectual history, the objective figure it traces on their social life. There are dangers in both courses.

The first is a matter, so to speak, of learning to 'think black', not imposing Western categories of understanding, but seeking to conceive of things as the blackfellow himself does.

In our modern understanding, we tend to see 'mind' and 'body', 'body' and 'spirit', 'spirit' and 'personality', 'personality' and 'name' as in some sense separate, even opposed, entities though we manage to connect them up in some fashion into the unity or oneness of 'person' or 'individual'. The blackfellow does not seem to think this way. The distinctiveness we give to 'mind', 'spirit' and 'body' and our contrast of 'body' versus 'spirit' are not there, and the whole notion of 'the person' is enlarged. To a blackfellow, a man's name, spirit and shadow are 'him' in a sense which to us may seem passing strange. One should not ask a blackfellow: 'What is your name?' To do so embarrasses and shames him. The name is like an intimate part of the body, with which another person does not take liberties. The blacks do not mind talking about a dead person in an oblique way but, for a long time, they are extremely reluctant even to breathe his name. In the same way, to threaten a man's shadow is to threaten him. Nor may one treat lightly the physical place from which his spirit came. By extension his totem, which is also associated with that place, and with his spirit, should not be lightly treated.

In such a context one has not succeeded in 'thinking black' until one's mind can, without intellectual struggle, enfold into some kind of oneness the notions of body, spirit, ghost, shadow, name, spirit-site and totem. To say so may seem a contradiction, or suggest a paradox, for the black-fellow can and does, on some occasions, conceptually isolate the 'elements' of the 'unity' most distinctly. But his abstractions do not put him at war with himself. The separable elements I have mentioned are all present in the metaphysical heart of the idea of 'person', but the overruling mood is one of belief, not of inquiry or dissent. So long as the belief in The Dreaming lasts, there can be no 'momentary flash of Athenian questioning' to grow into a great movement of sceptical unbelief which destroys the given unities.

There are many other such 'onenesses' which I believe I could substantiate. A backfellow may 'see' as 'a unity' two persons, such as two siblings or a grandparent and grandchild; or a living man and something inanimate, as when he tells you that, say, the woolybutt tree, his totem, is his wife's brother. (This is not quite as strange as it may seem. Even modern psychologists tend to include part of 'environment' in a 'definition' of 'person' or 'personality'.) There is also some kind of unity between waking-life and dream-life: the means by which, in Aboriginal understanding, a man fathers a child is not by sexual intercourse, but by the act of dreaming about a spirit-child. His own spirit, during a dream, 'finds' a child and directs it to his wife, who then conceives. Physical congress between a man and a woman is contingent, not a necessary prerequisite. Through the medium of dream-contact with a spirit an artist is inspired to produce a new song. It is by dreaming that a man divines the intention of someone to kill him by sorcery, or of relatives to visit him. And, as I have suggested, it is by the act of dreaming, in some way difficult for a European to grasp because of the force of our analytic abstractions, that a blackfellow conceives himself to make touch with whatever it is that is continuous between The Dreaming and the Here-and-Now.

The truth of it seems to be that man, society and nature, and past, present and future, are at one together within a unitary system of such a kind that its ontology cannot illumine minds too much under the influence of humanism, rationalism and science. One cannot easily, in the mobility of modern life and thought, grasp the vast intuitions of stability and permanence, and of life and man, at the heart of Aboriginal ontology.

It is fatally easy for Europeans, encountering such things for the first time, to go on to suppose that 'mysticism' of this kind rules *all* Aboriginal thought. It is not so. 'Logical' thought and 'rational' conduct are about as widely present in Aboriginal life as they are in the simpler levels of European life. Once one understands three things — the primary intuitions which the blackfellow has formed about the nature of the universe and man, those things in both which he thinks interesting and significant, and the conceptual system from within which he reasons about them — then the suppositions about prelogicality, illogicality and non-rationality can be seen to be merely absurd. And if one wishes to see a really brilliant demonstration of deductive thought, one has only to see a blackfellow tracking a wounded kangaroo, and persuade him to say why he interprets given signs in a certain way.

The second means of dealing with the notion of The Dreaming is, as I said, to try to relate it to things familiar in our own intellectual history. From this viewpoint, it is a cosmogony, an account of the begetting of the universe, a story about creation. it is also a cosmology, an account or theory of how what was created became an orderly system. To be more precise, it is a theory of how the universe became a moral system.

If one analyses the hundreds of tales about The Dreaming, one can see within them three elements. The first concerns the great *marvels* — how all the fire and water in the world were stolen and recaptured; how men made a mistake over sorcery and now have to die from it; how the hills, rivers and waterholes were made; how the sun, moon and stars were set upon their courses; and many other dramas of this kind. The second element tells how certain things were *instituted* for the first time — how animals and men diverged from a joint stock that was neither one nor the other; how the blacknosed kangaroo got his black nose and the porcupine his quills; how such social divisions as tribes, clans and language groups were set up; how spirit-children were first placed in the waterholes, the winds and the leaves of trees. A third element, if I am not mistaken, allows one to suppose that many of the main institutions of present-day life were *already ruling* in The Dreaming, for example marriage, exogamy, sister-exchange and initiation, as well as many of the well-known breaches of custom. The men of The Dreaming committed adultery, betrayed and killed each other, were greedy, stole and committed the very wrongs committed by those now alive.

Now, if one disregards the imagery in which the verbal literature of The Dreaming is cast, one may perhaps come to three conclusions.

The tales are a kind of commentary, or statement, on what is thought to be permanent and ordained at the very basis of the world and life. They are a way of stating the principle which animates things. I would call them a poetic key to reality. The Aborigine does not ask himself the philosophical-type questions: What is 'real'? How many 'kinds' of 'reality' are there? What are the 'properties' of 'reality'? How are the properties 'interconnected'? This is the idiom of Western intellectual discourse and the fruit of a certain social history. His tales are, however, a kind of answer to such questions so far as they have been asked at all. They may not be a 'definition', but they are a 'key' to reality, a key to the singleness and the plurality of things set up once-for-all when, in The Dreaming, the universe became man's universe. The active philosophy of Aboriginal life transforms this 'key', which is expressed in the idiom of poetry, drama and symbolism, into a principle that The Dreaming determines not only what life *is* but also *what it can be*. Life, so to speak, is a one-possiblity thing, and what this is, is the 'meaning' of The Dreaming.

The tales are also a collation of *what is validly known* about such ordained permanencies. The blacks cite The Dreaming as a charter of absolute validity in answer to all questions of *why* and *how*. In this sense, the tales can be regarded as being, perhaps not a definition, but a 'key' of truth.

They also state, by their constant recitation of what was done rightly and wrongly in The Dreaming, the ways in which good men should, and bad men will, act now. In this sense, they are a 'key' or guide to the norms of conduct, and a prediction of how men will err.

One may thus say that, after a fashion — a cryptic, symbolic and poetic fashion — the tales are 'a philosophy' in the garb of a verbal literature. The European has a philosophic literature which expresses a largely deductive understanding of reality, truth, goodness and beauty. The blackfellow has a mythology, a ritual and an art which express an intuitive, visionary and poetic understanding of the same ultimates. In following out The Dreaming, the blackfellow 'lives' this philosophy. It is an implicit philosophy, but nevertheless a real one. Whereas we hold (and may live) a philosophy of abstract propositions, attained by someone standing professionally outside 'life' and treating it as an object of contemplation and inquiry, the blackfellow holds his philosophy in mythology, attained as the social product of an indefinitely ancient past, and proceeds to live it out 'in' life, in part through a ritual and an expressive art, and in part through non-sacred social customs.

European minds are made uneasy by the facts that the stories are, quite plainly, preposterous; are often a mass of internal contradictions; are encrusted by superstitious fancies about magic, sorcery, hobgoblins and superhuman heroes; and lack the kind of theme and structure — in other words, the 'story' element — for which we look. Many of us cannot help feeling that such things can only be the products of absurdly ignorant credulity and a lower order of mentality. This is to fall victim to a facile fallacy. Our own intellectual history is not an absolute standard by which to judge others. The worst imperialisms are those of preconception.

Custom is the reality, beliefs but the shadows which custom makes on the wall. Since the tales, in any case, are not really 'explanatory' in purpose or function, they naturally lack logic, system and completeness. It is simply pointless to look for such things within them. But we are not entitled to suppose that, because the tales are fantastical, the social life producing them is itself fantastical. The shape of reality is always distorted in the shadows it throws. One finds much logic, system and rationality in the blacks' actual scheme of life.

These tales are neither simply illustrative nor simply explanatory; they are fanciful and poetic in content because they are based on visionary and intuitive insights into mysteries; and, if we are ever to understand them, we must always take them in their complex context. If, then, they make more sense to the poet, the artist and the philosopher than to the clinicians of human life, let us reflect on the withering effect on sensibility of our pervasive rationalism, rather than depreciate the gifts which produced the

Aboriginal imaginings. And in no case should we expect the tales, *prima facie*, to be even interesting if studied out of context. Aboriginal mythology is quite unlike the Scandinavian, Indian or Polynesian mythologies.

III

In my own understanding, The Dreaming is a proof that the blackfellow shares with us two abilities which have largely made human history what it is.

The first of these we might call 'the metaphysical gift'. I mean the ability to transcend oneself, to make acts of imagination so that one can stand 'outside' or 'away from' oneself, and turn the universe, oneself and one's fellows into objects of contemplation. The second ability is a 'drive' to try to 'make sense' out of human experience and to find some 'principle' in the whole human situation. This 'drive' is, in some way, built into the constitution of the human mind. No one who has real knowledge of Aboriginal life can have any doubt that they possess, and use, both abilities very much as we do. They differ from us only in the directions in which they turn their gifts, the idiom in which they express them, and the principles of intellectual control.

The blacks have no gods, just or unjust, to adjudicate the world. Not even by straining can one see in such culture heroes as Baiame and Darumulum the true hint of a Yahveh, jealous, omniscient and omnipotent. The ethical insights are dim and somewhat coarse in texture. One can find in them little trace, say, of the inverted pride, the self-scrutiny, and the consciousness of favour and destiny which characterized the early Jews. A glimpse, but no truly poignant sense, of moral dualism; no notion of grace or redemption; no whisper of inner peace and reconcilement; no problems of worldly life to be solved only by a consummation of history; no heaven of reward or hell of punishment. The blackfellow's afterlife is but a shadowy replica of worldly life, so none flee to inner sanctuary to escape the world. There are no prophets, saints or *illuminati*. There is a concept of goodness, but it lacks true scruple. Men can become ritually unclean, but may be cleansed by a simple mechanism. There is a moral law but, as in the beginning, men are both good and bad, and no one is racked by the knowledge. I imagine there could never have been an Aboriginal Ezekiel, any more than there could have been a Job. The two sets of insights cannot easily be compared, but it is plain that their underlying moods are wholly unlike, and their store of meaningfulness very uneven. In the one there seems an almost endless possibility of growth, and a mood of censoriousness and pessimism. In the other, a kind of standstill, and a mood which is neither tragic nor optimistic. The Aborigines are not shamed or inspired by a religious thesis of what men might become by faith and grace. Their metaphysic, assents, without brooding or challenge, to what men evidently have to be because the terms of life are cast. Yet they have a kind of religiosity cryptically displayed in their magical awareness of nature, in their complex totemism, ritual and art, and perhaps too even in their intricately ordered life.

They are, of course, nomads — hunters and foragers who grow nothing, build nothing, and stay nowhere long. They make almost no physical mark on the environment. Even in areas which are still inhabited, it takes a knowledgeable eye to detect their recent presence. Within a matter of weeks, the roughly cleared camp-sites may be erased by sun, rain and wind. After a year or two there may be nothing to suggest that the country was ever inhabited. Until one stumbles on a few old flint-tools, a stone quarry, a shell-midden, a rock painting, or something of the kind, one may think the land had never known the touch of man.

They neither dominate their environment nor seek to change it. 'Children of nature' they are not, nor are they 'nature's master'. One can only say they are 'at one' with nature. The whole ecological principle of their life might be summed up in the Baconian aphorism — *natura von vincitur nisi parendo*: 'nature is not to be commanded except by obeying'. Naturally, one finds metaphysical and social reflections of the fact.

They move about, carrying their scant possessions, in small bands of anything from ten to sixty persons. Each band belongs to a given locality. A number of bands — anything from three or four up to twelve or fifteen, depending on the fertility of the area — make up a 'tribe'. A tribe is usually a language or dialect group which thinks of itself as having a certain unity of common speech and shared customs. The tribes range is size from a few hundred to a few thousand souls.

One rarely sees a tribe as a formed entity. It comes together and lives as a unit only for a great occasion — a feast, a corroboree, a hunt, an initiation, or a formal duel. After a few days — at the most, weeks — it breaks up again into smaller bands or sections of bands: most commonly into a group of brothers, with their wives, children and grandchildren, and perhaps a few close relatives. These parties rove about their family locality or, by agreement, the territories of immediate neighbours. They do not wander aimlessly, but to a purpose, and in tune with the seasonal food supply. One can almost plot a year of their life in terms of movement towards the places where honey, yams, grass seeds, eggs, or some other food staple is in bearing and ready for eating.

The uncomplex visible routine, and the simple segmentation, are very deceptive. It took well over half a century for Europeans to realize that, behind the outward show, was an inward structure of surprising complexity. It was a century before any real understanding of this structure developed.

In one tribe with which I am familiar, a very representative tribe, there are about 100 'invisible' divisions which have to be analysed before one can claim even a serviceable understanding of the tribe's organization. The structure is much more complex than that of an Australian village of the same size. The complexity is in the most striking contrast with the comparative simplicity which rules in the two other departments of Aboriginal life — the material culture, on the one hand, and the ideational or metaphysical culture, on the other. We have, I think, to try to account for this contrast in some way.

Their creative 'drive' to make sense and order out of things has, for some reason, concentrated on the social rather than on the metaphysical or the material side. Consequently, there has been an unusually rich development of what the anthropologist calls 'social structure', the network of enduring relations recognized between people. This very intricate system is an intellectual and social achievement of a high order. It is not, like an instinctual response, a phenomenon of 'nature'; it is not, like art or ritual, a complex type of behaviour passionately added to 'nature', in keeping with metaphysical insight but without rational and intelligible purposes which can be clearly stated; it has to be compared, I think, with such a secular achievement as, say, parliamentary government in a European society. It is truly positive knowledge.

One may see within it three things: given customs, 'of which the memory of man runneth not to the contrary'; a vast body of cumulative knowledge about the effects of these customs on a society in given circumstances; and the use of the power of abstract reason to rationalize the resultant relations into a system.

But it is something much more: it has become *the source of the dominant mode of Aboriginal thinking*. The blacks use it to give a bony structure to parts of the world outlook suggested by intuitive speculation. I mean by this that they have taken some of its fundamental principles and relations and have applied them to very much wider sets of phenomena. This tends to happen if any type of system of thought becomes truly dominant. It is, broadly, what Europeans did with 'religion' and 'science' as systems: extended their principles and categories to fields far beyond the contexts in which the systems grew.

Thus, the blacks have taken the male–female social principle and have extended it to the non-human world. In one tribe I have studied, all women, without exception, call particular birds or trees by the same kinship terms that they apply to actual relatives. In the same way, all men without exception use comparable terms for a different set of trees or birds. From this results what the anthropologist calls 'sex totemism'. The use of other principles results in other types of totemism. An understanding of this simple fact removes much of the social, if not the ritual, mystery of totemism. Again, the principle of relatedness itself, relatedness between known people by known descent through known marriages, is extended over the whole face of human society. The same terms of kinship which are used for close agnatic and affinal relatives are used for every other person an Aborigine meets in the course of his life: strangers, friends, enemies and known kin may all be called by the same terms as one uses for brother, father, mother's sister, father's mother's brother, and so on. This is what an anthropologist means when he says 'Aboriginal society is a society of kinship'.

It might even be argued that the blacks have done much the same thing with 'time'. Time as a continuum is a concept only hazily present in the Aboriginal mind. What might be called *social* time is, in a sense, 'bent' into cycles or circles. The most controlled understanding of it is by reckoning in terms of generation-classes, which are arranged into named and recurring cycles. As far as the blackfellow thinks about time at all, his interest lies in the cycles rather than in the continuum, and each cycle is in essence a principle for dealing with social interrelatedness.

IV

Out of all this may come for some an understanding of the blackfellow very different from that which has passed into the ignorance and vulgarity of popular opinion.

One may see that, like all men, he is a metaphysician in being able to transcend himself. With the metaphysic goes a mood and spirit which I can only call a mood and spirit of 'assent': neither despair nor resignation, optimism nor pessimism, quietism nor indifference. The mood, and the outlook beneath it, make him hopelessly out of place in a world in which the Renaissance has triumphed only to be perverted, and in which the products of secular humanism, rationalism and science challenge their own hopes, indeed, their beginnings.

Much association with the blackfellow makes me feel I may not be far wrong in saying that, unlike us, he seems to see 'life' as a one-possibility thing. This may be why he seems to have almost no sense of tragedy. If 'tragedy is a looking at fate for a lesson in deportment on life's scaffold', the Aborigine seems to me to have read the lesson and to have written it into the very conception of how men should live, or else to have stopped short of the insight that there are gods either just or unjust. Nor have I found in him much self-pity. These sentiments can develop only if life presents real alternatives, or if it denies an alternative that one feels should be there. A philosophy of assent fits only a life of unvarying constancy. I do not at all say that pain, sorrow and sadness have no place in Aboriginal life, for I have seen them all too widely. All I mean is that the blacks seem to have gone beyond, or not quite attained, the human *quarrel* with such things. Their rituals of sorrow, their fortitude in pain and their undemonstrative sadness seem to imply a reconciliation with the terms of life such that 'peace is the understanding of tragedy and at the same time its preservation', or else that they have not sensed life as baffled by either fate or wisdom.

Like all men, he is also a philosopher in being able to use his power of abstract reason. His genius, his *métier* and — in some sense — his fate is that because of endowment and circumstance this power has channelled itself mainly into one activity, 'making sense' out of the social relations among men living together. His intricate social organization is an impressive essay on the economy of conflict, tension and experiment in a life situation at the absolute pole of our own.

Like all men, too, he pays the price of his insights and solutions. We look to a continuous unfolding of life, and to a blissful attainment of the better things for which, we say, man has an infinite capacity. For some time, nothing has seemed of less consequence to us than the maintenance of continuity. The cost, in instability and inequity, is proving very heavy. Aboriginal life has endured feeling that continuity, not man, is the measure of all. The cost, in the world of power and change, is extinction. What defeats the blackfellow in the modern world, fundamentally, is his transcendentalism. So much of his life and thought are concerned with The Dreaming that it stultifies his ability to develop. This is not a new thing in human history. A good analogy is with the process in Chinese poetry by which, according to Arthur Waley, its talent for classical allusion became a vice which finally destroyed it altogether.

A 'philosophy of life', that is, a system of mental attitudes towards the conduct of life, may or may not be consistent with an actual way of life. Whether it is or is not will depend on how big a gap there is, if any, between what life *is* and what men think life *ought to be*. If Ideal and Real drift too far away from one another (as they did at the end of the Middle Ages, and seem increasingly to do in this century) men face some difficult options. They have to change their way of life, or their philosophy, or both, or live unhappily somewhere in between. We are familiar enough with the 'war of the philosophies' and the tensions of modern life which express them. Problems of this kind had no place, I would say, in traditional Aboriginal life. It knew nothing, and could not, I think, have known anything of the Christian's straining for inner perfection; of 'moral man and immoral society'; of the dilemma of liberty and authority; of intellectual uncertainty, class warfare and discontent with one's lot in life — all of which, in some sense, are problems of the gap between Ideal and Real.

The Aborigines may have been in Australia for as long as 10 000 years. No one at present can do more than guess whence or how they came, and there is little more than presumptive evidence on which to base a guess. The span of time, immense though it may have been, matters less than the fact that, so far as one can tell, they have been almost completely isolated. Since their arrival, no foreign stimulus has touched them, except on the fringes of the northern and north-western coasts. To these two facts we must add two others. The physical environment has, evidently, not undergone any marked general change, although there has been a slow desiccation of parts of the centre into desert, and some limited coastline changes. The fourth fact is that their tools and material crafts seem to have been very unprogressive.

It we put these four facts together — an immensely long span of time, spent in more or less complete isolation, in a fairly constant environment, with an unprogressive material culture, we may perhaps see why sameness, absence of change, fixed routine, regularity, call it what you will, is a main dimension of their thought and life. Let us sum up this aspect as leading to a metaphysical emphasis on abidingness. They place a very special value on things remaining unchangingly themselves, on keeping life to a routine which is known and trusted. Absence of change, which means certainty of expectation, seems to them a good thing in itself. One may say, their Ideal and Real come very close together. The value given to continuity is so high that they are not simply a people 'without a history': they are a people who have been able, in some sense, to 'defeat' history, to become ahistorical in mood, outlook and life. This is why, among them, the philosophy of assent, the glove, fits the hand of actual custom almost to perfection, and the forms of social life, the art, the ritual and much else take on a wonderful symmetry.

Their tools and crafts, meagre — pitiably meagre — though they are, have nonetheless been good enough to let them win the battle for survival, and to win it comfortably at that. With no pottery, no knowledge of metals, no wheel, no domestication of animals, no agriculture, they have still been able not only to live and people the entire continent, but even in a sense to prosper, to win a surplus of goods and develop leisure-time occupations. The evidences of the surplus of yield over animal need are to be seen in the spiderweb of trade routes criss-crossing the continent, on which a large volume of non-utilitarian articles circulated, themselves largely the products of leisure. The true leisure-time activities — social entertaining, great ceremonial gatherings, even much of the ritual and artistic life — impressed observers even from the beginning. The notion of Aboriginal life as always preoccupied with the risk of starvation, as always a hair's breadth from disaster, is as great a caricature as Hobbes's notion of savage life as 'poor, nasty, brutish, and short'. The best corrective of any such notion is to spend a few nights in an Aboriginal camp, and experience directly the unique joy in life which can be attained by a people of few wants, an other-worldly cast of mind and a simple scheme of life which so shapes a day that it ends with communal singing and dancing in the firelight.

The more one sees of Aboriginal life the stronger the impression that its mode, its ethos and its principle are variations on a single theme — continuity, constancy, balance, symmetry, regularity, system, or some such quality as these words convey.

One of the most striking things is that there are no great conflicts over power, no great contests for place and office. This single fact explains much else, because it rules out so much that would be destructive of stability. The idea of a formal chief, or a leader with authority over the persons of others in a large number of fields of life — say, for example, as with a Polynesian or African chief — just does not seem to make sense to a blackfellow. Nor does even the modified Melanesian notion — that of a man becoming some sort of a leader because he accumulates a great deal of garden wealth and so gains prestige. There are leaders in the sense of men of unusual skill, initiative and force, and they are given much respect; they may even attract something like a following; but one finds no trace of formal or institutionalized chieftainship. So there are no offices to stimulate ambition, intrigue, or the use of force; to be envied or fought over; or to be lost or won. Power — a real thing in every society — is diffused mainly through one sex, the men, but in such a way that it is not to be won, or lost, in concentrations, by craft, struggle or coup. It is very much a male-dominated society. The older men dominate the younger, the men dominate the women. Not that the women are chattels — Dr Phyllis Kaberry in her interesting book *Aboriginal Woman* disposed of that Just-So story very effectively, but there is a great deal of discrimination against them. The mythology justifies this by tales telling how men had to take power from women by force in The Dreaming. The psychology (perhaps the truth) of it is as obvious as it is amusing. If women were not kept under, they would take over!

At all events, the struggle for power occurred once for all. Power, authority, influence, age, status, knowledge, all run together and, in some sense, are the same kind of thing. The men of power, authority and influence are old men — at least, mature men; the greater the secret knowledge and authority the higher the status; and the initiations are so arranged (by the old men) that the young men do not acquire full knowledge, and so attain status and authority, until they too are well advanced in years. One can thus see why the great term of respect is 'old man' — *maluka*, as in *We of the Never-Never*. The system is self-protective and self-renewing. The real point of it all is that the checks and balances seem nearly perfect, and no one really seems to want the kind of satisfaction that might come from a position of domination. At the same time, there is a serpent in Eden. The narrow self-interest of men exploits The Dreaming.

Power over things? Every canon of good citizenship and common sense is against it, though there are, of course, clear property arrangements. But what could be more useless than a store of food that will not keep, or a heavy pile of spears that have to be carried everywhere? Especially in a society in which the primary virtues are generosity and fair dealing. Nearly every social affair involving goods — food in the family, payments in marriage, intertribal exchange — is heavily influenced by equalitarian notions; a notion of reciprocity as a moral obligation; a notion of generously equivalent return; and a surprisingly clear notion of fair dealing, or making things 'level' as the blackfellow calls it in English.

There is a tilt of the system towards the interests of the men, but given this tilt, everything else seems as if carefully calculated to keep it in place. The blacks do not fight over land. There are no wars or invasions to seize territory. They do not enslave each other. There is no master–servant relation. There is no class division. There is no property or income inequality. The result is a homeostasis, far-reaching and stable.

I do not wish to create an impression of a social life without egotism, without vitality, without cross-purposes, without conflict. Indeed, there is plenty of all, as there is of malice, enmity, bad faith and violence, running along the lines of sex inequality and age inequality. But this essential humanity exists, and runs its course, within a system whose first principle is the preservation of balance. And arching over it all is the *logos* of The Dreaming. How we shall state this when we fully understand it I do not know, but I should think we are more likely to ennoble it than not. Equilibrium ennobled is 'abidingness'. Piccarda's answer in the third canto of the *Paradiso* gives the implicit theme and logic of The Dreaming: *e la sua volontate è nostra pace*, 'His will is our peace'. But the gleam that lighted Judah did not reach the Australian wilderness, and the blacks follow The Dreaming only because their fathers did.

15
Consciousness and Responsibility in an Australian Aboriginal Religion

DEBORAH BIRD ROSE

In 1965 Stanner wrote that the central task of the study of Australian religions was to break down 'the collocation of facts so that the components would be religiously intelligible' (1965:224). He was referring to approximately two centuries of study during which Aboriginal religious life had either been denied, addressed as a primitive form of religion, or reduced to sociological or other frameworks of analysis. In contrast, Eliade's work (1973, in particular) is deeply insightful and soundly based on a sensitive hermeneutic. Yet because his aim is to synthesize the few sources relevant to Aboriginal religious life, his work cannot do justice to the beauty and complexity of religion as it is lived.

In this paper I examine one facet of Aboriginal religion in the Northern Territory. One of the points I will be making is that in Aboriginal society and culture religion is part of every aspect of life. Religion underlies all actions, expressions and interpretations, for women and for men, in daily and ceremonial life, both public and secret. First, I briefly examine Ngaringman and Ngaliwurru cosmology, focusing primarily on the principles according to which the cosmos is believed to work. Secondly, I turn to ideas about life and consciousness, particularly in relation to cosmic principles. Thirdly, I examine concepts of responsibility toward self and cosmos. In conclusion I discuss some of the implications of these issues for the comparative study of religion.

In order to interpret religious understanding into western categories of knowledge and experience, one is faced with a problem of language, for Aboriginal languages implicitly define as unified many of those categories which westerners define as separate. Given the interpenetration of religion and all other categories of life, it is possible to approach the analysis of religion from any of several different directions. I have chosen to use terminologies which, in the west, are characteristic of ecology, cybernetics, and moral philosophy. My purpose however is not to reduce religion to these categories, but rather to use these categories as a means of producing a religious analysis.[1]

This paper was delivered to the Australian Association for the Study of Religions, Ninth Annual Conference, Canberra 24–28 August, 1984 and was first published in *Nelen Yubu*, 23.

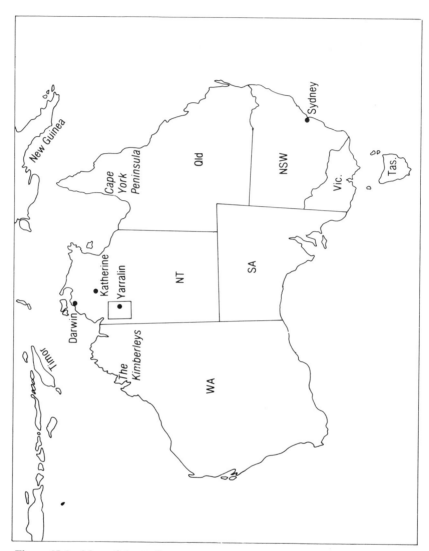

Figure 15.1   Map of Australia

The data 1 present here derive from twenty-four months of anthropological research with Ngaringman and Nagaliwurru speaking people in the Northern Territory.[2] I was studying cultural identity in an Aboriginal community called Yarralin on Victoria River Downs Station (Figures 15.1 and 15.2). The people with whom I worked have a century-long history of contact with Europeans, primarily pastoralists and police. They all speak pastoral English, are well versed in the intricacies of the cattle business and are rapidly becoming skilled at dealing with Europeans outside the pastoral context. At the same time, they have never been forced into reserves or missions, and have never been

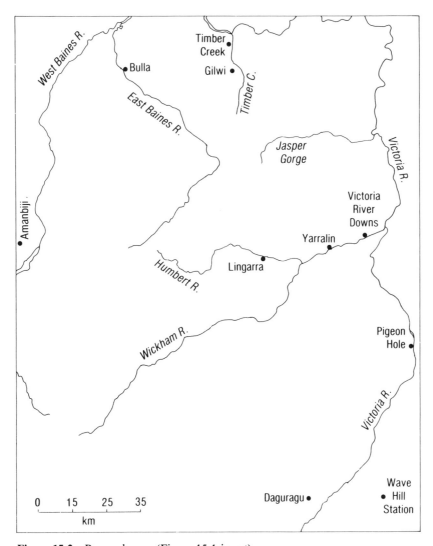

Figure 15.2 Research area (Figure 15.1 insert)

consistently exposed to Christian teachings. In fact, Victoria River Downs was until recently closed to both missionaries and anthropologists (Arndt 1965:243). Because Aboriginal labour was only required on cattle stations for about six months out of the year, people in this region spent the other half of the year very consciously teaching younger people the skills and knowledge necessary to all facets of Aboriginal life. Thus while European domination has necessitated many changes in Aboriginal life, people have maintained a continuity of traditional knowledge and culture. Yarralin people are thoroughly Aboriginal in their fundamental orientation towards such central issues of human life as the meaning and management of birth and death, life and the cosmos.

Cosmology

Ngaringman/Ngaliwurru cosmology can only be understood by reference to the Dreaming. As Stanner (1979:23–40) and many others state, this concept is the most central and yet the most elusive aspect of Aboriginal culture. According to Stanner (1979:24), this 'subtle conception' is many things in one: a narrative of the heroic past during which life came to be; a charter for the present; and a 'kind of logos or principle of order transcending everything'. It is this third concept, logos, that I focus on here.

Yarralin people speak frequently of Dreaming Law which they see as a set of unchanging moral principles through which life is assured. Dreaming Law was established in Dreaming Time — the heroic time which existed in the past and still exists today. The earth is thought of as a living female being who gave birth (out of caves) to all other living things, and who is still the ultimate source of life. The origins of all life thus derive from one mother, the earth. As such all life forms can be seen as kinsmen. This includes all humans, plants and animals, as well as other life forms which Yarralin people recognize, such as the sun, moon and rain, and several categories of human-like beings.

In the beginning, living things frequently walked in the shape of humans; in their actions and interactions they produced the set of pinciples now known as Dreaming Law.[3] The essence of Dreaming Law, expressed through myth, song cycles and so on, is that it shows how and why the cosmos constitutes a living system. Dreaming Law then is about life — about the principles by which life is maintained and enhanced in this system in which all parts are interrelated.

Intrinsic to Yarralin people's understanding of the cosmos is the idea that all parts of the cosmos are alive. All were alive in Dreaming Time and all are still alive. Each part is related to other parts, but in the beginning each part walked separately. It is on this basis that Dreaming Law is a law of autonomy: every life form that walked in the Dreaming Time walked as an autonomous creative power, and every modern descendent of an original Dreaming is still autonomous. And while each part is autonomous, each is equally part of a total system. The goal of the system as a whole is to reproduce itself as a living system, while the goals of each part are: (1) to reproduce itself as a part; and (2) to maintain the relationships between itself and other parts, for it is through these relationships that the cosmos as a whole is maintained.

These relationships are crucial, for without them life cannot continue. Aboriginal morality has to do with maintaining the cosmos as a life enhancing system. Moral rules concern these critical relationships between parts of the system. These relationships are based upon four principles which I identify as those of response, balance, symmetry and autonomy. Each part is autonomous as a fundamental feature of the integrity of life. Each part balances and is balanced by other parts. In order for parts to be balanced they must be symmetrical, that is, of equal power (physical, social, intellectual etc.). And in order for balance to be maintained, parts must communicate. They do this by acting (being alive) and responding. In action, parts assert their autonomy and strength; in responding, parts delimit the boundaries of other parts and thus implicitly their own boundaries. Each part of cosmos is thus seen as a moral agent and in behaving morally each part reproduces the relationships through which the whole system continues to enhance life.

This abstract delineation of cosmic principles can be more clearly understood by reference to a living example. The actions of the seasons illustrate these principle well. Sun and rain (Rainbow Snake) were walking in human form during the Dreaming. At that time they tested laws and ultimately they established the conditions of their present existence and of their relationship. The sun now lives in the sky, shines during the day, is hot and dry, and heats or 'cooks' the earth. Plants and animals grow to maturity through the strength of the sun's heat. Rain, characterized as the Rainbow Snake, lives in permanent waterholes, is wet and cool and washes the earth clean, thus renewing cycles of regeneration. Without sun the earth would be flooded, while without rain the earth would be burnt. In short, the sun has its own Law and rain has its own Law. The Law of their relatedness becomes more complex and is the topic of many myth segments. Put succinctly, as the sun dries and heats the country the flying foxes move from water to dry land, but as the sun becomes too hot they retreat to the waterholes. Flying foxes are said to be 'mates' with the Rainbow Snake; their presence 'tells' the Rainbow that it is time to move. It rises out of the water and spits, causing thunder, lightning and rain. Various other species join in calling up the Rainbow and urging it to create more rain. Eventually however, the rain becomes dangerous. Like the sun, what is necessary at one stage in the cycle becomes dangerous if allowed to become too powerful. At this point the wind intervenes, breaking the Rainbow's back, the sun burns it, and the Rainbow retreats to the rivers while the sun takes over the sky, initiating a cycle of growth.

Sun and rain exist independently of each other; they are autonomous beings. The sun, in acting as itself, begins to burn the earth. It thus tells the flying foxes to go to the river. They in turn tell the Rainbow Snake to rise up. Sun and rain are conceived of as two powerful and balancing forces, each one summarizing and expressing a great range of phenomena — hot and cold, wet and dry, growth and obliteration. Each in its own way expresses the powers of birth, death and renewal. They thus balance each other. Neither allows the other to go out of control. They are alive and conscious, they communicate and respond. In behaving morally they enhance all life.

Human beings do much the same thing. Ngaringman/Ngaliwurru people are active participants in a number of different social groups, each of which balances, and is balanced by, other groups. As members of groups based on language, for instance, people oppose and balance one language group against another. These groups can be divided into smaller groups based on smaller units of country, each of which is autonomous and is balanced by other, symmetrically defined, groups. Likewise, language groups can be brought together on the basis of co-ownership of ceremony lines, each of which is balanced by ·other ceremony lines.

In similar fashion, human groups are located in country and have intense moral responsibilities of locality. Each group should, at least: burn the grass, use the country, perform increase ceremonies at local Dreaming sites, and protect dangerous Dreaming sites so that no harm comes from them. In return, country takes care of its people, providing them with food, water and all the other necessities of life. This is a reflexive moral relationship of care through which the continuity of life for humans, for country and for plants and animals is assured.

In using country, humans also enter into relationships with other species. Women, for instance, hunt, fish and gather, taking care not to overuse any of the resources. They are resource managers with a deep knowledge of the ecological relationships on which moral action must be based. Women also give birth to children. These human children belong to specific country, grow up with specific responsibilities to people, country and other species, and are gradually taught the knowledge of how to participate responsibly in these systemic relationships. Other categories of human identity define people in relation to other species. One set of categories is the matrilineal species identity (totem) termed 'Dreaming' in Aboriginal English and *ngulu* in Ngaringman. For example, people who are flying fox *ngulu* are said to be 'countrymen' (close kin) of flying foxes and 'mates' with rain. They share a special relationship to flying foxes which is particularly evident when a flying fox person dies. At that time all flying foxes become taboo as food and it is only with the passage of time and with the permission of flying fox people that flying foxes may again be hunted. In earlier days these relationships were given special attention after death when the bones of a dead person were used to invigorate the Dreaming sites of species with which the individual had been identified in life.

In sum, this brief examination of cosmology indicates that Yarralin people see the cosmos as a system which was designed during the Dreaming Time with the goal of enhancing life. Each part of the system is seen to be a moral agent engaged in relationships which are nurturant and which are maintained according to a few principles: response, balance, symmetry and autonomy.

Species Intersubjectivity

I now turn to a finer examination of relationships between parts of the cosmic system. I use the term intersubjectivity to mean the ways in which one subject encounters another subject (Owens 1970:1) and I expand the general usage to include all life forms, while focusing primarily on animal/human relationships.

Westerners have engaged in seemingly endless speculation about what distinguishes us from animals, be it the gift of language, of consciousness, of foreknowledge of death, of the ability to speculate, imagine, plan and execute plans. Ngaringman/Ngaliwurru people have an answer to this question and it is an answer which they find satisfying. For them shape is the key.

According to Yarralin people all animals have language. That ordinary people cannot understand the language of birds is not surprising — we cannot even understand the language of other people if they come from far away. Likewise, all animals have ceremony. Brolgas are a good example. With their grey bodies and bright red heads they look painted for ceremony and when they dance they move about and stamp their feet as people do.

Boundaries are thought to be immutable as a result of Dreaming action. But they are not impenetrable. Clever people and clever animals can change their shape, disguising themselves as other species and learning to communicate with them. The fact that there are clever people and clever animals introduces the necessity of interpretation into Yarralin people's environment: one cannot know with certainty what a thing is just by looking at it. One must also observe behaviour and events and deduce the quality of being in this light. Yarralin people consistently do this and in their view all parts of the cosmos are doing the same thing.

To be the same, then, minimally, is to share a shape and hence the potential to share a culture. To be different is, initially, to have a different shape, a different physical being. Out of that shape emerge other differences — animals of one shape, one species, share a language, a set of ceremonies, certain kinds of food, a way of life. In Aboriginal English this specific way of life is termed 'culture'. According to this usage, culture is not specific to human beings. All animals have their own culture. We are not different from others by having culture which they lack; we are different in that our culture, like our shape, is different from theirs.

This analysis of species difference brings us to the crux of the matter. Each species has its own culture which in part defines those actions which the species must take to reproduce itself, its Law, and its relationships with other species. Brolgas do not imitate human culture; in their dancing they are manifesting their own culture.

Life then in Ngaringman/Ngaliwurru thinking *is the cosmos.* And to be alive is to be conscious — to know and follow one's own Law, to recognize that other consciousnesses exist and to interact responsibly with others. Yarralin people's environment is alive, conscious and paying attention. Human actions are noted, just as humans note the actions of other living beings. This cosmic awareness is only possible because all 'cultures' are subject to the same moral principles of response, balance, symmetry and autonomy.

It is not necessary for humans to know brolga culture in detail; it is sufficient to know that brolgas have their own culture. Human beings know this in several ways. First, it is known because myths from the Dreaming show brolgas to have been autonomous actors then. It follows logically that since there are still brolgas, they are autonomous. Secondly, brolga culture is known to exist because, like humans and all other species, brolgas can be seen to behave in ways that are regular, predictable and unique. Uniqueness indicates their autonomy — 'they have their own Law'. Regularity and predictability show that they follow their Law, their actions are not chaotic. Thirdly, clever people can communicate with brolgas. Fourthly, the fact that there are brolgas now indicates that they have been behaving as responsible moral agents — reproducing themselves, their Law, and their relationships. Their very existence thus proves their participation in a moral cosmos.

Modes of knowing the other thus become circular: myths tell that others exist according to law, while the fact that others can be seen to exist proves that they have their own Law and have been following it. Relationships are good because they are real and real because they are good. Ultimately, however, they can be defined as moral if the continued result is enhanced life. Once the continued life of any group becomes threatened, then it is clear that someone has been acting immorally. The wrong that is done is a wrong inflicted on the cosmos as a whole and the results affect everyone, including the wrongdoer (see Rose 1984b).

Responsibility

Responsibility in this system consists in acting according to a few moral principles which were laid out in the Dreaming Time and which, as Law and exegesis, constitute a vast portion of Aboriginal knowledge.

Yarralin people spend a great deal of their time maintaining their own portion of the system — arranging marriages, growing people from childhood to maturity, teaching younger people, managing birth and death, feeding themselves, taking care of their country and performing all those ceremonies through which cosmic life is regenerated. These are all moral activities aimed at reproducing human life, the relationships among humans and those between humans and other life forms. Ultimately then, they aim at nurturing the cosmos.

The point I would make here is that Ngaringman/Ngaliwurru people believe that all other species are doing much the same sorts of things (see Rose 1984a:456–73). When the brolgas dance, they too are performing ceremonies which regenerate the cosmos. When flying foxes tell the Rainbow Snake to bring rain they are helping to keep the sun in balance and thus to nurture life. If human beings bear a burden of responsibility for all life, so too do all living things. The ultimate goals of life — to nurture and enhance life — are goals which are shared by all living things.

Since all relationships involve mutual nurturance, it follows that the state of being of any portion of the cosmic system is evidence of the care exercised by relevant portions of the system. The state of country, for instance, offers concrete evidence of the responsibility which the owners have been exercising. Responsibility is grave; there is no hiding in a conscious universe.

Each part of the cosmos assumes responsibility as an act of will and in accordance with its own Law as set out in the Dreaming. We find here no heaven or hell, no punishment or reward. C. S. Lewis' (1964) concept of the Great Divorce is not applicable, nor are we talking about a marriage of heaven and hell. Rather we are talking about the exercise of will in a situation where the choice to deny moral action is to turn one's back on the cosmos and ultimately on one's self. The choice to assume responsibility is a multivalent one involving self-interest, reverence, morality and mysticism.

Self-interest lies in the fact that in enhancing cosmic life one assures one's own life. Thus when Yarralin people burn the grass at the end of the wet season they are performing an act from which they later reap the benefit of fat kangaroos and wallabies. Their own diet is improved through the care they put into country. At the same time, care requires an intelligent reading of what the system needs or does not need. Fertility is enhanced in some contexts but may need to be controlled in other contexts. Yarralin people protect a death adder site for instance, trying to assure that it not be damaged because any disturbance would result in an overpopulation of death adders.

The control of fertility is far more complex than this example suggests. Every Dreaming site is an 'increase' site, including those sites which contain potential human beings. Effective management involves knowing when to stimulate a given species and when to leave it alone. Much of what I know about this control is secret and cannot be discussed publicly.

Reverence for life is a quality which is fundamentally characteristic of Aboriginal life, pervading every aspect of daily and ceremonial life. Yet this quality seems frequently to have been overlooked by many Europeans. Generalized reverence is given form and expression in the relationship between people and the earth, for earth is the original mother of all life and a living, conscious being in and of herself. To harm or neglect 'the mother' is to be both rootless and witless — ignorant of one's origins, of the meaning of one's life and of one's place in the cosmos.

All the same time reverence is not just for the earth, but for all life. Death adders, for instance, are controlled but not obliterated. They have their own Law, their autonomy and their own right to be.

Many people of the world have identified reverence for life with abstention from killing and eating meat. For Aboriginal people, of course, this is not the case. Yarralin people see their predations on other species as part of their knowledgeable management of relationships between species. As I have said, there are times when foods become taboo; there are also times when people refrain from predation because they feel that a given species in a given area needs a chance to grow. But they also see that predation is part of maintaining a balance between parts of the cosmos. Overabundance is as much a problem as underabundance.

Yarralin people believe that they themselves are preyed upon by other species, such as a class of beings known as *Kaiya* (custodians of death). They regard these predations as terrifying and they try to avoid being captured by *Kaiya*, but they do not regard these predations as morally wrong any more than they regard their own hunting as morally wrong.

Morality thus lies in those actions which enhance life, given an intelligent assessment of the state of the system at any given point. For Yarralin people this is self-evident. They do not justify their sense of morality other than to point to facts of self-interest. Principles were determined in the Dreaming Time and these principles can be demonstrated to work for the system as a whole.

In the complex web of relationships which, in its totality, nurtures life, morality lies in enhancing all life. This moral code poses a problem when there is a difference between what is life enhancing for an individual and what is life enhancing for a group. The principle of response assures that others will enforce a balance even though it might be repugnant to an individual.

In the Ngaringman/Ngaliwurru view of morality however, 'right' is self-evident at the most general level. They know that some people appear not to understand that continued life on earth is a 'good' to be desired and that actions which enhance life are morally right. In their view such people (many Europeans, for example) are mad. To be 'good' is to be intelligent, knowledgeable and sane. It is also to be at one with the cosmos.

Finally, mysticism too is part of the Aboriginal sense of responsibility. James (1902:410) defines the mystical experience as the 'overcoming of all the usual barriers between the individual and the Absolute'. While this is the most simple and expressive definition of mysticism that I have found, it poses a certain difficulty in the Aboriginal context, for Yarralin people do not see barriers between themselves and the Absolute. The Absolute, in Ngaringman/Ngaliwurru cosmology, is the oneness of the whole cosmos. Yarralin people are born and educated to this sense of oneness, regarding it as their rightful heritage as living, conscious beings. All responsible acts are acts which place the individual in a state of harmony with the cosmos. Both daily and ceremonial life are expressive of this sense of oneness. In daily life people exercise the care and management of nurturant relationships between parts of the system. In ceremonial life they exercise management of time in such a way that the cycles of life are allowed to begin again. It is precisely through living in *this* world that Yarralin people achieve a oneness with the cosmos.

In sum, responsibility is an act of will, taken by conscious beings, deriving from and producing self-interest, reverence, morality and mysticism.

Religious Life

We are now in a position to return to questions relating to the category which westerners have called 'religion'. Unfortunately it is far easier to discuss Aboriginal religion in terms of what it is *not* than to effectively communicate what it is. The following discussion adopts a bit of both approaches. For purposes of comparison I want to show that some western notions of religion are not applicable in the Aboriginal context, yet at the same time I want to communicate that we are indeed talking about a profoundly moving representation of humanity's search for religious meaning. In particular, I will examine concepts of a supreme deity, of sacred and profane and of participation in religious life.

1. Stanner (1979:31) has stated that 'the Aborigines have no gods, just or unjust, to adjudicate the world'. In spite of many attempts to identify one or more 'high gods' in Aboriginal cosmologies (see Eliade 1973:1–42 for a thorough discussion), I am convinced that the people with whom I worked do not have, and do not wish to have, a supreme deity.[4] One of the most important moral principles of the whole cosmos is that the parts are autonomous. The monotheistic concept of an all-powerful deity would seem to deny this principle. Aboriginal concepts of consciousness and responsibility demand that each part of the cosmos take upon itself the responsibility for its own actions, as well as the responsibility for

managing its relationships to other parts of the system. The cosmos 'works' not because a supreme deity regulates it, but because all of the parts regulate each other.

Neither is there hierarchical ordering of parts of the cosmos. Rank is not an issue here, nor is it possible to suppose that the cosmos is human-centred. Rather each part of the cosmos must be seen as an independent moral agent. These parts share a commitment to life and assent to a set of principles through which life is nurtured. The cosmos is maintained and made through the actions of all its parts.

2. Eliade (1973:62) stated that for Australian Aborigines 'living as a human being is in itself a religious act'. He bases his statement on the understanding that 'men assume the responsibility of preserving the world ... through rituals, and especially through the 'increase ceremonies''' (ibid). While I thoroughly agree with the contention that the process of living is a religious act, I have shown that it is not only through rituals that human beings maintain contact with Laws and principles of creation.

I believe that for westerners religious acts are commonly determined to be different from other acts through reference to the sacred. Western concepts of religion thus depend on a contrast between the sacred and the profane. Many analysts have applied this distinction to Aboriginal life (Durkheim 1915; Kaberry 1939; and Warner 1937 offer exceptionally elegant analyses based on this distinction).

My argument is simple. I contend that as life is seen to be sacred, in the sense of having ultimate value and being an ineffable miracle, and as everything is seen to be alive, then there is no basis by which to distinguish between sacred and profane. Likewise, seemingly commonplace actions have a sacred significance, not because they reproduce the past as Eliade (1973:47) suggests, but because they nurture life, create balace and promote the future.[5]

For example, the process of burning the grass is, I believe, a religious act invested with ranges of symbolic meaning which incorporate many deep ideas about life and death. It is thus part of a cosmic cycle in which the balance between sun and rain is restored. It is equally part of a regenerative process in which the debris of past experience is cleared away to make place for new life. Through human action, cosmic forces of fertility and renewal are combined to produce continued life on earth. When Yarralin people burn at the right time of year a new crop of green grass appears, animals eat the fresh grass and grow strong on it, and humans eat some of the animals, making themselves strong. As I stated earlier self-interest, reverence, morality and mysticism combine. Burning provides food, nurtures the earth, recreates the Dreaming Law of balance and places people in harmony with the cosmos. It is an economic, ecological, political and mystical act.

3. I stated in the introduction that the analysis of Aboriginal religions poses a language difficulty. My reworking of conventional notions of sacred and profane is a case in point. A further difficulty arises when we turn to concepts of mysticism, for the paradox of the unity of sacred and profane is frequently taken to be a distinguishing characteristic of mystical experience (Eliade 1958:29; Stace 1960:253).

I have suggested that there is a difference between Aboriginal and other forms of mysticism. I think that this difference lies in the concept of barriers between the individual and the Absolute, a barrier which may also be expressed as the distinction between the sacred and the profane. And I have suggested that Yarralin people do not see a barrier between themselves and the cosmos. Where mysticism in the religions of the great traditions leads people out of this world and toward a transcendent experience of unity beyond, Aboriginal religion leads people into this world and toward an immanent experience of unity in the here and now. This is a unity of time, life and place in which human beings are responsible conduits for life and at the same time are pivotal actors in cosmic processes.

The statements I have made about human participants in life processes are equally true for other life forms. Human beings act as moral agents to nurture and enhance their own life, the life of others, and the relationships between themselves and others. Other life forms are doing the same thing, creating themselves and others through participation in religious life.

Life is sacred and in the Ngaringman/Ngaliwurru cosmology, as I have said, everything is alive. For this reason I contend that it is not only human beings who are participants in the religious life. All parts of the cosmos act responsibly and engage in mystical union with the cosmic whole.

Notes

1. For purposes of my discussion in this paper, I think the best definition is that proposed by Madariago: 'the relatively modest dogma that God is not mad' (quoted in Geertz 1973:99).
2. Research funded by the Australian Institute of Aboriginal Studies, the National Science Foundation (USA) and Bryn Mawr College, Department of Anthropology.
3. Yarralin people possess a vast body of myth relating these actions. Each myth or myth segment discusses relationships between life forms and physical, ecological, social and cultural facts. The analysis of these relationships yields a rich exegesis of human life in particular, and of the life of the cosmos in general. In order to become adept at understanding myths, one must become adept at much of Ngaringman/Ngaliwurru culture in general, for myths make constant reference to social facts and are incomprehensible without an understanding of these referents. The analysis of myth is a complex and detailed study which is most rewarding. However, since my purpose here is to elucidate fundamental principles, I bypass the complex area of myth and draw on Yarralin people's understanding of the major portions of the cosmos: seasons, humans, plants and animals.
4. When the Christian God is discussed in terms of Aboriginal cosmology, Yarralin place him in the category of ancestral human being. They say that the Lord Jesus was a man so his father, God, must also have been a man. They both belong to the Dingo-Human branch of life forms.
5. I have implied that the language and categories of religious studies may not be the best for analysing Aboriginal religion. Here I think that this contention can be seen clearly, for the analysis of myth and ritual has led to a focus on the past which can indicate a rather mechanical approach to life. Stanner (1979:40), for instance, states that Aborigines 'follow the Dreaming only because their fathers did' (see also Eliade 1973:47). In contrast, I contend that Yarralin people use

principles derived from the past as guides to action in the present, in order to produce a certain kind of *future*. The future to be produced is, of course, one in which the same principles will still be applicable, and thus in which life will continue.

References

ARNDT, W (1965), 'The Dreaming of Kunukban', *Oceania*, **35**(4):241–258.

DURKHEIM, EMILE (1915), *The Elementary Forms of the Religious Life*, New York: The Free Press.

ELIADE, MIRCEA (1958), *Patterns in Comparative Religion*, London: Sheed & Ward.

—— (1973), *Australian Religions: An Introduction,* Ithaca: Cornell University Press.

GEERTZ, CLIFFORD (1973), *The Interpretation of Cultures*, New York: Basic Books.

JAMES, WILLIAM (1902), *The Varieties of Religious Experience*, New York: Modern Library.

KABERRY, PHYLLIS (1939), *Aboriginal Woman: Sacred and Profane,* London: George Routledge & Sons.

OWENS, THOMAS J. (1970), *Phenomenology and Intersubjectivity. Contemporary Interpretations of the Interpersonal Situation*, The Hague: Martinus Nijhoff.

ROSE, DEBORAH (1984a), Dingo Makes Us Human; Being and Purpose in Australian Aboriginal Culture, PhD dissertation.

—— (1984b), The Saga of Captain Cook: Morality in European and Aboriginal Law, manuscript in preparation for publication.

STACE, W. T. (1960), *Mysticism and Philosophy*, Philadelphia: J. B. Lippincott.

STANNER, W.E.H. (1965), 'Religion, Totemism and Symbolism' in R. M. & C. H. Berndt (eds), *Aboriginal Man in Australia,* Sydney: Angus & Robertson.

—— (1979), 'The Dreaming' (1953), in W. E. H. Stanner (1973), *White Man Got No Dreaming*. Canberra; ANU Press.

WARNER, LLOYD (1937), *A Black Civilization*, Gloucester, Mass.: Peter Smith (1969 reprint).

16
Aboriginal Women's Religion: A Shifting Law of the Land

DIANE BELL

My father was *kurdungurlu* for that place. It was his to look after. He looked after the two places, Waake and Wakulpu and then I lost him; he passed away. Now it is up to me looking after my own country, Jarra Jarra and also Waake and Wakulpu. As my father could not go on to that country so from when I was a young girl I kept on doing the *yawulyu* [women's ceremonies], looking after the country ... My sisters, Mona and Nancy, they are looking after that country too ... We do that *yawulyu* for Wakulpu all the time ... for fruit. So it will grow up well, so that we can make it green, so that we hold the Law forever. My father instructed me to hold it always this way, so I go on holding *yawulyu* for that country. Sometimes we dance, man and woman together. For Wakulpu. So we can 'catch him up', 'hold him up'. (Mollie Nungarrayi, 1981, quoted in Bell 1983a:119, 132)[1]

This testimony, given in the context of a central Australian land claim,[2] aptly summarizes the nature of women's relationship to and responsibility for country, and takes us to the very heart of Aboriginal religion: the focus on kin and sacred sites, the integration of spiritual with economic life in ritual celebration, generational transmission of knowledge and a sex division of labour (see Bell 1983a, 1987c). It is the latter, the sex division of labour, and the existence of sex-specific bodies of secret-sacred knowledge, that render research and analysis of Aboriginal women's religious beliefs and practices so problematic (see Berndt 1965:241–7; Bell 1983a:229ff.; Goodale 1971:338; Hamilton 1987:45–9; Maddock 1982:139–40). To gain access to the intimate ritual worlds of women, one needs to be female (and, as I suggest below, not just any female). There have been few women in the field and not all have been interested in women, let alone religion.[3] Those who have written of women's lives faced a dilemma in the presentation of their data.[4] How do the worlds of women and men articulate? How are contradictory sex-specific perceptions to be accommodated? Is it sufficient to accept the ideology of male dominance as a timeless, enduring actuality? What of regional differences? How do our own assumptions regarding gender relations shape our fieldwork experiences and subsequent analyses?

First published in Arvind Sharma (ed.), *Today's Woman in World Religions*, New York: State University of New York Press, 1994.

From the testimony of Mollie Nungarrayi another aspect of Aboriginal life, which impinges on any discussion of religion, is plain. The contemporary contexts within which we may learn of women's commitment to 'hold onto' traditional knowledge are limited, and often hostile to hearing what women have to say on serious matters. Nungarrayi spoke in a legal context, an environment that does little to put women at ease. Land claims are a telling example, albeit one of many, where the constraints on recognition of women's contribution to Aboriginal society are manifest (see Bell 1984–5, 1988c). The politics of knowledge and gender relations in Aboriginal society, and the points of articulation with institutions of the wider Australian society, shape our approaches and appreciations of Aboriginal women's religious beliefs and practices (Bell 1983a:240–6, 1989:6–9; Bell and Nelson 1989:408–11). Indeed, the politics of Aboriginal religion and the politics of the study of Aboriginal religion have intertwined so intricately that to write of religion necessarily entails engaging with local politics, academic politics and those of the nation-state (see Bell and Marks 1990:98–104). As these domains are ones in which women's voices are muted, to focus on women is to call attention to the situatedness of the ethnographic voices.

A Feminist Ethnography of Aboriginal Religion

Here I address two basic questions: what are women doing in the ritual domain, and what does this mean for our understanding of Aboriginal religion? I begin from within the ritual worlds of women and map their contribution to the religious domain. But we cannot leave it there, for Aboriginal religion is the political forum within which women and men negotiate authority, power, meaning and relationships. Thus I explore ceremonial contexts within which women and men participate in the construction of representations of Aboriginal religion. My field methodology — participant observation — is necessarily situated, perspectival, relational and contextual, and my rendering of my field experience in the writing of ethnography is similarly framed. This, I suggest, is so of all ethnography, but where ethnographic reporting has produced images consonant with those cherished by the dominant society, and consonant with current scholarly theorizing about gender and women, the relation of the anthropologist to his or her field remains unscrutinized (Hondagneu-Sotelo 1988). In other words, the epistemology is undeclared; male experience is privileged; reality is presented as unmediated by the observer, and the voices of the less powerful are muted (Mascia-Lees *et al.* 1989). The difference for feminist anthropologists is that we cannot feign disinterest, and, as I am arguing here, the sex division of labour in the religious domain presents an enigma which feminist critiques of 'culture' and 'gender relations' illuminate (Moore 1988: 186ff.).

I have chosen an ethnographic presentation for several reasons. First, there is little written on Aboriginal women's ritual life.[5] Second, what does exist variously ignores women; is blind to the historical transformation of gender relations; non-reflectively endorses as holy writ male expressions of power and social reality; or categorically excludes woman's activities from the religious domain.[6] Third, by beginning with a detailed account of one region, one where the separation of the sexes is particularly marked, it is possible to demonstrate that much of the generalizing about women's religious life has been premature and its sureness of vision has constrained research.[7] Finally, a woman-centred ethnography reveals that certain behaviours of women, which appear anomalous if religion is mapped with male as ego, are part of a consistent, coherent set of practices.

I begin with the assumption that what women are doing, and say they are doing, is worth recording; that differences between male and female interpretations of religion are not necessarily evidence that one has erred, but a challenge for the anthropologist to find ways of writing of a society with gendered views. My position is that an ethnography which is explicitly feminist in giving voice to women not only illuminates women's worlds but also leads us to a more dynamic reading of Aboriginal religion, and thereby to a critique of the ways in which we represent our fieldwork. In addressing these issues, I am in open dialogue with current feminist debates concerning reflexivity, politics and epistemology (Caplan 1988; Clifford 1988; Hawkesworth 1989; Mascia-Lees *et al.* 1989). Following Caplan (1988:10), I am arguing that we can be both 'reflexive and political' and that to acknowledge our power as ethnographers is not to forgo our interest in the foundations of knowledge.[8] It is a profoundly political act to decentre man ethnographically as subject, or authority, and the terms in which feminist analyses have been reviewed in Australia are ample evidence of this.[9]

Although Aboriginal beliefs and practices are not consistent across the continent, at core is the concept of the dreamtime (*jukurrpa, altjirra, wongar, bugari*), a moral code that informs and unites all life. The dogma of dreaming states that all the world is known and can be classified within the taxonomy created by the ancestral heroes whose pioneering travels gave form, shape and meaning to the land (Stanner 1979). Here a rocky outcrop indicates the place where the ancestral dog had her puppies, there a low ridge the sleeping body of the emu; the red streaks on the cliff face recall the blood shed in a territorial dispute; ghost gums stand as mute witnesses to where the lightning brothers flashed angrily at their father rain; the lush growth of bush berries is the legacy of prudent care by two old grandmothers; the clear, sweet waterholes, the home of the rainbow serpent, which may only be approached by those schooled in the 'business' (the term used for the work necessary to maintain the law of the dreamtime), remain pure.

The law binds people, flora, fauna and natural phenomena into one enormous interfunctional world. It is the responsibility of the living, who trace direct relationships to these ancestors, to give form and substance to this heritage in their daily routines and their ceremonial practice: to keep the law, to visit sites, to use the country and to enjoy its bounty. It is in the living out of the dreamtime heritage, particularly in the ceremonial domain, that we see how the past is negotiated in the present, how women and men position themselves *vis-à-vis* each other and *vis-à-vis* the law. Staging ceremonies which celebrate the dreamtime heritage is a sacred trust shared by men and women, both of whom have sacred boards, the title deeds to land; both of whom know songs and paint designs which, in cryptic graphics, encode knowledge of the dreamtime. The common core concerns the structural level of knowledge of ancestral activity (the major sites and their spiritual affiliations), the rights of living descendants and the responsibilities of the ritual bosses of the business.

How each sex then fleshes out this common core of beliefs and knowledge, as 'men's business' and 'women's business', is dependent upon their perception of their role and of their contribution to society. These are elaborated in sacred sex-specific spaces (the ceremonial ground and the ritual storehouse) before being brought into shared spaces. Thus this portrait of Aboriginal religion stresses the sex division of labour, but as a mode of maintaining a complex system of beliefs and practices, and a means of revitalizing the common core of knowledge of the dreaming. By exploring the contexts in which meanings are negotiated and decisions made by men and women, we can see the importance of the existence of separate power bases. Separation does not necessarily entail fixed hierarchies, but rather generates shifting context-dependent moments. Aboriginal society presents a fascinating dilemma for the anthropologist who is willing to struggle with situated ethnographies and grapple with cultural models which accommodate societies where women and men have separate residential structures, ceremonial cycles, social strategies, and where there is no clearly defined public domain in which to 'balance' one view against the other.

The politics of place and person, age and ambition, ceremony and sentiment, knowledge and kin, shape ritual practice. As each generation works with the resources at hand, it is important that we locate our studies historically and geographically. This ethnography draws on field-work (both lengthy periods of participant observation and shorter periods of applied research) undertaken in central and northern Australia since 1976, and is sensitive to the contexts within which Aboriginal women make known their religious belief and practices. In an oral culture, the law can only be given meaning through the expressions of the living which, in the Aboriginal case, are inscribed on the land itself. As long as one has contact with the land and control over the sites, the dreamtime as the ever-present, all encompassing law can be asserted to be reality. Under these conditions the dreamtime is enduring and timeless: women and men negotiate common ground within a closed system. But land, as the central tablet, as the sacred text, is no longer under Aboriginal control across the continent. Ritual politics must now encompass a dramatically changed cast of players and forces.

A critically important change, which impacts dramatically on religion, is the shift from a hunter–gatherer mode of subsistence to a more sedentary one (Bell 1983a:94–106). Aborigines must now deal with the state, its agencies, its policies, its laws and modes of distribution. Dispossessed of their land by the British in 1788, Aborigines' struggle for land rights has brought Aboriginal beliefs into the public arena. Under existing Northern Territory legislation, to gain title to their land Aborigines must now prove traditional ownership in an Australian court, and this entails demonstrating their religious ties to land.

Aborigines in Australian Society

At the time of the arrival of the British in Australia in 1788, there were hundreds of different languages spoken, by the million or so persons who were the undisputed owners of the continent.[10] The colonization of the land was uneven: Aboriginal groups in the south-east bore the brunt of the first wave of the invasion and for many peoples of northern Australia intensive contact with whites dates only from this century. It is still possible to attend Aboriginal ceremonies that proceed in a way that is very close to those observed by men such as Spencer and Gillen (1899) at the turn of the century. However, the context has changed dramatically. Alternative land use by pastoralists, miners, urban and rural developers, has shattered the nexus between economic and spiritual practice. Once Aboriginal religion offered a comprehensive reading of the rhymes and rhythms of the world, and set the parameters of social, economic and political life. Now, dependent on social security, subject to Australian laws, poorly housed and nourished, Aborigines suffer high rates of imprisonment, infant mortality and interpersonal violence; endure low levels of educational certification and employment. The sense of self and community derived from religion today is thus markedly different from a century ago, and the shaping factors are not all amenable to religious interpretation and manipulation.

Aborigines constitute approximately 1.4 per cent of the Australian population (i.e. about 200 000 people), but apart from indicating their electorally weak standing, this statistic reveals little of their situation, and nothing of the issues facing women. Indeed analyses that give salience to gender are resisted as not in the interests of the new elites, or in the interests of the wider society (Bell and Nelson 1989:414–15; Bell and Marks 1990:98–104). The highest proportion of Aborigines to non-Aborigines is in the north, but even there residential sites range from urban, the fringes of the town, to cattle stations (ranches), missions, government reserves, homeland centres and Aboriginal land. What is consistent is that this is frontier society, a man's world, and the positions of power, the ability to name, and to confer meaning, in the emerging political order are not for women (Bell 1983a:249–50). The official policy is self-management but this is a colonial artifact, which reverberates with paternalism and sexist practices (Bell and Ditton 1980:5–15; Bell and Nelson 1989:413–15).

Across the tropical north of Australia (Queensland, the Northern Territory and Western Australia) and into the desert regions of central Australia there are large tracts of land where Aborigines are the dominant population, and in some areas, where they have land rights, they are able to exclude outsiders. It is in these regions that ceremonial life is intense. Freed from the constant threat of intrusion, on their own land, and able to manage much of their own affairs, the impact of dispossession of land and disruption of family life is ameliorated. The shift from a hunter–gatherer life to a more sedentary one, the establishment of centres of population where groups who would not have sustained close relations are in daily inter-action, has had a mixed impact on religious practice, and more particularly on women. New possibilities for sustained ceremonial life arise, but there are also new possibilities for tensions, jealous fights and conflicts over distribution of the resources that flow from the politics of self-determination. There are important differences for those resident on cattle stations, settlements, missions, outstations and towns (Bell and Ditton 1980:29–90; Bell 1983a:76–81).

One of the resources generated at the interface of the two cultures is the authorative documentary accounts of Aboriginal life. These reflect the preoccupations and purposes of the writers as surely as they reflect the lives of Aborigines. Men's roles and perceptions have been well documented; women's are rather less well known. However, this has not inhibited generalizations (Bell 1984; Gross 1987:41–2). Many of those that deal with religion in a contemporary context acknowledge that Aboriginal religion is a political domain, but tend to cast men as the politicians and women as the pawns (Bern 1979a, 1979b). Les Hiatt (1978:186), in the face of evidence from feminist anthropologists, acknowledged that women had a voice, but cast men as setting the agenda and women as resisting. Clearly there is an unease in dealing with reports of vocal, powerful women, and as Ken Maddock (1982:140) allows in revising his 1972 text, 'the established position' that men hold the keys to cosmic order (Munn 1986:213) is under siege. We are poorly served in our search for meaning if we begin with the assumption that women are the profane and the passive, that men command and women comply. If we are prepared to look beyond assertions that men control the religious domain, and beyond the promise of security contained in the dreamtime dogma of immutability, to the reality of the persons, passions and politics that generate current religious practice and shape beliefs, to map the activities which maintain Aboriginal religion, and to trace how ritual decisions are negotiated, we move into a more dynamic, albeit problematic, exploration of Aboriginal religion.

The community in which my children and I lived between 1976 and 1978 was home to some 750 Aboriginal persons of four different language groups (Alyawarra, Kaytej, Warlpiri and Warumungu) and about 75 whites. The settlement of Warrabri (now Ali-Curang), established in 1954 under a heavily assimilationist policy, was an unhappy place where intergroup rivalries shaped daily life (Bell 1983a:73–94). Around the periphery of the settlement service core, where whites ran and controlled the police station, store, post office, garage, hospital, school and power plant, were the Aboriginal camps. People whose land was to the east lived in camps oriented to that country; likewise those on the west oriented their camps to their traditional lands. An 'elected' all-male village council, who administered funds from the federal Department of Aboriginal Affairs, 'ran' the settlement.[11] Much remained outside the ambit of council decision making, but its presence and resources were factors in the balancing of power between groups, between men and women, between young and old. The settlement area is now Aboriginal land, and people settled there against their will several decades ago have moved away to nearby towns, and onto adjacent traditional lands, which have been secured under the Land Rights Act. The shift from a hunting and gathering subsistence mode to welfare dependency and local enterprises registers differently on women and men. Thus, in writing of Aboriginal women and religion in contemporary contexts, I must necessarily take account of the impact of 200 years of colonization of desert lands, government policy, legal reform, of the embeddedness of Aboriginal society in the wider Australian society. Here we see that the law, the state, religion are not gender blind in Australian society, any more than in Aboriginal society.

Women's Worlds

At Ali-Curang, some younger women were engaged as teaching aides, house girls, assistants and nursing assistants, but for most, having left school early, married and begun a family, their choices were limited. Even those who had completed high school found that they had few options, and to get employment usually meant moving to town. The older generation of women who had grown up on the local missions, ration depots and cattle stations, but still enjoyed a relatively mobile life, mourned the loss of youth to the 'new law' (gambling, alcohol, television). Nonetheless, conscientiously and rigorously, they instructed the young girls in the ways of the law. Much of their daily life was taken up with work in family camps and women's camps, in hunting and gathering, and in ritual.

Instruction in 'women's business' occurs in all-female groups and the most prominent setting is the *jilimi*, the all-female camps, which are taboo to men. *Jilimi*, a Warlpiri term (also used by Kaytej), is often translated as 'single women's camp', but this has pejorative overtones of the place being peripheral, transient, junior and lacking power. In fact the *jilimi* is home to the ritually important senior women. It is a symbol of women's independence, a refuge, the locus of daily activity, and information exchange (Bell 1983a:16–17, 82–4, 110–36). At any given time up to 25 per cent of the adult female population of the settlement could be found there. At the residential core of the *jilimi* was the older and respected ritual leaders, who are usually divorced, widowed or separated, and their dependent female relatives, women visiting from elsewhere; women who for any reason are not living with a man; women who are ill, too young for marriage, or reluctant to enter a marriage. During the day the *jilimi* was the focal point of women's activities; during the evenings it provided a refuge.

Because of the sex-segregated nature of Aboriginal society, it is extremely inappropriate (and in terms of in-depth fieldwork unproductive) to attempt to work equally with men and women. Usually one is identified with members of one's own sex and is able to move freely within that sphere. Fortunately for my study, women considered my position agreeable for one who sought ritual instruction. Had I been working with teenage girls, the relations established would have been very different. As a divorced woman in receipt of a government pension (pensioners are important people in Aboriginal communities), I was in a similar position to the ritual 'bosses' of the Warlpiri and Kaytej *jilimi* with whom I worked: I was economically and emotionally independent of men and therefore potentially safe with women's secrets. Further, the social status I enjoyed by virtue of my two outgoing and energetic children allowed me access to the world of adult women. Ritual knowledge resides with the older women who, once freed from the immediate responsibilities of child care, devote their time and energies to upholding and transmitting their spiritual heritage to successive generations.

By being around the knowledgeable women of the *jilimi*, one learned through direct experience: there is no concept of vicarious learning, no hypothetical puzzles by which one is instructed. When young girls do not hunt with their female kin, they do not learn survival skills and 'women's law' in an integrated fashion. Competing calls on the time of young girls have reduced quality teaching opportunities. One of the most dramatic losses of knowledge is that of sign language, which is learned through exposure to groups of older women who are communicating in this way. When a close relative dies, part of the mourning ritual requires that women do not speak and the taboo lasts for up to two years (Bell 1983a:115; Kendon 1988). But because young girls no longer spend so many hours in women's company they do not learn the signs, and consequently the speech taboo period is shortened so that there can be communications with younger women. Thus learning time is curtailed, and the practice falls into disuse for want of skilled 'speakers'. The knowledge of sign language, like knowledge of the environment, was once an integral part of religious observances, but is being lost in a downward spiral: ceremonial observations associated with mourning and subsistence activities informed by mythological narratives of place are truncated.

Participation in the ceremonial life of women made it possible to explore aspects of ritual practice and belief at first hand. I was learning in the appropriate manner but I had quite a bit to cram. I was incorporated in the kinship system and, as a classificatory mother, sister and mother-in-law to various young men, participated in their initiations; as an older woman with two children — a son who was seen to be nearing the age of initiation, and a daughter approaching marriageable age — I was admitted into the ritual world of women and participated in many women's ceremonies. Further, because I had a roadworthy vehicle, was literate, and willing to assist with telecommunications, I was considered well resourced, and by settlement standards, for a woman, I was. When I later worked as anthropologist for the Aboriginal Sacred Sites Protection Authority, as consultant to the Aboriginal Land Councils, Legal Aid Services, the Aboriginal Land Commissioner and the Law Reform Commissions, and gave evidence in cases involving customary law, I was able to draw on the knowledge of ceremonial practice and women's strategies learned in one place to enter women's ceremonial worlds in others. Regional differences were made plain to me and a constant source of amusement for women in fieldwork sites north of Ali-Curang was to ask me to dance in the 'desert style'.

On the occasions when I was engaged in applied anthropological research, my resources and my relationships to community members were of a different order from those of a long-term fieldworker. My position in terms of mediating between two cultures was more transparent; my motives in seeking knowledge recognizably part of the era of self-determination. The points of articulation between the gender politics of the wider society and Aboriginal society were nonetheless a critical factor

(Bell 1984–5, 1987a, 1987b; Bell and Ditton 1980; Bell and Nelson 1989). This was not so much a consideration for local peoples as it was for their representative organizations, the bureaucratic agencies with responsibility in the area of Aboriginal affairs, and institutions and individuals dispensing academic patronage and fieldwork funds.

My documentation and analysis of central Australian Aboriginal women's worlds draw mainly on Warlpiri, Kaytej and Alyawarra ceremonies, but I also attended Warumungu, Pintupi, Gurinji, Pitjantjatjarra and Aranda ceremonies when, in the company of women I knew at Ali-Curang, we visited other communities. In their religious rituals women emphasized their role as nurturers of people, land and relationships. Their responsibility to maintain harmoniously this complex of relationships between the living and the land is manifest in the intertwining of the ritual foci of health and emotional management. Through their *yawulyu* (land-based ceremonies) they nurture land; through their health and curing rituals they resolve conflict and restore social harmony; and through *yilpinji* (love rituals) they manage emotions. In *yilpinji*, as in their health-oriented *yawulyu*, women seek to resolve and to explore the conflicts and tensions which beset their communities. In centres of population concentration where Aborigines now live, jealous fights, accusations of infidelity and illicit affairs occur on a scale impossible a century ago when people lived in small mobile bands. Thus today, women's role in the domain of emotional management, like their role in the maintenance of health and harmony, is truly awesome (Bell 1983a:145–62).

In central Australia, ceremonies may be classified as: those staged by women, which are secret and closed to men; those in which men and women participate; and those staged by men, which are closed and secret to women. Most analyses begin from within the latter. If, however, we begin from within woman's ceremonial world and explore her ritual domain, we find that women see their lives as underwritten by their independence and autonomy of action. These self-evaluations are not easily dismissed for they are legitimated by women's direct access to the dreamtime. Men and women politic to achieve personal ends, to establish favourable alliances between families and countries, and with fieldworkers whose analyses become part of other political campaigns — be the forum the law courts, the academy or the bureaucracy.

Yawulyu

The *jilimi*, which is the focus of womens daily activities, is also where women begin to make plans for *yawulyu* activity. At the core of each *jilimi* are key individuals for a particular country and the *jilimi* is known by that name. In *yawulyu*, it is relations to land which are being stressed also. In central Australia, women and men alike trace their descent from the dreamtime through two distinct lines and here I am using the Warlpiri terms. From one's father and father's father a person has the rights and responsibilities of *kirda*; through one's mother and mother's father those of *kurdungurlu*. From one's mother's mother one also enjoys a special relationship to what is called one's *jaja* (granny) country. Other interests in land are stated in terms of conception dreamings, residence, marriage, place of death, burial and sentiment. Through these overlapping and interlocking modes of expressing how one is 'of the land', central Australian women and men locate themselves within the ancestral design (Bell 1983a:264–6).

Place names, dreaming affiliations and the relationship of particular individuals to land may be discussed within the *jilimi*, but when women wish to engage in *yawulyu*, or serious discussion concerning *yawulyu* places, women retire to their ceremonial ground. Situated within walking distance of the *jilimi*, but conceptually 'in the bush', and thus beyond the settlement, are the ritual storehouse, bough-shelter and 'ring place', ceremonial ground (Berndt 1950:43). This area is inaccessible by road, and not visible from the residential camps. Men travel circuitous routes to avoid even sighting the general area, and women, if disturbed by children during ritual activity at the 'ring place', will carry through disciplinary threats which at other times, because of the high levels of personal autonomy enjoyed by children, are not enforced.

The women's ritual area has two main divisions. One is a large clearing where women may sit to paint, display their boards, dance and occasionally sleep. The second area, facing east, the site of more serious work, backs onto the 'ring place' and has a storehouse where the ritual paraphernalia (sacred boards, stones, painting sticks, bleached feathers, ochres, hair string and headbands) are stored, often on a ledge in one of the recesses of the structure. The area opens out into a bough shade, a private, secure place, from where the women keep all activity in the *jilimi* under surveillance and signal through only those visitors they wish to see. Gone is the ribald joking of the *jilimi*; instead women speak of the importance of caring for their treasures and the need to 'hold' them always.

In the past women's 'ring places' were where offenders were brought to trial and disputes resolved by ritual means. Men refer to their ceremonial ground as the 'ring place' and it also has a function in dispute resolution. Important meetings concerning women are held in their 'ring place'. On occasions when I was putting together a background briefing on disputes which had found their way into Australian courts, I knew the matter entailed serious infringement of the law if I was invited to the 'ring place' for discussion. Although many of the functions have now been usurped by school, hospital, church and police, the 'ring place' is still considered to be a therapeutic place to sleep during trying times. For one thing, it is away from the daily hubbub of the camps and the demands of children and husbands, but it is also where women may state their authority and ability to manage their own lives, and to influence community affairs.

The atmosphere at the 'ring place', while handling the sacred objects, is one of hushed reverence for the traditions being evoked. Introduced items, such as store-bought cleaners, wool, dripping (cattle fat) and cash, which have been incorporated through use are treated as if they were the stone-derived bleaches, hair string, emu fat and exchange items. The availability of certain items has facilitated ceremonial activity. For example, once 'hair string' could only be obtained through exchanges at initiation; now women may buy wool, red ochre it, and use it in ceremonies. On becoming part of the store, it is indistinguishable from ritual hair string. Now that women may buy small handle tomahawks in the store, they can cut wood for ritual poles with ease. Store-bought fat means ritual activity is no longer constrained by the availability of goanna or emu fat from hunting. Cash is incorporated into ritual exchanges and, to an extent, it is brought under the law. But inflation is rampant because, unlike traditional exchange items, money is not produced by the participants.

In the past the contents of the storehouse moved with the ritual bosses (larger items remained at sacred sites), but today, where people are living in population-intensive settlements, women want brick museums to protect their sacred paraphernalia from fire, theft and accidental intrusion. Men have had success in gaining funding from government agencies and enjoyed support from local councils in obtaining such structures. However, when a women's submission comes before a male council, members of which have cause to fear the growing strength of women's ceremonies, or a government bureaucrat ignorant of women's business, funding is problematic (Bell and Ditton 1980:6). Further, it is improper for women to be asking men for assistance in 'women business'.

At one level the lack of outside support has meant that women have had less prying into their affairs than have men, but at another it means they are not taken seriously in the resource allocation that flows from the implementation of government policies of self-determination and management. Access to vehicles is a good example. Men, as drivers and owners of vehicles, have been able to consolidate and extend their social and ceremonial networks. Women, with fewer vehicles and little driving experience, have trouble visiting neighbouring women and 'mustering' women for ceremonies.[12] Thus while population-intensive settlements and readily available materials facilitate the staging of *yawulyu*, other factors limit the impact and efficacy of the activity. Whereas once separation of women's and men's activities assured that women were consulted, because their resources were necessary for male activities, now it is the means of their marginalization. The political domain, in which resources are distributed, has become the male domain and women have been relegated to the domestic. The latter is an imposed category with no real traditional correlate save that which is generated by assuming that when women go out to gather food, they are engaged in 'women's business' for women's benefit, not the production of the means of survival of the whole group (Bell 1983a:54–6). Or, that when women talk in their own camps, it is the 'gossip' of 'highly vocal' 'toothless old hags' (Hart and Pilling 1960:14, 20; Meggitt 1962:236), not the reflections of ritual sages (Bell 1983a:16–17).

I had been in the community more than nine months before I moved with any ease in the 'ring place'. I needed to know a great deal of kinship relations, actual and classificatory, and these can be difficult to distinguish, but are a critical indicator of ritual politics. I needed to know the history of group movements, to have access to sites, and to know the range of country associated with individuals and groups. My clearest instruction included the structural level of interrelations of sites, persons and dreamings — the grand design of mythological activity in the area. This was accompanied by visiting the sites, *yawulyu*, sand maps and careful monitoring of my behaviour to ensure that I spoke only of those matters of which it was proper to speak. I was being tested to see if I understood the politics of knowledge. It was not what I knew, but rather what I verbalized, to whom and in what context, that was critical. I was guided carefully, for to blunder would have been to endanger myself and others, and protected by always being in the company of other women, particularly my 'sisters', with whom I shared major kin avoidances (Bell 1983a:25).

Alongside the macro-level of learning of what I have termed the 'common core' were finer-grain analyses of song texts, designs and gestures. These were only forthcoming after I had participated; were sometimes quite elliptical; and usually built on the broader appreciations of the macro-level. Once I began to take greater responsibility within the 'ring place', and had been taken to visit the women's sites, I was expected to 'know' more and was instructed accordingly. It was like having the outline coloured in. The revelation of the details of ancestral activity through interaction with country is also one way in which women validate their rights and authority over the land and it bounty, both spiritual and economic (Bell 1983a:110–28).

Yawulyu performances tend to cluster around the preparation for special events, during times of social unrest and illness. At other times women simply gather to work on ritual items, to plan, to share information. Although I have been present at some eighty *yawulyu*, generalizations are difficult for one group, let alone region or the continent. Nonetheless, it is possible to identify key aspects of the structure of women's ceremonies in desert regions which are also manifest in the practice of women further to the north. All the *yawulyu* I have attended included a period of preparation which was sacred and secret, a 'calling in' transition, a relatively open performance, and a solemn 'finish up'. All had an overt function — Nangala was ill; Nakamarra needed to visit a site; there was a land claim, a school excursion, a sacred site registration. Someone had to ask for *yawulyu* and being able to pin performances to external bodies alleviated tensions generated by jealous fights if one person 'put herself up' as in charge. There is a difference between assuming that role and being 'mistress of ceremonies'. When powerful interests are at stake, it is wise to be the one responsible for resolving conflict, but folly to claim responsibility for initiating the action. A similar mode of deflection of responsibility is manifest in the way in which women will say they 'learned' of a particular ceremony: it came from elsewhere (especially powerful *yilpinji*); it was 'found' in a 'dream'; or it was in the mythology. Underpinning the stated ceremonial agenda, there were always deep simmering, long-standing 'troubles', ones which were rarely voiced, and are only known in the unfolding of individual and group histories, which spanned generations implicating the unborn and deceased.

The preparation for *yawulyu* usually begins early in the afternoon. Women gather at the 'ring place' where they sit close, and speak softly as they take their sacred objects from the store. The objects are fondled, named and then passed to the appropriate person for preparation. The women begin by greasing their own bodies with fat, and then the senior *kurdungurlu* begin the body painting of the *kirda*. More junior persons may then try their hand under the guidance of older women. Painting is a group activity, which allows novices to acquire the necessary knowledge and expertise. Onto the fat, on the upper torso, legs and back, red ochre is applied, and with broad brush strokes of the index finger, the painter maps out the basic contours of the design in black, yellow or red (Berndt 1950, 1965; Munn 1986:36ff.). Then with small painting sticks, the white enclosures are applied to produce dramatic symbolic representations of land, myth and relationships. Bleached white headbands are painted with symbols from the same repertoire as those on the body and boards. The ritual pole is dressed in the same manner as the human participants — white cockatoo feathers in the headband, designs running along the body of the board, and hair-string skirt. The particular designs being used depend on the site(s) and dreaming activity on which the *yawulyu* is focused.

While the women are preparing the ritual items and painting, they sing gently and harmoniously of the dreamtime experience, which validates their use of the objects. During this activity, the range of songs, harmonies and symbolic meanings is far more extensive and complex than during the open and public singing which may follow in the 'ring place'. It is a private time when children and outsiders are not welcome and the songs known as 'dear ones' — that is, old and cherished — are sung; it is also when verbal instruction occurs, when ritual roles are sorted out and when new information may be incorporated. For example, in the narratives of the places Waake and Walapanpa, the ancestor rain, an extremely important dreaming in the desert, is manifest as younger and older brother. This relationship should be reflected in the seniority of the lineages of the current generations with responsibility for the sites. But there is room for adjustment. The seniority of lineages is not reckoned by chronological age, but rather by sibling relations at the parent level, or more often grandparent generation level, and these relatives may be actual or classificatory. Thus the living ritual celebrants have room to manoeuvre and the status of seniority is conferred on the most able, most active, best positioned, ritual politicians. Once done, it is ratified by the law and thus not open to speculation by mortals.

When the body painting is completed, the boards are greased, the feathers are glistening and the headbands are brilliant white, the women move to the dancing place, sit facing west, and begin to sing the songs which call in those who may watch, which welcome strangers and which begin the process of 'bringing' the dreamings to the ceremonial ground. The fire in the centre of the ground, a symbol of ritual continuity, is rekindled in the embers of previous fires. Following the 'calling in' songs, the *kurdungurlu* introduce the country with several songs, which allude to, rather than explicate, ancestral activity. Then the senior *kirda*, holding the painted boards on high for all to see, dance forward in single file, until they arrive at the fire. This 'wakens' the *kirda* and activates the power of the *jukurrpa* at that ceremonial site.

The seated *kirda* and *kurdungurlu* sing of the site at which the dreaming rests or visits, while senior *kurdungurlu* 'plant' the boards. The power of the dreaming is thus brought to the 'ring place', and is active for the duration of the ceremony. The past moves concurrently with the

present. The planted boards are called by name and addressed affection-
ately by the kin terms. In this way both the ritual relationship and the
deep emotional personal tie to country are given expression. The
kurdungurlu dance flanking the *kirda* and thus re-enact the way in which
the ancestors made known these ritual roles. One narrative tells how little
black birds danced alongside black berry in his tiring journey to Wakulpu.
The meandering track of their travels is symbolized in the designs for this
yawulyu, and is imprinted on the land by the dancing feet of the *kirda* and
kurdungurlu.

The sacred board or ritual pole becomes the focus of the dancing as the
kirda and *kurdungurlu* weave patterns in the sand, which spell out the
interactions of the dreamings. The broad design can be grasped by an
outsider, but the rich texturing of the information in the songs is only
available if one has been given previous ritual instruction. The *yawulyu*
performance is short, alludes to the preparation, but in no way spells out
the nature of the negotiations. The dance is the time to confirm the ritual
roles to the assembled public, to tell a story for the pleasure of all present:
it is truly a celebration of the dreamtime. A favourite *yawulyu* segment
concerns the adventures of two 'grandmothers' who were out collecting
berries. As they filled their wooden dishes with fruit, young girls who
were out playing in the country crept up from behind the older women
and stole berries. When they discovered the loss, the grandmothers were
surprised and turned this way and that looking for an explanation. The
dance sequence is repeated several times for the further amusement of
those present, and as a way of giving younger girls a dancing part in
yawulyu.

In the final segment of *yawulyu*, the mood shifts back to one of hushed
reverence. The dancing finished, the women sing the dreamings back into
the ground and expect visitors to leave. Senior women smooth over all
traces of where the boards have been, throw dirt to nullify any remaining
power, and rub the painted boards onto their bodies to reabsorb the power.
This transference of power is extremely dangerous, and when the *yawulyu*
has resolution of conflict as a goal, constitutes the most sacred moment.
Once stripped of their designs, the boards are returned to the storehouse.
Some women return to the *jilimi* to sleep, others remain at the ground.
The body paint is allowed to wear off, and often the fading designs are
the only sign that women have been engaged in ritual.

Within the *yawulyu* context, ritual segments may directly address the
needs of group members. For example, when the *yawulyu* is for health
reasons, the fun performance is omitted and only the gathering of women
at the 'ring place' occurs. The power evoked is that of women's relationships to land and their power to restore the harmony necessary for good
health of individuals and communities. Through these ceremonies women
may seek to achieve resolution of conflict or more specific symptomatic
relief. There has, I think, been a subtle shift in the structuring of these
health and well-being ceremonies, which are now organized according to
the complementary lines of descent of relations to land and *yawulyu*, but
once emphasized matrilineality more strongly (Bell 1983a:152–4). This
line, through the mother, is important in nurturance especially in matters
of birthing and feeding. And, as I have argued elsewhere, the shift in the

nature of conflict post-contact, and especially on settlements, registers ceremonially (Bell 1983a:248–9).

If the particular *yawulyu* focuses upon emotions (and these are closely linked to health), *yilpinji* songs will be included and the 'secrecy' and 'sex-exclusivity' indexes will be higher: only those directly involved can participate. The songs concern attraction, resistance, pacification, arousal, infidelity, abiding affection and rejection, indeed the whole gamut of emotions manifest in male/female relations. A woman may request *yilpinji* if she is having trouble in a relationship, wishes to attract a new lover, or ensure the absent spouse will be faithful. The decision to stage *yilpinji* is not taken lightly, for women believe that their actions are not only efficacious, but release potent forces which, if handled improperly, may cause illness, conflict and impotence. Emotions, it is acknowledged, are serious matters in which to delve and their management is part of women's business.

In the literature *yilpinji* is often glossed 'love magic' (Bell 1983a:176–9). For central Australia, if the songs are taken out of context this may be sustainable, but if they are analysed within *yawulyu* then it is the broader management of emotions rather than an explicit concern with sex and sexuality which is being managed. Of course sex and sexuality are often at the base of fights and disturbances, and it is not surprising that they are richly represented in women's ritual symbolism. I have explored elsewhere the agenda (scholarly and indigenous) which supported the designation 'love magic' and its pejorative overtones (Bell 1983a:176–9). For the purposes of this discussion, suffice it to say that *yilpinji* deals with 'troubles', a gloss which includes, but is not limited to, matters of sex. However, by giving a shorthand explanation of the activity as 'love magic', older women deflect attention from other ritual agenda, and restrict younger women's access to certain ritual knowledge until they have the wisdom to use it 'properly'.

If we shift from the reading of woman as sexual object, and from the physical realm of reproduction to the symbolic constructions of woman in women's ceremonies, different interpretations of Aboriginal religion are available, and a different portrait of gender relations is generated. When women hold aloft their sacred boards on which are painted ideational maps of their country, when they dance hands cupped upward, they state their intention and responsibility to 'grow up' country and kin. To Aboriginal women, as the living descendants of the dreamtime, the physical acts of giving birth and lactation are important, but are considered to be one individual moment in a much larger design. Their wide-ranging and broadly based concept of nurturance is modelled on the dreamtime experience, itself one all-creative force. When women rub their bodies with fat in preparation for the application of body designs which, like the boards, symbolically encode information about sites, dreamings and estates and when they retrace in song and dance the travels of the mythological heroes they become as the ancestors themselves. Through ritual re-enactment women establish direct contact with the past, make manifest its meaning and thereby shape their worlds. The past is encapsulated in the present; the present permeates the past. In women's rituals the major themes of land, love and health fuse in the nurturance motif, which encapsulates the growing up of people and land, and the maintenance of the complex of land–people relationships.

There are occasions when *yawulyu* performances are oriented to incorporating or instructing men, and do so by actively engaging men in the performance. The most extensive ceremonial presence of men at a woman-controlled, woman-initiated series of ceremonies that I have observed occurred on a cattle station and involved three distinct groups of women. Two were extremely knowledgeable and had an extensive ritual repertoire. The third, the local group, were desirous of extending their ceremonial authority, and by linking it to that of the other groups, accessing their expertise. This was accomplished over a series of visits and required that the men 'witness' the authorative statements of the women in a performance which occurred at the final meeting of the groups. In a 'surprise' which delighted the women, the men brought a short, compact and dramatic ceremonial segment concerning the major dreaming being celebrated to the women's ground. Another example of men's participation in women's ceremonies concerns *jarrarda*, the name given to women's *yawulyu/yilpinji*, farther north.

Yungkurru

Moving from women's *yawulyu* to ceremonies which entail co-operation of women and men, in *yungkurru* we find an excellent forum in which to explore commonalities and differences in male and female practice. In *yungkurru* women bring their ceremonial expertise to a ground shared with men. During these joint ceremonies, the sexual politics of ritual are evident. Each sex vies with the other in its brilliant display of knowledge. At the same time, each is constrained by the need to represent the dreamtime experience with meticulous fidelity and not to provoke jealous fights. Ceremonies at which men and women are present have the dual function of permitting monitoring of the activities of the other, and providing a forum of display to the other. Attendance means that the division of labour is made explicit and the physical layout of ceremonial activity is shared. Each is able to elaborate their interpretations of the common core of knowledge and to ensure neither errs is the necessary and continuous process of reinvention. It is at such times that the unity of the law, which underwrites the separation of the sexes, is open to observation, and it is possible for an anthropologist to learn what each knows of the practice of the other. In this context, common ground concerned the structural aspects of ancestral activity in land, the name of the *kirda* and *kurdungurlu* for the area and the sites and the major dreamings; sex-specific explanations concerned the content of the activity and the interpretation of the songs. Negotiations concerned who will be told what, when, by whom and for what purpose: the politics of knowledge and gender were intertwined.

According to the participants, *yungkurru* ceremonies occurred infrequently, perhaps averaging one every three to four years. *Yungkurru* were to 'make young men'. They have as their focus one particular site and its interrelations with a number of intersecting dreamings. There needs to be an occasion worthy of the staging of a *yungkurru*, and settlement politics, rather than exclusively traditional concerns, generate rich contexts. It is, for instance, a way of introducing new people into the dreamtime design, and then declaring it to have always been thus. It is a way of redistributing knowledge, of sorting out ambiguous ritual relations by establishing, through practice, that this is 'the woman' or 'the man' of a particular place.

The *yungkurru* I was able to follow from beginning to end in 1977 was easily recognizable as the *ingkurra* of Spencer and Gillen (1899:271ff.) and *inkura* of Strehlow (1947:100ff.). Unlike their documentation, the one I saw was not associated with a particular initiation but it was focused on a particular sacred site, and it was a means by which changes and new information were injected into the repertoire of practice and knowledge. Throughout, the participants were able to maintain the continuity of tradition by reference to an ancestral event that legitimated their activity. It was politically charged as needs, ambitions and alliances were being negotiated, but superbly crafted as 'the law' in the final performance.

The external reference point, which protected the instigators from being the subject of jealous fights, was the centennial celebrations at Hermannsburg, a Lutheran mission, south-east of Alice Springs. One of the then rising political stars of the settlement was from that mission and was seeking integration in the Ali-Curang community. It was in the interests of the Kaytej to accommodate this man, for if he were to become president of the settlement their interests would be well represented at the community level. The keen rivalry for his affections was obvious when the presiding council created difficulties over access to the community bus, needed for the trip to Hermannsburg.

The more deeply entrenched political agenda of the ceremony concerned the need to recruit men to an area of country to the west of the settlement. Nungarrayi, the woman whose father had been *kurdungurlu* for that country, and whose father's mother's father — that is, *kirda* for that country — had appeared to her in a 'dream'.[13] In the 'dream' Jampijinpa had instructed Nungarrayi in the use of *jungkurru* songs; told her to take the business to the 'ring place'; to build a brush shelter for the men; to hold the boards high so all could see; and then to make everyone sit and wait in the way the little birds had for bush berry in the dreamtime.

Women routinely use a 'dream' to introduce, or more properly to reintroduce, information into the ritual realm. When a person dies part of the 'sorry business' (mourning rituals) requires that all personal things are set aside, and this includes use of ritual objects, songs, designs, mythology intimately associated with the individual. After a period of three or more years, a woman, usually in the *kurdungurlu* line, but certainly of the ritual cohort of the deceased, will have a 'dream' in which the parent or grandparent of the deceased appears and instructs the 'dreamer' to go forth and perform the ceremonies, and use the items which henceforth will be associated with her. In this way the living may shape current ceremonial activity while maintaining that nothing changes. On the occasions when I have been able to observe the first reuse of a song, a number of women who had been present at previous performances gathered, and while the new 'owner' intoned the words these experts discreetly guided the action. Henceforth it was the law.

In the 'dream' of Nungarrayi for the *yungkurru*, the interdependence of the roles of *kirda* and *kurdungurlu* were marked, the interrelations of the dreamings complex. Unity was achieved by Nungarrayi in her display of the sacred pole as Nangala, the daughter of the Jampijinpa of the dream, as the object which would be at the centre of the dancing. Nungarrayi was able to show the men in the *kirda* line what had been revealed to her, thereby incorporating them within that frame, and extending their existing dreaming tracks into that country. This was anxiously sought by an older man who was her father's classificatory 'mother's father' and it was an agenda she endorsed. One other consequence of the ceremonies, only apparent some ten years later, is that Nungarrayi was able to strengthen her daughter's relation to the dreamings and to make sure she would be able to marry into that country. Nungarrayi's daughter's children would then be in the *kirda* line for the country. Also she was able to establish a rationale for her relation to land as *kurdungurlu* through a line of descent which was unusual (through father's mother). She was of the right patrimoiety and this facilitated her playing that role, but to be a first-order *kurdungurlu* she needed a more direct link. This strategizing by important women to position favoured kin within their ritual worlds is not unusual. However, it is not pursued in an aggressive fashion — it just unfolds.

The *yungkurru* ceremony lasted for over a week, drew heavily on the resources of all involved, entailed the making of new boards and the generation of new designs. All the designs were within the given symbolic repertoire, but by rearranging the colours (red, black and white representing different manifestations of the dreamings) and the elements (circles, semicircles, dots and lines representing the presence of the dreamings at three sacred sites) Nungarrayi generated greater diversity for the ceremonial painting of bodies, boards and headbands. Nungarrayi directed which boards the women would make and which would appear at Hermannsburg. Again this was a subset of the total production. In all the ceremonies I have attended, there have always been possibilities for further learning and future exchanges. Retention of objects and holding back of knowledge maintains power in the hands of the persons hosting the ceremony. Indeed ceremonies are often 'cut short' on the basis that the 'next time we will be able to do that part', but just for now there is 'not enough time'.

Each afternoon the men and women gathered on a newly cleared ground to prepare materials and participants. The women worked as if these were *yawulyu* preparations, but the performance was on a shared ground and involved women and men singing and joint displays. The women invested a great deal of time and energy in the *yungkurru* and were quick to remind the men, if they were not taking up their share of the work, that it was they who wanted to be 'level' with the women. In the *yungkurru* the differences in public and private behaviour, in terms of what each sex admits to knowing, was pronounced. One old man asked Nungarrayi for information and she responded: 'Don't ask me, I'm a woman'. Half an hour before she had been teaching the women just those details. What she was prepared to show were the designs she had elaborated. The men had expressed jealousy of the extent of her knowledge, and had she fallen ill this would have been given as a reason. She had already shed a certain amount of knowledge and bestowed associated paraphernalia on a neighbouring group of women to allay such fears (Bell 1983a:157–79).

In transforming a section of wood to a ritual object, the women chose an area from which it should be cut — one where the dreamings intersected — and thus the object could be a centrepiece for the travels of any of these dreamings, and could serve as a focal point for the ceremonial retracing and extension of the ancestral travels. The women rubbed the board with red ochre, sang it into the area, dressed it as a person, and henceforth it was known as Nangala. Each of the key participants could trace a relationship along a dreaming track to Wakulpu. These radiated outward and constituted extensions of the country already known and claimed. But it was through the 'dream', as related by Nungarrayi, that the dreamtime design was made explicit.

In the performance the women were quick to distinguish those *yawulyu* songs of Nangala for Wakulpu, which concerned mythology, from those *jungkurru* songs of Jampijinpa for Wakulpu, which concerned display. In terms of the maintenance of the dreamtime heritage, the *yungkurru* was an occasion on which women and men engaged in co-operative work. The final performance, which was viewed by many outsiders, black and white, was short, showed a fraction of what had been 'rehearsed', and by itself gave no indication of the many ambitions, passions and politics of the ceremony.

Initiation

Initiation is a time when the whole society pauses, when all resources are directed at 'making your men'. However, while old men 'make' boys into young men through the ritualized death and rebirth of circumcision, and thereby celebrate their role as spiritual procreator, old women organize the feeding of the boys, sit in all-night vigils with the boys, stage *yawulyu*, which celebrate the continuity of land and people associated with the boys, and nominate the mothers-in-law for the boys. Women make manifest their rights — which flow directly from the *jukurrpa* — by providing links between groups through marriage; by their ritual incorporation of outsiders; by their extension of knowledge through ritual action; and at initiation by nominating the mother of the girl the boy will eventually marry. Thus, women engage in key decision making, which affects both ritual procedure and the aftermath of initiation. When we focus on the world of men and treat women's rituals as a subset, we blur the playing out of independence and interdependence of the sexes in the spiritual domain.

One conceptual difficulty in accounts of initiation is that woman's participation has been analysed in terms of her kin ties to the initiate and not in terms of her relationship to the *jukurrpa* (Bell 1983a:238). Once the ritual correlates of the kin roles are recognized, it is then possible to see the ways in which women's participation overlaps, extends and complements that of the men. One of the consequences of seeing women as ritual status holders at initiation is that their role in marriage arrangements becomes an integral part of initiation for, like the act of circumcision, they are hedged in with ritual politics and serve to create new webs of relationships within the society.

A second problem in coming to an appreciation of initiation from a womancentric view has been that one must participate in the role of mother, mother-in-law, sister, grandmother, cross-cousin in order to follow the action. It is inappropriate to ask what is happening if one has not been present, and one may only seek guidance from those involved; it is dangerous to speak of the business of others. Questions regarding initiation are not hypothetical, but involve real choices being made about actual persons, and this is not something about which one speculates. When I asked about a mother's role at initiation, I would be answered with questions: Which mother? Where is she from? Where did this happen? Thus, only after I had sat in the all-night vigils with the mothers, been red-ochred and danced all night, answering the men's calls with a shrill trill for my 'brother', did the design in the patchwork of women's participation emerge. Once it was assumed 'I knew' the structure, my questions were often answered with reference to my own children, and my adoptive family would make claims as 'aunts', 'uncles', and in one memorable moment as 'father-in-law'.

During the periods spent in the field between 1976 and 1980, I attended the initiations of some twenty boys (often two or three boys of the same subsection classification would be initiated at the one ceremony).[14] Having boys to initiate is an indication of the strength of the law and some groups are said to be 'rich' in young men. The ceremonies I attended were for Warlpiri, Warumungu, Alyawarra and Kaytej peoples. While there are significant differences in the sequencing of the events, it is possible to identify a structure that holds for all. The differences speak to variations in marriage arrangements, land tenure and kinship systems. While these are intriguing, especially for tracking the nature of the velocity (speed and direction) of change, they are outside the scope of this article (Bell 1980, 1988b). Here I highlight the moments which women emphasized as critical. One concerned decision making: men decide who will be the circumcisor, women who will be the mother-in-law, and it was the latter decision which interested women. The decisions are made independently, yet ideally the woman and man chosen should be wife and husband. The action moves back and forth, and there are many negotiations, but the ideology says each decision is a surprise to the other. This is yet another example of the politics of knowledge in an oral culture.

The timing of initiation is one key decision which illustrates a particular patterning of ritual decision making. Within family camps, husbands and wives discuss the forthcoming initiation season. A mother's decision that her son is ready is based on her assessment of his physical and emotional maturity, the availability of potential mothers-in-law with whom she may wish to establish an alliance, the availability of food to feed the influx of visitors and the necessary resources for extended periods of ritual activity. There are considerable pressures on women to have adult sons and benefits accrue, but if a woman wishes to delay for a year, that is acceptable. Women should appear reluctant to lose their sons, should cry and worry about their safety, but in reality the boys have been living in single-sex peer groups for some time, and have been the bane of everyone's existence, mothers included. However, once the decision is made, it is no longer open to scrutiny. Only when boys are 'grabbed' by neighbouring groups in a hostile act are the merits of timing debated after the fact (Bell 1983a:215–16).

The capture of the boys by the red-ochred men, who swoop through the camps to the sound of blood-curdling whoops, 'grab' the boys and take them to the men's ceremonial ground, where they are held 'captive', is also supposed to be a surprise. But, because a number of observances are necessary, it cannot be too much of a surprise. For instance, one must not be on the 'wrong side' of the party of captors. After a while I learned to read the signs of an imminent capture: the women would be sitting around quietly in their camps, there would be no hunting, no visiting and the store would be virtually empty. These behaviours cannot be maintained for long: food cannot be stored for any time, people need to move around to chat and to keep news alive.

After the capture, which is often in the early morning, women dance at the initiation ground for a short period 'to soften the ground'. This will ease the pain of the boys and prepare the area for the subsequent week of dancing. The women then return to their own camps (ones specially constructed for the duration of the ceremony) where they begin preparation of the ritual paraphernalia for their dancing that evening. On this occasion the mother is clearly directing the action, and it is the designs of her country (the ones for which the boys are *kurdungurlu*) that feature, and her daughter (his sister, who shares the boys' ritual affiliations) receives special attention.

At dusk the women return to the men's ceremonial ground, build a fire, one for the family of each initiate, and sit waiting for nightfall. The men send small concave boards to the women, which they hold until the end of the ceremony. A large cleared area, on an east–west axis, is prepared by the men for each year's initiations. To the east, the men sit singing behind the shallow semicircular windbreak. The women sit to the west. A deep groove made by the *kurdungurlu* joins the men's windbreak to a small fire and break at the western end. The long leafy poles, which will be stripped on the penultimate night of the week-long dancing, are visible on now overgrown initiation grounds of previous years.

On this first night the women dance all night in a formation that locates mothers, fathers' sisters (female fathers) and classificatory mothers-in-law at the centre, with sisters flanking the huddle of dancers. Thereafter there are three or four 'half-nights' of dancing by the women. Somewhere in the middle of this sequence there is a day of rest to allow the 'visitors' to arrive, preparations for the finale and routine business to be done. Prior to each 'half-night' of dancing, the sisters and fathers' sisters — that is, co-*kirda* with the boys — stage *yawulyu*. Women who are visiting are incorporated at the level of patrimoiety and thus assigned affiliations with those present. By participating they extend their knowledge of country into the sites and stories of the local families. It is during these nights that the mother refines her decision regarding the mother-in-law, and this is evident in the order in which women are painted.

After the women's dancing at the men's ground, but before they return to their camps, is a feeding ritual in which women make plain they bore the child, nurtured him and will now marry him. In Warlpiri initiations, the women carry the boy on their shoulders to a special area where, sitting on his mother's lap, he is fed by his sisters. The surrounding symbolism of this short sequence evokes birth: there are the smoky leaves and exhortations to grow strong. Rather than initiation being a time when women are negated as life-givers, the women co-operate in the symbolic rebirth. The Alyawarra practice, which makes explicit women's nurturance role, occurs during the capture of the boys: the women present the men with bags of flour to sustain the participants in their work. This compares with Warlpiri practice where the women provide food daily.

Nomination of the mother-in-law is a decision made by the mother of the boy in consultation with the mother of the girl, who will be the future mother of the boy's promised wife. The two mothers (of the boy and of his future mother-in-law) are likely to be of a similar age. Ideally the girl should be under twenty, not married, or if married have no children, and the mother-in-law should like the potential daughter-in-law. It is for young women one of the first opportunities to participate in ceremonial activities, and the person chosen must be willing to learn. She must also be present on the night when the fire-stick is passed. Thus young girls may exercise a degree of control over the choice. These personal and pragmatic constraints nestle within a constellation of factors dealing with ritual and country. The choices made are part of a wider pattern of reciprocation given form in marriage alliances and land affiliations which implicate three generations. 'Keeping the families straight' is part of the women's responsibility (Bell 1980, 1983a:269–72). Men ponder aloud who may be nominated, but it is not until the passing of the fire-stick that the choice is made public.

The Alyawarra procedure whereby the nomination is made known is a good example of the joint responsibilities and interaction of roles at initiation. At dusk the women go to the men's ground where they sleep until after midnight. On the call of *wadja* they move through to the dancing ground where mothers and mothers-in-law dance in a tight formation, flanked by sisters and mothers' mothers; the sisters call out to the brothers who answer. The patterns made by the dancing feet echo the groove cut by the men. At about 1 am the women move to an area a little separate from the main ground and sit beside a fire lit by the men. Shields painted by the men with the country of the mother are laid on the blanket around which the women are sitting. A brother brings a fire-stick and gives it to the mother who passes it to the mother-in-law she has chosen. The sisters hold a torch to illuminate the mother-in-law's face. Mothers and mothers-in-law dance briefly together and then the brother places the white ritual fluff on the mother-in-law's head. The sisters then position themselves between the men and the mother-in-law and dance until dawn twirling a bunch of head scarfs (traditionally possum tails).

At dawn the boys are escorted to the blanket where they sit in front of the mothers-in-law who rub their ochred bodies against the boys, in the way women rub sacred objects in their *yawulyu*. The boys are returned to the men's space where the women rush, fall upon the boys and then, mothers supporting the mothers-in-law, depart to their own secluded area. Movement is restricted, speech and food taboos apply. The mothers-in-law are in a liminal state until the final 'finish up', when weeks later payments and counterpayments are made to those who participated and all taboos are lifted.

While this structure is well known to all and could be generated from a reading of the classic desert ethnographies, the events taking place in the women's ritual area are not visible to male participants or observers. What is generally reported is the conclusion of the intensive ceremonial activity at the men's 'ring place' with two nights of men's dancing. On the first night the men bring out the long poles and dance, and the following night the boys are circumcised. A male observer would see the women appear and disappear, but could not track them into their ceremonial camps. Here working from women's domain out, we see initiation is a time when women make certain statements about their importance in the presence of men, and do so in a way consonant with their construct of woman in *yawulyu*.

In my analysis of initiation, I have juxtaposed the men's circumcision of the boy with the women's nomination of the mother-in-law. Both are acknowledged as key events; both serve to crystallize male and female roles; both are political acts based on the ritual rights, responsibilities and ambitions of the participants. Therefore, while at initiation the values of the society are writ large, it is a *complex* of values that is being celebrated. Initiation entails both separate ritual actions and co-operative endeavours: young men cannot be made without the assistance of women. There are male–female negotiations, and decisions that are the prerogative of each. Women continue to assert their nurturing role, not just as mothers, but within the context of relations to land in the *yawulyu*; to people in the choice of co-workers; and to their dreamtime heritage in the transmission of power by direct and indirect contact with the boys.

My ethnography of initiation is a far cry from depictions of initiation as an exercise in male power, as the time of negation of women, whose heads cowered, in fear of death, run to and from the male initiation ground. Nothing I observed at the male ceremonial ground was substantially at odds with the observations of Meggitt (1962), Strehlow (1947) and Spencer and Gillen (1899). What was radically different was the way in which I was being guided to see and understand it. When the women 'ran away', they went to their ceremonial ground where they worked on their ritual relations, which impacted on the male world of making young men. Further, behaviours which had mystified men like Spencer and Gillen (1899:366–68, 374, 380) are rendered intelligible. The presence of women at men's ceremonies could not be accommodated within their analysis of ceremonies as male affairs and the 'anomalous' behaviour was left as noted in passing, but did not stimulate further questions.[15]

The ceremonies I have so far discussed were documented during a period of in-depth fieldwork in central Australia and reflect the politics of large settlements. One of the consequences of contact is that extended ceremonies are held in the times when other demands on Aborigines' time are limited: thus initiation tends to coincide with the long summer break from schools and the stand-down for the wet season (summer months) in the cattle industry. This period is only six weeks to two months, and therefore the period of exclusion of the boys from heterosexual society has been shortened. Similarly the extended bush tours of the novice have been curtailed to accommodate time constraints. This is no longer on foot, and the route taken is constrained by the demands of vehicles for fuel, passable roads, and the competing needs of the participants to make no contact with 'civilization' but to collect welfare cheques to pay for the travel.

The period of initiation has gone from being a time of education to an abrupt transition from boyhood to manhood. The deprivations, which once taught men to respect women as a precious resource, no longer apply. Punitive aspects of initiation are now emphasized by initiating boys at a younger age. This is aimed at 'settling down' wild boys, and the ceremonies do not include full instruction. This is intended as punishment, but also means boys with significant 'knowledge deficits' become men. Respect for the knowledge of elders has diminished, as it is evident that they no longer are in control. As marriages have become between persons closer in age, and fewer are the result of promises made at initiation, the standing of woman as spouse has changed. Once marriage is about choices based on attraction, not about productive relations and family alliances, women lose the network of powerful older women and initiation promises, which implicate kin networks, and must operate as individuals. They become dependents in households with a nominal male head, no longer independent producers in a hunter–gatherer economy (Bell 1980, 1988b).

Legislative Contexts and Self-determination

In this section I am shifting from material generated by in-depth field-work in central Australia to comparative material generated by applied research farther north. The existence of special-purpose legislation for Aborigines[16] has created novel forums in which to learn of women's religious life, but the existence of a weighty body of literature detailing the overriding importance of men in the religious domain has been a significant impediment to women's full participation in the new order (Bell 1984–5). Finding appropriate ways of bringing information regarding women's spiritual rights and responsibilities into the courts, and sensitizing the bureaucracy to the need to consult with women, has been fraught. One strategy pursued by women has been to allow ignorance of their rituals to go unchallenged, because they have feared loss of control if they are drawn into forums where the rules governing transmission of knowledge do not accommodate 'women's business'. This strategy has consequences where documents, such as registers of owners or beneficiaries of a particular action, are drawn up and assume a life of their own (Bell 1983b).

From 1978 to 1987, I worked on some seven land claims and prepared exhibits which dealt especially with the rights and responsibilities of women in land (Bell 1981, 1982, 1984–5, 1987a). Women preferred to give evidence in ceremonial form, for that is the clearest way of answering the question 'Who is the "owner" of this land?'. The problem for me, as consultant anthropologist, then became how to render this information in a form which would be considered evidence by the court, and to do so in a way which would not jeopardize women's secrets in a public place. Segments of performances could be adapted for mixed company, but the private, secret part of the preparations could not, and that was where much of the critical information was to be found. We found ways of scaling down the court, of making it less intimidating for women, but still there remained the problem that women were giving less than a full account, because the court was predominantly male, and ultimately their evidence had to be seen by a male judge (Bell 1984–5). In the process of registering a sacred site, the material was to be reviewed by a male authority (Bell 1983b). This legislation has recently been amended and women now sit as members of the authority.

In 1981, as anthropologist to the newly formed Aboriginal Sacred Sites Protection Authority in Darwin, I was able to record and participate in a week-long *jarrarda*, a secret women's ceremony, held at a cattle station (ranch) in the Roper River area and attended by women from far-flung communities (Bell 1982; see also Berndt 1950:30–7, 44, 1965:254). In song and dance, in gesture and design, the assembled women celebrated the travels of the Munga-Munga ancestral women who pioneered the country from Tennant Creek to Arnhem Land. These female ancestors scattered across the Barkly Tablelands; they travelled from Macarthur River and from the junction of the Wilton and Roper rivers to a site on Hodgson River and thence to Nutwood Downs, where their tracks divide, one following the 'road' to Alice Springs, the other to a site on Brunette Downs. The Munga-Munga assumed different forms, met with, crossed over, absorbed and transformed the essence of other ancestors; their influence infused country with the spiritual essence of women.

In subsequent discussions of the ceremony with the participants, they retraced in sand maps the patterns made by the dancing feet on the ceremonial ground, and explained that Munga-Munga mapped the country for women; they were everywhere; they changed form, language and style as they forged links between groups in the dreamtime. Within the context of this overarching responsibility for the dreaming, women also stated their responsibility for particular tracts of land and emphasized certain themes and, as with central Australian women, emotional management and health were the principal ones. At one level women gave form to a generalized notion of their responsibility for land, its dreamings and sites in expressions such as 'we must hold up that country', 'not lose him'. At another level the ceremony allowed certain divisions of labour for responsibility for country to be played out.

Although the terms are different, the multiplicity of ways of tracing a relationship to land remained a salient feature of the ceremonial activity.[17] Those who traced their relationship from their father and father's father as *minirringki* and from their mother and mother's father as *jungkayi*, and from their mother's mother as *dalyin*, had a particular role, and the overlap with the division of labour of *kirda* and *kurdungurlu* in central Australian *yawulyu* was considerable. Men were rigidly excluded from the ceremony at the women's 'ring place', but at the conclusion of the activity on the women's ground, the women entered the main camp where the men had been sitting quietly. A gift exchange between men and women then took place. In this way the interdependence of men's and women's worlds was celebrated.

The northern literature, where it makes mention of women's rituals, speaks of crisis of life ceremonies (Berndt 1965:238–43). Catherine Berndt (1950) writes of *tjarada, jawalju* and *ilbindji*, but the emphasis in the literature on religion concerns the regional cults of Kunapipi and Yabaduruwa at which women have a shadowy presence. Bern (1979a, 1979b), Elkin (1961) and Berndt (1951) provide fine-grain ethnographic descriptions and analyses of male-controlled activities at which women are necessary, but their role is supportive: they cook; they are drawn to the verge of knowing men's secrets, but their own participation is limited (Bern 1979a:418–19). The most confident generalizations regarding woman's profanity, and women's exclusion from all things sacred, have come from anthropologists working in these regions (Warner 1937; Maddock 1972; Bern 1979a, 1979b). Writing of Arnhem Land, Lloyd Warner (1937:6) had summarized that women made little sacred progress through life but remained largely profane. Despite Kaberry's (1939:221) counter that 'men are the uninitiated at women's ceremonies', Warner has become the 'Australian case'.[18]

Through working with women in these contexts, having participated in women's ceremonies in the Roper River, Victoria River Downs and Daly Rivers areas, and held meetings with women in eastern Arnhem Land, I would suggest that the central Australian material provides as good a basis for generalization as the more popular northern fieldwork. By beginning with the desert material, we gain a different perspective on separation of the sexes. The work of Hamilton (1979, 1987) in the Western Desert would also offer interesting contrasts, where to infiltrate women's autonomous ritual world in the Western Desert men need to undermine the mother–daughter tie, because endogamous generation moieties organize ritual life.[19] The ceremonial life in central Australia consists of separate and shared ground, but as we move further north to the Roper River, Victoria River Downs and Daly Rivers region and onto Arnhem Land, the markers of separation of the sexes are less dramatic. There are still women's grounds, and there is still 'women's business', but there is not the same high level of independence structuring women's economic and ritual life. Men produce a greater percentage of the reliable diet, polygyny rates are higher and age difference at first marriage greater.

More work is necessary on the Munga-Munga and *jarrada* before we can discuss women's ceremonies in this area as dealing with 'personal reactions to physiological stress' (Maddock 1972:155). In the revised edition of *The Australian Aborigines* Maddock (1982:139) took into account that in central Australia there were women's ceremonies other than those focusing on crises of life, and that the evidence of land claims supported my ethnography. However, he noted that the scale of women's ceremonies does not rival that of men, and it seems unlikely the underreporting is a case of male bias. He wisely added that scale is not necessarily an indicator of importance or merit. Clearly we need to ask new questions of the material.

One question worth reflection raised by the *jarrarda* I witnessed is: Could it be that the Munga-Munga is a women's regional cult, now truncated to a *jarrarda*? Certainly the ceremony encompassed a number of groups, covered vast tracts of land and could travel from site to site. It had not been performed for many years and it is worth noting why this was so and why it was staged in 1981 (Bell 1982). This is an area where the logistic constraints on women's ceremonial life are marked. Women, isolated from each other on a number of cattle stations, needed access to transport to bring together the necessary personnel. Munga-Munga is dangerous business and released wild and uncontrollable forces, not ones that give men any great joy, and for the duration of the ceremony they were under certain restriction of movement. To stage a *jarrarda* for Munga-Munga, women needed a compelling rationale. The activities of the Sacred Sites Authority provided a rationale and access to vehicles driven by women for the journey to the ceremonial ground required woman-specific activities and negotiations. The ceremonial activity had another prompt from the impending land-claim hearing to the north of the cattle station, and that was one supported by the local land council.

In terms of the 1981 ceremony there was an interesting overlap in politics: women ritual 'bosses', resident on the cattle station, were anxious to confirm their claim to the area, and this could be achieved through ceremonial activity on a site as a Munga-Munga place. If this site were protected by legislation, then it would be respected by station managers and visitors alike. It would give women a negotiating position in the politics of self-determination in that they would be registered, and therefore would be more likely to be consulted. And as John Bern's (1979a) exploration of politics in the Roper River region helpfully indicated, power plays drive ceremonial action. However, he excluded women as players because in his analysis religion is the business of men (1979a:47). Here I am suggesting we factor women into the resource wrangles that characterize much of the institutional politics of the region.

As anthropologist to the Sacred Sites Authority, I was anxious to begin the task of alerting developers to the existence of women's sites and the need to consult with women. There had already been a lengthy dispute over a site in Alice Springs where, too late, women who controlled aspects of the site were acknowledged (Bell 1983b:284). On that occasion, all reports had been done by men talking to men, and it was only when the site was about to be flooded that the importance of the women became apparent. Had the site not been threatened, the women's side would have remained unknown; secrecy had been the preferred strategy. Part of my work in 1981 entailed explaining the existence of the new sacred sites legislation and giving people and option of registering sites if they thought it offered protection. For the most part, if they could protect sites by keeping them out of the public eye, that was the path chosen. However, the situation was delicate, for once sites became the subject of disputes there was always the suspicion, on the part of developers and the state, that they had been 'invented' to thwart their work. Stopping development for a woman's site was even more problematic as the image of woman as excluded from the religious domain and as persons punished for violating sacred sites (Strehlow 1971:340) is pervasive.

The things left 'undone' in 1981 *jarrarda* were addressed again in 1983 and 1984, but on these occasions the bureaucratic support was more intrusive (Merlan 1989) and the ritual agenda different: the site had already been confirmed as a Munga-Munga place. In 1981 we had asked the women initiating the ceremony who should be invited and what should be said in telegrams, a favoured way of communicating between communities. We travelled with one of the bosses and at each community we asked again who should go, and attended meetings in family groups. Men were interested in what the women were doing, but made no attempt to attend. The preliminaries took longer than the ceremony and involved many decisions which then set the parameters for the ceremony. Had we been a mixed group, the ceremony would have been different; had the Sacred Sites Authority not had a specific agenda regarding women, it would have been different. What distinguished this occasion was that there were resources available to women. Had the ceremony involved only men, it would have been part of a known history of ceremonies in the area. The recourse to external bodies to resolve ritual politics has led to an increasing level of engagement with bureaucratic politics and submissions for funding. The ceremonies staged will reflect these factors, but will also be driven by territorial disputes and a contesting of leadership. It is not particularly helpful to promote one ritual agenda as more authentic, untouched or apolitical than another. However, I would suggest that the long history of women being denied (overtly or covertly) the means to gather for ceremonies has benefited male politicking through ceremonies.

My next example is from the Daly River where I had the opportunity to work with women on a land claim and to participate in a series of closed and secret women's ceremonies (Bell 1981). The ceremonial cycle had engaged the services of all the women in the community, and was glossed as a girl's 'puberty rite'. Five girls were put through the ceremonies, but, as I had already learned in central Australia, there was likely to be a broader political agenda, and indeed there was and it was relevant to a local land claim. The site on which the ceremony focused was a woman's site and without documenting its importance one area of the claim would have failed. I could only discuss structure, not content of the rite, with a fellow male anthropologist who had worked in the area, and I very much wanted to know what he had been told of such ceremonies (Bell 1987c:238). The particular ceremony was similar to *yawulyu*: there was the private, women-only segment of preparation, painting, handling of sacred objects (including hair string); the performance and confirmation of the ritual status in a wonderfully staged segment, the stress on kin — the mother was in charge and the sister-in-law was classified as 'wife'. What I had not expected in a 'crisis of life' ceremony was the invocation from the ritual 'boss': 'Help me in my ceremony. Make me happy for this land'.

In terms of separation of the sexes, the men knew the ceremonies were in progress and one of the girls was the daughter of a principal claimant in the impending land claim. He was anxious to have another adult women in his group. In the focused segments of the puberty rituals, the women worked in their own space. On the day when all women were welcome, they gathered in large numbers in a public space. The men had all vacated the mission for the day, and in a parade, bold and dramatic, the women brought their business through the main camp. The cries they let out were to warn anyone nearby not to look, and were reminiscent of those of the red-ochred men at the capture of the boys in initiation. The final segment of the ceremony involved the men and gift exchanges. The community now had more adult women and the men thanked the women for their work.

My evidence concerning these activities for the land-claim hearing was carefully negotiated with the women. It fell into two parts: there was a submission, which dealt with the structure of the ceremony without referring to actual content, and a second containing photographs and descriptions of the meanings. This was to be available only to the judge and to female counsel. Establishing this 'precedent' was another interesting illustration of the problems of gendered knowledge for a culture without the parallel legal structures: there was no women's 'ring place' to which we would retire for a ruling. In the interests of fairness, the judge allowed the women's submission to be restricted to women. In so doing, he granted the women the same privileges that men's restricted submissions have always enjoyed (Bell 1984–5:357–9). However, men's submissions have not had to declare their masculinist bias, because they present little disruption to a court.

Although the women's movement has had some impact on the practice of law, for the most part patriarchal values permeate Anglo-Australian law. Courts of law are not accommodating of women, and legal means of establishing rights present special problems for Aboriginal women (Bell 1984–5; Bell and Ditton 1980/4). Similarly, within the academy, although feminist scholarship constitutes a fundamental challenge to the pursuit of knowledge as value-free, women are marginalized, co-opted, treated as tokens, or their work dismissed as of concern for women only (Moore 1988; Mascia-Lees *et al.* 1989).

Other contemporary contexts in which we may learn of women's ceremonial life are ones where an external authority is the initiator: tourist performances; opportunities generated by film crews; historic occasions marked by a 'traditional' celebration; the opening of a gallery; or an exhibition in an urban centre. The contexts for ceremonial life continue to change. Berndt (1950) noted this some forty years ago, but her focus was on dimensions of cultural contact. In the 1990s Aboriginal women are moving into regional networks and the politics driving these new interactions are those of the institutions of self-determination. The politics concern, among others, the state, statutory authorities and development lobbies (Bell and Marks 1990). It is my impression that with the politicization of Aboriginal affairs, the drawing of Aborigines into the bureaucracy, and the indigenization of service industries, a 'brain drain' is occurring. Women ritual leaders now travel to Norway to address conferences on indigenous art, not to the next *jilimi* to negotiate *yawulyu*. The resources at hand are different, and so are the needs. Religious practice has always had the capacity to adapt, absorb and accommodate change. Ceremonial life continues but its association with land as spiritual and economic giver of life is attenuated.

It is no longer possible to write of Aboriginal religion as if it existed in a closed world, isolated from the politics of the nation-state, or gender relations as if independent of the wider Australian society. Making explicit the broader factors which impact on the Aboriginal groups whose religious practice is the subject of enquiry is a complex task and more elusive than merely speaking of 'bias'. I am endorsing the analysis which holds that the religious domain is where power, status, authority, resources are negotiated and distributed, but I am arguing that women engage in these politics not just as pawns but as players; that if we begin with the ethnography (what women are doing), and build from there to map women's strategies, we are writing a special kind of situated ethnography, one where the participant observation is with women, and one which relies on what can be learned from women of women's business. This is an exercise in power, and when it has the effect of bringing women's lives into sharper focus, it raises questions of knowing, knowers and the known (Hawkesworth 1989).

The feminist ethnography presented in this article demonstrates that much of the earlier generalizing was premature: we know too little of actual practice, it varies regionally, and impact of contact has been dramatic. What does emerge is that there are common features to women's ceremonies across regions from the desert to the tropical north; that the structuring principles are age, kin and ritual status; that ceremonies celebrate relations to land and sacred sites; that the religious domain constitutes an arena for political negotiations; that ceremonies manifest a division of labour which entails exclusions and interrelations with the men, exchanges of knowledge, power and goods; that the focus of ceremonies shifts according to needs. There are regional variations, as there are in men's ceremonial life, in terms of the land that is being celebrated, the sustenance it provides and the contexts in which it is made known. What varies is the basis of women's separation, the context of the ceremonies and the contexts in which we learn of religious beliefs and practices.

Notes

1. This article draws substantially on the central Australian ethnography presented in *Daughters of the Dreaming* (1983) and I gratefully acknowledge the permission of George Allen & Unwin to reprint the material. In writing of women's religious beliefs and practices, one walks a fine line, for much is secret. I have consulted (and continue to consult) with the women who are the 'owners' of the knowledge discussed here. I am using only material that the women with whom I worked have cleared as 'open' knowledge. Recently in Australia there have been objections raised by certain urban Aboriginal women regarding the propriety of anyone other than Aboriginal women writing about certain matters — this was with reference to rape — but on

other occasions has included religion and already published material (Bell and Nelson 1989:415 n2). There are problems with descriptions of ceremonies in earlier works and I have avoided direct quotations from sources other than those I know to be 'open'.

2. The Kaytej, Warlpiri and Warlmanpa land claim was heard before Mr Justice Toohey in 1981. Under the *Aboriginal Land Rights (Northern Territory) Act 1976*, title to Aboriginal reserves was transferred to Aborigines and the conditions under which Aborigines could make claim to vacant crown land (and land in which all interests were held by or on behalf of Aborigines) were specified. Under the Act, Aborigines must demonstrates that they satisfy the criteria of traditional ownership and this entails presenting evidence of spiritual responsibility and affiliations to the land and its sites. The claims are heard before a judge who sits as the Aboriginal Land Commissioner.

3. See Rohrlich-Leavitt *et al.* (1975), Bell (1983a:229–46) and Gross (1987) for literature reviews from feminist perspectives; and compare Merlan (1988). Phyllis Kaberry (1939) provided the first monograph on Aboriginal women in which she presented important data on women's ceremonies in the Kimberley region of western Australia as closed, secret and sustaining, and a refutation of Durkheim's dichotomy as promoted by Lloyd Warner (1937). However, Elkin, writing the preface to Kaberry's work (xxix–xxx), significantly under-cuts her analysis. In various articles Catherine Berndt (1950, 1965) presents material on women's closed, secret ceremonies across northern and western Australia and also engaged with Durkheim. Jane Goodale (1971) detailed Tiwi ceremonies and her final chapter explores male and female world views. Nancy Munn's (1973/86) symbolic analysis of desert iconography offers much regarding women's ceremonial life, but privileges the male experience. Annette Hamilton (1979, 1987), working with Pitjantjatjarra in the Western Desert, has explored the impediment to consolidation of male power represented by women's secret ritual and indicated the ways in which men seek to infiltrate women's worlds. In the last decade or so, a number of women have begun or completed PhDs and some have begun to publish: Victoria Burbank (1989), Gillian Cowlishaw (1979), Françoise Dussart (1988), Barbara Glowczewski (1983), André Grau (1983), Jan Lauridsen (1990), Helen Payne (1988), Deborah Bird Rose (1984). Few have engaged with feminist questions or written explicitly situated ethnographies.

4. Kaberry (1939) and Goodale (1971), for instance, presented theirs in the format of a life cycle. In this context one should note that Hart and Pilling's *The Tiwi* (1960) remains *the* ethnography although it is based on work with men. Similarly, Mervyn Meggitt's *Desert People* (1962) although about men is *the* desert ethnography.

5. When Rita Gross (1987:41–2) surveyed the Australian literature, she noted that there were many interpretations, but scanty fieldwork. This is indicative of the slow filtering of Australian material to international markets, but also of the way in which what exists is classified. For instance, in the catalogue of the AIAS, the major research funding body in Australia, there is no category for women (Hill and Barlow 1985). In other bibliographic sources I find my work classified under 'social change', 'special problems', 'welfare'.

6. Unfortunately Annette Hamilton's (1979) PhD, which is a most exacting analysing of the shifting ground on which ethnographic observations were made at the time of first contacts in the Western Desert, remains unpublished. Hamilton (1987) offers a glimpse of this material. See Leacock (1978), Bell (1980, 1983a:41–106, 246–50, 1988b) for other ethnographic examples.

7. In his review of the literature addressing the study of Aboriginal religion, Stanner (1979) noted that a world view is hard to dislodge, and even in the face of strong evidence to the contrary, scholars continued to write of Aborigines

as primitives with nothing worthy of the name religion. The critical edge of anthropology has dug deeper in ethnocentrism than sexism, and feminist anthropologists are now exploring the intersection of gender and race (Moore 1988). The theoretical preoccupations, research design and the nature of the discipline in Australia have all conspired to relegate women to a position of marginality within Aboriginal society and within the discipline (Bell 1983a, 1984).

8. Hawkeworth's (1989:535) critique of the divergent arguments concerning the premises of a feminist epistemology points to the need to move beyond merely declaring interest and bias, to questioning the bases of our knowledge, but is troubled by the tensions this presents for a feminist politic (ibid.:556–7). The 'postmodernist turn' in anthropology (Marcus and Fischer 1986; Clifford 1988), while claiming self-reflexivity, fails to acknowledge the range of feminist theorizing and ethnographic experimentation, or that critical readings of gendered subjects have long been a central concern of feminist theory (Bell 1983a; Mascia-Lees *et al.* 1989; Moore 1988; Hondagneu-Sotelo 1988; Stacey 1988; Caplan 1988). Reflexive anthropologists such as Clifford and others have set gender aside as too difficult, and severely underrepresent the contribution of feminist anthropologists. Certainly the relationship between feminism and anthropology is not simple (Strathern 1985; Moore 1988; Caplan 1988), but the dialogue belongs in mainstream, and the work of feminists is a fundamental critique. Engaging in this debate is another article, but I am flagging it here for the reader as a shaping force in the debates concerning anthropological practice.

9. One tactic has been to ignore it — Mayne's (1986) bibliography contains no reference to women — or to suggest that womancentric work lacks balance. In reviewing the last twenty-five years of anthropology in Australia, the AIAS commissioned overview papers; Berndt and Tonkinson (1988:6) write of the 'earlier feminist anthropological writings' as 'overcorrection'. Francesca Merlan's (1988) review of gender, which follows their introduction, ignores the intellectual and political importance of feminism as a context for anthropologists, but observes that it is mostly women writing on gender. Her suggestion is a return to the issues of sex, sexuality and reproduction (ibid.:35ff.). See also Burbank (1989) who quotes Merlan approvingly. Anna Yeatman (1983) is also interested in modelling gender in this way and is content to draw on ethnography such as that of Spencer and Allen. She finds nothing in the feminist ethnography to dissuade her.

10. The Aboriginal population at contact is contested and ranges from as low as 150 000 to millions (Bell and Marks 1990:6–12).

11. The composition of village councils is an excellent example of the intersection of gender politics of Aboriginal society and Western notions of representation as gender blind. In many communities, especially in central Australia, it is inappropriate and dangerous for men and women to gather in large meetings. Administrators have looked to men to represent the views of communities (Bell and Ditton 1980/4:44).

12. For a number of reasons women are less likely to hold a driver's licence than men. They have had fewer opportunities to learn. Men were engaged as drivers during World War II and assisted in stock work, but these work contexts were not routinely available to women.

13. The experiences spoken of as a 'dream' do not necessarily occur in sleep, but in a thinking back on an earlier time. Women sometimes have these 'dreams' while in especially important country. This use of 'dream' in English is not to be confused with 'dreaming' or 'dream time'.

14. The subsections system (also called 'skin-system') has eight divisions, into which one is born according to affiliations of one's parents and is a shorthand

form of expressing social relationships (Meggitt 1962:168; Bell 1983a:260–4). Siblings will fall within the same subsection but not all members will be siblings. The system is generated by three crosscutting moiety divisions: parti, matri and generational.

15. In his notes of their trip, Gillen (1968) records the episodes on which the later jointly authored works of Spencer and Gillen are based. Women appear as more vocal and engaged in these accounts but their activities are classified as squabbles or food-getting, and thus further questions are not asked. There is ample evidence in this source that women's relationship to land mirrored that of men, but this material did not find its way into their ethnography (Bell 1983a:24–5).

16. The Aboriginal Sacred Sites Protection Authority was a statutory body established under Northern Territory legislation, the *Sacred Sites Act 1978*, which is reciprocal legislation to the federal land rights Act in 1976, but has been significantly amended. Under the *Aboriginal Land Rights (Northern Territory) Act 1976*, land councils, also statutory authorities, were established to handle land claims and represent Aborigines in matters of land.

17. Much debate concerning local and social organization and land tenure systems in Australia focuses on this region, but woman's relationship to land and to ancestors is often explained as derivative of her relationship to someone else, for example her husband or her father, but not as the mirror image of the male system. In the literature there has also been a stress on patrilineal descent as the basis of group membership. However, evidence forthcoming in land claims where Aboriginal witnesses provide direct statements concerning land supports the position I have outlined here (Bell 1982; Maddock 1982).

18. Feminist anthropologists (Collier and Rosaldo 1981), arguing the universality of sexual asymmetry, have taken Warner in this way also.

19. It is in the shattering of the ritually maintained nexus of land as resource and land as spiritual essence that I have located a shift from female autonomy to male control, from an independent producer to one dependent on social security (Bell 1980, 1983a, 1988b). Thus while Hamilton (1979, 1987) and I are concerned to explore the changing nature of the relations between the sexes from a historical perspective, we have focused from rather differing conceptions of time and place, and upon different institutions and sets of relationships.

References

BELL, DIANE (1980), 'Desert politics: choices in the "marriage market"', in Mona Etienne & Eleanor Leacock (eds), *Women and Colonization: Anthropological Perspectives*, New York: Praeger.

—— (1982), 'In the tracks of the Munga-Munga', Submission to Cox River Land Claim, prepared on behalf of the Northern Land Council, Darwin, Exhibit No. 27 (35 pp.).

—— (1981), 'Daly River (Malak Malak) Land Claim: women's interests', Submission to the Daly River (Malak Malak) Land Claim prepared on behalf of the Northern Land Council, Darwin, Exhibit No. 8 (34 pp.); Exhibit No. 65 (12 pp.) (restricted).

—— (1983a), *Daughters of the Dreaming*, Sydney: Allen & Unwin.

—— (1983b), 'Sacred sites: the politics of protection', in Nicolas Peterson & Marcia Langton (eds), *Aborigines and Land Rights*, Canberra: AIAS.

—— (1984), 'Women and Aboriginal religion', in Max Charlesworth, Ken Maddock, Diane Bell & Howard Morphy (eds), *Religion in Aboriginal Australia*, St Lucia: Queensland University Press.

—— (1984–5), 'Aboriginal women and land: learning from the Northern Territory experience', *Anthropological Forum*, **5**(3):353–63.

—— (1987a), 'Aboriginal women and customary law', in Bradford W. Morse & Gordon R. Woodman (eds), *Indigenous Law and the State*, Holland: Foris.

—— (1987b), 'Exercising discretion: sentencing Aborigines for murder in the Northern Territory', in Bradford W. Morse & Gordon R. Woodman (eds), *Indigenous Law and the State*, Holland: Foris.

—— (1987c), 'Aboriginal women and the religious experience', in W. H. Edwards (ed.), *Traditional Aboriginal Society: A Reader*, Melbourne: Macmillan. (First published 1982.)

—— (1988a), 'The politics of separation', in Marilyn Strathern (ed.), *Dealing with Inequality*, Cambridge: Cambridge University Press.

—— (1988b), 'Choose your mission wisely: Christian colonials and Aboriginal marital arrangements on the northern frontier', in Deborah Bird Rose & Tony Swain (eds), *Aboriginal Australians and Christianity*, Adelaide: AASR.

—— (1988c), 'We are hungry for our land', in Verity Burgman & Jenny Less (eds), *A Most Valuable Acquisition*, Melbourne: McPhee Gribble/Penguin.

—— (1989), 'The sacred and the profane revisited: religion and gender in Aboriginal Australia', Roundtable presentation, AAR Annual Conference, Anaheim, Calif., November.

—— (1992), 'Considering gender: are human rights for women too?', in Abdullahi An-Na'im (ed.), *Human Rights in Cross Cultural Perspectives*, Philadelphia: University of Pennsylvania Press.

BELL, DIANE & DITTON, PAM (1980/4), *Law: The Old and the New*, Canberra: Aboriginal History.

BELL, DIANE & MARKS, GENÉE (1990), *Aborigines and Australian Society*, Paris: UNESCO.

BELL, DIANE & NELSON, TOPSY NAPURRULA (1989a), 'Speaking about rape is everyone's business', *Women's Studies International Forum*, **12**(4):404–16.

BERN, JOHN (1979a), 'Politics in the conduct of a secret male ceremony', *Journal of Anthropological Research*, **35**(1):47–60.

—— (1979b), 'Ideology and domination', *Oceania*, **50**(2):118–32.

BERNDT, CATHERINE (1950), 'Women's changing ceremonies in Northern Australia', *L'Homme*, **1**:1–87.

—— (1965), 'Women and the "secret life"', in R. M. & C. H. Berndt (eds), *Aboriginal Man in Australia*, Sydney: Angus & Robertson.

—— (1970), 'Digging sticks and spears, or, the two-sex model', in Fay Gale (ed.), *Women's Role in Aboriginal Society*, Canberra: AIAS.

BERNDT, R. M. (1951), *Kunapipi*, Melbourne: Cheshire.

BERNDT, R. M. & TONKINSON, R. (1988), 'Foreword: a contemporary overview', in R. M. Berndt & R. Tonkinson (eds), *Social Anthropology and Australian Aboriginal Studies*, Canberra: Aboriginal Studies Press.

BURBANK, VICTORIA (1989), 'Gender and the anthropological curriculum: Aboriginal Australia', in Sandra Morgen (ed.), *Gender and Anthropology: Critical Reviews for Research and Teaching*, Washington: AAA.

CAPLAN, PAT (1988), 'Engendered knowledge', *Anthropology Today*, **14**(5):8–12; **14**(6):14–17.

CLIFFORD, JAMES (1988), *The Predicament of Culture*, Cambridge, Mass.: Harvard University Press.

COLLIER, JANE & ROSALDO, MICHELLE (1981), 'Politics and gender in simple societies', in Sherry B. Ortner & Harriet Whitehead (eds), *Sexual Meanings: The Cultural Construction of Gender and Sexuality*, London: Cambridge University Press.

COWLISHAW, GILLIAN (1979), 'Woman's Realm: a study of socialisation, sexuality and reproduction', PhD thesis, University of Sydney.

Dussart, Françoise (1988), 'Warlpiri women's yawulyu ceremonies: a forum for socialization and innovation', PhD thesis, ANU, Canberra.

Elkin, A. P. (1961), 'The yabuduruwa', *Oceania*, **31**:166–209.

Gillen, Francis James (1968), *Gillen's Diary: The Camp Jottings of F. J. Gillen on the Spencer and Gillen Expedition across Australia, 1910–2*, Adelaide: Libraries Board of South Australia.

Glowczewski, Barbara (1983), 'Death, women and "value production": the circulation of hairstrings among the Walpiri of the Central Australian Desert', *Ethnology*, **22**(3):225–39.

Goodale, Jane (1971), *Tiwi Wives*, Seattle: University of Washington Press.

Grau, Andrée (1983), 'Dreaming, dancing, kinship: the Melville and Bathurst Islands, North Australia', PhD thesis, Queen's University of Belfast, Northern Ireland.

Gross, Rita (1987), 'Tribal religions: Aboriginal Australia', in Arvind Sharma (ed.), *Women and World Religions*, Albany: SUNY Press.

Hamilton, Annette (1979), 'Timeless transformations: women, men and history in the Australian Western Desert", PhD thesis, University of Sydney.

—— (1987), 'Dual social systems: technology, labour and women's secret rites in the eastern Western Desert of Australia', in W. H. Edwards (ed.), *Traditional Aboriginal Society: A Reader*, Melbourne: Macmillan. (First published 1980.)

Hart, C. W. M. & Pilling, A. R. (1960), *The Tiwi of North Australia*, New York: Holt, Rinehart and Winston.

Hawkesworth, Mary E. (1989), 'Knowers, knowing and known: feminist theory and claims of truth', *Signs*, **14**(3):533–7 (see also commentaries and reply, *Signs*, 1990, **15**(2):417–28).

Hiatt, L. R. (1987), 'Aboriginal political life', in W. H. Edwards (ed.), *Traditional Aboriginal Society: A Reader*, Melbourne: Macmillan. (First published 1984.)

Hill, Marji & Barlow, Alex (1985), *Black Australia 2: An Annotated Bibliography and Teachers' Guide to Resources on Aborigines and Torres Strait Islanders*, Canberra: AIAS.

Hondagneu-Sotelo, Pierrette (1988), 'Gender and fieldwork: review essay', *Women's Studies International Forum*, **11**(6):611–18.

Kaberry, Phyllis M. (1939). *Aboriginal Women: Sacred and Profane*, London: George Routledge and Sons.

Kendon, Adam (1988), *Sign Language of Aboriginal Australia: Cultural Semiotic and Communicative Perspectives*, Cambridge: Cambridge University Press.

Kuhn, T. S. (1970), *The Structure of Scientific Revolutions*, Chicago: University of Chicago Press.

Lauridsen, Jan (1990), 'Women's jarata of North Central Australia', manuscript.

Leacock, Eleanor (1978), 'Women's status in egalitarian society', *Current Anthropology*, **19**(2):247–75.

Maddock, Kenneth (1982), *The Australian Aborigines: a Portrait of their Society* (second edition), Ringwood: Penguin (first edition 1972).

Marcus, George E. & Fischer, Michael M. J. (1986), *Anthropology as Cultural Critique*, Chicago: University of Chicago Press.

Mascia-Lees, Frances E., Sharpe, Patricia & Cohen, Colleen Ballerino (1989), 'The postmodern turn in anthropology: cautions from a feminist perspective', *Signs*, **15**(1):7–35.

Mayne, Tom (1986), *Aborigines and the Issues*, Sydney: Australian Council of Churches.

Meggitt, M. J. (1962), *Desert People: A Study of the Walbiri Aborigines of Central Australia*, Sydney: Angus & Robertson.

Merlan, Francesca (1988), 'Gender in Aboriginal social life: a review', in R. M. Berndt & R. Tonkinson (eds), *Social Anthropology and Australian Aboriginal Studies*, Canberra: Aboriginal Studies Press.

—— (1989), 'The objectification of "culture": an aspect of current political process in Aboriginal affairs', *Anthropological Forum*, **6**(1):105–16.

MOORE, HENRIETTA (1988), *Feminism and Anthropology*, Minneapolis: University of Minnesota Press.

MUNN, NANCY D. (1973/1986), *Walbiri Inconography: Graphic Representations and Cultural Symbolism in a Central Australian Society* (with a new after-word), Chicago: University of Chicago Press.

PAYNE, HELEN (1988), 'Singing a sister's sites: women's land rights in the Australian Musgrave Ranges", PhD thesis, University of Queensland.

RÓHEIM, GEZA (1933), 'Women and their life in Central Australia', *RAIJ*, No. 63:207–65.

ROHRLICH-LEAVITT, RUBY, SYKES, BARBARA & WEATHERFORD, ELIZABETH (1975), 'Aboriginal woman: male and female anthropological perspectives', in *Towards an Anthropology of Woman*, Rayna Reiter (ed.), New York: Monthly Review Press.

ROSE, DEBORAH BIRD (1984), 'Dingo makes us human: being and purpose in Australian Aboriginal culture', PhD thesis, Bryn Mawr College.

SPENCER, Baldwin & GILLEN, F. J. (1899), *The Native Tribes of Central Australia*, London: Macmillan.

STACEY, JUDITH (1988), 'Can there be a feminist ethnography?', *Women's Studies International Forum*, **11**(1):21–7.

STANNER, W. E. H. (1979), 'Religion, totemism and symbolism', in *White Man Got No Dreaming*, Canberra: ANU Press. (First published 1962.)

STRATHERN, MARILYN (1985), 'Dislodging a world view: challenge and counter challenge in the relationship between feminism and anthropology', *Australian Feminist Studies*, No. 1:1–25.

STREHLOW, T G. H. (1971), *Songs of Central Australia*, Sydney: Angus & Robertson.

WARNER, LLOYD W. (1969), *A Black Civilization: A Social Study of an Australian Tribe*, Glouchester, Mass.: Peter Smith. (First published 1937, Harper and Row.)

WHITE, I. M. (1975), 'Sexual conquest and submission in Aboriginal myths', in L. R. Hiatt (ed.), *Australian Aboriginal Mythology*, Canberra: AIAS.

YEATMAN, ANNA (1983), 'The procreative model: the social ontological bases of the gender-kinship system', *Social Analysis*, No. 14:3–30 (see also comments and rejoinder, *Social Analysis*, 1984, No. 16:3–43).

17
Exploring an Aboriginal Land Ethic

DEBORAH BIRD ROSE

The term 'land ethic' was coined in 1949 by Aldo Leopold. In *A Sand County Almanac* Leopold spoke of the 'land ethic' as an extension of the ethics that prompt individuals to co-operate with fellow members of their community. He argued that 'the land ethic simply enlarges the boundaries of the community to include soils, waters, plants, and animals'.[1] In borrowing his felicitous term I emphasize the vision he expressed. Leopold's ideas were of his time, but also ahead of it. Working with a theory of evolution that incorporated teleological notions of progress, he came to the belief that an ethic was gradually evolving that would allow human beings to treat their environment as a moral community.

More recently, it has been shown that the kind of land ethic proposed by Leopold was already to be found among American Indians. Books such as T. C. McLuhan's *Touch the Earth*[2] bear eloquent testimony to American Indians' feelings about, and attitudes toward, the 'natural world'. Similar testimony is to be found among Aboriginal Australians. Guboo Ted Thomas, for example, discusses concepts of mother earth and reverence for life, comparing the natural world to a Christian cathedral.[3] Other anthropologists have made similar points, and David Bennett has provided an excellent analysis in a philosophical mode.[4]

There is always the possibility that people who perceive a lack in their own culture will be drawn to a romantic and nostalgic glorification of other cultures and seek to transplant another culture's ethical system into their own. The attempt is misguided. Every culture is the product of particular beings living particular lives within the particular options and constraints of their own received traditions, their mode of production and so on, none of which can be readily transplanted. Furthermore, the attempt to appropriate another culture's ethical system is self-defeating because it is self-contradictory: the act of appropriation is so lacking in the respect which is the basis of the desired ethic that the appropriation becomes annihilation.

It remains true, however, that moral philosophers, conservationists and other concerned people are querying Western values and attempting to formulate a new system of ethics. This entails a profound shift; as William Godfrey-Smith has argued, it requires 'a whole change in the way of *seeing*

First published in *Meanjin*, **47**(3), 1988.

our social world ... not just a change in behaviour, but a change in perception'.[5]

For several millennia now, the Western tradition has been dominated by various human-centred views of the cosmos. Nature has progressively been defined as ever more distant from human culture. The decline and 'death of nature' has been traced by Carolyn Merchant, who analyses the way organic metaphors have been replaced by mechanical cultural constructs in expressing the relationships between cosmos, society and self.[6] Reactions against the personal, social and ecological costs of these changes have drawn on metaphors developed in non-Western cultures. Yet, in spite of the many eloquent statements by American Indians, Aboriginal Australians and others, we have very little idea of what a non-human-centred cosmos looks like and how it can be thought to work.

My purpose here is to outline the beginnings of such an understanding by discussing a land ethic expressed by Ngarinman and Ngaliwurru people in the communities of Yarralin and Lingara in the Northern Territory. For convenience, I will use the terms Ngarinman and Yarralin to refer to the broader categories of people in both communities. I am concerned here with exploring domains and modes of analysis rather than with presenting conclusions.

My present study, which is still in progress, builds on previous intensive research in the Yarralin/Lingara area during 1980–82. At the start, I was particularly interested in questions of Aboriginal religion, ontology, moral philosophy and moral practice. I came to understand that Ngarinman people believe that human life exists within the broader context of a living and conscious cosmos. Humans' responsibility lies in actions that nurture and enhance human life, the life of other species (plants and animals) and the relationships between humans and between humans and others. Other animal species are believed to be acting equally responsibly. People, other animals and other categories of beings are moral agents. The whole cosmos is maintained through the conscious and responsible actions of different lifeforms. Conflict is recognized as a basic component of this system, and responsible conflict is directed toward asserting a balance. It is impossible to justify the annihilation of groups or species.

My current research focuses on Yarralin people's understanding of ecosystems. I began the work by documenting their botanical knowledge with the assistance of two botanists, David Cooper and Jock Morse. I found that Yarralin people frequently discussed plants according to use. Although not a major means of classification, use-value does provide a window to the extensive dimensions of Yarralin people's ways of thinking about the world. Of 119 separate plants, 106 were said to have some sort of use to somebody. Eighty-one of the 119 plants were useful either to humans alone or to both humans and animals; twenty-five were useful but not to humans; and thirteen were said to be no use to anybody. Many of the plants that were said to have no use were termed *walayinkari*, which was glossed as 'just the rubbish' or 'just the nothing'. However, many people pointed out that at least some of these 'rubbish' plants have a use in producing seeds, which grow more plants of the same species; such plants are useful to themselves, regardless of the use others make of them.

Plants may be useful to humans for food, as material from which tools are made, for firewood, shade or medicines. They may also provide food and shade for other animals, and in many cases these categories of use overlap. For example, a type of plum called *karayijkarayij* (*Ziziphus quadulocularis*) was described as 'good tucker for everybody. Emu, birds, everybody eats it.' Many plants were described as foods for very particular animals. Two trees were said to be food for black cockatoos, another to have berries that are food for turtles and leaves that are food for flying foxes. Other plants with 'pretty flowers' were said to be food for native bees; a few plants were distinguished by whether they would become ground sugarbag or tree sugarbag (native honey).

Dreaming trees are a particularly salient and instructive category of plants. All of the Dreaming plants that I have been shown are trees. Some of these apparently acquire their Dreaming status by growing in a place where a Dreaming was active in the past. For example, all the trees around a billabong called Wuyang on Humbert River Station are classed as Dreaming trees. The billabong is a Dreaming site for the 'little boys' (uninitiated males) who stopped there during their travels. One tree is identified as the 'old man' or 'boss'. When I first visited this site in 1981 the 'old man' was dead and had been so for some time. On a recent visit I was told that a new tree has been identified to take over the position of 'old man'.

Another instance is of several trees near Lingara. One is dead, one is a living shitwood, and one a living Leichhardt. They are all Dreaming trees for the plant also called lingara (*Fimbristylis oxystachya*), a grass seed that was once found throughout the area. The trees mark a site of increase: they are the source of life for this plant. The grass seed plants have not fared well under the impact of cattle. They are still available, but their range is now highly restricted. I will return to the question of decline later.

I also encountered a number of trees that were identified as Dreaming trees because they were living outside their proper habitat. On one cross-country trip we stopped to look at a tree that we had not seen before, growing near a billabong. I was told that it was a Dreaming tree because it is a type that properly belongs in stony hill country. As it is in the area where the 'little boys' had been travelling, it was identified as a 'little boy', and it was said to be there by Dreaming, because it would not have gone there on its own. Another tree that was identified individually as a Dreaming tree (again a 'little boy') was a snappy gum, said to be 'different' because it formed part of a long line of snappy gums that are 'pegged out just like a fence' running along part of the Dreaming track of the 'little boys'. On the basis of this information, it seems that trees are likely to have Dreaming significance if they are out of place ecologically or are distributed in what appears to be a non-tree-like fashion.

Seasonality

For Yarralin and Lingara people, all animals are spoken of and treated as moral agents; so too are some 'natural' phenomena such as sun, moon and rain; and so are some categories of beings that Westerners do not recognize, but which are important parts of the Ngarinman cosmos. Ngarinman people see the cosmos as a whole as being conscious, as are most, if not all, of its parts.

The question I want to address here is this: where is responsibility for seasons located? If we asked this question of a Western-trained meteorologist, he might find it a bit baffling. But, ignoring the deeper questions of responsibility, he would no doubt point to such phenomena as the tilt of the earth, its orbit around the sun, high and low pressure systems and so on. Westerners also use the calendar as an external frame of reference; weather is judged to be normal or abnormal according to patterns developed over time. So we get 'record highs' and 'record lows', 'the first rain in three months' and so on. Our expectations are partly conditioned by our sense of calendar time and our ideas about statistical normality. These expectations do not work very well in the tropics; even in the temperate zones they may work far less well than we are conditioned to think.

Over the years I have attempted to elicit terms for seasons from Yarralin people, but without success. I now believe the problem arose from the fact that my questioning was constrained by my Western ideas of what a system of seasons would look like. I found that Yarralin people recognize and have a term for the cold time of year (the dry, in English). Their term is simply *makuru*, meaning cold. They also have a term for the hot time of year, which is *ngarap*, glossed as 'hot weather, more hot and hot' (build-up, in English), In addition there is a term for the time of big rains: *Mayiyul* (the wet, in English). Beyond this, I was taught a generic term for rain, and a set of terms to refer to all the different types of rains: the cold-weather rain, the hot-weather rain, the first rain after the really hot time of year, and the smell of the first rain. There are also different coloured rains, which relate to matrilineally defined categories of people. Rain is conceptually related to all water, and different coloured rains are conceptually linked to different coloured river water. Again, different coloured river water relates to the action of the rainbow snake, as does the rain itself. So there is a complex and interconnected set of ideas about water that relate to the rainbow snake.

But the rainbow snake is not alone; it has its allies in the turtles, fish, frogs, tadpoles and flying foxes. In a normal course of events, rain comes because the flying foxes have told the rainbow snake that the earth is getting very hot, the trees are all getting dry, the flowers that are food for the flying fox are gone. They 'say' this by going to roost along the river. So one portion of the seasonal cycle is conceptually linked to a range of faunal species. Many of these species are associated with human beings through matrilineally derived categories of identity. In this way, humans, animals and seasons are brought together as part of a system. I know far less about the other portions of this cycle, but they incorporate a similar range of associations.

These three types of weather — cold, hot and rainy — indicate a division into broad segments that generally follow a predictable sequence and are punctuated by different types of rain. Yarralin people, however, know far more about what is happening at any given time of year than this broad outline would suggest. Their knowing depends on correctly interpreting the messages that plants and animals communicate through their behaviour.

Seasonal knowledge here is based on a logic which asserts that two separate but simultaneous events stand in a communicative relationship to each other. Sally Bijibiji, a most knowledgeable woman, told me: 'March flies are telling you the [crocodile] eggs are ready'. The value of this kind of information is manifest: the moment at which crocodiles start to lay eggs is quite unpredictable by the Western calendar, but it is entirely predictable if one pays attention to march flies. Furthermore, to be bitten by march flies, one need not be in a place where crocodiles are likely to lay eggs; but the bites are a signal that it is time to go and look for crocodile eggs.

I have recorded many bits of this type of information. The other type of biting fly tells you that the bush plums are ready. 'When the brolga sings out, the *jarlalka* (dark catfish, associated with flood waters) starts to move.' 'When the little bird *nini* starts crying, it's hot weather time and a good time to kill emu.' 'When the flowers of the *jangarla* tree (*Sesbania formosa*) fall into the water, the barramundi are biting.'

This system of information is based on messages sent out by different agents within the system, 'telling' about the system. In this context, the kind of things that people want to know are indications of when certain plant foods will be ripe and ready for harvesting, when animals will be at their peak condition, when certain kinds of fish will be available and so on. There is an immediately discernible pragmatism here: if human beings are to forage with greatest success and minimal outlay of energy, they must know what is happening at any given time. Beyond simple pragmatics, however, there are further questions regarding the political economy of knowledge, and the intellectual requirements of responsible human behaviour. In order to act responsibly, humans and others must be constantly alert to the state of the systems of which they are a part. Awareness is achieved by learning basic sets of messages, and by continually observing and assessing what is happening around them.

We have here a category of information that Yarralin people recognize as being a matter of parts of a system telling about the state of the system. And the very existence of this category of information can tell us something about the organization of information and responsibility in a conscious cosmos. If we pause for a moment to consider the implications of living in a sentient cosmos inhabited by many different categories of moral agents, whose moral agency has as a basic element the taking of responsibility for those portions of the system in which they operate, it becomes clearer what is going on with concepts of seasonality. Those who know how to interpret the messages that are always being sent are then able to respond to these messages. But the messages themselves are not organized into a centralized, hierarchical structure. Information is dispersed throughout the cosmos. Specifics emerge from a background of broader categories; simultaneous emergence indicates a shared ontological status. From this perspective, the cosmos cannot be seen as human-centred. The march flies' messages are not telling people to go and dig up crocodile eggs. They are simply saying that the crocodiles are laying their eggs.

In an article appropriately entitled 'Rhizome',[7] Deleuze and Guattari discuss the concept of acentred systems. The model of acentred systems offers some useful insights into how a system such as the one I am concerned with here might work. For example, Deleuze and Guattari state that an acentred society 'rejects any centralizing, unifying automaton as "an asocial intrusion"' (p. 61). What they are suggesting leads us to a position profoundly removed from our own notions of power, hierarchy and external frames of reference. At least since Durkheim, following through Radcliffe-Brown and continuing into the present in much (though not all) social and cultural analysis, there has been an assumption, implicit or explicit, that every society is made up of isolated individuals who must be brought into some sort of social cohesion. Centralization of some sort is seen as the unquestionable basis for the existence of any society. What Deleuze and Guattari are asking us to do is to consider a radically different idea: that some societies may not only be politically acentred, but may conceive of themselves and their relationships to the cosmos as acentred, may conceive of mutually independent parts, and may resist centralization as being asocial. 'Local initiatives', they contend, 'are coordinated independently of a central instance' (p. 69).

This analysis has resonances with Eric Michaels's analysis of the Warlpiri graphic system. Paraphrasing Michaels, we might say that information about the cosmos is coded and transmitted so as not to undermine the autonomous ontological status of different sets of actors in the cosmos.[8]

This concept of the cosmos as an acentred information system has implications for decision making. Yarralin people are reluctant to intervene in ecological processes except in limited and localized ways, or in ways that are authorized by accumulated experience, expressed as Dreaming or Law. I suggest that their reluctance derives from the facts that no individual or species has a monopoly on information, that responsible action can only be based on knowledge, and that it takes time to accumulate sufficient knowledge to arrive at an understanding of complex events.

Wilderness

David Brower, first executive director of the Sierra Club and founder of Friends of the Earth, stated in 1978 that he had often thought 'along with Mrs Malaprop, that wilderness is a place where the hand of man had not set foot'. In Australia, there is no wilderness according to this definition. Aboriginal people were everywhere. Yet the Northern Territory Conservation Commission and many other bodies consistently justify the acquisition of land because it is, or represents, wilderness. They then go on to develop this land in a way that will allow them to market the wilderness experience to tourists. The contradictions are manifest.

In the area I am concerned with, the new Gregory National Park is being marketed in this way: its historic, prehistoric and 'wilderness' features simultaneously contradict each other and are presented as its value. In 1986, some 150 keen young people participating in Operation Raleigh 'explored' the park area. The irony (to use a fairly neutral term) is that these young people were 'exploring' an area that is, in fact, someone else's home. The land in question belongs to Wardaman, Ngaliwurru, Nungali and Ngarinman people. They know it intimately and have spent their lives attempting to take care of it properly.

In recent years some fine literature has appeared describing and analysing Aboriginal peoples' active participation in the ecosystem as resource managers. Allen's work on faunal change, Williams and Hunn's *Resource Managers*, Rhys Jones's work on fire, Kimber's work on cultivation and Stevenson's work with the Tiwi are excellent examples.[9] The point has been made quite clearly enough: there need be no further talk of Aborigines as 'parasites on nature'. However, we are as yet only beginning to understand that people's intimacy with the 'natural' world is not itself somehow 'natural'. Scholars such as Jane Goodale and Rhys Jones have shown with considerable sophistication that intimacy is achieved through cultural constructions of the environment based on close observations accumulated through time. There is a great deal to be learnt about 'the facts' that Aboriginal people have observed, and more to be learnt about their managerial strategies. There is even more to be learnt of the cultural construction of the environment, for it is through moral and ontological systems that Aboriginal people have achieved and sustained their skilled ecological management strategies.

Yarralin people have not been very successful in managing much of their country. This is because for the past 100 years the area has been entirely allocated to pastoral leaseholders. Fortunes have been made in the cattle industry in this area. The unrecorded cost has been borne by Aboriginal people, and by the plants, animals, soils and water systems.

Our ethnobotanical research revealed some devastating losses in plant life. Although I have not made an equivalent study of animal life, it is apparent that a detailed study would show a parallel picture of loss, particularly among the smaller marsupials such as possums, bandicoots and native cats.

Most of the plants that I have been told about and have been unable to document are food items, primarily seeds and tubers. Among the species that I have been unable to locate are several types of tubers — *kayalarin*, *kamara* and *janata* — that were staple foods until they became unavailable. Other food items of which I was able to locate specimens (often after much searching and many false leads) are now highly restricted in their distribution. I have been told of billabongs that 'always' used to have lilies, and of places where a variety of perhaps four or five tubers 'always used to grow'. Some areas have been described as 'like a big garden', so rich were they. Now one is lucky to find a few isolated specimens, and many of these 'gardens' appear to exist no longer.

As Yarralin people began listing disappearing plant species, shrinking resource locations, and the disappearance of the once-flourishing exchange of bush foods, they expressed anger and sorrow, and offered some very perceptive insights into what is going on. They spoke of the damage that cattle do: eating seeds so that plants cannot reproduce, pulling up plants by the roots so that nothing remains, making the ground hard and breaking up billabongs. People also suggested that introduced plants — 'improved pasturage', rubber and brigalow bushes, for example — may be pushing out native plants. Finally, people stated that before the mid-1950s the country was much more open, with far fewer fences and bores. They suggested that the altered land use may have intensified, or brought to a critical level, the damage that cattle were doing to the country. I have elicited approximate dates for many of the disappearances and for the introduction of noxious weeds. I am also collecting European descriptions, both early and recent, of the country and its vegetation. Meteorological records and station records will allow me to fill out this chronology in considerable detail, and I have a few enclosures in place which may allow me to document changes over the next few years.

The point I want to make in the midst of this wealth of detail is this: the area that the Conservation Commission describes so enthusiastically as wilderness is actually home for a fair number of people who know it intimately. The same country has also been pastoral property for the last eighty years or more, and it has suffered terribly during that time. Parts of it have been so degraded that they are now true badlands. It is nothing like what it was a century ago.

As part of the documentation of degradation, I made a short video of some of the most badly affected areas. I asked one of the senior custodians of this country what he called the degraded area. He looked at it for a while and said, 'It's the wild, just the wild.' He then went on to speak eloquently of the lack of care in this area and to contrast this wild country with another area that he termed 'quiet'.

On the basis of how this one man, Daly Pulkara, spoke of country, it is possible to suggest an analogy: the Western distinction between wilderness and degraded country parallels Daly Pulkara's distinction between quiet and wild country. The distinction between wilderness and degraded land opposes European concepts of natural or untouched country and damaged or spoilt country. The quiet/wild distinction opposes Ngarinman concepts of country that is cared for and spoilt country. This analogy highlights the contrasts between European and Aboriginal ways of talking about similar phenomena. It is here that we begin to perceive something very interesting. Daly Pulkara is telling us that his country is becoming a 'wilderness' — a man-made and cattle-made wilderness where nothing grows, where life is absent, where all the care, intelligence and respect that generations of Aboriginal people have put into the country have been eradicated in a matter of a few short years. In contrast, he tells us that country that is cared for, that is unspoilt by the encroaching wilderness, is 'quiet'.

The term 'quiet' is a Kriol term. It means tame, domesticated, not dangerous, under control The inescapable irony, and the hurt for many Aboriginal people, is this: the country Europeans would want to see as 'untouched wilderness' is the country that Daly Pulkara and others regard as properly cared for. Quiet country is country in which those who know how to read the signs see human action of the most responsible sort.

This research suggests several pointers towards the development of an indigenous Western land ethic. It is clear that any land ethic that is not human-centred must involve knowledge of other living species and of living systems. Responsible action can only be based on a sound understanding of what is going on in all parts of the system. Deeply embedded notions of hierarchy, centralization, specialization and progress are inimical to a land ethic that is not human-centred. We have to realize how deeply these ideas are embedded in Western cultures. One intellectual approach that challenges many of these notions is that of biologists such as Stephen

Jay Gould and Jacques Monod. We should be taking them very seriously. And, as a final point, I think that if an acentred land ethic is to be developed in the West, it will not be developed in wilderness but in our own back yards, farms and stations. At this point, we do not so much need to understand the seemingly exotic as to learn to know and care for the ecosystems with which we interact on a daily basis. It is here that we can develop an ethic that encompasses both theory and praxis. We can't write ourselves out of the system any more than we can define ourselves as its ultimate focus.

Notes

My current research has been funded by the Australian Institute of Aboriginal Studies. It builds upon my research in the area beginning in 1980 and on David Cooper's work in the area as a field officer for the Aboriginal Sacred Sites Protection Authority. There is a much broader domain of kin-like relationships between people and plants, seasons and animals than I have indicated here. These and other points are discussed more fully in my PhD dissertation, 'Dingo Makes Us Human: Being and Purpose in an Australian Aboriginal Culture' (Bryn Mawr, 1984), and articles: 'The Saga of Captain Cook', *Australian Aboriginal Studies*, 1984, and 'Consciousness and Responsibility in an Australian Aboriginal Religion', in W. Edwards (ed.), *Traditional Aboriginal Society* (Melbourne, 1987), pp. 257–69.

1. Aldo Leopold (1949), *A Sand Country Almanac*, London.
2. T. C. McLuhan (1971), *Touch the Earth: A Self-Portrait of Indian Existence*, New York.
3. Guboo Ted Thomas (1987), 'The land is sacred: renewing the Dreaming in modern Australia', in G. Trompf (ed.), *The Gospel is Not Western*, Maryknoll.
4. David Bennett (1986), *Inter-species Ethics: Australian Perspectives*, Canberra: Department of Philosophy, ANU.
5. William Godfrey-Smith (1980), 'The rights of non-humans and intrinsic values', in D. Mannison *et al.* (eds), *Environmental Philosophy*, Canberra Department of Philosophy, ANU.
6. Carolyn Merchant (1980), *The Death of Nature: Women, Ecology and the Scientific Revolution*, London.
7. Gilles Deleuze and Felix Guattari (1981), 'Rhizome', in *I & C*, **8**:49–71.
8. Eric Michaels (1988), 'Hollywood iconography: a Warlpiri reading', paper presented to the Australian Institute of Aboriginal Studies Biennial Conference, May.
9. See Harry Allen (1983), *Nineteenth-century Faunal Change in Western N.S.W. and North-west Victoria*, Working Papers in Anthropology, Archaeology, Linguistics, Maori Studies, No. 64, Department of Anthropology, University of Auckland; Richard Kimber (1984), 'Resource use and management in central Australia', *Australian Aboriginal Studies*, **2**:12–23; Rhys Jones (1969), 'Firestick farming', *Australian Natural History*, **16**, 7, September: 224–8; Paul Stevenson (1985), 'Traditional Aboriginal resource management in the wet-dry tropics: Tiwi case study', *Proceedings of the Ecological Society of Australia*, **13**:309–15; Nancy Williams and Eugene Hunn (eds) (1982) *Resource Managers: North American and Australian Hunter–Gatherers*, Boulder, Colorado.

18
Continuities of Wiradjuri Tradition

GAYNOR MACDONALD

Wiradjuri is a traditional Aboriginal society. More properly, it is a traditional Aboriginal nation, a federation of approximately twenty communities who collectively call themselves Wiradjuri. Within these communities, all aspects of daily life are informed by traditions which stem from classical Wiradjuri culture, from the practices and beliefs of Wiradjuri ancestors who lived in and owned Wiradjuri country at the time it was colonized by the British in 1788 or, in practice, from 1815, when the Blue Mountains west of Sydney ceased to be a barrier to colonial expansion. On the other side were the vast plains, rolling hills and rivers of Wiradjuri.

The simple and evident (to someone who has lived in a Wiradjuri community) fact that contemporary Wiradjuri culture is informed by Wiradjuri tradition is not, however, one which has found its way into popular thinking about Aboriginal societies. It is more common to hear that Wiradjuri, as with other societies in 'settled' Australia, has 'lost its culture', is 'non-traditional' or 'de-tribalized'. Bowler (1902:28) said of Wiradjuri in 1902 that 'it is only the old customs and manners that are of any interest'. He was not only voicing the belief that the 'old' ways were fast disappearing, but also reflecting the attitudes of his time. For many decades they were not studied at all, regarded as unworthy of the anthropological gaze. They were of interest only in so far as they could shed light on 'the past', the imagined primitiveness from which Europeans saw themselves as having emerged into the light of 'civilization'. Acceptance of the 'Aboriginality' of such societies in recent years has prompted anthropological and historical analyses of their resistance to colonial dominance, their encapsulation within debilitating and racist structures, their political activism, and the construction of new identities of Aboriginality. This has put them back on the map, but few of these studies concede that such societies have strong continuities with their classical forebears, that they are just as much a part of their own traditions as they are of structures of European domination, that the dynamics of colonialism have always interacted with the internal dynamics of lifeways based on traditions.

The 'old customs and manners' (or, at least, those ones in which Europeans were interested) were defined as 'traditions', negating the processes whereby Wiradjuri drew upon deeply engrained ontologies and moral systems so as to adjust those customs and manners to the exigencies of their colonial situation, and so to reconstitute their socialities in terms of these as *ongoing* traditions. Instead of 'tradition' being seen as the dynamic by which Wiradjuri peoples were able to maintain or transform their identity and presence as 'Wiradjuri', popular use of the concept in Australia has been locked into fixed and static ideas of indigenous cultures, which deny both the fact and the legitimacy of change. To have changed has implied 'loss': the inability to remain Wiradjuri, cultured or to have traditions.

Implicit in my approach is, therefore, a critique of theories of social change in anthropology, including notions of 'traditionality', which have neither developed creative models of change, adaptation, modification or transformation, nor challenged the erroneous depiction of people such as the Wiradjuri as devoid of culture and tradition. As Chase (1981:27) maintained many years ago, in what is still perhaps the most incisive critique of change and tradition in the Aboriginal literature: 'No person has an absence of traditions, or else he can no longer be a human social being'. Whatever changes are introduced into our lives, it is only through resources we already have that these changes can be assimilated at all. It is through the learnings of the past that we process the present. Our traditions (as practices, beliefs, values, attitudes, objects brought forward from our past) are the filtering, mediating, translating, enabling mechanisms by which we continually produce and reproduce our living cultures. Wiradjuri are not cultureless, nor are they merely 'human social beings'. They are *Wiradjuri* social beings, located in a distinctive and meaningful social and spatial world within which they are constituted as Wiradjuri. The traditions which inform their lives are not just those of any human social being's past, they are rooted in a *Wiradjuri* past, a past shaped by their colonial experiences *and* their classical, pre-colonial culture. What has been handed down, why and how, differs from one Aboriginal society to another: they each have different histories, different experiences of the impact of colonization in particular.

It is time to challenge the selective and invidious way in which 'traditionality' has been understood and valued in anthropology and in Australia more generally. Not all Wiradjuri practices and beliefs survived the violence of the European takeover of their lands. But many did, including key features which defined their relations to each other and to place. Popular, as well as past anthropological, assessment of Aboriginal cultures has defined some characteristics as definitional, others not. 'Real' Aboriginal people — those allowed to call themselves 'traditional' — were those who retained, for instance, language fluency, particular physical characteristics, ritual observance and religious beliefs.

In a recent study of continuities of tradition among the Peak Hill Wiradjuri on the upper Bogan River, I concluded that:

> ... whilst there have been many enforced changes in Wiradjuri lifestyles, Wiradjuri people have responded to these in such a way as to enable continuation of the three key cultural principles which define their corporate life. The first is a kinship system through which their relations to their ancestors and to each other are articulated in a principle of direct descent, and which ensures succession. The second is the continuing identification of this community of descent with the upper Bogan River area within which these

social relations are constituted, and through which landedness itself is constituted. Third is the body of moral law, belief and custom which are able to be expressed and maintained through the pathways that are provided by kinship and landedness for the practice and transmission of cultural traditions. There is, in addition, a Wiradjuri world view (ontology) which draws these social practices into a coherent intellectual system of belief as well as practice. This world view makes the identity of people and place inseparable: the existence of one is defined in terms of the existence of the other. The terms 'Wiradjuri' or 'Bogan River Wiradjuri' or the 'Peak Hill mob' are spatial as well as social referents, and vice versa. Through this integral intellectual and social system, rights and interests to land are both held and passed on from one generation to another. (Macdonald 1996: 204)

This article will focus on Wiradjuri kinship, but against a backdrop of kinship studies entrenched in traditionality and constructed from fieldwork in remote areas of Australia. These have tended to act against the interests of understanding the dynamics of kinship in Wiradjuri country. Models of kinship are a good example of the linking of traditionality to a static and unchanging 'culture', locked in classical times. Aboriginal kinship studies have rarely examined the dynamic and responsive ways in which kinship systems have been transformed so as to maintain a continuity of traditions, as shifting systems of shared meanings based on mutual experience. The focus has been on the highly elaborated structures associated with classical societies. As recently as 1988, Keen's review of anthropological studies of kinship ignored studies in south-east Australia. Ironically, he begins by citing John Barnes's note of censure: 'These formal structures have considerable aesthetic appeal and comprehending their logical properties tests the intellectual agility of those who analyse them. Many anthropologists have, alas, been mesmorised by them'. As Barnes pointed out, aesthetics have had more appeal than lived lives, or even how these systems work in practice. Structures do not have to be highly elaborated before they are seen to constitute a social system as a system, nor do they have to be inflexible: clans and moieties are merely evidence of a system rather than its definition. And there are significant differences in the ways in which Aboriginal kinship systems have been and are structured. However, the highly elaborated has exotic appeal and has been privileged as evidence of 'tradition'.

To Wiradjuri people themselves, kinship is not a matter of structure, although they are clearly aware of the frameworks within which they operate. It is firstly a matter of relationships. Structural analyses tend to emphasise form — clans or genealogies for instance. But these are secondary to the way in which people are in relationship with each other. Kinship is thus about how one identifies with and invigorates the collective world of shared meanings. It is about dropping in for a cuppa, catching up on stories, cadging $10, and going to funerals. Nor are Wiradjuri people necessarily aware of the relationship between past and present practices, as is true of most peoples who do not systematically have available a study of their own histories. But they consistently and frequently refer to differences between their own experiences of kinship and those of non-Aboriginal people.

Reay (1963) in her earlier studies of Aboriginal kinship in New South Wales made a useful distinction 'between "family structure", meaning the general build of social relationships within the family, and "familial culture", meaning the way of life a particular family pursues' (but, note the shift to the sociological concept of *family* as a denial of the legitimacy of using the conventional anthropological notion of *kinship*):

> Using these two dimensions, it becomes apparent that the major difference between the [A]boriginal family and the white Australian family is a significant difference in the relationship between social structure and culture in the context of the family. The white Australian family is remarkably uniform in structure, and the [A]boriginal family is remarkably diverse; the familial cultures of white Australia are diverse, and those of [A]boriginal Australia uniform. (Reay 1963:19)

The difference is significant because so much of the literature on nineteenth century Wiradjuri kinship emphasizes the manifest structure (sections and clans) while largely ignoring familial culture. Yet familial culture is not only remarkably uniform across Wiradjuri country, but it is also remarkably uniform over time. It is this capacity to maintain familial culture regardless of changes in family structure which is a major means by which Wiradjuri societies have been able to transform in the midst of upheaval. Changes have taken place at the surface level in trans-formations of structure so as to accommodate the enduring familial culture so definitional of Wiradjuri styles of relating.

Ontological Traditions in Wiradjuri Kinship

Kinship is a key social expression of the moral and ontological foundations of Wiradjuri society. It has also been, from a non-Wiradjuri perspective, their most visible form. The references to 'dysfunctional' families which are common throughout 1930s to 1970s literature, and references to the 'failure' of assimilationist programs, are, I contend, actually recognitions of the different system within which Wiradjuri and other New South Wales Aboriginal people operated, albeit not understood as such. Theoretical blinkers of the time limited the analysis of Wiradjuri kinship to comparison with European ideals of the middle class white family. This was both the yardstick and the desired direction of change. It is clear, once the different bases of Wiradjuri society are recognized, that Wiradjuri people were not concerned to conform to these European expectations except in so far as not to do so attracted punitive measures from white authorities. I argued ten years ago that (1986: Ch 1.2):

> The Wiradjuri kinship system is not merely the *ad hoc* vestige of a traditional system glossed as an 'extended family': it is a system in its own right . . . This system . . . is fundamental to understanding the organisation of the Wiradjuri domain, relations of people over time, residence and mobility patterns, and forms of exchange. It is possible to discern the transformation of past principles of kinship in the different environments moulded by European-introduced constraints.

Colonial events impacted on Wiradjuri lifeways in a variety of complex ways. There was no uniform 'destruction'. The loss of control of certain preferred social practices did not mean loss over others. Some features were specifically targeted by Europeans: the prevention of marriage between older men and younger women was an early target of missionaries who deliberately wished to destabilize both the traditions of marriage and the power exerted by senior members of Wiradjuri societies. An older Cowra Wiradjuri man has spoken of his grandparents' stories about being stoned for using their own language. Nowadays, Wiradjuri speak predominantly English, interspersed with a small Wiradjuri lexicon. Initiation ceremonies, although held occasionally until the 1890s, were increasingly difficult to organize when travel between societies became dangerous and a high death rate robbed people of significant ritual leaders (see also Rose (1985) on the impact on ceremonies of the non-availability of key participants in the Victoria River district). Such rituals were also deplored by many European observers. Under less scrutiny were funerals which, with a ritual content changed to that of Christianity, continue to bear the hallmarks of Wiradjuri tradition. As the most significant of contemporary Wiradjuri ceremonies, they continue to bring together hundreds and occasionally thousands of kin.

Throughout colonial history, kinship has remained the foundation, setting up the pathways by which other spheres of social life, including political and economic relations, find expression in ways distinctive of Aboriginal societies. The Wiradjuri moral and ontological orders inform political, legal, economic, belief and other features of Wiradjuri social life, and all of these are expressed through the structures and familial cultures of kinship. In this way, Wiradjuri people have been able to respond to colonial encounters creatively and in their own terms to a greater extent than is generally appreciated. At the same time, the emphasis in this study is not meant to diminish the impact of the violence Wiradjuri people and their lifeways were also, and continue to be, subject to. But violence, resistance and racism are only one part of the Wiradjuri story. Indeed, it is often the fact of the durability of Wiradjuri traditions which contributes to the fuelling of racist and derogatory attitudes on the part of the dominant society which does not legitimize their expression.

Wiradjuri people perceive themselves as part of a social whole in which people are not sharply distinguished from each other as in the European tradition. A person is a social being, constituted socially and without meaning if separated from the social. 'Kinship' is the formal label applied to the ways in which social relations are organized within a holistically conceived system. Wiradjuri people are more likely today to use terms such as 'my people', 'my mob'/'the Narrandera mob', or 'my relations'. The medium of kinship allows and fosters discreet expressions of what it means to be Wiradjuri; what it means to belong to an entity far more important that any individual life. This is not to say that individual lives are not unique and worthy of the utmost respect. It is more an expression of what it means to identify as part of a life entity, one which is continuous yet is constantly renewing itself to accommodate changing circumstances and conditions.

The existential framework which allows for individuation (the process of becoming a unique, autonomous individual within the social body) is provided through the network of familial relations. The framework dictates certain responsibilities and obligations but it also allows for a person to negotiate their sense of meaning within the existential conditions provided by that framework. More simply, these systems of kin-connectedness allow the individuation process to take place. This is contrary to European notions of individualism which tend to retard the individuation process because they are dependent upon institutional recognition. Throughout the history of capitalism it is possible to observe the continual shift in the ways in which people of northern European origin identify themselves. In very general terms, people in classical European societies were recognized from birth because of the emphasis on collective identification. In modern capitalist societies people are not recognized until they have achieved, or have 'become' something within the institutional sphere. Wiradjuri people have expressed cynicism to me at the way in which Aboriginal people, athletes in particular, are held up by Europeans as examples of what 'Aborigines can achieve', while others go unrecognized. Recognition is not dependent for them on kinds of 'achievement': one just 'is'. 'Doing things for 'one's own people' is more important than becoming well known. One may 'achieve' in life and this is seen as a good thing but one does not have to achieve to be recognized. Recognition among 'Westerners' is a teleological process, because a person has to achieve social recognition via the medium of abstract institutional structures (school, competitive arenas, work). For an institutionally based society this is important so that the institutionalization of identity from an early age can inhibit ways of individuating which may be counterproductive to life in the institutional sphere. The contrast in Aboriginal societies is startling, as most anthropological fieldworkers know. People are recognized from birth because the bases of recognition are different: they are grounded in the extreme value place on the social entity. One can therefore undergo the individuation process knowing that one will always be recognized for being unique yet part of an important life entity. To put it simply, you are allowed to be who you are.

In this sense, the Wiradjuri 'self' is a social self. One is not merely related to others but constituted as part of the same social body/entity. This results in a great tolerance of autonomy, individual differences and of different activities in which people engage, including conflict. One does not have to be 'the same' or 'good' to belong. Belonging, however, does require that one fulfil one's social obligations, one of which is continuing to identify with that social body. A 'blood tie' alone is insufficient to constitute one as a part of the social body. A person has to activate the social obligations which their blood-relatedness has done no more than make possible. Blood ties and genealogies provide pathways. They do not provide social guarantees.

This core moral/ontological position has caused consternation among European-Australians who criticize Wiradjuri people for their apparent lack of desire to 'get on in life'. They are often unable to understand how Wiradjuri people can find personal and social value in 'just being' or being a part of the Wiradjuri social body. This has implications for the understanding of various facets of Wiradjuri lifeways, as well as for conflicts, misunderstandings and pejorative stereotypes found among European-Australians. It is particularly evident when Europeans comment on practices such as sharing income with kin instead of investing (without examining the relationship between investment in material well-being in a materially oriented society and investment in sociality in a socially oriented society), or people not relocating to take up a job, even a promotion, because they want to stay with kin and in their own country.

Kinship informs and is informed by moral codes which provide a conceptual framework which allows people's humanness to come into being. The kinship system maximizes Wiradjuri processes of individuation in such a way as to benefit the social. The social takes precedence over the individual in moral terms but without collapsing or compromising the autonomy of persons. Kinship is thus the key form of Wiradjuri social organization which allows for and provides pathways for a distinct Wiradjuri way of being in the world.

Structures of Kinship

The continuities of Wiradjuri social life centre on and are enabled by the kinship structures which organize people *vis-à-vis* each other. It is through a vast network of people defined as 'relations' in some way or another that the processes of Wiradjuri life can be understood. Kinship is a reference to systems of classification whereby Wiradjuri people organize their social world. It is because the pathways provided by kinship structures are so important that Wiradjuri people themselves speak as if kin are their whole world, and kinship is so dominant in literature about them. Everything is expressed through — but not reduced to — the structures and familial culture of kinship.

Kinship structures provide pathways for the sharing of meaning and experience, and also for identification. They locate a person within the social entity in such a way that they 'belong': they are recognized as having a social place. A key way of locating people in all kinship systems is through naming practices. Three of these are briefly examined here: first, the way individuals are socially placed through the use of kin terms, and identified through personal names; second, the way in which social groupings of kin are identified with each other through the use of surnames; and, third, the way kin-based groupings are associated with a particular country. Each of these is an important structural principle within the Wiradjuri domain.

The range of people any individual Wiradjuri person counts as kin or 'relations' is extensive. The range alone points to the distinctiveness of this system and the reasons why it continues to dominate the majority of Wiradjuri social interactions. Although commonly referred to in New South Wales literature as an 'extended family', this nomenclature in no way captures either the extent of an individual's kin network or the complex of social roles performed by various kin. These roles encompass all facets of social life, 'public' as well as 'domestic' — distinctions which are not made within a Wiradjuri world view. It is rarely possible to contrast a sphere of 'family' with spheres of life in which family/kin relations are not a factor.

A simple exercise can identify people Wiradjuri count as kin. Ask a person to list those kin with whom they have had some contact over the previous two years (only), including personal encounters, phone calls, correspondence and so on. It proves an onerous task! Usually people are willing to do so at first but no sooner do they get started than they realize what is being asked of them. Most then give up. One woman in Peak Hill, with three children and six grandchildren, started to redefine the task to make it manageable. First she chose to limit her list to one year:

> She started and then restricted it to kin she had had close social dealings with, excluding anyone met through meetings (she has a number of community involvements). She then decided to also exclude kin met at funerals. Her limited list came to over a 100 people. She commented that the task would take forever otherwise as it would be 'about a thousand, even two thousand people!' This is no exaggeration. (Macdonald 1996)

I have done similar studies formally and informally with Wiradjuri people over several years. One done in Cowra (genealogical linkages are reported in Macdonald 1986: Ch. 6) produced a 'short' list of 268 kin compiled by an unmarried teenager without children, who did not know a lot about her mother's side of the family. She designated 145 of these kin as 'close', 123 as 'distant'. Close and distant are only partly based on genealogical reckoning and they take the activation of the relationship into account as well.

This extensive world of kin is a clear continuity with the classical Wiradjuri world in which the entire socially significant universe of people would have been defined as kin. Not to be kin was to be an enemy or stranger. While a Wiradjuri person's universe today includes many non-kin — non-Aboriginal people, co-workers, migrants who have moved from other areas — these relationships have not detracted from the significance of kin. On the contrary, and as in the past, non-kin relationships which are valued are likely to be incorporated as fictive kin into the kinship universe (which also binds the otherwise 'outsider' into relations of obligation and accountability.)

Kin terms

Kin terms describe genealogically based relationships as well as rights, responsibilities and obligations associated with particular kin dyads. Although English terms are used, they do not always correspond in meaning to conventional Australian English usage, particularly terms of address. Wiradjuri people employ them in a distinctive way so as to accommodate their wider socially significant sphere of kin. Wiradjuri do not follow the classical practice of grouping kin exactly (based on the equivalence of siblings) but have retained elements of it which are useful in a contemporary sense. For instance, 'aunty' includes MZ, FZ, MBW, FBW but also one's mother's and father's first and second cousins, and spouses of anyone called uncle. Siblings and close cousins are frequently merged as 'sis' or 'bro'. Wiradjuri kin classification has been modified through the use of English kin terms, and changes in the roles that kin play.

While kin terms reflect a genealogically defined model of relationships, they are also used to specify the recognition and activation of a set of reciprocal obligations, privileges and responsibilities between the two people using the terms. Thus a 'mother' should perform the social role expected of a 'mother'. The term is a package of information about what is expected in a *social* relationship. The terms are thus extended to people of other genealogical relationships who do perform these roles. A person reared by a grandmother may address her as 'Mum', for instance, even if referring to her as 'my grandmother'. If extended to people not in a conventional genealogical relationship, including non-Aboriginal people, they are assumed to carry the same package of meanings — and thus the same expectations of the relationship. A person is called 'brother' in the desire that they be prepared to act as a brother should. Kin terms of address such as 'Mum', 'sister/sis', 'brother/bro' and 'cuz' are also linked to the expectations of the relationship. So, in one case, a Wiradjuri man rejected his mother's (genetrix) request for money which she had expressed as, 'Go on, son, give your old mother a few bob for a drink.'. He retorted, 'Go on, you've never been a mother to me!' He had, in fact, been raised by his mother's brother, whose wife he addressed as 'Mum', more usually calling his actual mother by her first name or 'Mother'. It is an important feature of the kin terminological system that rights associated with the use of particular terms are not automatically acquired through genealogical connectedness. They must be backed by action. Many conflicts arise because kin are not seen to be 'doing the right thing'. In familial custom, 'Mum' and 'daughter', in contrast to European usage, are not used merely to refer to a state of being in a bio-genetic relationship but also to a social role. A genealogical connection may be acknowledged in biological terms but denied in practice: 'Well, she is a cousin but I don't think of her that way'; 'She may be my sister but she sure doesn't act like one — she's as mean as hell!'; or people counted as kin because of their behaviour: 'Uncle Billy — well, he's not my uncle really but he's been more of an uncle to me than my real uncle'.

The use of nicknames is also a strong Wiradjuri tradition. They were often recorded by Europeans in the nineteenth century and there is obviously humour and irony attached to some names, although the distance of time makes it hard to decipher the intent. Wiradjuri stories recall, for instance, Cobborn Jacky (*kobon*, big/large). Genanagie Jack (*genanagie*, human excrement), Charlie Goolagong (Genanagie and Goolagong being contemporary place names), and Billy Wandong (*Wandong* is a reference to a greatly feared Wiradjuri spirit). It is common for names to be handed down from one generation to another. Parents name children for their own parents, their siblings and themselves. This leads to some 'old fashioned' names so some young people are steering away from this tradition, or using family names as 'middle names'.

Surnames

Surnames are used to link people to other groups of kin and to specific areas of country. Some surnames become well known as 'Wiradjuri names' throughout New South Wales, even though obviously shared by non-Wiradjuri and non-Aboriginal people as well. Examples in the Wiradjuri genealogical population would include, for instance, Coe, Bamblett, Bell, Dargin, Lyons, Towney and Williams. Each of these will refer, first, to people who share kin links with others associated with that name, and, second, to an association with a core area with which that name is linked: Wellington in the case of Bell: Narrandera in the case of Bamblett and Lyons; Peak Hill in the case of Dargin and Towney. In the Coe case, there are two 'cores': the 'Cowra Coes' and the 'Condo (Condobolin) Coes'.

Surnames package information about kin relatedness and place identification, encoding information about social and spatial belonging. However, the patrilineal form of surname succession introduced by Europeans has proved too limiting a system of nomenclature without adjustment in usage. When people speak of 'the Williams' or 'the Towneys' they may be specifically referring to people who carry that surname, or to a nuclear family household, as is common in Australia. But the use of 'the Towney *mob*' is not merely a reference to people of that surname or to people of an agnatic group but to a wider constellation of cognatic kin, who may or may not bear the name 'Towney', but are all regarded as part of 'the Towney mob'. 'The Keed mob' will include people who use the name Keed as well as descendants who use other surnames because of the adoption of patri-surnames.

Surnames can thus be used to designate a family as the smallest significant kin-defined grouping or a very large grouping. Either way, someone associated with a surname 'mob' is assumed to be close, to share the attributes and responsibilities associated with that constellation, and so on. The group is not formally defined, or socially or geographically bounded. In some cases it can be ambiguous. As most people have access to at least two surnames (mother and father) and women may also acquire a marital surname, they can stress one rather than the other, or alternate depending upon circumstances. One reason for alternating is that surnames not only identify a person with 'a mob' of people, but also with country. They locate a person spatially as well as socially, which can be important in introductions in which people desire to find forms of connectedness upon which to base their relationship.

Kin networks

Wiradjuri people use terms such as 'my relations' or 'all the rellies' to refer to their kin networks today. Members of a kin network will often refer to themselves in terms of a key surname which is identified with Bogan River Wiradjuri or Narrandera Wiradjuri but various surnames may be used within the network. 'I belong to the Nadens' or 'I come in through the Williams' are ways of locating oneself within a descent network, irrespective of one's actual surname. An individual has a personal network of kin, the range referred to briefly above, and will also orient to a core family within it. A kin network is the genealogically structured grouping of living kin, overlapping parts of which will be an individual's activated network.

Members of a kin network may live in various different places and will not always interact with each other. Most kin networks have a core kin group or family who are seen as the focus of that network. This may be the household of the oldest surviving member of the network, or a significant household which has tended to be a gathering place for kin within this network. Frequently a core is identified with key authority figures, often grandparents who are held in high regard and seen as influential throughout the network. These people have a kind of centripedal social force, centring kin attention.

When kin networks take deceased members into account, including immediate and distant ancestors, they can be referred to as a 'descent network'. A descent network is, therefore, a cognatic group which traces common ancestry to known or assumed ancestors. Within a descent network, descent is defined bilaterally, through one's mother and/or father. As in the case of kin networks, the term 'network' rather than 'group' is used to indicate the unbounded nature of descent network membership, as well as to recognize the options of affiliation which exist for its members (see below).

The notions of kin networks ('my people' or 'my relations'), surname groups ('my mob') and locality groups ('the Peak Hill mob') describe different structures within which kin and land connectedness are played out. These structures of relationship influence who goes to funerals, who responds in crises, who has rights to speak and on what, who one will be associated with, and where one 'belongs'. Within each of these structures, individuals relate to each other in relations defined by the use of kin terms.

These networks are not equivalent to residential groups. The distinction made in classical Wiradjuri studies between kin-based groupings (often described in superclass terms) and residential entities (bands comprised of hearth groups) is also made today between kin networks (see also Macdonald 1986:Ch. 6) and residential communities. Kin networks are geographically extensive and rarely, these days, include all those in the community of residence. Wiradjuri people used to call these their 'communities' or their 'mob'. Since the term community was introduced in the 1970s by government agencies, the mixed residential population is now referred to as a community. Residential communities are comprised of local and non-local people, kin and non-kin, landed and non-landed, just as bands would have been in the past.

Descent and Landedness

There are two broad ways in which Wiradjuri people have always associated with their country. The first can be termed identity, and includes landedness established by descent, spiritual and social associations, and the regulation of relations with neighbours. The second can generally be termed economic, including occupation and a continuous tradition of foraging activity of varying significance, as well as contemporary economic activities. The descent network is the crucial Wiradjuri vehicle for establishing relationships to country. To be recognized as 'landed', one must be descended from named ancestors who were themselves regarded within the group and by neighbouring peoples as having rights to land. By tradition, the genealogical depth of knowledge required for such assertions is short, as each generation can assume that the law of succession is such that only eligible people can succeed to rights. One's own immediate links — to parents and grandparents — are taken as sufficient confirmation of rights established through descent. Wiradjuri traditions of land tenure are characterized by the privileging of descent over short-term choices such as a history of residence. This deeply rooted essentialism produces stability and a basis for assessing the lawfulness of who may claim rights to country. Detailed studies in three northern Wiradjuri communities suggest that landed identity cannot be based on birth in an area, marriage, co-residence, friendship, or close association with an area.

Land connectedness is an important tradition by which all Aboriginal people identify themselves and it is clear that Wiradjuri people have been concerned to ensure that their social structures continued to provide the means by which landedness could be protected and preserved, even within a colonial context that would appear to have left them few options. To be 'Wiradjuri' is to be located within a constellation of social relations both spatially as well as socially. There are no exceptions to the picture developed in other parts of indigenous Australia that Aboriginal people understand themselves as integrally constituted in terms of particular areas of country. This applies as much to the local communities of descent within the Wiradjuri nation as it does between Wiradjuri and its neighbours.

It is through succession principles that kinship is able to maintain pathways to land in terms of both ownership rights and rights to speak for the community and its country. But, as in the case of using kin terms, descent refers only to one's genealogical *potential* to claim rights. It must also be combined with social activation of the responsibilities and obligations that this potential demands in order for it to be fully recognized. As the principle of activation is based on social knowledge, it is assumed that social knowledge can only be based on social experience. To actually claim rights, people must be genealogically connected to ancestors of that place in addition to showing, through their practice, that they have an ongoing concern for and (relevant) knowledge for that place. People need to be involved in some way. The *activation* of social roles is a theme which permeates Wiradjuri societies. If people are said to have 'done the wrong thing by their people', to have 'done the dirty on someone', or if they 'had to shoot through', the use of such expressions implies these people have not met social obligations in some way. It is more often described negatively since participation is the 'taken for granted' way to behave in a culture that emphasizes the 'belongingness' of each person to the social whole — the significant emphasis of

Wiradjuri ontologies. The right to make claims of any kind — kin support, community support, rights to anything going on in the community, access to knowledge, land — depends not only on where one fits in to social structures but also on the familial culture which insists that people do the right thing by the relationships in question.

Land is not the only right or benefit to which one succeeds through kinship structures. A person's totems are also handed down from parent to child. Membership of a Wiradjuri totemic division in the past was inherited from a person's mother and it is still the mother's totem which is seen as particularly valued, although not all Wiradjuri have been able to inherit their totems, and they do not organize themselves in terms of totemic divisions. Two people with the same totem were seen as 'one blood' and could not marry, whatever their genealogical distance. These marriage rules are expressed more informally today. Because not all people know their totems, marriage with all close kin is discouraged, especially closer than third cousins, and sometimes including them. Although totems are not used in social organization so much, the custom of totem inheritance is important because of other features of the totem. A totem (most usually an animal or a bird) watches over a person, and warns them of danger to themselves or others close to them. This caring characteristic of one's own totem is of great importance and also links in with Wiradjuri traditions of belief in the caring visits of deceased ancestors, as well as other spirits and signs and their presence in the landscape.

Continuities and Transformations in Wiradjuri Systems of Kinship and Landedness

I have focused on the Wiradjuri kinship system to illustrate the continuity of Wiradjuri traditions because kinship is commonly and rightly understood as a cornerstone of all Aboriginal social systems and Wiradjuri are no exception in this respect. It is also a reflection of the importance of the pathways which kinship provides that it continues to open up a great variety of social, political, economic and other opportunities for Wiradjuri people. It is through kinship that other systems also characteristic of Wiradjuri tradition, such as political and economic relations, find expression in ways distinctive of this culture.

While it might be legally and politically acceptable at the present moment to emphasize the extent of Wiradjuri traditions, their very continuity has constituted 'a problem' to the colonizers of Wiradjuri country. Many features of these traditions are in conflict with the values of the dominant Anglo-Australian society; many non-Aboriginal people — and also Aboriginal people — refuse to recognize or legitimate the validity of the cultural demands which stem from traditions — both because their presence as tradition is denied, and because, in a modern nation-state, the ambiguity can be useful to people wanting to play off one system against the other. Valued traditions which have roots in classical Wiradjuri lifeways are also an affront to a mainstream society which expected that Wiradjuri and other Aboriginal peoples would 'inevitably', and want to, adopt Anglo-European values. Wiradjuri people have refused to disappear in accordance with the history books.

On the one hand, kinship is celebrated as a strong feature of Aboriginal life because the European tradition has placed a particular value on 'family', distinguishing it from the seemingly rougher aspects of political and economic life. On the other hand, kin also make 'huge demands', which Europeans have long seen as debilitating as they limit the possibility for Aboriginal people to enter into capitalist relations. But these are inseparable realms in the Wiradjuri context. Wiradjuri people work well in kin groupings, as 'natural' cultural social formations within which both the rules of co-operation and of limitations of demands are circumscribed. Economic and political relations, likewise, are understood in terms of rules associated with kinship. The demands that kin make of each other are valued for the extent to which they are able to 'share and care' for each other (Macdonald 1996). The precedence which should, by Wiradjuri tradition, be given to kin is in direct conflict with certain values and practices of the dominant society. From a European point of view, the extension of kinship into non-familial realms (non-familial by European definition) is illegitimate. Such practices are ranked as 'nepotism' or 'cronyism' when engaged in by Aboriginal people. This is, of course, despite the fact that a majority of small businesses in Australia are family owned and run, and the 'old school tie' networks are alive and well. At one moment Australians are enjoined to respect 'Aboriginal culture' more, the next they are imposing bureaucratic values they do not adhere to in their own business life — an example of what von Sturmer (1995) refers to as 'human rights colonisation'.

But if Anglo-Australians only selectively recognize and legitimize the Wiradjuri kinship system, they maintain denial of continued Wiradjuri relations to land, which that kinship system has made possible. Authority in Wiradjuri communities has long been associated with kin and country relations. The outsider or migrant, no matter how long they have lived locally, is rarely conceded the right to speak for the community, and more particularly for its land. In this realm as well, tradition has not only not been recognized as a continuity, it has been legally denied expression in legislation that accords rights to all residents irrespective of their origins (Macdonald 1996). Because conflicts within a community are also a means of withholding funds or may prompt a greater degree of surveillance, people who regard themselves as having traditional rights but who have become minorities because of resettlement programs either become 'trouble makers', opt out, or maintain the illusion of democratic and egalitarian harmony required of them by funding bodies. Landed identity is not recognized as a source of intra-community conflict because Europeans have long assumed that landedness has not endured.

In any kin-oriented society the 'rules' of kinship almost if not always allow for some kinds of social flexibility and fluidity. What has been underestimated is the extent to which these simple but powerful principles by which people can be included or excluded in meaningful social relationships are one of the most powerful ways in which Wiradjuri cultural practices were able to continue despite extensive changes to their social and material environment brought about by colonization. In general, the specificities of Wiradjuri life have become more diffuse as a result of their colonial history. The contemporary kinship structure is less formally elaborated than was the case in the past, and some rituals have changed or been discarded. Many of the tasks towards which this elaboration was oriented were rendered impractical or irrelevant. In particular, this applies to the religious sphere which suffered the most impact of all features of classical Wiradjuri life. But theirs is not a story of destruction. Rather it should be seen as a celebration of the creativity of human cultures in their responses to violent change. The capacity of Wiradjuri traditions to sustain their lifeways in the face of all odds would have been a proper study for anthropology rather than a stylized image of the 'old ways'.

Briefly, what I have aimed to describe here are ways in which Wiradjuri traditions have both continued unchanged, as absolute continuities (after Sutton 1996) or as transformations of classical customs which reveal continuities in the deep structure despite surface changes. It is the surface changes which are all too often read and misinterpreted in the assessment of the extent to which Wiradjuri society is informed by traditions which belong to its own classical past. Not only have Wiradjuri people been told for decades by non-Aboriginal academics that they have lost their culture, they have been denied the right to celebrate their own distinctive lifeways on the grounds that these do not conform to those of Anglo-Australian society.

The fact that Europeans have privileged highly elaborated structures in their valuing of Aboriginal traditions should no longer be allowed to obscure the significance of other features of their cultures. The Wiradjuri kinship system clearly continues to act as an important vehicle for personal identity and the process of individuation, and for meaningful social interactions based on sets of obligations and responsibilities which bind people to each other. As in the past, it continues to inform and limit the obligations of sociality, establish parameters for marriage prohibitions, and enable the delineation of rights to succession. It also continues to provide pathways for political and economic interactions, setting the parameters for acceptable social behaviour and supervising transgressions. And these features and functions continue despite at times extensive pressure from the dominant society to extinguish them. It is time to value this as a statement of Wiradjuri intent and value and not, as earlier literature would have it, as something dysfunctional to their assimilation or modernization. I do not subscribe to the view that these are vestiges of the past which only continue to have efficacy because they have tided people over in conditions of poverty. This is to miss the point with which I started: that kinship itself is an expression of deep moral and ontological perspectives which can be seen to have been amazingly impervious to the strictures of the colonial regime. The Wiradjuri continue to affront and surprise, as all Aboriginal societies have done over the past two hundred years, by their refusal to adopt the contradictory moralities and increasingly desocializing ontologies of their colonizers.

Note
I am much indebted to Mark Winters for his input to my thinking in this article. We have worked together on concepts developed for Wiradjuri Native Title cases, in particular those of traditionality and individuation.

References
BOWLER, S. C. R. (1902), 'Aboriginal customs', *Science of Man*, **5**:28.
CHASE, ATHOL (1981), 'Empty vessels and loud voices: views about aboriginality today', *Social Alternatives*, **2**(2):23–7.
KEEN, IAN (1988), 'Twenty-five years of Aboriginal kinship studies', in R. M. Berndt & R. Tonkinson (eds), *Social Anthropology and Australian Aboriginal Studies: A Contemporary Overview*, Canberra: Aboriginal Studies Press.
MACDONALD, GAYNOR (1986), *The Koori Way: The Dynamics of Cultural Distinctiveness in 'Settled' Australia*, unpublished PhD thesis, University of Sydney.
——— (1996), *Bogan River Wiradjuri: Anthropology Report*, report commissioned by NSW Aboriginal Land Council for Peak Hill Native Title Claim.
MACDONALD, GAYNOR & WINTERS, MARK (nd), *Continuity and Transformation*, unpublished manuscript.
REAY, MARIE (1963), 'Aboriginal and white Australian family structure: an enquiry into assimilation trends', *Sociological Review* (NS), **11**(1):19–47.
ROSE, DEBORAH BIRD (1985), 'Christian identity versus Aboriginal identity in the Victoria River District', *Australian Aboriginal Studies*, 1985/2:58–61.
SUTTON, PETER (1996), 'Native title anthropological concepts: systems of Aboriginal law and custom', paper prepared for the NSW Aboriginal Land Council Native Title Unit, Aldgate, SA.
VON STURMER, JOHN R. (1995), 'R stands for . . .': an extract from a Mabo diary', *Australian Journal of Anthropology*, **6**(1&2):101–15.

Index